# ADVANCES IN MANAGEMENT ACCOUNTING

# ADVANCES IN MANAGEMENT ACCOUNTING

Series Editors:

Volumes 1–25: Marc J. Epstein and John Y. Lee
Volume 26: Marc J. Epstein and Mary A. Malina

Recent Volumes:

ADVANCES IN MANAGEMENT ACCOUNTING
VOLUME 26

# ADVANCES IN MANAGEMENT ACCOUNTING

EDITED BY

## MARC J. EPSTEIN
*Rice University (retired), USA*

## MARY A. MALINA
*University of Colorado Denver, USA*

United Kingdom – North America – Japan
India – Malaysia – China

Emerald Group Publishing Limited
Howard House, Wagon Lane, Bingley BD16 1WA, UK

First edition 2016

Copyright © 2016 Emerald Group Publishing Limited

**British Library Cataloguing in Publication Data**
A catalogue record for this book is available from the British Library

ISBN: 978-1-78441-652-2
ISSN: 1474-7871 (Series)

ISOQAR certified
Management System,
awarded to Emerald
for adherence to
Environmental
standard
ISO 14001:2004.

ISOQAR
REGISTERED

Certificate Number 1985
ISO 14001

INVESTOR IN PEOPLE

# CONTENTS

# LIST OF CONTRIBUTORS

| | |
|---|---|
| *Chris Akroyd* | College of Business, Oregon State University, Corvallis, OR, USA |
| *Ranjith Appuhami* | Department of Accounting and Corporate Governance, Macquarie University, Sydney, Australia |
| *Kevin Baird* | Department of Accounting and Corporate Governance, Macquarie University, Sydney, Australia |
| *Sharlene Sheetal Narayan Biswas* | Department of Accounting and Finance, University of Auckland, Auckland, New Zealand |
| *Sharon Chuang* | PwC, Auckland, New Zealand |
| *Sven Grollmuss* | Karlsruhe Institute of Technology, Karlsruhe, Germany |
| *James W. Hesford* | Ecole hôtelière de Lausanne, HES-SO, University of Applied Sciences Western Switzerland, Lausanne, Switzerland |
| *Mary A. Malina* | The Business School, University of Colorado Denver, Denver, CO, USA |
| *Lasse Mertins* | Carey Business School, Johns Hopkins University, Baltimore, MD, USA |
| *Susana Morales* | Karlsruhe Institute of Technology, Karlsruhe, Germany |
| *Nuraddeen Abubakar Nuhu* | Department of Accounting and Corporate Governance, Macquarie University, Sydney, Australia |

| | |
|---|---|
| *Mina Pizzini* | McCoy College of Business, Texas State University, San Marcos, TX, USA |
| *Michael Scheer* | Karlsruhe Institute of Technology, Karlsruhe, Germany |
| *Chandra Subramaniam* | University of Texas at Arlington, Arlington, TX, USA |
| *Marcia Weidenmier Watson* | University of North Carolina at Charlotte, Charlotte, NC, USA |
| *Lourdes Ferreira White* | Merrick School of Business, University of Baltimore, Baltimore, MD, USA |
| *Marc Wouters* | Karlsruhe Institute of Technology, Karlsruhe, Germany and University of Amsterdam, Amsterdam, The Netherlands |

# EDITORIAL BOARD

# STATEMENT OF PURPOSE AND
# REVIEW PROCEDURES

*Advances in Management Accounting (AIMA)* is a publication of quality applied research in management accounting. The journal's purpose is to publish thought-provoking articles that advance knowledge in the management accounting discipline and are of interest to both academics and practitioners. The journal seeks thoughtful, well-developed articles on a variety of current topics in management accounting, broadly defined. All research methods including survey research, field tests, corporate case studies, experiments, meta-analyses, and modeling are welcome. Some speculative articles, research notes, critiques, and survey pieces will be included where appropriate.

Articles may range from purely empirical to purely theoretical, from practice-based applications to speculation on the development of new techniques and frameworks. Empirical articles must present sound research designs and well-explained execution. Theoretical arguments must present reasonable assumptions and logical development of ideas. All articles should include well-defined problems, concise presentations, and succinct conclusions that follow logically from the data.

## REVIEW PROCEDURES

*AIMA* intends to provide authors with timely reviews clearly indicating the acceptance status of their manuscripts. The results of initial reviews normally will be reported to authors within eight weeks from the date the manuscript is received. The author will be expected to work with the Editor, who will act as a liaison between the author and the reviewers to resolve areas of concern. To ensure publication, it is the author's responsibility to make necessary revisions in a timely and satisfactory manner.

# EDITORIAL POLICY AND MANUSCRIPT FORM GUIDELINES

1. Manuscripts should include a cover page that indicates the author's name and affiliation.
2. Manuscripts should include a separate lead page with a structured abstract (not to exceed 250 words) set out under four to seven sub-headings; purpose, methodology/approach, findings, research limitations/implications (if applicable), practical implications (if applicable), social implications (if applicable), and originality/value. Keywords should also be included. The author's name and affiliation should not appear on the abstract.
3. Tables, figures, and exhibits should appear on a separate page. Each should be numbered and have a title.
4. In order to be assured of anonymous reviews, authors should not identify themselves directly or indirectly.
5. Manuscripts currently under review by other publications should not be submitted.
6. Authors should e-mail the manuscript in two WORD files to either of the editors. The first attachment should include the cover page and the second should exclude the cover page.
7. Inquiries concerning *Advances in Management Accounting* should be directed to either of the following editors:

Marc J. Epstein
epstein@rice.edu

Mary A. Malina
mary.malina@ucdenver.edu

# INTRODUCTION

After more than 10 years, John Y. Lee has stepped down as Editor of *AIMA*. We would like to express sincere gratitude to John for his dedicated service to the journal. Mary A. Malina has joined Marc J. Epstein as Editor. Mary is an Associate Professor of Accounting at University of Colorado Denver.

This volume of *Advances in Management Accounting (AIMA)* represents the diversity of management accounting topics, methods, and author affiliation which form the basic tenets of *AIMA*. Included are papers on traditional management accounting topics such as performance measurement and cost behavior, as well as papers on broader topics of interest to management accountants such as employee turnover and new product development. The papers in this volume utilize a wide variety of methods including archival data analysis, survey, experiment, qualitative field study, quantitative field study, and structured literature review. Finally, the diversity in authorship is apparent with affiliations from Australia, Germany, New Zealand, Switzerland, and the United States.

This volume begins with a paper by Mertins and White that uses an experimental design to examine biases in performance evaluation that result from the presentation and use of multiple measures in a balanced scorecard. The study concludes that presentation of BSC in a graph (as opposed to a table) results in a more efficient evaluation mechanism, but, conversely, results in more bias in the ratings as well. The study also shows that evaluators make judgments consistent with the performance on nonfinancial measures when the performance on all six non-financial measures varies from the performance on the two financial measures.

The next paper by Hesford, Malina, and Pizzini uses a quantitative field study to investigate the impact of employee turnover on unit-level financial performance. They investigate outcomes associated with the turnover of unskilled workers (hotel housekeepers and front desk attendants), isolating its effects on revenue, cost, and profit. They challenge the assumption that voluntary turnover is categorically harmful and the results for front desk attendants support the view that organizations choose turnover levels that maximize performance. The authors also provide new evidence on the effects of involuntary turnover. Contrary to the established notion that dismissing less able employees should improve performance, they find that involuntary turnover has negative consequences.

Nuhu, Baird, and Appuhami use a survey to study the extent of use and the impact of two packages of management accounting (contemporary and traditional) on organizational change and organizational performance in the public sector. Prior research has examined these packages in private industry and some research has examined isolated practices. This paper targets a gap in the literature by examining packages of controls in public organizations. The findings indicate that while the prevalence of traditional practices is still dominant, such practices were not associated with organizational change or performance. Rather, those organizations that use contemporary management accounting practices to a greater extent experienced greater change and stronger performance.

The next paper by Akroyd, Biswas, and Chuang uses a qualitative field study to provide an in-depth description and analysis of how a company used management controls in new product development (NPD). The focus is on the tension between strategic objectives of sales growth versus product profitability. For managing this tension, responsibilities are divided between different departments (i.e., Marketing and NPD) and decision-making processes are clearly structured along a stage-gate process. While the alignment of product development projects to corporate strategy is not easy, this study shows how it can be enabled through the use of a number of management control practices.

The next paper by Wouters, Morales, Grollmuss, and Scheer provides an overview of research on cost management methods in new product development published in the innovation and operations management. The authors build on their previous structured literature review that was published in Volume 24 of *AIMA* which focused solely on the management accounting literature. They help bridge the gap between management accounting and other management disciplines studying new product development. This paper is a worthwhile attempt at finding the common thread that will be helpful for future management accounting research.

The final paper by Subramaniam and Watson uses archival data analysis to help resolve the conflicting results on sticky cost behavior in prior literature. Large sample studies in cost behavior find costs are sticky, that is, costs are less likely to decrease when activity decreases than to increase when activity increases. In contrast, studies limited to one industry find little or no sticky cost behavior. To resolve these differences, they examine sticky cost behavior across four major industry groups characterized by different production and operating environments and find that sticky cost behavior is industry specific, both in the magnitude of activity changes that give rise to sticky cost behavior and in the determinants that drive the behavior. Their results may explain why, contrary to large sample studies, single industry studies find little or no sticky behavior in costs.

We believe the six papers in this volume represent relevant, theoretically sound, and practical studies that can greatly benefit the management accounting discipline. They manifest our commitment to providing a high level of contribution to management accounting research and practice.

Marc J. Epstein
Mary A. Malina
*Editors*

# PRESENTATION FORMATS, PERFORMANCE OUTCOMES, AND IMPLICATIONS FOR PERFORMANCE EVALUATIONS

Lasse Mertins and Lourdes Ferreira White

## ABSTRACT

Purpose — *This study examines the impact of different Balanced Scorecard (BSC) formats (table, graph without summary measure, graph with a summary measure) on various decision outcomes: performance ratings, perceived informativeness, and decision efficiency.*

Methodology/approach — *Using an original case developed by the researchers, a total of 135 individuals participated in the experiment and rated the performance of carwash managers in two different scenarios: one manager excelled financially but failed to meet targets for all other three BSC perspectives and the other manager had the opposite results.*

Findings — *The evaluators rated managerial performance significantly lower in the graph format compared to a table presentation of the BSC. Performance ratings were significantly higher for the scenario where the manager failed to meet only financial perspective targets but exceeded targets for all other nonfinancial BSC perspectives, contrary to the usual*

Advances in Management Accounting, Volume 26, 1–34
ISSN: 1474-7871/doi:10.1108/S1474-787120150000026001

1

*predictions based on the financial measure bias. The evaluators reported that informativeness of the BSC was highest in the table or graph without summary measure formats, and, surprisingly, adding a summary measure to the graph format significantly reduced perceived informativeness compared to the table format. Decision efficiency was better for the graph formats (with or without summary measure) than for the table format.*

Originality/value − *Ours is the first study to compare tables, graphs with and without a summary measure in the context of managerial performance evaluations and to examine their impact on ratings, informativeness, and efficiency. We developed an original case to test the boundaries of the financial measure bias.*

**Keywords:** Presentation format; performance evaluation; BSC; informativeness; efficiency; financial measure bias

# INTRODUCTION

For over two decades, management accounting researchers and practitioners have been advocating the use of multiple performance measures in managerial evaluations (Kaplan & Norton, 1992). The use of these measures is expected to increase the fairness of performance appraisals and motivate managers to act in ways that will benefit the organization in the long run (Merchant & Van der Stede, 2012). Both financial and nonfinancial performance measures can be combined in Strategic Performance Measurement Systems (SPMS), to remedy several shortcomings present in evaluations that focus only on financial performance measures. In particular, the Balanced Scorecard (BSC), a widely adopted SPMS tool, is designed as an integrated set of financial and nonfinancial measures consistent with organizational strategy, to help translate strategy into action by establishing measures that lead managers to achieve strategic goals (Kaplan & Norton, 2001).

For the BSC to promote such strategy-directed behavior, all performance measures included in the BSC that meet certain criteria such as controllability and goal congruency (see review in Libby, Salterio, & Webb, 2004) should be considered relevant in managerial evaluations. There is growing evidence, however, that the implementation of the BSC is often accompanied by practical limitations, and evaluators routinely fail to integrate all relevant performance measures. Neglect of unique, strategy-driven measures (Banker, Chang, & Pizzini, 2004; Lipe & Salterio, 2000), or overemphasis of financial measures (Cardinaels & Van Veen-Dirks, 2010) are judgment biases related to BSC use that have been well-documented in the management accounting literature (Kaplan, Petersen, & Samuels, 2012).

In our study we examine how various presentation formats of BSC information may mitigate biases in performance evaluations by calling evaluators' attention to both financial and nonfinancial measures. We contribute to the extant performance measurement literature in three ways. First, we compared three BSC presentation formats (table, graph without summary measure, and graph with summary measure) to evaluate their impact on evaluators' judgments. Secondly, we developed an original case and used it in an experiment designed to test the boundaries of the financial measure bias. The case included a scenario where a manager excelled in all nonfinancial BSC perspectives but failed to meet targets for the financial perspective, and another scenario where the managers had the opposite results. Instead of replicating tests based on the same clothing retail industry and performance measures used in Lipe and Salterio (2000), as it has been a common practice in management accounting research for the past 10 years (e.g., Banker et al., 2004; Cardinaels & Van Veen-Dirks, 2010; Kaplan et al., 2012; Neumann, Roberts, & Cauvin, 2010, 2011), we tested whether presentation format and performance outcomes influence performance appraisals in the carwash industry, a simple business setting familiar to most people. Thirdly, we explored how presentation formats may affect other aspects of performance appraisal, such as the relative informativeness of the three types of BSC presentation formats and decision efficiency.

Presentation formats for performance evaluation have become an important issue for practitioners (Neumann et al., 2011). Performance evaluations play a critical role in motivating and retaining top talent in any organization, and presenting performance measures in ways that reduce bias and increase evaluation efficiency can significantly contribute to organizational success (Dilla & Steinbart, 2005). Some companies have chosen to present BSC data in the form of simple tables, while others use color and performance markers that indicate positive and negative variances from target (Azofra, Prietro, & Santidrian, 2003; Bauer, Tanner, & Neely, 2004). More complex presentation formats incorporate graphical attributes such as length and size of bars to highlight differences in performance (Card, Mackinlay, & Shneiderman, 1999). Based on information-processing theory (Libby, 1981), Cardinaels and Van Veen-Dirks (2010) found that markers facilitate the information-processing task and help evaluators pay attention to nonfinancial performance measures.

Developments in commercially available software allow users to engage in interactive data visualization whereby the user chooses which information to view and whether it is displayed in a table or graph format (Active Strategy, 2009; Edwards, 2005; Microsoft, 2013; SAP, 2010). For example, QPR Scorecard (QPR, 2014) allows users to select from an array of supplementary displays of BSC data. According to Dilla, Janvrin, and Jeffrey (2013), most large public company annual reports present key financial variables in graph formats. By some estimates, 80−90% of companies in western developed countries use graphs to report performance data (Beattie & Jones, 2008). In their investor relations websites, companies now offer users the options of selecting which financial data to display and the format of the presentation (Dilla, Janvrin, & Raschke, 2010).

Although this proliferation of ways of visualizing data is often advertised as a benefit to users of BSC software, researchers have just begun to assess the effect of various BSC display formats on decision quality (Dilla & Steinbart, 2005; Hirsch, Seubert, & Sohn, 2015; Schauß, Hirsch, & Sohn, 2014). We hope to contribute to this research effort.

This paper is organized as follows: The next section presents a literature review and introduces our hypotheses, followed by a section that describes the research methods for data collection and analysis. Further, we dedicated a section to reporting and discussing the results. A summary of the implications of this study for performance measurement research and practice appears in the last section.


## LITERATURE REVIEW AND HYPOTHESES DEVELOPMENT

For the BSC to be truly balanced, evaluators need to consider all relevant BSC performance measures, both financial and nonfinancial. A central research question in our study is whether presentation formats, to the extent that they influence an evaluator's ability to extract information from an evaluation report, can significantly impact the quality of the evaluator's judgment and decision making (JDM).

The psychology literature has provided rich insights into how human cognition processes are influenced by presentation formats. This line of research has examined how graphs (or pictures) compare with tables (or words and numbers) in terms of the accuracy, speed, and difficulty of information extraction and integration. Graphs facilitate tasks when "we need to reason about a graph by comparing a value to some expected or standard value ... (i.e., how big is this relative to that?)" (Zacks, Levy, Tversky, & Schiano, 1998, p. 136). Cognitive psychologists have also found that the placement of salient anchors can severely affect the extent of estimation errors (Poulton, 1985). An anchoring bias occurs when a decision maker forms a preliminary estimate based on an initial value (usually displayed in a salient or prominent way), and then proceeds to make partial adjustments based on subsequent information (Epley & Gilovich, 2002; Tversky & Kahneman, 1974), while still "anchored" on the initial estimate. One defining characteristic of this anchoring/adjustment cognitive process is that the piece of information presented most saliently can bias the overall decision, because additional information leads the decision maker to adjust the initial estimate only partially. Such an anchoring effect holds true even if the anchoring piece of data is uninformative or irrelevant (Kahneman, 2011). This persistent anchoring bias has spurred ongoing research into the way humans process information based on the specific format in which it is presented.

More recently, psychology researchers have examined specifically how people form mental representations based on information displayed in tables versus graphs in order to make a decision. Graphs are found to help people engage in perceptual processing, whereby subjects perceive cues in a context, while tables induce analytical processing, with subjects processing cues as discrete data points in a decontextualized way (Amit, Algom, & Trope, 2009).

When a judgment task requires significant cognitive effort to process multiple cues, especially under conditions of uncertainty, people are expected to resort to heuristic strategies or shortcuts (Epley & Gilovich, 2002). In contrast with rational strategies, where an individual considers all cues and their relative degree of association to each alternative judgment, heuristic strategies "assume that people apply simple rules that often rely on a subset of available information" (Bryant, 2014, p. 97). This selective information processing is characteristic of intuitive thinking and associated with heuristics (Epley & Gilovich, 2002). Tables, by presenting information in more abstract, decontextualized ways such as words (Rim et al., 2015) engender rational strategies, while graphs provide more concrete, simplified pictures that elicit heuristic thinking, by "reducing the amount of information considered and, potentially, the complexity of computations performed" (Bryant, 2014, p. 108).

These differences between tables and graphs have also prompted information system research into which presentation formats, based on available technologies, offer the best fit with the requirements of the tasks being executed. An early version of cognitive fit theory posited that when the presentation format elicits a type of mental representation that is appropriate for the type of task at hand, cognitive fit is achieved and decision outcomes such as accuracy and efficiency improve (Umanath & Vessey, 1994; Vessey, 1991; Vessey & Galetta, 1991). Inasmuch as tables induce analytical thinking, they offer a better fit than graphs when symbolic tasks are carried out (such as, calculating profit from rows of sales and cost information). Graphs, on the other hand, since they induce perceptual thinking, offer the best fit for spatial tasks (e.g., comparing bars in a graph to determine the year with highest sales). Later information system research expanded cognitive fit theory to address task complexity, task environment, information overload, and decision maker characteristics (Kelton, Pennington, & Tuttle, 2010). Still, after dozens of studies and decades of research, information system studies have not been able to establish the precise circumstances under which graphs may be better or worse than tables for JDM quality (Jarvenpaa & Dickson, 1988).

Some breakthroughs on presentation format research have come from its application to the marketing domain. Jarvenpaa (1990), when studying consumer decision making, identified that the type of presentation format "appears to have some effect not only on the temporal order in which information on attributes is acquired, but also on the relative attention given to information on attributes during the early phases of decision making" (Jarvenpaa, 1990, p. 247). She described that the first stage of decision making is marked by automatic, pre-attentive data acquisition, "driven by sensory features such as color, size and form" (Jarvenpaa, 1990, p. 251), followed by a second stage when an individual focuses attention and draws from prior knowledge about the task, acquiring information consciously. A graphic display is more appropriate for pre-conscious decision making, when the individual is intuitively focusing on how various items are physically different from one another, because a graph facilitates information acquisition based on the visual salience of the attributes (Hoffman, 1978). On the other hand, an alpha-numeric display (such as tables) facilitates information acquisition based on the importance weights associated with each attribute. The limitations of graphs were also apparent in more recent marketing studies (e.g., Lurie & Mason, 2007), where graphs were found to increase efficiency but not accuracy of decision making. Graphs helped consumers limit their choices to a smaller set of alternatives, by increasing salience of some cues, but also led to biases when consumers evaluated information less relevant for their decisions. Based on the literature review mentioned earlier, we summarized the main implications of the differences between table versus graph presentation formats for JDM purposes in Table 1.

In the accounting area, where complex tasks often require processing multiple cues, by comparing values as well as integrating them into calculated amounts, cognitive effort may be high, and the need for presentation formats to improve JDM takes on special significance. Yet, Libby (1981) argued that accountants in general, including management accountants, have given little systematic thought about how the way accounting data are displayed can influence JDM inside organizations. Companies increasingly generate tabular and graphic reports in various formats, and accountants routinely rely on "using data printed out in almost random format by the computer" (Libby, 1981, p. 116).

Since Libby's statement, the type of presentation format has been found to influence accounting-based JDM in a variety of contexts such as predicting bankruptcy (Smith & Taffler, 1996), pricing and allocating resources (Cardinaels, 2008), auditing of complex estimates (Backof, Thayer, & Carpenter, 2014) and reporting production efficiency (Mertins & White, 2014). Other accounting studies found no significant or mixed results on the effect of presentation format on JDM (e.g., Dilla et al., 2013; Kaplan, 1988). This study expands previous research findings by examining how the presentation format of outcomes in a BSC may impact managerial performance evaluations.

***Table 1.*** Differences in Presentation Format.[a]

| Characteristics of Presentation Formats | Tables | Graphs |
| --- | --- | --- |
| Integration strategy | Analytical | Perceptual |
| Level of abstraction | Higher | Lower (concrete) |
| Type of data | Symbolic (words and numbers) | Spatial (pictures) |
| Access to underlying data | Direct | Indirect |
| Categorization of data | Broader, more inclusive | Narrower, less inclusive (selective) |
| Relationships among data points | Discrete values | Interrelated values |
| Cognitive effort | Higher | Lower |

[a]Based on information from Amit et al. (2009), Bryant (2014), Dilla et al. (2010), Jarvenpaa (1990), Rim et al. (2015), Umanath and Vessey (1994), Zacks et al. (1998).

## *Presentation Format and Performance Evaluations*

In the context of performance evaluations, evaluators are faced with a complex, multi-attribute task. First, they need to extract individual data on targets and actual results; next, they compare the relative sizes of variances from targets and evaluate these variances in terms of positive versus negative values; finally, they integrate this information for multiple performance measures into one overall performance rating. For BSC users, this task becomes even more complex because evaluators have to consider targets and results for several performance measures in the four perspectives of the BSC (financial, customer, internal business, and learning and growth). When facing this type of high-cognitive-load task, it is critical that evaluators see the BSC data presented in a well-organized format. However, because performance evaluations are essentially integrative tasks (not just symbolic or spatial), it becomes difficult to determine the presentation format that would best "fit" these task characteristics. JDM for performance evaluations is often subjective in practice, and typically there are no readily available "right answers" for researchers to assess JDM accuracy or cognitive fit in this context.

To date, few accounting studies have examined the effect of presentation format of performance data on managerial evaluations. Lipe and Salterio (2002) and Cardinaels and Van Veen-Dirks (2010) investigated different ways of organizing BSC data and found significant effects of presentation format on evaluations; however, both studies used only tabular presentations. Dilla and Steinbart (2005) compared tabular and graphical displays of BSC data provided as supplements to traditional BSC divisional performance results, and obtained mixed results regarding judgment consensus, and consistency between evaluation and bonus decisions. Banker, Chang, and Pizzini (2011) tested if supplemental BSC information depicted graphically in BSC strategy maps led evaluators to consider strategic objectives and concluded that these supplemental BSC maps did influence evaluator decisions as predicted. Van Der Heijden (2013) examined the use of a performance anchor and pictorial charts to evaluate performance of a hospital emergency room, and participants perceived the anchor supplemented by the pictorial chart as the most informative and attractive display. Hirsch et al. (2015) showed that the addition of a graph to a table with financial and nonfinancial performance results increases the accuracy of performance evaluations, if the goal is to assign equal weights to all performance measures; the supplemental graphic display did not improve self-reported confidence on the evaluation decision.

In our study, we attempted to replicate realistic task environment conditions, by allowing evaluators to decide how to integrate target and actual data provided for each performance perspective. BSC data are displayed either in table or graph formats, to compare the effect of those presentation formats on evaluation decisions.

We employ bar graphs with columns presented horizontally because of their popularity in practice and their ability to depict both positive and negative variances of actual performance from targets (Beattie & Jones, 2008). According to basic bar graph conventions (for a review, refer to Beattie & Jones, 2008), a scale should be carefully chosen so that even unskilled users can easily interpret the graph specifiers (i.e., the length of the columns). In a bar graph comparing variances from target, the scale uses target levels as the zero point, shown as a vertical axis, with negative variances displayed as horizontal column bars departing from the zero gridline toward the left side and positive variances displayed as horizontal column bars to the right of the zero gridline. Following a perceptual pattern, and beginning from left to right (as conditioned by reading habits), graph users engage in a visual routine of finding an anchor point in the negative columns in the left and scanning other specifiers to the right (or column lengths) (Simkin & Hastie, 1987). Even before engaging in more cognitive activities such as scale or label reading, the user can visually compare the sizes of the variances by concretely inspecting the column lengths. Consistent with heuristic thinking supported by graphs, users thus reduce cognitive effort by lowering the amount of information they need to process and the number of computations performed (Bryant, 2014).

Based on the literature reviewed above, particularly with respect to anchoring (Fay & Montague, 2015; Tversky & Kahneman, 1974), we expect that evaluators presented with a graph first focus on the negative variances saliently displayed on the left side, and anchor their initial judgments on this negative information, then proceed to make partial adjustments to the initial evaluation judgments using information about positive variances displayed on the right side of the graph. Tables, on the other hand, elicit an analytical strategy of extracting discrete data items from each row, top to bottom, without considering comparisons among the data points (Dilla et al., 2013). The use of tables is expected to support the inclusion of more data than graphs, and, primed with symbolic information provided in tables, decision makers are more likely to engage in greater global processing of information presented sequentially (Rim et al., 2015). Therefore, due to the anchoring effect, and the differences between cognitive processing of data displayed in tables versus graphs, evaluators are hypothesized to combine performance results from multiple dimensions into lower performance ratings when using graphs than tables. We formulate this hypothesis as:

**Hypothesis 1a.** The graph format for presenting performance measures is associated, on average, with lower performance ratings than the table format.

For the purpose of our study, we also consider a common variation in the graph format by adding a summary measure that averages the performance results across all four dimensions of the BSC. In conversations with controllers and other management accounting professionals during a recent annual conference of the Institute of Management Accountants, we found that organizations routinely report an overall performance index that combines all performance results into one score instead of letting individual evaluators tailor the weights attributed to financial and nonfinancial measures to the unique strategies of the business units.

Summary measures can serve as a decision aid to assist decision makers in integrating information from the multiple performance cues. While the creators of the BSC did not recommend specific ways for performance evaluators to combine results from financial and nonfinancial measures (Kaplan & Norton, 1996), there is evidence in the accounting literature that decision aids, even if redundant, can "help reduce task complexity by reducing the amount of information a person has to process" (Bonner, 2008, p. 342). Decision aids, by definition, are task-specific tools that facilitate information gathering, processing and analyzing (Brown & Eining, 1996). Furthermore, Mertins (2014) hypothesized, based on heuristic processing and the tendency of evaluators to employ shortcuts to reduce cognitive effort, that evaluators tend to focus on summary measures that are salient (Haynes & Kachelmeier, 1998); the evidence supported this hypothesis, and evaluators were found to direct their attention to the summary measure while ignoring additional information.

We expect that a summary measure, when added to the graph format for performance measures, will help mitigate some of the rating difference between the graph and table formats described earlier, by providing a salient, easy-to-access index that incorporates the information content from all performance measures, compensating in part for the anchoring effect of negative variances. However, given that evaluators are still using a graph format, we hypothesize that the graph with summary measure format leads to lower performance ratings than the ones obtained with the table format. Thus the second part of our first hypothesis states:

**Hypothesis 1b.** The graph with summary measure format for presenting performance measures is associated, on average, with higher performance ratings than the graph format without a summary measure, but lower performance ratings than the table format.

## Financial versus Nonfinancial Performance

Kaplan and Norton (1992) explicitly intended the BSC to combine financial and nonfinancial measures in order to provide a more complete evaluation of historic (lagging) as well as future-oriented (leading) performance factors that impact strategic business units within organizations. However, just a few years after pioneering organizations started implementing the BSC, researchers started documenting the financial measure bias by demonstrating that evaluators systematically ignore nonfinancial measures in favor of financial ones, especially when performance results conflict along different dimensions (Kaplan & Norton, 1996; Simons & Davila, 1998). In their seminal paper, Lipe and Salterio (2000) found that evaluators tend to focus on performance measures that are common across business units (mostly financial measures) and ignore unique measures that are based on strategic considerations (the "common measure bias"). As summarized in Wong-On-Wing, Guo, Li, and Yang (2007), other research has suggested ways to reduce the common measure bias by introducing strategy maps (Banker et al., 2004), disaggregating measures included in the BSC (Roberts, Albright, & Hibbets, 2004), and providing both process accountability and quality assurance for the measures (Libby et al., 2004). More recently, Kang and Fredin (2012) demonstrated that performance evaluation feedback attenuates the common measure bias.

Several explanations exist for overemphasizing financial measures: Evaluators, who are subject to cognitive limitations, reduce their cognitive load by focusing on the more familiar financial measures; those measures inspire more confidence because they rely on audited financial statements; and they are easier to collect and process. Furthermore, the "outcome effect" from the psychological literature suggests that evaluators place more weight on financial measures because they reflect the outcome of managerial decisions, thereby neglecting nonfinancial measures that are typically input-based or process-oriented (Brown & Solomon, 1987; Ghosh & Lusch, 2000; Mitchell & Kalb, 1981). Even when nonfinancial measures are not neglected, the "halo bias" of focusing primarily on financial measures appears to influence how evaluators perceive nonfinancial results (DeBusk, Killough, & Brown, 2005). Cardinaels and Van Veen-Dirks (2010) show that using the BSC may actually exacerbate the financial measures bias: compared to evaluators using an unformatted list of measures, evaluators presented with a BSC tend to make more extreme judgments when divisions differ in their financial performance, but not when divisions differ along other performance perspectives.

Several studies that reported a BSC financial bias have employed a similar instrument: a BSC with at least four measures per BSC perspective, with financial measures representing 20 to 25% of the total number of measures (e.g., DeBusk et al., 2005; Cardinaels & Van Veen-Dirks, 2010). Another study designed a BSC instrument with an equal number of four financial and four nonfinancial measures and found mixed results regarding the financial measure bias (Neumann et al., 2011). Depending on the purpose of the study, evaluators were asked to consider scenarios where the manager exceeded targets for all performance measures by different amounts (e.g., Lipe & Salterio, 2000) or beat targets and underperformed for an equal number of measures (e.g., Kaplan et al., 2012).

In our study, we are interested in exploring the boundaries of the financial measure bias by investigating how evaluators respond when a manager either fails to meet targets for the financial perspective only or achieves financial perspective targets but fails on all other nonfinancial BSC perspectives (which typically comprise the majority of the BSC measures). If cognitive load is reduced by limiting the number of measures so that evaluators can consider all measures (financial and nonfinancial), we expect that their performance ratings will follow the direction of the majority of the variances in the nonfinancial perspectives (either positive or negative). Thus our second hypothesis states:

**Hypothesis 2.** Managers who excel in all three of the nonfinancial BSC perspectives but fail to meet targets only for the financial perspective receive higher performance ratings than managers who excel only in the financial perspective but fail to meet targets for all three of the nonfinancial BSC perspectives, regardless of presentation format.

In Table 2, we summarized the implications of this hypothesis concerning the financial measure bias. In the "Above Target" condition, if evaluators respond with a low overall performance rating, that would be strong evidence of financial measure bias because the manager did exceed targets in the majority of measures. Conversely, in the "Below Target" condition, if evaluators still rated the manager's performance highly, that would also be strong evidence of the financial measure bias, because the manager

***Table 2.*** Boundaries of Financial Measure Bias.

| Manager Excelled in Financial Perspective? | Low Overall Performance Rating | High Overall Performance Rating |
|---|---|---|
| No, but excelled in all nonfinancial perspectives ("Above Target") | Strong evidence of financial measure bias | No evidence of financial measure bias |
| Yes, but failed in all nonfinancial perspectives ("Below Target") | No evidence of financial measure bias | Strong evidence of financial measure bias |

missed targets for the majority of measures. The other two possible combinations would indicate that no financial measure bias was evident, as predicted in H2.

### Informativeness

For the purpose of this study, we adopt the definition of informativeness proposed by Christensen and Demski (2003): "the capacity of information to make a difference in a decision by helping users to form predictions about the outcomes of past, present, and future events or to confirm or correct prior expectations" (Christensen & Demski, 2003, p. 427). This concept of informativeness was used by Van Veen-Dirks (2010) to assess the role performance measures play in facilitating decisions regarding periodic evaluations. Similarly, Van Der Heijden (2013) characterized informativeness as the facility with which actual results may be compared with targets.

According to Holmstrom's informativeness criterion (Holmstrom, 1979), based on agency theory, any measure that offers additional information regarding the agent's actions should be used by the principal in performance evaluations. However, empirical research has shown that presentation formats influence perceived informativeness of performance measures in complex ways. Dilla and Steinbart (2005) found that a tabular format showing results as percentages above or below targets is the most informative format for the evaluation of divisional performance (this is consistent with results from Fennema & Kleinmuntz, 1995; Kleinmuntz & Schkade, 1993; Schkade & Kleinmuntz, 1994). On the other hand, Blocher, Moffie, and Zmud (1986) found that graphs, compared to tables, improved auditor judgments in an experimental forecasting task. Yet Dilla and Steinbart (2005) found strong support for the conclusion that users perceived graphs to be less informative than tables when rendering judgments about performance evaluations and bonuses.

One argument in favor of tables being more informative than graphs during performance appraisals is that tables allow evaluators to access specific data points more easily (Lusk & Kersnick, 1979). Furthermore, tables preserve the global features of the information (Backof et al., 2014). Even though tables, compared to graphs, require more cognitive effort to process the data, they offer the advantage that the evaluator has direct access to the underlying data (Lusk & Kersnick, 1979) which can lead to a perception of increased informativeness and thus improve user experience (Amer, 1991). Graphs, while requiring less cognitive effort, "do not present discrete data values directly ... the data in graphs are accessed using perceptual processes" (Umanath & Vessey, 1994, p. 805). Such perceptual processes lead users to pay more attention at salient attributes and disregard others in a selective processing of information (Jarvenpaa, 1990). Previous information systems research found that, for higher level decision activities, graph users have demonstrated less understanding of the information gathered than table users (Jarvenpaa & Dickson, 1988), which would make graphs less informative for complex tasks such as evaluation decisions. We expect that evaluators using graphical displays of performance data may perceive their informativeness as lower than those using a tabular format.

In our study we are also interested in assessing the informativeness of graphs that are supplemented with a summary measure. Based on salience theory (Haynes & Kachelmeier, 1998; Mertins, 2014), we expect that a summary measure calculated on the basis of all variances from target will alter the salience of the different dimensions of the data set. Jarvenpaa (1990) found that displaying adjacent bars in a graph was enough to alter the salience of the differences among the attributes of divisional performance. In a multi-attribute, multi-choice task, participants focused only on the graphical displays with a salient cue and not on how relevant the attributes were or how they were weighted. Pomerantz (1981) introduced the concept of an "emergent feature" to explain why users will focus on a novel grouping of parts that can be perceived without prior recognition of its components. Consequently, we expect graphs with a summary measure (while still less informative than tables because of perceptual processing of the graphical format) will be perceived as more informative than graphs without such salient information. We state our third hypothesis as:

**Hypothesis 3.** Evaluators rate the informativeness of performance reports using the table format higher than those using the graph format with a summary measure, which, in turn, rate informativeness higher than those using a graph without a summary measure.

## *Efficiency*

Given the limited amount of time that supervisors can take away from day-to-day operations to evaluate subordinates, efficiency in the use of time is a desirable outcome of decisions based on performance data. Time spent on a task is, in fact, frequently used as a dependent variable to measure desirable decision outcomes in data representation research (Dilla et al., 2010). Decision latency or speed is a typical variable of interest in accounting information systems research (see Amer, 1991) because even small improvements in the time it takes for managers to make regular decisions may cumulatively result in significant resource savings.

Van Der Heijden (2013) tested whether a pictorial or verbal presentation format of hospital performance data led to differences in time spent on the experimental task. While task duration was found to have no significant impact on evaluation scores across different presentation formats, variations in presentation format were associated with changes in time spent on the evaluation.

As discussed in the introduction, the lack of objective, formula-based procedures for evaluations in most BSC settings (Banker et al., 2011) causes evaluators to spend time considering which measures to use and how to weigh them. This is particularly true of a tabular presentation format, given that it requires more cognitive effort from decision makers to extract information, analyze it and make an overall judgment. A graphical representation can facilitate problem comprehension by summarizing information (Desanctis & Jarvenpaa, 1989). This ability of graphs to summarize information is consistent with evidence about time on task and its effect on investors' judgments about earnings performance (Dilla et al., 2013). Graphs can make evaluation decisions more efficient by allowing "simultaneous processing of numerous data points" (see review by Backof et al., 2014, p. 11).

The comparative advantage of graphs over tables in terms of processing time relates to the ability of graphs to elicit perceptual strategies for information acquisition and evaluation (Umanath & Vessey, 1994). By allowing users to perceive data at a glance, graphs support quicker comparisons among data points, compared to the analytical, step-by-step strategies required by tables. As Umanath and Vessey (1994) argued, "the dominant characteristic of the perceptual processes used in association with graphs is that they lead to fast responses ..." (p. 805). Their study, however, found no significant difference in time between graphs and tables used for a bankruptcy prediction task.

Furthermore, early psychological studies concluded that small variations in graph styles can result in significant differences in the time needed to make certain types of judgments (Lohse, 1993; Pinker, 1990; Zacks et al., 1998). A graph with a summary measure, to the extent that it reduces cognitive load by providing a ready-to-use way of integrating performance data, is expected to reduce time on task even more than graphs without such summary measures. Thus our fourth hypotheses is:

**Hypothesis 4.** Performance ratings require most time when results are presented in a table format, followed by graph formats without a summary measure and graphs with a summary measure.

# METHODOLOGY

## *Participants*

A total of 135 participants took part in this experiment. In regard to the subject selection, we followed Cardinaels' (2008) approach of recruiting business students as participants in a similar decision-making experiment. A mix of undergraduate and graduate students who were enrolled in two public universities in the mid-Atlantic area of the United States participated in our study; participation was voluntary and could be discontinued at any point during the experimental task. All of the students were taking management accounting courses at the time of the survey and received course credit for their participation. The subjects were on average 23.90 years old and had 3.74 years of work experience. 48.89% of the students were females. All of the students had some experience with BSCs that they acquired during their management accounting courses, and there were no differences in BSC knowledge among the experimental groups. Table 3 summarizes the demographics of the participants.

## *Experimental Design*

We employed a 3x2 factorial design. The two independent variables were Presentation Format (between-subject design) and Performance Outcomes (within-subject design). First, the BSC information was displayed to the participants in three different "*Presentation Formats*": (a) "Table" format; (b) "Graph" format; and (c) "Graph with Summary Measure" format. Each participant was randomly assigned to only one of the three

**Table 3.** Demographic Data.

| Attribute | Scale | Overall | Table | Graph | Graph with Summary Measure |
|---|---|---|---|---|---|
| Number of participants | | 135 | 44 | 44 | 47 |
| Age | Years | 23.90 | 23.89 | 23.37 | 24.40 |
| Gender (females) | Percentage | 48.89% | 50.00% | 40.91% | 55.32% |
| Work experience | Years | 3.74 | 3.18 | 3.80 | 4.21 |
| Evaluator experience | Percentage | 12.59% | 18.18% | 11.36% | 8.51% |
| Evaluatee experience | Percentage | 60.74% | 56.82% | 63.64% | 61.70% |
| Self-perceived BSC knowledge | Rating 1–10[a] | 5.28 | 5.18 | 5.05 | 5.57 |

[a] 1 – lowest score; 10 – highest score.

presentation formats. The second independent variable was "*Performance Outcomes*" referring to the performance of the two carwash store managers to be evaluated. In the "Above Target" condition, the manager of the "Light Street" store exceeded target in the six nonfinancial measures, but came short of the target in the two financial measures. Because six of the variances were positive, the summary measure also displayed a positive overall variance (thus the label "Above target" for this condition). On the other hand, in the "Below Target" condition ("Main Street" store), the manager exceeded the targets for the two measures in the financial perspective, but came short of the targets for the six measures in the Customer, Internal Business, and Learning & Growth perspectives.

"*Performance Evaluation Rating*," "*Informativeness Rating*," and the "*Time to Perform Evaluation*" were the dependent variables in our study. The first two dependent variables were measured using a 0 (worst) to 100 (best) scale. The online survey tool that we employed allowed us to measure the time that the participants took to submit the evaluation.

### Experimental Tasks

The experimental instrument asked the participants to complete performance evaluations of store managers of two carwash locations (Light Street and Main Street) using a BSC framework. One manager exceeded all six targets for the nonfinancial BSC perspectives but underperformed financially (Light Street), while the other manager exceeded the two financial perspective targets but underperformed in six of the eight measures

(Main Street). The majority of the participants (119 students) completed the survey during regular class hours in a computer lab. The remaining 16 students were online students who completed the experiment outside of class.

The experiment consisted of an original case developed by the authors about a carwash company's performance evaluation system. We pilot tested this instrument with 20 MBA students that had BSC knowledge. Based on their feedback, we revised the instrument before distributing it to the participants in this study. The case company used a BSC with eight measures (two measures in each of the four BSC perspectives: Financial, Customer, Internal Business, and Learning & Growth). We employed the following eight measures: two financial measures for the financial perspective (Sales Growth and Cost per Carwash), two nonfinancial measures for the customer perspective (Customer Satisfaction Rating, and Repeat Visits per Customer per Year), two nonfinancial measures for the internal business perspective (Average Wait Time per Customer, and Preventive Maintenance Hours per Year), and two nonfinancial measures for the learning and growth perspective (Number of Training Hours per Year and Employee Retention). These measures were used to evaluate the store managers' overall performance, their bonuses, and promotions. We selected those BSC measures and their corresponding targets based on a review of carwash industry statistics online (US Census Bureau, 2014) and trade publications. We also reviewed three Harvard Business School teaching cases (Bruns, 1999; Gompers, 2010; Jerez & Miller, 2011) and one business simulation (Ernst, 2012) to define the performance measures as they are typically used in the carwash industry. Performance measures were selected carefully to reflect factors that are within the control of a carwash manager.

After reading information about the company, its strategy, and its store managers, the participants received the BSC results for one of two stores of the carwash company. The BSC for the "Light Street" location showed positive variances for the two financial measures (Sales Growth and Cost per Carwash) and negative variances for the remaining six nonfinancial measures. In contrast, the BSC for the "Main Street" shop displayed positive variances for the two financial measures and negative variances for the nonfinancial measures. Positive variances were color-coded in green and negative variances color-coded in red for all three presentation formats. We examined several BSCs used by corporations prior to developing the instrument and found that it was common to color-code positive variances in green and negative variances in red. We randomized the order of the two

BSC conditions, that is, some participants received the "Light Street" BSC first, others the "Main Street" scorecard.

The participants were randomly assigned to one of three presentation formats. The "Table" format presented the BSC results as a list separated into the four perspectives. The measures in the four BSC perspectives were visually separated and the three columns contained the target values, actual values, and the variances from the target. The "Graph" format displayed the same measures within the same perspectives. However, this format did not display the actual and target values. Instead, it showed the variances in form of eight bar graphs. The length of the variance bars increased with the magnitude of variances; the percentage values (positive and negative) were also displayed inside the bar graphs. Finally, the "Graph with Summary Measure" condition consisted of the same graph as in the "Graph" format, but it also included a summary measure at the bottom of the BSC displaying the mean variance of all eight measures.

The subjects were asked to take on the role of the regional manager who evaluates store managers on a yearly basis. Therefore, after examining the first scorecard, the participants were asked to (1) rate the overall performance of the respective store manager, (2) recommend the manager for a bonus, (3) recommend the store manager for a promotion, and (4) rate the informativeness of the respective BSC. Then the second scorecard was presented, followed by the same four questions. After that they were asked to answer two questions: (a) a manipulation check question ("Did the Balanced Scorecard include an Overall Average Measure?") and (b) a question intended to check their information retention ("How many individual measures were in the Clean and Shiny Carwash's Balanced Scorecard?").

Next, we asked the participants about the importance of each measure for their evaluations, but we did not report these results here because this part of the experiment is outside the scope of this study. Finally, the participants completed a short seven-question quiz about BSC concepts and rated their self-perceived level of BSC knowledge. The last section of the instrument included several demographic questions. We did not place any time pressure on the participants; they were allowed to take as much time as they needed to complete the tasks.

*Analysis*

We employed a 3x2 Analysis of Variance (ANOVA) to test our hypotheses. For H1, H3, and H4, additional *t*-tests were conducted to compare mean results of the three experimental groups. In all hypotheses tests, "Presentation Format" and "Performance Outcome" are the independent variables. In the H1 and H2 analysis, "Performance Evaluation Rating" is the dependent variable. "Informativeness Rating" and "Time to Complete Evaluation" are the dependent variables in the H3 and H4 analyses, respectively.

In addition we conducted several analyses to examine whether personal characteristics (e.g., gender, work experience, etc.) impact the performance ratings in the three presentation formats.

# RESULTS

## *Manipulation Check*

We included a manipulation check question in our experiment to examine if the participants recalled whether their instrument included an overall summary measure. The instrument did not include a summary measure in the "Table" and "Graph" groups. Most of the participants in the "Table" (89%) and the "Graph" (77%) conditions correctly answered this question. Seventy percent of the participants in the "Graph with Summary Measure" group remembered that they had a summary measure at the bottom of their BSC. When the participants who failed this manipulation check were removed from the analysis, the results were still qualitatively the same.

## *Hypothesis 1*

In H1a, we anticipated that individuals assign lower performance ratings in a graph format than in a table format. The results on the last row labeled "Total" in Table 4, Panel A, reveal that the ratings for managerial performance (64.77) are significantly higher in the "Table" format than in the "Graph" (49.16) format. The results from the ANOVA (Table 4, Panel B) show that the mean differences between the "Table" format and the two graphical formats are statistically significant at the $p < 0.05$ level in terms of performance evaluation ratings. The $t$-test reported in Table 4, Panel C, confirms that performance ratings for the table format are significantly different ($p < 0.05$) from the graph format. Therefore, H1a is supported.

According to H1b, evaluators in the "Graph with Summary Measure" group would provide higher ratings than the participants in the "Graph"

***Table 4.*** ANOVA: The Impact of Presentation Format and above/below Target Performance on Performance Evaluation Ratings.

Panel A: Mean Performance Ratings (and Standard Deviation)[a]

|  | Table | Graph | Graph with summary measure | Total |
|---|---|---|---|---|
| Above target[b] | 77.52 | 64.77 | 68.36 | 70.18 |
|  | (12.56) | (17.09) | (21.97) | (15.24) |
| Below target[b] | 52.02 | 33.55 | 38.64 | 41.34 |
|  | (19.85) | (19.73) | (22.38) | (20.78) |
| Total | 64.77 | 49.16 | 53.50 | 55.76 |
|  | (20.91) | (24.15) | (21.97) | (23.23) |

Panel B: Analysis of Variance for Main Effects ($n = 270$)

| Source of variation | df | Sum of squares | Mean square | F | p-value[c] |
|---|---|---|---|---|---|
| Presentation format | 2 | 11,462.625 | 5,731.312 | 19.615 | 0.000 |
| Performance | 1 | 55,998.739 | 55,998.739 | 191.656 | 0.000 |
| Presentation format × Performance | 2 | 389.142 | 194.571 | 0.666 | 0.515 |
| Error | 264 | 77,136.293 | 292.183 |  |  |

Panel C: *t*-Test

|  | Difference in perf. ratings | p-value[d] |
|---|---|---|
| Table versus graph | 15.61 | 0.000 |
| Graph versus graph with summary measure | 4.34 | 0.206 |
| Table versus graph with summary measure | 11.27 | 0.001 |

[a]Dependent variable: performance evaluation rating on a 0−100 Scale.
[b]*Above Target* = 2 financial measures below target, 6 nonfinancial measures above target; *Below Target* = 2 financial measures above target, 6 nonfinancial measures below target.
[c]One-tailed.
[d]Two-tailed.

group, but lower ratings than the participants in the "Table" group. The results in Table 4 reveal that the average ratings in the "Graph with Summary Measures" (53.50) were indeed in between the "Table" (64.77) and "Graph" (49.16) ratings. However, while the difference in means is significant when comparing performance ratings in the "Graph with Summary Measure" to the "Table" group ($p < 0.05$; Table 4; Panel C), the difference in mean ratings is not significant when comparing the "Graph with Summary Measure" and the "Graph" conditions ($p > 0.05$). Therefore, H1b is only partially supported.

These results are important for organizations striving to design performance evaluation systems that utilize alternative presentation formats such as graphs. A graphical format may seem an attractive alternative presentation format of a manager's achievements because it summarizes the performance in one bar per measure (when it is displayed in a bar graph). However, the results of this study suggest that evaluations are significantly lower when the BSC is presented in a graphical versus tabular format. This occurs in both the below and the above target conditions. This result does not mean that the ratings in a graphical format are more or less accurate than in tabular format because it is impossible to determine the "perfect evaluation assessment" in a subjective performance evaluation environment. Nevertheless, these results suggest that, compared to the most common format (the tabulated BSC with four perspectives), using a bar chart format to display the variances from the target will lead to lower performance ratings on average. The display of a summary measure in the graph format only partially reduces the difference between performance ratings for the table versus graph format.

This may have a significant impact on the evaluatee's compensation and career if her or his evaluation ratings tend to be lower as a result of the presentation format choice. Managers need to be aware of this tendency. Given that we did not directly assess JDM quality, we cannot determine based on our results whether the table or the graph format leads to a more accurate evaluation.

*Hypothesis 2*

Previous studies suggest that the BSC is not very balanced because evaluators base their evaluations primarily on the financial measures (e.g., DeBusk et al., 2005; Ittner, Larcker, & Meyer, 2003). We examine the boundaries of this financial measure bias in our experiment. Does the financial measure bias still exist when all nonfinancial measures exhibit variances from targets in the opposite direction of the variances from financial targets? In the Light Street scenario ("Above Target"), only the two financial variances are negative, while in the Main Street scenario ("Below Target"), the two financial measures are the only ones showing a positive variance. If the financial measure bias existed in either scenario, then evaluators would focus primarily on the two financial measures and evaluate the manager more positively in the "Below Target" condition and more negatively in the "Above Target" condition. However, we predicted that the financial measure bias is mitigated or non-existent when a majority of nonfinancial measures show a variance that is opposite to the financial measures variance.

The results in Table 4, Panel A, reveal that evaluators rate the carwash manager's performance significantly higher in the "Above Target" group for all three presentation formats (77.52, 64.77, 68.36) than the managers in the "Below Target" group (52.02, 33.55, 38.64). The average rating for the "Above Target" condition (70.18) is significantly higher than the average rating for the "Below Target" condition (41.34), as indicated by the ANOVA results for the performance main effect in Panel B ($p < 0.05$). This shows that the six nonfinancial measures combined have a larger impact on the performance ratings than the two financial measures, consistent with H2.

While these results provide evidence against the financial measure bias, they may not hold for other organizational contexts. It is reasonable to assume that nonfinancial performance is more important at the level of carwash managers because they have little control over financial performance. As one moves up the hierarchical ladder, or perhaps in a different industry setting, financial measures can increase in importance, thereby also increasing the likelihood of the financial measure bias.

## *Hypothesis 3*

BSCs are generally presented in a table format. However, we examine in this study whether individuals consider certain presentation formats as more informative than others. Specifically, we anticipated in H3 that the "Table" format would be perceived as being more informative than the "Graph" and the "Graph with Summary Measure" formats. The last row of Table 5, Panel A, shows that individuals in the "Table" group rated the perceived informativeness of their BSC format (69.94) higher than the individuals in the "Graph" (68.18) and the "Graph with Summary Measure" (62.89) groups. This difference in means is significant at the $p < 0.10$ level ($p = 0.074$; Table 5, Panel B). However, the $t$-tests in Panel C reveal that the statistical significance stems from the difference in the means between the "Table" and "Graph with Summary Measure" conditions. Therefore, H3 is only partially supported.

The finding that the "Graph with Summary Measure" format is perceived to be not more informative than the "Graph" format is surprising because the overall summary measure, as a decision aid, should provide additional relevant information. However, it seems that "less" is perceived

**Table 5.** ANOVA: The Impact of Presentation Format and above/below Target Performance on Perceived Informativeness.

Panel A: Mean Perceived Informativeness (and Standard Deviation)[a]

|  | Table | Graph | Graph with summary measure | Total |
|---|---|---|---|---|
| Above target[b] | 70.80 | 68.00 | 64.38 | 67.65 |
|  | (19.59) | (20.96) | (24.15) | (21.71) |
| Below target[b] | 69.09 | 68.36 | 61.40 | 66.18 |
|  | (20.07) | (20.83) | (23.64) | (21.74) |
| Total | 69.94 | 68.18 | 62.89 | 66.91 |
|  | (19.73) | (20.77) | (23.82) | (21.70) |

Panel B: Analysis of Variance for Main Effects ($n = 270$)

| Source of variation | df | Sum of squares | Mean square | F | p-value[c] |
|---|---|---|---|---|---|
| Presentation format | 2 | 2,468.298 | 1,234.149 | 2.630 | 0.074 |
| Performance | 1 | 139.809 | 139.809 | 0.298 | 0.586 |
| Presentation format × Performance | 2 | 128.670 | 64.335 | 0.137 | 0.872 |
| Error | 264 | 123,903.403 | 469.331 |  |  |

Panel C: t-Tests

|  | Difference in informativeness | p-value[d] |
|---|---|---|
| Table versus graph | 1.76 | 0.565 |
| Graph versus graph with summary measure | 5.28 | 0.113 |
| Table versus graph with summary measure | 7.05 | 0.032 |

[a]Dependent Variable: Perceived Informativeness on a 0–100 scale.
[b]*Above target* = 2 financial measures below target, 6 nonfinancial measures above target; *Below target* = 2 financial measures above target, 6 nonfinancial measures below target.
[c]One-tailed.
[d]Two-tailed.

as "more" in this condition. The participants may focus on this summary measure and therefore primarily make their judgment based on that single summary measure instead of the mix of measures in addition to the summary measure. This lack of incremental informativeness of graphs with summary measures is consistent, however, with an argument from early cognitive theory work by Amer (1991). He suggested that a graphic display with an emergent feature may actually make it difficult for users to pay attention to a single information cue that is required for the task. Glover, Prawitt, and Spilker (1997) argued that, in some situations, a structured decision aid may encourage decision makers to rely on the decision aid assuming that it accounts for all relevant cues and minimize effort by ignoring additional information.

These results are very relevant for practice. One would think that each piece of additional information would increase perceived informativeness, but in this case it has no effect on perceived informativeness. Individuals may have perceived the information provided in the BSC graph format as sufficient and did not think that the overall summary measure added more relevant information to the BSC.

*Hypothesis 4*

In H4, we expected that evaluators in the "Table" format would need longer to make an evaluation judgment than evaluators in the "Graph" and "Graph with summary measure" groups. We measured the time it took the evaluators to submit the evaluation page (in seconds), excluding the time devoted to other parts of the instrument such as the case, or demographic questions. The time we tracked for the purpose of testing H4 included only the time the subject spent on the evaluation page, while the evaluators examined the BSC results and made a judgment about the carwash manager's performance, bonus, and promotion. However, to prevent skewed data, we first removed outliers based on Tukey's "Outlier Labeling Rule." Tukey's "Outlier Labeling Rule" is a common method to detect outliers. The initial method used a multiplier of 1.5, but more recent studies suggested that a multiplier of 2.2 is more appropriate. Therefore, we applied a multiplier of 2.2 in our outlier calculations (Hoaglin & Iglewicz, 1987; Tukey, 1977).

Since each of the 135 participants made two performance judgments (Main Street and Light Street), the total data points were 270. After removing the outliers, we had 85 data points in the "Table" condition, 84 in the "Graph" condition, and 91 in the "Graph with Summary Condition." The data analysis in Table 6, Panel A, shows that it took the individuals in the "Graph" group the shortest amount of time to complete the performance evaluation (83.80 seconds), then the "Graph with Summary Measure" group (87.70 seconds), and the "Table" condition was the slowest with 105.39 seconds on average.

The ANOVA in Table 6, Panel C, reveals that the participants in the "Table" condition needed significantly longer to rate the manager's performance ($p < 0.05$) than the participants in the two graphical groups, consistent with H4. The *t*-tests in Panel C further indicate that the time for the

***Table 6.*** ANOVA: The Impact of Presentation Format and above/below Target Performance on Performance Evaluation Efficiency.

Panel A: Mean Time to Complete Performance Evaluation (and Standard Deviation)[a]

|  | Table | Graph | Graph with summary measure | Total |
|---|---|---|---|---|
| Above target[b] | 103.15 | 89.03 | 91.82 | 94.64 |
|  | (60.52) | (58.07) | (53.42) | (57.19) |
| Below target[b] | 107.57 | 78.81 | 83.66 | 89.87 |
|  | (58.84) | (46.38) | (48.71) | (52.64) |
| Total | 105.39 | 83.80 | 87.70 | 92.22 |
|  | (59.37) | (52.35) | (50.97) | (54.87) |

Panel B: Analysis of Variance for Main Effects ($n = 260$)

| Source of variation | df | Sum of squares | Mean square | F | p-value[c] |
|---|---|---|---|---|---|
| Presentation format | 2 | 22,285.443 | 11,142.722 | 3.758 | 0.025 |
| Performance | 1 | 1,404.321 | 1,404.321 | 0.474 | 0.492 |
| Presentation format × Performance | 2 | 2,681.846 | 1,340.923 | 0.452 | 0.637 |
| Error | 254 | 753,173.780 | 2,965.251 |  |  |

Panel C: $t$-Tests

|  | Difference in time (sec.) | p-value[d] |
|---|---|---|
| Table versus graph | 21.59 | 0.013 |
| Graph versus graph with summary measure | 3.90 | 0.618 |
| Table versus graph with summary measure | 17.69 | 0.035 |

[a]Dependent Variable: time to complete performance evaluation in seconds.
[b]*Above Target* = 2 financial measures below target, 6 nonfinancial measures above target; *Below Target* = 2 financial measures above target, 6 nonfinancial measures below target.
[c]One-tailed.
[d]Two-tailed.

"Table" condition was significantly longer than for either the "Graph" or the "Graph with Summary Measure" conditions, while there was no significant difference in average times in the "Graph" versus the "Graph with Summary Measure" conditions.

These results suggest that graphs seem to lead to more efficient performance evaluations. The graphs summarize the variances and make it easier for the evaluator to make performance judgments. However, as the analysis for H1 showed, the evaluation ratings differ between the table and the graph formats. Therefore, performance system designers must decide whether the increase in evaluation efficiency from graphic displays is worth the risk of having a downward shift in performance ratings.

*Additional Analysis*

Finally, we examined whether personal characteristics influenced the way the participants rated managerial performance in the three presentation formats. We added the following variables to the ANOVA individually to analyze whether they had an impact on the results: Gender, Age, Work Experience, Area of Concentration (Accounting/Finance versus Non-Accounting/Finance), Collegiate Level (Undergraduate versus Graduate Student), and Perceived BSC Knowledge. None of these variables had a significant effect on the results. Therefore, the results can be considered robust across these characteristics.

# CONCLUSIONS

This study has several important implications for practice and theory. Organizations have many choices of how they design their managerial performance evaluation systems, including the choice of presentation format of the performance measures. Technology has also afforded users the option of interactive data visualizations, whereby each user can choose which performance information to use and the presentation format. Traditionally, the BSC is displayed in the form of a table that separates the measures into the four BSC perspectives. In this study, we tested whether a graphical format of the BSC would impact the performance evaluation ratings, affect the perceived informativeness of the BSC, and increase evaluation efficiency. The tabular display has the advantage that BSC users are familiar with this type of format and it contains all the detailed information about performance variances (i.e., target value, actual value, and variance value). On the other hand, graphs already summarize some of the variance information and therefore should decrease the information-processing load of the evaluator. In addition, graphs emphasize more clearly the difference between positive and negative variances and the relative magnitude of those variances.

In our analysis, we found that evaluations ratings are higher when they are based on a tabular representation of the BSC than when they are based on a graphic format. This is an important finding because the same level of managerial performance is interpreted differently based on the type of presentation format. That does not mean that the evaluations are more or less accurate, but evaluators must be aware of this phenomenon when they select an appropriate presentation format for their BSC using interactive data visualization technologies. Our research suggests that the ability of users to choose the presentation format, an increasingly more common feature available in BSC software, may lead to significantly skewed performance ratings across organizational units. A limitation of this study was that we did not assess judgment quality of each format so as to determine which one leads to more accurate evaluations. Future research may take on this task of defining the accuracy of various performance evaluations and investigating which presentation format leads to a more accurate performance assessment. We examined the perceived informativeness of the three presentation formats and found that the table format was perceived to be the most informative way to present BSC information.

A surprising result was that adding a summary measure to the graph format did not significantly impact the level of perceived informativeness compared to a graphic display without a summary measure. One would expect that adding more information would lead to an increase in perceived informativeness, but the results suggest otherwise. In addition, a summary measure at the end of the BSC does not increase the efficiency of the performance evaluation process. One would think that evaluators only need to focus on the overall summary measure to make their performance judgment. It would be easy for evaluators to justify their ratings based on that summary measure. The results revealed, however, that this expectation was not correct, as there were no significant differences in time required for the graphical displays with or without a summary measure. A potential limitation in our study is that placing the summary measure below all variances made it less salient, as suggested by 30% of subjects in the "Graph with Summary Measure" group not being able to recall if their performance reports contained a summary measure or not. By displaying the summary measure at the bottom of the BSC we may have inadvertently reduced its informativeness and potential time-saving benefit. Participants in our study may have first examined the individual measures and then processed the information contained in the summary measure. It would be interesting to analyze in future research whether the results change if the summary measure is provided at the top of the BSC.

Nonetheless, it took the participants in the two graph conditions less time to complete their performance evaluations than in the table format. We can, therefore, conclude that a BSC in a graph format leads to a higher level of performance evaluation efficiency. This finding creates a dilemma for performance evaluation designers. On the one hand, a graphical presentation of the BSC measures increases efficiency. That is important because managers often do not have much time to complete performance assessments. On the other hand, evaluation ratings in the graph format tend to be lower than the ratings provided in the table format. Future research could examine how one can design a performance evaluation system that increases efficiency but is still consistent in regards to evaluation ratings across presentation formats.

Finally, we explored the boundaries of the financial measure bias. Previous studies usually had the same or a similar amount of positive versus negative variances for their financial and nonfinancial measures. Those studies consistently found a financial measure bias in BSC-based performance assessments. In our study, we had six positive (negative) nonfinancial performance outcomes versus only two negative (positive) financial performance outcomes.

In our experiment, we did not find a financial measure bias. The results could have been driven by industry factors or the fact that our case focused on the first-level of supervisory responsibility. For higher level managers, financial measures are more controllable and may gain greater importance. The evaluation ratings in our study were in the direction of the predominantly positive or negative variances of the six nonfinancial measures. Future research could look for the ratio of financial versus nonfinancial performance at which the financial measure bias takes over. In addition, we color-coded the positive variances in green and negative variances in red, following best practices in performance management (Cardinaels & Van Veen-Dirks, 2010). However, we were not able to disambiguate the effect of positive and negative variances on the results regarding financial measure bias because of the potentially confounding effect of color-coding on the evaluation decisions. Future research could examine whether color-coding of positive and negative variances impacts the perceived importance of financial versus nonfinancial measures.

Overall, our study calls attention from researchers and practitioners to the power of presentation format in influencing managerial evaluations in significant ways. If the proverbial "picture is worth a thousand words," our results caution performance evaluation designers to consider carefully how evaluators will process the pictures and words contained in performance reports. Especially in settings where users can interactively select their own preferred presentation format, performance evaluation designers must intentionally anticipate the advantages and disadvantages of each alternative display, and not give them just an afterthought.

# REFERENCES

Active Strategy. (2009). *Scorecards vs. dashboards.* Plymouth Metting, PA: ActiveStrategy Inc. Retrieved from http://www.activestrategy.com/what-we-do/

Amer, T. (1991). An experimental investigation of multi-cue financial information display and decision making. *Journal of Information Systems, 5*(2), 18−34.

Amit, E., Algom, D., & Trope, Y. (2009). Distance-dependent processing of pictures and words. *Journal of Experimental Psychology: General, 138*(3), 400−415.

Azofra, V., Prietro, B., & Santidrian, A. (2003). The usefulness of a performance measurement system in the daily life of an organisation: A note on a case study. *The British Accounting Review, 35*(4), 367−384.

Backof, A. G., Thayer, J. M., & Carpenter, T. (2014, May 29). *Auditing complex estimates: Management-provided evidence and auditors' consideration of inconsistent evidence.* Retrieved from http://ssrn.com/abstract=2279138 or http://dx.doi.org/10.2139/ssrn.2279138

Banker, R., Chang, H., & Pizzini, M. (2004). The balanced scorecard: Judgmental effects of performance measures linked to strategy. *The Accounting Review, 79*(1), 1−23.

Banker, R., Chang, H., & Pizzini, M. (2011). The judgmental effects of strategy maps in balanced scorecard performance evaluations. *International Journal of Accounting Information Systems, 12,* 259−279.

Bauer, J., Tanner, S., & Neely, A. (2004). Developing a performance measurement audit template - A benchmarking study. *Measuring Business Excellence, 8*(4), 17−25.

Beattie, V., & Jones, M. (2008). Corporate reporting using graphs: A review and synthesis. *Journal of Accounting Literature, 27,* 71−110.

Blocher, E., Moffie, R. P., & Zmud, R. W. (1986). Report format and task complexity: Interaction in risk judgments. *Accounting, Organizations and Society, 11*(6), 457−470.

Bonner, S. (2008). *Judgment and decision making in accounting.* Upper Saddle River, NJ: Pearson Prentice-Hall.

Brown, C. E., & Solomon, I. (1987). Effects of outcome information on evaluations of managerial decisions. *The Accounting Review, 62*(3), 564−577.

Brown, D., & Eining, M. (1996). The role of decision aids in accounting: A synthesis of prior research. *Advances in Accounting Information Systems, 4,* 305−332.

Bruns, W. (1999). *PDQ manufacturing.* Case study number 9-199-045. Boston, MA: Harvard Business School Publishing.

Bryant, D. J. (2014). Strategy selection in cue-based decision making. *Canadian Journal of Experimental Psychology, 68*(2), 97−110.

Card, S., Mackinlay, J., & Shneiderman, B. (1999). *Readings in information visualization − Using vision to think.* San Francisco, CA: Morgan Kaufman.

Cardinaels, E. (2008). The interplay between cost accounting knowledge and presentation formats in cost-based decision making. *Accounting, Organizations and Society, 33*(6), 582−602.

Cardinaels, E., & Van Veen-Dirks, P. M. (2010). Financial versus non-financial information: The impact of information organization and presentation in a Balanced Scorecard. *Accounting, Organizations and Society, 35*(6), 565−578.

Christensen, J. A., & Demski, J. S. (2003). *Accounting theory: An information content perspective.* Boston, MA: McGraw-Hill.

DeBusk, G. D., Killough, L. N., & Brown, R. M. (2005). Financial measures bias in the use of performance measurement systems. *Advances in Management Accounting, 14*, 61–89.

Desanctis, G., & Jarvenpaa, S. L. (1989). Graphical presentation of accounting data for financial forecasting: An experimental investigation. *Accounting, Organizations and Society, 14*(5/6), 509–525.

Dilla, W. N., Janvrin, D. J., & Jeffrey, C. (2013). The impact of graphical displays of pro forma earnings information on professional and nonprofessional investors' earnings judgments. *Behavioral Research in Accounting, 25*(1), 37–60.

Dilla, W. N., Janvrin, D. J., & Raschke, R. (2010). Interactive data visualization: New directions for accounting information systems research. *Journal of Information Systems, 24*(2), 1–37.

Dilla, W., & Steinbart, P. (2005). Relative weighting of common and unique balanced scorecard measures by knowledgeable decision makers. *Behavioral Research in Accounting, 17*, 43–53.

Edwards, J. (2005). Picture this. *CFO Magazine*, November 1. Retrieved from http://www.cfo.com

Epley, N., & Gilovich, T. (2002). Putting adjustment back in the anchoring and adjustment heuristic. In T. Gilovich, D. Griffin, & D. Kahneman (Eds.), *Heuristics and biases: The psychology of intuitive judgment*. Cambridge: Cambridge University Press.

Ernst, R. (2012). *Operations management exercise: Balancing process capacity*. Georgetown University Teaching note 4306. Boston, MA: Harvard Business School Publishing.

Fay, R. G., & Montague, N. R. (2015). Witnessing your own cognitive bias: A compendium of classroom exercises. *Issues in Accounting Education, 30*(1), 13–34.

Fennema, M. G., & Kleinmuntz, D. N. (1995). Anticipations of effort and accuracy in multiattribute choice. *Organizational Behavior and Human Decision Processes, 63*, 21–32.

Ghosh, D., & Lusch, R. (2000). Outcome effect, controllability, and performance evaluation on managers: Some field evidence from multi-outlet businesses. *Accounting, Organizations and Society, 25*, 411–425.

Glover, S. M., Prawitt, D. F., & Spilker, B. C. (1997). The influence of decision aids on user behavior: Implications for knowledge acquisition and inappropriate reliance. *Organizational Behavior and Human Decision Processes, 72*(2), 232–255.

Gompers, P. (2010). *Car wash partners, Inc.* Case study number 9-299-034 and Teaching note 5-299-058. Boston, MA: Harvard Business School Publishing.

Haynes, C. M., & Kachelmeier, S. (1998). The effects of accounting contexts on accounting decisions: A synthesis of cognitive and economic perspectives in accounting experimentation. *Journal of Accounting Literature, 17*, 97–136.

Hirsch, B., Seubert, A., & Sohn, M. (2015). Visualization of data in management accounting reports: How supplementary graphs improve every-day management judgments. *Journal of Applied Accounting Research, 16*(2), 221–239.

Hoaglin, D. C., & Iglewicz, B. (1987). Fine-tuning some resistant rules for outlier labeling. *Journal of the American Statistical Association, 82*, 1147–1149.

Hoffman, J. E. (1978). Search through a sequentially presented visual display. *Perception and Psychophysics, 23*, 1–11.

Holmstrom, B. (1979). Moral hazard and observability. *Bell Journal of Economics, 10*, 74–91.

Ittner, C. D., Larcker, D. F., & Meyer, M. W. (2003). Subjectivity and the weighting of performance measures: Evidence from a balanced scorecard. *The Accounting Review, 78*(3), 725–758.

Jarvenpaa, S. L. (1990). Graphic displays in decision making – The visual salience effect. *Journal of Behavioral Decision Making, 3,* 247–262.

Jarvenpaa, S. L., & Dickson, G. W. (1988). Graphics and managerial decision making: Research based guidelines. *Communications of the ACM, 31*(6), 764–774.

Jerez, F., & Miller, K. (2011). *ProntoWash: Washing the world's cars to a tango beat.* Case study number 9-108-037. Boston, MA: Harvard Business School Publishing.

Kahneman, D. (2011). *Thinking, fast and slow.* New York, NY: Farrar, Strauss, Giroux.

Kang, G. G., & Fredin, A. (2012). The balanced scorecard: The effects of feedback on performance evaluation. *Management Research Review, 35*(7), 637–661.

Kaplan, R. S., & Norton, D. P. (1992). The balanced scorecard: Measures that drive performance. *Harvard Business Review, 70*(January-February), 71–79.

Kaplan, R. S., & Norton, D. P. (1996). *The balanced scorecard: Translating strategy into action.* Boston, MA: Harvard Business School Press.

Kaplan, R. S., & Norton, D. P. (2001). *The strategy-focused organization: How balanced scorecard companies thrive in the new business environment.* Boston, MA: Harvard Business School Press.

Kaplan, S. E. (1988). An examination of the effect of presentation format on auditors' expected value judgments. *Accounting Horizons, 2*(3), 90–95.

Kaplan, S. E., Petersen, M. J., & Samuels, J. A. (2012). An examination of the effect of positive and negative performance on the relative weighting of strategically and non-strategically linked balanced scorecard measures. *Behavioral Research in Accounting, 24*(2), 133–151.

Kelton, A. S., Pennington, R. R., & Tuttle, B. M. (2010). The effects of information presentation format on judgment and decision making: A review of the information systems research. *Journal of Information Systems, 24*(2), 79–105.

Kleinmuntz, D., & Schkade, D. (1993). Information displays and decision processes. *Psychological Science, 4*(4), 221–227.

Libby, R. (1981). *Accounting and human information processing: Theory and applications.* Englewood Cliffs, NJ: Prentice-Hall.

Libby, T., Salterio, S. E., & Webb, A. (2004). The balanced scorecard: The effects of assurance and process accountability on managerial judgment. *The Accounting Review, 79*(4), 1075–1094.

Lipe, M., & Salterio, S. (2000). The balanced scorecard: Judgmental effects of common and unique performance measures. *The Accounting Review, 75*(3), 283–298.

Lipe, M., & Salterio, S. (2002). A note on the judgmental effects of the balanced scorecard's information organization. *Accounting, Organizations and Society, 27,* 531–540.

Lohse, G. L. (1993). A cognitive model for understanding graphical perception. *Human-Computer Interaction, 8,* 353–388.

Lurie, N. H., & Mason, C. H. (2007). Visual representation: Implications for decision making. *Journal of Marketing, 71,* 160–177.

Lusk, E. J., & Kersnick, M. (1979). The effect of cognitive style and report format on task performance: The MIS design consequences. *Management Science, 25*(8), 787–798.

Merchant, K. A., & Van der Stede, W. A. (2012). *Management control systems: Performance measurement, evaluation, and incentives* (3rd ed.). London: Prentice Hall.

Mertins, L. (2014). The effects of outcome presentation on performance evaluation ratings. Presented at 2014 Mid-Atlantic Region in King of Prussia, PA, April 2014.

Mertins, L., & White, L. (2014). The impact of production variance presentation method on employees' working behavior. *Advances in Management Accounting, 23,* 149–179.

Microsoft. (2013). *2013 annual report.* Retrieved from https://www.microsoft.com/investor/annualreports/default.aspx

Mitchell, T. R., & Kalb, L. S. (1981). Effects of outcome knowledge and outcome valence on supervisors' evaluations. *Journal of Applied Psychology, 66*(5), 604–612.

Neumann, B. R., Roberts, M. L., & Cauvin, E. (2010). Information search using the balanced scorecard: What matters? *Journal of Corporate Accounting & Finance, 21*(3), 61–66.

Neumann, B. R., Roberts, M. L., & Cauvin, E. (2011). Stakeholder value disclosures: Anchoring on primacy and importance of financial and nonfinancial performance measures. *Review of Managerial Science, 5*(2–3), 195–212.

Pinker, S. (1990). A theory of graph comprehension. In R. Freedle (Ed.), *Artificial intelligence and the future of testing* (pp. 73–126). Hillsdale, NJ: Erlbaum.

Pomerantz, J. (1981). Perceptual organization in information processing. In M. Kubovy & J. Pomerantz (Eds.), *Perceptual organization* (pp. 141–180). Hillsdale, NJ: Eribaum.

Poulton, E. (1985). Geometric illusions in reading graphs. *Perception & Psychophysics, 37,* 543–548.

QPR. (2014). *QPR scorecard introduction.* Retrieved from http://www.qpr.com/Downloads/Brochures/QPRBalancedScorecardFactSheet.pdf

Rim, S., Amit, E., Fujita, K., Trope, Y., Halbeisen, G., & Algom, D. (2015). How words transcend and pictures immerse: On the association between medium and level of construal. *Social Psychological and Personality Science, 2*(6), 123–130.

Roberts, M. L., Albright, T. L., & Hibbets, A. R. (2004). Debiasing balanced scorecard evaluations. *Behavioral Research in Accounting, 16*(1), 75–88.

SAP. (2010). *Framing your view of the business.* Retrieved from http://www.sap.com/solutions/sapbusinessobjects/large/business-intelligence/dashboard-visualization/brochures/index.epx

Schauß, J., Hirsch, B., & Sohn, M. (2014). Functional fixation and the balanced scorecard. *Journal of Accounting & Organizational Change, 10*(4), 540–566.

Schkade, D. A., & Kleinmuntz, D. N. (1994). Information displays and choice processes: Differential effects of organization, form, and sequence. *Organizational Behavior and Human Decision Processes, 57*(3), 319–337.

Simkin, D., & Hastie, R. (1987). An information-processing analysis of graph perception. *Journal of the American Statistical Association, 82*(398), 454–465.

Simons, R., & Davila, A. (1998). How high is your return on management? *Harvard Business Review, 76,* 70–81.

Smith, M., & Taffler, R. J. (1996). Improving the communication of accounting information through cartoon graphics. *Accounting, Auditing and Accountability Journal, 9*(2), 68–85.

Tukey, J. W. (1977). *Exploratory data analysis.* Reading, MA: Addison Wesley.

Tversky, A., & Kahneman, D. (1974). Judgment under uncertainty: Heuristics and biases. *Sciences, 185*(4157), 1124–1131.

Umanath, N. S., & Vessey, I. (1994). Multiattribute data presentation and human judgment: A cognitive fit perspective. *Decision Sciences, 25*(5/6), 795–824.

United States Census Bureau. (2014). *Professional carwashing and detailing.* Retrieved from http://www.statisticbrain.com/car-wash-car-detail-industry-stats/. Accessed on January 1, 2014.

Van Der Heijden, H. (2013). Evaluating dual performance measures on information dashboards: Effects of anchoring and presentation format. *Journal of Information Systems, 27*(2), 21–34.

Van Veen-Dirks, P. (2010). Different uses of performance measures: The evaluation versus reward of production managers. *Accounting, Organizations and Society, 3*, 141–164.

Vessey, I. (1991). Cognitive fit: A theory-based analysis of the graphs versus tables literature. *Decision Sciences, 22*(2), 219–240.

Vessey, I., & Galetta, D. (1991). Cognitive fit: An empirical study of information acquisition. *Information Systems Research, 2*(1), 63–84.

Wong-On-Wing, B., Guo, L., Li, W., & Yang, D. (2007). Reducing conflict in balanced scorecard evaluations. *Accounting, Organizations and Society, 32*(4), 363–377.

Zacks, J., Levy, E., Tversky, B., & Schiano, D. J. (1998). Reading bar graphs: Effects of extraneous depth cues and graphical context. *Journal of Experimental Psychology: Applied, 4*(2), 119–138.

# TURNOVER AND UNIT-LEVEL FINANCIAL PERFORMANCE: AN ANALYSIS OF THE COSTS AND BENEFITS OF VOLUNTARY AND INVOLUNTARY TURNOVER IN UNSKILLED JOBS

James W. Hesford, Mary A. Malina and Mina Pizzini

## ABSTRACT

Purpose — *We investigate outcomes associated with the turnover of unskilled workers, isolating its effects on revenue, cost, and profit. Little attention from researchers has been given to unskilled workers, a significant portion of the workforce.*

Methodology/approach — *This study investigates the relation between turnover among unskilled workers and financial performance using data from 527 hotels owned by the same lodging chain. The workers in our sample are full-time housekeepers and front desk attendants.*

Findings — *We find that the relation between turnover and performance differs by turnover type (voluntary vs. involuntary) and category of*

Advances in Management Accounting, Volume 26, 35–65
ISSN: 1474-7871/doi:10.1108/S1474-787120150000026002

*unskilled worker, reiterating the need to differentiate between turnover type and the importance of context in studying turnover. We challenge the assumption that voluntary turnover is categorically harmful and our results for front desk attendants support the view that organizations choose turnover levels that maximize performance. We also provide new evidence on the effects of involuntary turnover. Contrary to the established notion that dismissing less able employees should improve performance, we find that involuntary turnover has negative consequences.*

Research limitations/implications — *Our results demonstrate the importance of distinguishing voluntary turnover from involuntary turnover and the need to include both in models predicting turnover's performance effects.*

**Keywords:** Voluntary turnover; involuntary turnover; financial performance; customer satisfaction

# INTRODUCTION

Employee turnover is one of the most widely studied topics in the organizational sciences. The overwhelming majority of turnover studies conducted in the last 50 years address the determinants of turnover (Hausknecht & Trevor, 2011; Holtom, Mitchell, Lee, & Eberly, 2008). Implicit in these studies is the assumption that turnover is an important organizational problem that should be measured, and can be resolved by identifying and addressing its causes (Glebbeek & Bax, 2004; Staw, 1980; Ton & Huckman, 2008). Consistent with this assumption, many firms include turnover in their balanced scorecards as a key "learning and growth" metric to be minimized (Eaglen, Lashley, & Thomas, 2000; Gumbus & Johnson, 2003; Ulrich, 1997). In the past decade researchers have used large-sample, archival data to test the relationship between employee turnover and organization-level performance (Batt & Colvin, 2011; Glebbeek & Bax, 2004; Kacmar, Andrews, Van Rooy, Steilberg & Cerrone, 2006; Shaw, Gupta, & Delery, 2005; Siebert & Zubanov, 2009; Ton & Huckman, 2008). In general, these studies find that turnover is negatively associated with customer outcome and productivity measures; however, there is little support for the expectation that turnover affects net profit (Glebbeek & Bax, 2004; Shaw et al., 2005; Ton & Huckman, 2008). While the accounting literature has documented customer and productivity measures as leading indicators of revenues and profits (Anderson, Fornell, & Mazvancheryl, 2004; Banker, Potter, & Srinivasan, 2000; Fornell, Johnson, Cha, & Bryant, 1996; Ittner & Larcker, 1998; Rust & Zahorik, 1993), customer and productivity measures fail to capture all direct and indirect financial effects of turnover. Holtom et al. (2008, p. 236) note that many of the direct costs of turnover are "buried in line items like recruitment, selection, temporary staffing and training"; and, Sailors and Sylvestre (1994) contend that the bulk of turnover's potential costs and benefits are indirect. Accordingly, we investigate the association between turnover (voluntary and involuntary) and financial performance.

Employee turnover is a measurement and reporting issue that has largely been addressed by management scholars. Accounting scholars, however, can add value to the management of employee turnover through our role of attention-directing, problem solving, and score keeping (Simon, Guetzkow, Kozmetsky, & Tyndall, 1954). By separately identifying voluntary and involuntary turnover's effects on both revenues and costs, we provide guidance to managers on how to address turnover. Moreover, turnover can be viewed as a fundamental management control issue as evidenced by its frequent inclusion in balanced scorecard models. Turnover undermines control over operations by redirecting resources away from the provision of goods and services to controlling membership (Price, 1977). Examining turnover in unskilled service jobs enables us to investigate turnover's effects on organizational control over service provision. Hospitality service chains evolve around branded and standardized offerings to customers, making consistent employee performance an essential element of business strategy (Lashley, 2001). Strong organizational control over service provision is necessary for firms to replicate their offerings in geographically-dispersed outlets.

Our study makes several important contributions. First, we adopt the view that turnover can yield benefits; firms must find a balance between the benefits and costs of turnover (Abelson & Baysinger, 1984; Glebbeek & Bax, 2004; Staw,1980). To this end, we investigate the detrimental and beneficial outcomes associated with turnover by isolating its effects on revenues and costs, which, in turn, determine profit. Most large-scale empirical studies examine proximal performance measures (customer outcomes and productivity) that capture only the negative aspects of turnover. In particular, higher turnover rates have been associated with inferior service quality (Kacmar et al., 2006; Subramony & Holtom, 2012; Ton & Huckman, 2008), lower sales (Shaw, Duffy, Johnson, & Lockhart, 2005; Siebert & Zubanov, 2009), higher accident rates (Shaw et al., 2005), and lower efficiency

(Kacmar et al., 2006; Shaw et al., 2005). Few studies recognize that new employees are paid lower wages and receive fewer benefits than longer-tenured employees (Glebbeek & Bax, 2004; Shaw et al., 2005). Therefore, we investigate whether the costs associated with lower sales and lower efficiency arising from turnover-induced declines in customer outcomes and productivity exceed the accompanying reductions in wages and benefits costs.

Second, this study examines the performance effects of both voluntary and involuntary turnover. With the exception of McElroy, Morrow, and Rude (2001) and Batt and Colvin (2011), prior studies on turnover's consequences use total or voluntary turnover rates. Hausknecht and Trevor (2011, p. 368) contend that "combining the two rates into a total turnover rate may mask any theoretical or empirical inferences that are specific to either of the two turnover types." Furthermore, failure to control for involuntary turnover in tests of the relation between voluntary turnover and performance may confound results if the two turnover types are correlated.

Third, by analyzing unskilled jobs requiring little firm-specific knowledge, we can largely attribute turnover's effects to organizational-level processes, rather than the job performance, human capital, or social capital of the individual workers who separate. The simple, routinized tasks inherent in unskilled work create little opportunity for performance variation, and theories on human and social capital primarily apply to high-skill jobs in knowledge-based, network intensive organizations (Becker, 1975; Boudreau, 1992; Dess & Shaw, 2001; Leana & Van Buren, 1999). Moreover, the highest levels of turnover take place in unskilled jobs, which constitute the majority of employment in the United States (U.S. Department of Labor, Bureau of Labor Statistics, 2012). Accordingly, it is important to study turnover's effects on this segment of the workforce.

Lastly, from a methodological perspective, we bring knowledge from the field to augment the quantitative analyses. Numerous field interviews and site visits were conducted and used in developing our hypotheses and interpreting our results. Quantitative methods need valid conceptual grounding and qualitative methods are critical to understanding social phenomena (Malina, Nørreklit, & Selto, 2011).

The hospitality industry provides an interesting and empirically-powerful setting for studying turnover. According to the U.S. Bureau of Labor Statistics (2012), the leisure and hospitality industry led domestic industries in turnover, with rates that ranged between 49% and 60% over the past decade. Studies that examine the costs of employee turnover in the lodging industry generally conclude that turnover increases costs and reduces customer satisfaction; therefore, hospitality managers should actively seek to reduce turnover (Cascio, 1999; Hinkin & Tracey, 2000; Simons & Hinkin, 2001; Tracey & Hinkin, 2008). Yet, high levels of turnover persist in many top-performing hospitality firms, suggesting that turnover may not categorically hinder performance. Accordingly, it is important to understand whether the performance effects of turnover are strictly negative in unskilled jobs, which constitute the majority of employment within the hospitality industry.

We analyze the relation between turnover and performance using six years of data from 527 hotels within a single lodging chain. The hotels are of similar size and staffing, offer the same service, and are subject to the same corporate policies and procedures. Despite the high degree of operational homogeneity, performance and turnover vary widely across the sample. Analyzing different units within the same firm enables us to control for firm-level characteristics (e.g., training, pay practices, human resource policies) that may confound multi-firm studies (Simons & Hinkin, 2001). Market data specific to the hotel industry provide strong controls for regional differences in demand, room prices, labor market conditions, and competition. Finally, employees in this sample – housekeepers and front desk attendants – are critical to the customer experience, and they constitute a significant portion of the workforce (77%) at each location. Accordingly, this setting is particularly conducive to isolating the relation between turnover and profit, should one exist.

We find that voluntary turnover is associated with both lower service quality and lower costs. Consistent with prior studies on service quality, higher voluntary turnover for both types of employees is associated with more customer complaints; however, only housekeeper quits lead to reduced revenues. In contrast to prior literature, voluntary turnover of both housekeepers and front desk attendants is associated with significantly lower costs. In the case of housekeepers, reductions in revenues stemming from voluntary turnover exceed the corresponding savings in costs arising from turnover so that profit falls significantly ($p < 0.05$, two-sided) as voluntary turnover increases. In the case of front desk attendants, the reductions in costs stemming from voluntary turnover lead to marginally significantly ($p < 0.10$, two-sided) higher profits.

Contrary to the established notion that dismissing less able employees should improve performance, we find that involuntary turnover negatively affects all of our performance measures. As with voluntary turnover, higher involuntary turnover for both types of employees is associated with more customer complaints, and housekeeper dismissals are associated with lower revenues and profits. In contrast to the results for voluntary turnover, controllable costs are positively associated with dismissal rates, and this association is significant ($p < 0.01$, two-tailed) for front desk attendants.

# LITERATURE REVIEW

The extant literature has investigated turnover's effects on organizational performance by examining the job performance of individual workers who separate and by examining how turnover affects an organization's overall resource consumption (e.g., spending on recruitment and training) and operational processes (e.g., efficiency). Below, we briefly review research conducted at the individual and organizational levels. We argue that in our sample of unskilled workers, the job performance of workers who separate (a top performer or a marginal performer) will have relatively little effect on organizational performance. Thus, the performance effects of turnover will be driven by how turnover impacts an organization's resource consumption and operational processes.

*Turnover at the Individual Level*

The relation between turnover and organizational performance depends at least in part on the individual performance of workers who leave and those who replace them (Dalton, Todor, & Krackhardt, 1982). The extant literature generally assumes that the loss of high achievers is detrimental to the organization, while the exit of marginal employees should improve organizational performance. This fundamental insight initiated a long stream of research that sought to identify the job performance of those who quit (i.e., voluntary turnover), and those who were dismissed (i.e., involuntary turnover).

Despite extensive investigation, the relation between individual job performance and voluntary turnover has not been conclusively identified (Batt & Colvin, 2011). Traditional theory contends that voluntary turnover is highest among poor performers and lowest among strong performers because the greater institutional rewards given superior performers bind them to employment. Conversely, Jackofsky (1984) argues that both below- and above-average performers are more likely to leave voluntarily relative to average performers; and therefore, the performance-turnover relation is u-shaped. Marginal performers leave because of perceived or actual threat of administrative action, while high performers are lured away by outside opportunities.

Meta-analyses of early studies have consistently estimated a negative, linear individual performance-turnover relationship (Bycio, Hackett, & Alvares, 1990; Griffeth, Hom, & Gaertner, 2000; McEvoy & Cascio, 1987; Williams & Livingstone, 1994). However, recent research implies that conclusions regarding a negative-linear relationship may be premature because many early studies did not investigate nonlinearity (Salamin & Hom, 2005). In particular, several studies that test for quadratic relationships find strong support for a u-shaped relation between individual job performance and turnover (Jackofsky, Ferris, & Breckenridge, 1986; Salamin & Hom, 2005; Sturman, Shao, & Katz, 2012; Sturman & Trevor, 2001; Trevor, Gerhart, & Boudreau, 1997). In summary, the performance level of those who leave voluntarily has not been conclusively determined, thus, it is not clear how the performance of voluntary leavers affects organizational outcomes.

Research on involuntary turnover demonstrates that the performance of those dismissed from the organization is lower than that of those who voluntarily leave (Bycio et al., 1990; McEvoy & Cascio, 1987). This result is consistent with economic theory on job matching, which contends that dismissals arise from selection errors. Since worker efficiency and effectiveness can only be known imperfectly at the time of hiring, some level of involuntary turnover is beneficial because it is rational for the employer to maintain the employment contract only if workers' output is matched by their pay (Jovanovic, 1979). However, the scant empirical evidence on involuntary turnover does not support the assumption that turnover of low performers improves organizational performance (Batt & Colvin, 2011; McElroy et al., 2001).

The unresolved issue of who exits a firm should have relatively little impact on organizational performance in our sample of unskilled workers because the standard deviation of performance tends to be lower in simple jobs than in complex jobs (Boudreau, 1992). From the firm's standpoint, the loss of a superior performer is not very different from the loss of a marginal performer. Accordingly, we expect that the most significant effects of turnover in our sample will arise from direct human resource costs, organization-wide disruption, and other organization-level factors that are independent of the performance level of the individual workers who leave.

## Organizational Costs of Turnover

Prior literature has shown several costs associated with employee turnover. Turnover, regardless of its source, increases direct human resources costs, disrupts operations and results in the loss of firm-specific human and social capital (Alexander, Bloom, & Nuchols, 1994; Becker, 1975; Dess & Shaw, 2001; Price, 1977; Staw, 1980). The direct costs of turnover include advertisements for replacements, recruitment fees, training expenses, and overtime payments to cover unexpected vacancies. Simons and Hinkin (2001) and Tracey and Hinkin (2008) argue that the direct financial costs of turnover within the hospitality industry can be substantial.

Perhaps more significant than the direct costs of turnover are its indirect costs (Sailors & Sylvestre, 1994). Collective turnover disrupts operations and undermines workplace rules that form the basis of organizational control (Alexander et al., 1994; Price, 1977; Staw, 1980). An evolving workforce redirects resources away from the provision of goods and services to controlling membership (Price, 1977). Experienced workers are diverted from their daily work to train and socialize novices; and, firms may increase manager-to-worker ratios in order to monitor new employees. Even with the increased attention of experienced workers and managers, productivity may drop until new employees become fully proficient (Batt, 2002). Accordingly, research suggests that high levels of employee "churn" result in less efficient output, higher accident rates and errors, theft, and policy violations (Gelade & Ivery, 2003; Hatch & Dyer, 2004; Kacmar et al., 2006; Thoms, Wolper, Scott, & Jones, 2001).

Finally, losses of firm-specific human capital and social capital are often cited as sources of significant, but unmeasured, turnover costs. Human capital refers to the knowledge and skills specific to the firm that employees acquire through accumulating experience in the firm and firm-specific training (Becker, 1975). Social capital is defined as an asset embedded in relationships that is developed when relationships facilitate instrumental action among employees (Leana & Van Buren, 1999). Theory posits that turnover negatively impacts organizational performance through the loss of the knowledge, skills, and key relationships specific to the firm. Human capital and social capital losses are generally minimal in unskilled jobs which require little training, institutional knowledge, or interpersonal networks. Thus we expect that in the current study, turnover's negative effects will primarily stem from direct human resource costs and operational disruptions.

### Organizational Benefits of Turnover

Both voluntary and involuntary turnover can also be viewed as a beneficial human resource process that reduces wage and benefits costs, capitalizes on the increased motivation that new workers often bring to the job, and improves financial flexibility (Abelson & Baysinger, 1984; Batt & Colvin, 2011; Glebbeek & Bax, 2004; Staw, 1980).

Wage and benefits costs can be significantly lower for new employees. Even when two individuals perform the same job, wages may differ substantially based on tenure. Moreover, companies typically require new employees to serve a predetermined period of time before they become eligible for employer-paid benefits. According to the U.S. Bureau of Labor Statistics, employer-paid benefits amounted to 25% of a service worker's average wage of $11.78 per hour (U.S. Department of Labor, 2012). In addition to higher wages and benefits, Glebbeek and Bax (2004) contend that there may be indirect costs associated with tempting workers to stay, such as flexible working hours and high autonomy.

Job skill is generally assumed to increase with organizational tenure; however, effort and motivation may be highest immediately after an individual is hired (Staw, 1980). The relative importance of skill and effort in completing job tasks determines when performance is highest during an employee's tenure. This suggests that, for physically demanding, unpleasant, or highly routinized unskilled jobs, such as janitorial and food service positions, efficiency and effectiveness peaks shortly after the employee joins the organization. Meta-analysis shows that the beneficial effects associated with tenure drops most rapidly in low-complexity jobs (Sturman, 2003).

The financial flexibility created by turnover is particularly beneficial for industries that experience large cyclical or seasonal fluctuations in demand, such as lodging and retail (Siebert & Zubanov, 2009). During economic downturns or seasonal drops in business, managers can simply postpone the replacement of workers to a future time when business picks up again. If voluntary turnover alone is not sufficient to reduce the labor force to an optimal level, companies can either retain the excess capacity or resort to layoffs.

### Turnover Type: Voluntary and Involuntary Turnover

In summary, involuntary and voluntary turnover have both negative and positive implications for organizational performance. The extant literature has focused on the relation between voluntary (or total) turnover and proximal measures of performance, such as customer outcomes, productivity, and efficiency. Empirical evidence generally favors a negative relationship;

however, this finding is not universally supported, is sometimes contingent upon moderators or mediators, and is not always linear (see Hausknecht & Trevor, 2011 for a review of this literature). Relatively few studies examine the direct relationship between voluntary (or total) turnover and net profit, a distal and comprehensive performance measure; and here, the results are equivocal. Some studies find a positive turnover-profit relationship (Glebbeek & Bax, 2004; McElroy et al., 2001; Morrow & McElroy, 2007; Peterson & Luthans, 2006; Simons & Hinkin, 2001; Ton & Huckman, 2008), while others report mixed or null results (Huselid, 1995; Koys, 2001; Riordan, Vandenberg, & Richardson, 2005; Van Iddekinge, Ferris, Perryman, Blass, & Heetderks, 2009).

In contrast to the growing literature on voluntary turnover's performance effects, corresponding research on involuntary turnover is quite sparse and its dynamics are not well understood. Theory posits that involuntary leavers are poor performers that cannot fulfill the basic requirements of the job and can be replaced with workers who are at least average performers (Dalton et al., 1982; McElroy et al., 2001). Accordingly, involuntary turnover is viewed as beneficial, or functional, and should be positively correlated with customer outcomes, productivity, and financial performance. However, neither of the two studies that investigates involuntary turnover (Batt & Colvin, 2011; McElroy et al., 2001) finds support for this prediction. This is not surprising because neither study controls for the number of sub-par performers (i.e., performers who should be dismissed) at the start of the sample period. The prediction of a positive involuntary turnover-performance relation assumes that each organizational unit begins the period with same number of sub-par performers; thus, firms that dismiss more sub-par performers (and replace them with average workers) should exhibit better performance over the sample period.

Despite presumptions that involuntary turnover is functional, Hausknecht and Trevor (2011, p. 369) develop two distinct perspectives that suggest the opposite. First, employee "churn" itself, regardless of who leaves can erode productivity. While erosion of productivity is expected to be greater for voluntary leavers, even the loss of less valuable (involuntary leavers) can disrupt operations. Second, involuntary turnover rates may signal the extent to which the workforce is dysfunctional. Barring changes in selection procedures or a shift in the relevant labor market, an organization that experienced high levels of involuntary turnover in the past will tend to, following the replacement of leavers, again be composed of a workforce that is likely to require a high rate of terminations.

# RESEARCH SITE AND HYPOTHESES

## *Research Site*

We gained access to data and employees of an international lodging firm. We focus on the firm's economy properties operating in a single country, and offering only one product: the provision of rooms. Employees at our research site perform work that directly impacts the customer experience.

A typical property has 108 rooms and is staffed by a general manager, a head housekeeper, a maintenance worker, six housekeepers, and four front desk attendants. General managers possess a significant degree of autonomy over the management of their properties including employee recruitment, sales, and marketing. To hire staff, the general manager (GM) may, for example, place ads in the local paper, register with a local unemployment bureau, and/or post a sign at the property. Although practices vary considerably, GMs often fill vacant positions by asking current employees if they know someone who is looking for work.

Employees in our study are full-time housekeepers and front desk attendants. Housekeepers change linens and towels and clean rooms. Housekeepers' work is supervised by a head housekeeper who verifies cleanliness of finished rooms and trains new housekeeping staff. Front desk attendants greet guests, assign rooms, check guests in and out of rooms, answer the phone, and respond to customer concerns. Front desk attendants must have adequate communication and interpersonal skills, and they must exercise sound judgment in responding to customer concerns and requests. Additionally, they often have the authority to make small adjustments to room prices in specialized circumstances when the GM is not present. The front desk position requires greater skill and ability than the housekeeper position. Accordingly, front desk attendant wages are 18% higher than housekeeping wages. The GM hires, trains, and supervises front desk staff.

Housekeepers and front desk staff perform highly routine tasks that can be mastered within a matter of days. The company staffs these positions with low-cost workers and pays them an hourly wage. Both types of employees can be classified into a control work system, in which the employer exerts low effort in selecting employees, offers little opportunity for career development, and is highly dependent on the external labor market (Bamberger & Meshoulam, 2000).

*Hypotheses*

In addition to theory and prior literature (summarized in Table 1), we use insights from our field research to guide our hypotheses. Along with extensive interactions with corporate senior management, one of the researchers visited 24 properties, interviewing managers and staff at 19 of these properties. Like the literature, senior management's view of the impact of employee turnover is mixed. A slight majority view turnover as a method of controlling labor costs. Since employees are quickly trained, turnover has little impact on effectiveness and efficiency. As mentioned previously, housekeepers and front desk staff are recruited by low-cost methods including signs on the property, advertisements at unemployment

*Table 1.* Foundation for Hypotheses Development.

| | Impact Expected in Research Setting? | Proximal Outcome | Expected Impact of Turnover on Proximal Outcome | |
| --- | --- | --- | --- | --- |
| | | | Voluntary | Involuntary |
| *Impact of turnover at the individual level* | | | | |
| Difference in performance level between leavers and new hires | No | | | |
| *Organizational costs of turnover* | | | | |
| Increases in direct costs | Yes | Controllable costs | Positive | Positive |
| Disruptions in operations | Yes | Controllable costs | Positive | More positive |
| | Yes | Customer complaints | Positive | Positive |
| Loss of firm-specific human and social capital | No | | | |
| *Organizational benefits of turnover* | | | | |
| Reduces wages and benefits costs | Yes | Controllable costs | Negative | Negative |
| Increase in motivation of new workers | Yes | Controllable costs | Negative | Negative |
| impact on efficiency | Yes | Customer complaints | Negative | Negative |
| Improves financial flexibility | Yes | Controllable costs | Negative | Negative |

offices, "word of mouth," and newspaper ads. Selection costs are also low because the company does not require drug tests, credit checks or criminal background checks. Accordingly, most senior managers perceive that turnover's benefits outweigh its costs.

The minority view holds that high levels of turnover disrupt operations and divert significant amounts of GM effort away from the provision of services. GMs spend time replacing and training personnel, and they fill in during periods of staff shortages. As a result, less time is available to focus on normal supervision (e.g., "walking the property") and making sales calls to local businesses in order to increase revenue. Accordingly, several senior managers perceive that the costs of turnover outweigh its benefits.

*Turnover, Customer Satisfaction and Revenue*
We begin our analysis of revenue with a discussion of customer outcomes because housekeepers and front desk attendants impact revenue through customer satisfaction (Heskett, Jones, Loveman, Sasser, & Schlesinger, 1994). Hospitality service operations, in particular, evolve around branded and standardized offerings to customers so that consistent employee performance becomes an essential element of business strategy (Lashley, 2001). Favorable guest experiences lead to repeat business and attract new customers through positive recommendations and ratings on travel websites. Housekeepers and front desk attendants significantly affect the guest experience. In the budget hotel segment, the majority of customer complaints (approximately 40%) pertain to the cleanliness of the room, which is the direct responsibility of the housekeeping staff. Another frequent driver of complaints is poor hospitality and service (approximately 20% of complaints), which generally refers to guest interactions with front desk staff. Thus we use customer complaints to measure customer satisfaction.

Recent large-sample studies find that total turnover is negatively associated with unit-level customer outcomes and revenues. Higher total turnover is associated with longer customer wait times (Kacmar et al., 2006) in Burger King restaurants and less favorable service quality perceptions in Barnes & Noble retail stores (Ton & Huckman, 2008). Using data from a large UK clothing retailer, Siebert and Zubanov (2009) investigate the relation between sales per store and total turnover for both full-time and part-time employees. Consistent with their predictions, sales are lower when full-time employee turnover is higher; and, sales exhibit an inverted-U shaped relation with turnover of part-time employees.

The relation between turnover and both complaints and revenues rests on whether the costs or benefits of turnover have a larger effect on complaints and on revenue. The detrimental effects of both voluntary and involuntary turnover on customer complaints stem from disruptions in operations while the benefits come from the increased motivation of new workers (see Table 1). In the context of our research site, voluntary and involuntary turnover disrupts operations by redirecting managerial attention away from service provision and sales to recruiting, selection, training, and monitoring new employees. Time that the head housekeeper devotes to training new employees pulls her away from inspecting rooms, monitoring the remaining workers and responding to special cleaning requests. Similarly, GMs typically "shadow" a new front desk attendant for the first few shifts. This diverts GM effort and attention away from marketing the property and making off-site sales calls.

The benefit of voluntary and involuntary turnover on customer complaints lies in increased motivation of new workers. While a number of general managers remarked that new employees — especially housekeepers — are more motivated than experienced employees, this "honeymoon" period fades quickly. Since the positions do not provide much in terms of job enrichment, employees who were initially pleased at being employed, grow tired of the job. Experienced housekeepers learn "tricks" that allow them to clean a room that will pass inspection with a minimum of effort expended. For example, one quality manager remarked that most new housekeepers, while perhaps not as efficient, work according to the corporate standards. Many experienced housekeepers, he said, do not clean under beds, replace dirty shower curtains when needed, clean under toilet rims, etc. Shortcuts like these are difficult for the head housekeeper to detect during inspections, allowing the housekeeper to shirk. Over a longer term, the deterioration in cleaning impacts quality and, consequently, customer complaints and revenue. Accordingly, it is unclear to many managers whether experienced employees are better, especially with their correspondingly higher wages, benefits, and injuries.

The previous discussion holds equally for both voluntary and involuntary turnover. With respect to voluntary turnover, the only benefit is that arising from the short "honeymoon" period in which new employees worker harder than experienced employees. Even if effort levels are significantly higher for new employees, it is unlikely that additional levels of effort over a short period will translate into lower complaints and higher sales. Accordingly, we predict that the negative effects arising from the diversion of managerial attention away from service provision and operational disruptions will exceed the benefits arising from the "honey-moon" period, as stated in the following hypotheses:

**H1a.** Voluntary front desk and housekeeping turnover is positively asso-ciated with customer complaints.

**H1b.** Voluntary front desk and housekeeping turnover is negatively associated with revenue.

As with voluntary turnover, the only benefit arising from involuntary turnover is the short "honeymoon" period. However, dismissals may be more disruptive to the organization than quits because they require the head housekeeper and GM to carefully document absenteeism, perfor-mance reprimands, and service quality problems for legal purposes. It can take several weeks of poor performance and absenteeism before a GM has gathered enough evidence to dismiss an underperforming worker.

Both senior managers and operational managers at the research site view involuntary terminations as undesirable. Poor performing or "bad" employ-ees are costly in many different ways. Nearly 85% of terminations can be attributed to three causes: excessive absenteeism (22%), low performance (32%) and policy violations (31%). Absenteeism is disruptive and often forces overtime, which is particularly costly. Poor performance reduces effi-ciency. Major policy violations, which include theft and the falsification of hours worked, divert significant managerial attention away from service provision to problem detection and resolution. The longer an employee who is ultimately fired remains on staff, the more damage the hotel suffers.

Only Batt and Colvin (2011) and McElroy et al. (2001) separately con-sider the effects of voluntary and involuntary turnover on customer satis-faction. In a cross-firm sample of 337 call centers, Batt and Colvin (2011) find that customer satisfaction scores are negatively associated with volun-tary and total turnover, but not dismissals. The explanatory power across all of their models is quite low, with $R$-squared values ranging from under 0.01 to 0.10. McElroy et al. (2001) analyze 31 subunits (regions) of a mort-gage bank and find that customer satisfaction scores are decreasing in both voluntary and involuntary turnover.

Given the organizational disruption and additional administrative effort created by involuntary turnover, we expect that involuntary turnover will negatively affect the customer experience and revenues, as stated in H2a and H2b:

**H2a.** Involuntary front desk and housekeeping turnover is positively associated with customer complaints.

**H2b.** Involuntary front desk and housekeeping turnover is negatively associated with revenue.

*Turnover and Costs*
Relatively few studies consider turnover's effects on organization-level costs. Organization-level costs encompass wages, benefits, and other labor-related costs, and they are affected by employee efficiency. Shaw et al. (2005) find that voluntary turnover leads to greater efficiency, but is not associated with the operating expense margin. In a study of nurses in 333 hospitals, Alexander et al. (1994) report that costs per patient-day are positively associated with total turnover. McElroy et al. (2001) and Morrow and McElroy (2007) find that cost per loan is positively correlated with both voluntary and involuntary turnover among a heterogeneous group of mortgage bank employees.

In our research site, both voluntary and involuntary turnover have relatively few negative implications for individual hotel costs. Recruitment and selection costs are minimal. Since new employees can master their job task within a few days, costs associated with training and assimilating new hires into the hotel's service provision cycle are low. For example, during a new housekeeper's initial days at a location, he generally takes a little longer to clean a room and the head housekeeper works additional hours to train and monitor new hires. New front desk personnel are trained either by the GM or by an experienced front desk attendant. Training requires the GM or experienced attendant to shadow the new employee. While the GM receives no additional pay, there are opportunity costs (e.g., fewer sales calls and less monitoring of operations) associated with the GM's shadowing. If another front desk attendant trains the new worker, then there is an additional outlay for the extra hours worked by the trainer.

Turnover, however, can benefit the organization by reducing wage and benefits costs. Housekeepers and front desk attendants receive small increases in wages with tenure and become eligible for health insurance and retirement benefits after six months. Furthermore, as discussed previously, the organization can use turnover to lower labor costs when occupancy is down by waiting to replace a worker who has quit or been dismissed. Given turnover's favorable implications for cost control and the short period of time it takes for new employees to master their jobs, we expect that costs will be negatively associated with both voluntary and involuntary turnover. As discussed in the development of H2, involuntary turnover may be more disruptive to operations and require greater supervisory attention than voluntary turnover. The head housekeeper and GM devote additional effort to monitoring under performers, detecting policy viola-tions, and resolving personnel problems associated with "bad" employees. Therefore, we expect the negative relation between turnover and controlla-ble costs to be weaker for involuntary turnover than it is for voluntary turnover. The previous discussion leads to the following hypotheses.

**H3a.** Voluntary front desk and housekeeping turnover is negatively associated with costs.

**H3b.** Involuntary front desk and housekeeping turnover is negatively associated with costs, but to a lesser degree than voluntary turnover.

*Turnover and Profits*

Extant literature has yet to establish a strong link between turnover and profit. Ton and Huckman (2008) find that total turnover is negatively asso-ciated with profit margin, *after controlling for total payroll costs*. Hence, their analysis eliminates a key advantage of turnover: lower wage and bene-fits costs. In a study of 110 offices of a Dutch temporary services firm, Glebbeek and Bax (2004) show mixed support for a negative relation between total turnover and net profit per office. Shaw et al. (2005) find no relation between voluntary turnover and profit. In a cross-firm study of 98 hotels, Simons and Hinkin (2001) report that total turnover is negatively related to gross operating profit. However, they fail to control for key firm-level characteristics (e.g., training, pay practices, human resource policies, managerial talent) and market-level factors (e.g., unemployment, competi-tion) that are likely correlated with both turnover and profit. Finally, in small-sample studies, Koys (2001) finds no relation between total turnover and profit, while McElroy et al. (2001) report that both voluntary and involuntary turnover are negatively associated with profit.

The ultimate relation between turnover and profit depends on the mag-nitude of its effects on revenues and costs. We expect that both voluntary and involuntary turnover will lead to lower revenues and costs, but make no prediction as to which effect will dominate. Accordingly, we make no directional predictions in the following hypotheses:

**H4a.** Front desk and housekeeping voluntary turnover is associated with profit.

**H4b.** Front desk and housekeeping involuntary turnover is associated with profit.

# RESEARCH DESIGN

To study the impact of turnover on customer satisfaction and financial performance, we gathered employee information as well as annual data on complaints, costs, revenues, profits, and market conditions. The panel data covers the period 2005–2010, inclusive.

## Dependent Variables

The dependent variables are *Complaints, Revenue, Controllable Costs*, and *Controllable Profit*. Descriptive statistics and correlations are contained in Table 2. The firm tracks the number of customer complaints for each property (*Complaints*). Customer complaints originate for many reasons such as cleanliness, noise, billing errors, and unresponsive front desk attendants. The mean number of complaints is 19.9 with a standard deviation of 13.3. *Revenue* includes revenues from room rentals, vending, internet access, telephone, in-room movies, and laundry. Across all years, mean revenue is $845,939 with a standard deviation of 282,465. *Controllable Cost* is defined as wages and benefits expense of all property personnel, supplies (cleaning, uniforms, linens, etc.), repairs and maintenance (plumbing, roofing, landscaping, etc.), energy (water, gas, electricity, etc.), utilities (trash, sewer, telephone, etc.), security, advertising, and local marketing expenses. Across all years, mean controllable cost is $368,615 with a standard deviation of 82,829. *Controllable Profit* is defined as total revenue minus controllable costs. Across all years, mean profit is $477,324 with a standard deviation of $224,768. More than 99% of properties are earning a profit using this measure.

## Turnover Measures

Turnover is calculated for housekeepers and front desk staff. Turnover is the number of employees terminated during the year divided by the average number of full-time employees throughout the year. The firm maintains records on the reason for turnover, enabling us to determine voluntary and involuntary turnover. Mean voluntary (involuntary) turnover for housekeepers (*HK Voluntary TO* and *HK Involuntary TO*) is 171.5% (55.2%) with a standard deviation of 142.8 (64.9). Mean voluntary (involuntary) turnover for front desk staff (*FD Voluntary TO* and *FD Involuntary TO*) is

**Table 2.** Descriptive Statistics and Correlations.

Panel A: Descriptive Statistics

| Variables | N | Mean | Std. Dev. | Median | Minimum | Maximum |
|---|---|---|---|---|---|---|
| HK Voluntary TO | 3,260 | 171.5 | 142.8 | 133.6 | 0.0 | 626.4 |
| HK Involuntary TO | 3,260 | 55.2 | 64.9 | 32.7 | 0.0 | 300.1 |
| FD Voluntary TO | 3,259 | 90.2 | 78.6 | 71.6 | 0.0 | 346.7 |
| FD Involuntary TO | 3,259 | 53.3 | 57.0 | 37.5 | 0.0 | 248.0 |
| GM Tenure | 3,260 | 2.3 | 1.7 | 1.7 | 0.4 | 10.8 |
| HHK Tenure | 3,260 | 3.7 | 2.7 | 3.4 | 0.2 | 29.5 |
| Complaints | 3,260 | 19.9 | 13.3 | 17.0 | 0.0 | 104.0 |
| Rooms Available | 3,260 | 39,351.8 | 8,537.1 | 39,420.0 | 15,330.0 | 63,684.0 |
| Occupancy | 3,260 | 65.5% | 10.9% | 65.4% | 27.4% | 99.2% |
| Revenue | 3,260 | 845,938.8 | 282,464.9 | 800,583.4 | 265,475.9 | 2,314,061.0 |
| Controllable Cost | 3,260 | 368,615.2 | 82,829.2 | 356,871.7 | 188,906.5 | 842,584.9 |
| Controllable Profit | 3,260 | 477,323.6 | 224,768.1 | 440,579.3 | -73,285.0 | 1,701,619.0 |
| Unemployment | 3,156 | 6.6 | 3.0 | 5.6 | 2.1 | 25.3 |
| Market REVPAR | 3,079 | 24.4 | 7.7 | 23.2 | 8.3 | 67.0 |

Panel B: Correlations

| Variables | 1 | 2 | 3 | 4 | 5 | 6 | 7 | 8 | 9 | 10 | 11 | 12 | 13 | 14 |
|---|---|---|---|---|---|---|---|---|---|---|---|---|---|---|
| 1. HK Voluntary TO | | **0.49** | **0.36** | **0.19** | **-0.17** | **-0.37** | **0.20** | **-0.09** | -0.04 | **-0.14** | **-0.16** | **-0.11** | **-0.39** | 0.01 |
| 2. HK Involuntary TO | **0.41** | | **0.18** | **0.38** | **-0.21** | **-0.32** | **0.24** | **-0.08** | **-0.08** | **-0.15** | **-0.10** | **-0.15** | **-0.25** | -0.04 |
| 3. FD Voluntary TO | **0.36** | **0.18** | | **0.39** | **-0.21** | **-0.24** | **0.27** | **0.06** | 0.03 | **0.06** | **0.05** | **0.07** | **-0.31** | **0.07** |
| 4. FD Involuntary TO | **0.16** | **0.42** | **0.36** | | **-0.27** | **-0.23** | **0.31** | **0.06** | 0.01 | **0.07** | **0.11** | **0.05** | **-0.26** | 0.03 |
| 5. GM Tenure | **-0.14** | **-0.18** | **-0.17** | **-0.25** | | **0.19** | **-0.26** | 0.00 | -0.04 | -0.03 | **-0.07** | -0.01 | **0.16** | -0.04 |
| 6. HHK Tenure | **-0.31** | **-0.24** | **-0.20** | **-0.18** | **0.17** | | **-0.24** | 0.01 | 0.03 | 0.03 | **0.05** | 0.02 | **0.30** | 0.02 |
| 7. Complaints | **0.18** | **0.22** | **0.25** | **0.30** | **-0.24** | **-0.23** | | **0.31** | **0.10** | **0.30** | **0.41** | **0.23** | **-0.27** | **0.08** |
| 8. Rooms Available | **-0.06** | **-0.05** | **0.08** | **0.08** | 0.00 | -0.02 | **0.31** | | **-0.30** | **0.51** | **0.68** | **0.39** | -0.04 | **-0.06** |
| 9. Occupancy | **-0.05** | **-0.09** | 0.03 | 0.02 | -0.06 | 0.02 | **0.11** | **-0.31** | | **0.48** | **0.14** | **0.55** | **-0.23** | **0.48** |
| 10. Revenue | **-0.13** | **-0.14** | **0.08** | **0.08** | **-0.05** | 0.03 | **0.31** | **0.53** | **0.48** | | **0.77** | **0.97** | **-0.28** | **0.56** |
| 11. Controllable Cost | **-0.16** | **-0.09** | **0.05** | **0.12** | **-0.09** | **0.05** | **0.40** | **0.69** | **0.16** | **0.77** | | **0.56** | **-0.13** | **0.20** |
| 12. Controllable Profit | **-0.11** | **-0.14** | **0.08** | **0.05** | -0.04 | 0.02 | **0.24** | **0.41** | **0.55** | **0.97** | **0.60** | | **-0.30** | **0.62** |
| 13. Unemployment | **-0.36** | **-0.23** | **-0.29** | **-0.25** | **0.17** | **0.30** | **-0.26** | -0.03 | **-0.23** | **-0.25** | **-0.12** | **-0.26** | | **-0.34** |
| 14. Market REVPAR | -0.02 | **-0.05** | **0.06** | 0.03 | **-0.05** | 0.03 | **0.11** | **-0.07** | **0.49** | **0.59** | **0.25** | **0.65** | **-0.29** | |

Notes:
Panel A: Turnover and unemployment amounts are percentages. Tenure amounts are in years. Financial amounts are in USD.
Panel B: Pearson's r below the diagonal and Spearman's rank correlations above the diagonal. Bolded figures are significant at p < .01.

considerably less, 90.1% (53.3%) with a standard deviation of 78.6 (57.0)., To model a nonlinear relationship between voluntary turnover and the dependent variables, we add a squared term. To eliminate multicollinearity, we center the four voluntary turnover measures.

## Control Variables

We include several variables to control for differences in hotel size, managerial ability, and market conditions. We control for hotel capacity and sales volume with the number of rooms available (*Rooms Available*) and the occupancy rate (*Occupancy*). The occupancy rate is calculated by dividing the number of rooms rented during the year by the number of *Rooms Available* during the year.

We use GM and head housekeeper tenure as proxies for management quality because more experience typically leads to better management of employees. Mean tenure for general managers (*GM Tenure*) was 2.29 years with a standard deviation of 1.72. Mean tenure for head housekeepers (*HHK Tenure*) was considerably higher at 3.71 years with a standard deviation of 2.66.

To control for differences in market conditions, we compute average revenue-per-available-room (REVPAR) for each hotel's local market area using data for each hotel's "competitive set." For a single hotel, REVPAR is computed as revenue divided by available rooms. The hospitality industry commonly uses REVPAR to evaluate performance because it captures the combined effects of price and capacity utilization. The "competitive set" is comprised of similar economy hotels within close proximity of the company's hotel. *Market REVPAR* is the sum of the property and competitor revenues divided by the sum of the property and competitor available rooms. Higher values for *Market REVPAR* indicate better market conditions.

We also control for general economic conditions that may impact our variables of interest. To control for labor market conditions, we obtain annual unemployment data (*Unemployment*) for each year and region. To adjust for price changes over the 2005–2010 period, currency amounts are scaled by a consumer price index. Data on unemployment and price levels come from the Bureau of Labor Statistics.

Finally, we include an indicator variable for each year, and an indicator variable for the state of California (*California*). A large proportion of its hotels are located in California. Management informed us that the California hotels tended to outperform hotels in other states.

# RESULTS

To test our hypotheses, we model unit level performance as a function of voluntary turnover, voluntary turnover squared, involuntary turnover, and a set of control variables as shown in Eq. (1).

$$
\begin{aligned}
Performance = {} & b_0 + b_1\ HK\ Voluntary\ TO + b_2\ HK\ Voluntary\ TO^2 \\
& + b_3\ HK\ Involuntary\ TO + b_4\ FD \\
& Voluntary\ TO + b_5\ FD\ Voluntary\ TO^2 \\
& + b_6\ FD\ Involuntary\ TO + b_7\ Occupancy \\
& + b_8\ Rooms\ Available + b_9\ HHK\ Tenure \\
& + b_{10}\ GM\ Tenure + b_{11}\ Unemployment \\
& + b_{12}\ Market\ REVPAR + b_{13}\ California + b_{14}2006 \\
& + b_{15}\ 2007 + b_{16}\ 2008 + b_{17}\ 2009 \\
& + b_{18}\ 2010 + \varepsilon
\end{aligned}
\tag{1}
$$

Performance is one of the following variables: *Complaints, Revenue, Controllable Cost,* or *Controllable Profit.*

*Hypotheses 1 and 2: Customer Complaints and Revenue*

The first set of hypotheses predicts that housekeeper and front desk voluntary turnover is positively associated with customer complaints and negatively associated with revenue. A Poisson regression model is used with complaints because complaints are count data (StataCorp, 2011). Results, presented in column 1 of Table 3, support H1a. Voluntary turnover terms for both housekeepers and front desk attendants are positively and significantly ($p < 0.01$, two-sided) associated with complaints. The negative ($p < 0.05$ and $p < 0.10$, two-sided) coefficients on both squared turnover terms indicate that as voluntary turnover increases, complaints are increasing, but at a decreasing rate.

**Table 3.**   Regressions of *Complaints, Revenue, Controllable Cost*, and *Controllable Profit* on Measures of Voluntary and Involuntary Turnover.

| Variables | Expected Sign | Complaints | Revenue | Controllable Cost | Controllable Profit |
|---|---|---|---|---|---|
| *HK Voluntary TO* | +/−/−/? | 0.004*** | −0.068*** | −0.058** | −0.049** |
|  |  | (0.006) | (0.002) | (0.014) | (0.047) |
| *HK Voluntary TO²* | −/+/+/? | −0.003** | 0.009 | 0.008 | 0.011 |
|  |  | (0.039) | (0.590) | (0.630) | (0.549) |
| *HK Involuntary TO* | +/−/−/? | 0.005*** | −0.063*** | 0.016 | −0.070*** |
|  |  | (0.000) | (0.001) | (0.362) | (0.000) |
| *FD Voluntary TO* | +/−/−/? | 0.005*** | 0.017 | −0.056*** | 0.036* |
|  |  | (0.000) | (0.827) | (0.005) | (0.069) |
| *FD Voluntary TO²* | −/+/+/? | −0.002* | 0.003 | 0.037** | −0.007 |
|  |  | (0.080) | (0.860) | (0.030) | (0.697) |
| *FD Involuntary TO* | +/−/−/? | 0.005*** | 0.024 | 0.060*** | 0.004 |
|  |  | (0.000) | (0.944) | (0.001) | (0.824) |
| *Occupancy* |  | 0.011*** |  | 0. 355*** |  |
|  |  | (0.000) |  | (0.000) |  |
| *Rooms Available* |  | 0.017*** | 0.569*** | 0.812*** | 0.454*** |
|  |  | (0.000) | (0.000) | (0.000) | (0.000) |
| *HHK Tenure* |  | −0.006*** | 0.028 | 0.017 | 0.021 |
|  |  | (0.000) | (0.178) | (0.446) | (0.332) |
| *GM Tenure* |  | −0.008*** | 0.008 | −0.027 | 0.029 |
|  |  | (0.000) | (0.647) | (0.110) | (0.113) |
| *Unemployment* |  | −0.007*** | −0.117*** | −0.107*** | −0.112*** |
|  |  | (0.000) | (0.000) | (0.000) | (0.001) |
| *Market REVPAR* |  |  | 0.516*** |  | 0.562*** |
|  |  |  | (0.000) |  | (0.000) |
| *California* |  | 0.000 | 0.181*** | 0.185*** | 0.172*** |
|  |  | (0.975) | (0.000) | (0.000) | (0.000) |
| *Year Controls* |  | Yes | Yes | Yes | Yes |
| Wald chi²/*F*-test |  | 765.650 | 128.636 | 92.230 | 109.486 |
| *R*-squared |  | 0.211 | 0.719 | 0.661 | 0.664 |
| *N* |  | 3,155 | 2,981 | 3,155 | 2,981 |
| Number of clusters |  | 527 | 511 | 527 | 511 |

*Notes*: Coefficients are standardized values. Robust standard errors are calculated by clustering at the property level. Significance levels are shown in parentheses. For the Poisson regression, Wald chi² is reported. For the other models, an *F*-test is reported. Pseudo-*R*-squared is reported for the Poisson regression and adjusted *R*-squared is reported for the remaining linear regression models. ***, **, and * indicate two-tailed significance levels of 0.01, 0.05, and 0.10, respectively. *Year controls*, as mentioned in the text, means that we have year-specific dummy variables. Since these are of no economic significance, we do not report the coefficient values in the interest of saving space. The model sample size (*N*) is smaller for the two regressions that incorporate the *Market REVPAR* variable because the firm did not retain market data for 16 properties that it later sold.

Tests of H1b, which predicts that voluntary turnover is negatively associated with revenues, are contained in column 2 of Table 3. Results for housekeeping turnover support H1b, while those for front desk turnover do not. The coefficient for *HK Voluntary TO* is negative and significant ($p < 0.01$, two-sided) and the coefficient *HK Voluntary TO²* is not significant, indicating that the negative relation between voluntary turnover and revenue is linear.

H2a and H2b predict that housekeeper and front desk involuntary turnover is also positively associated with complaints and negatively associated with revenue. The results, which are highly consistent with those for voluntary turnover, show strong support for H2a and mixed support for H2b. As shown in column 1 of Table 3, coefficients for involuntary housekeeper and front desk turnover are positively and significantly ($p < 0.01$, two-sided) associated with complaints. Consistent with H2b, involuntary housekeeping turnover is also negatively and significantly ($p < 0.01$, two-sided) associated with revenue, while involuntary front desk turnover is not. The size of the coefficients on the voluntary and involuntary turnover terms within each job type and model does not differ significantly, and thus suggests that voluntary and involuntary turnover are equally detrimental to the customer experience.

Taken together, the results indicate that both types of turnover (voluntary and involuntary) in both positions (housekeepers and front desk attendants) negatively impact the customer experience. However, only housekeeper turnover (voluntary and involuntary) is associated with lower revenue. Housekeeper turnover will have a stronger effect on revenue than front desk turnover if customers value room cleanliness more than they value the efficiency and professionalism of the front desk attendant. This is consistent with complaint data, which shows that the majority of complaints pertain to room cleanliness. Accordingly, unclean rooms lead to lower repeat business and unfavorable ratings on websites, while poor customer service at check-in or check-out has little effect on a potential customer's purchase decision.

*Hypothesis 3: Controllable Cost*

The third set of hypotheses predicts that both voluntary and involuntary turnover are negatively associated with controllable costs, but the negative association is weaker for involuntary turnover. Consistent with H3a, controllable costs are significantly lower when housekeeper ($p < 0.05$, two-sided) and front desk ($p < 0.01$, two-sided) voluntary turnover is higher (Table 3, column 3). The squared term for voluntary housekeeper turnover is not significant, indicating a linear relationship. Conversely, the squared term for voluntary front desk turnover is significant ($p < 0.05$, two-sided), indicating a curvilinear relationship. These findings differ from prior studies of nurses (Alexander et al., 1994) and mortgage bank employees (McElroy et al., 2001), which find that costs increase as turnover increases. This difference is likely due to the nature of the jobs studied. Nurses and bank employees possess relatively high levels of firm-specific capital and social capital, and the direct costs of recruiting, selecting, and training these workers significantly exceed the corresponding costs for hotel employees.

Contrary to H3b, involuntary turnover is positively associated with controllable costs and this association is significant ($p < 0.01$, two-tailed) for front desk attendants. The cost-related benefits of turnover (reduction in wages and benefits and financial flexibility) exceed its detrimental effects (direct turnover costs, operational disruption) only when turnover is voluntary. This suggests that involuntary turnover is more disruptive to operations than voluntary turnover. The additional disruption inherent in involuntary turnover completely offsets its potential benefits for housekeepers and significantly exceeds its benefits for front desk attendants.

These results are consistent with senior management's view that involuntary turnover is universally undesirable and can be attributed to hiring errors. Involuntary turnover of front desk attendants is particularly costly because these individuals have significantly greater responsibility than housekeepers. Most front desk attendants (43%) are dismissed for policy violations, while most housekeepers (33%) are dismissed for poor performance. Policy violations generally involve theft or fraud. For example, the front desk attendant may give away free rooms, accept cash for a room without recording the sale, or falsify guest refunds. GMs generally detect such behavior relatively quickly through the company's internal control procedures (e.g., matching rooms key issuances to revenues); however, such violations are quite disruptive to operations.

*Hypothesis 4: Controllable Profit*

Our final set of hypotheses (H4a and H4b) posits that voluntary and involuntary turnover are significantly associated with controllable profit, but makes no prediction as to the direction of the association. As shown in the last column of Table 3, the results for housekeeper turnover support H4a and H4b, while those for front desk turnover are mixed. Higher levels of voluntary and involuntary housekeeper turnover are associated with significantly lower profits ($p < 0.05$ and $p < 0.01$, two-sided, respectively). Involuntary turnover has a significantly ($p < 0.01$, two-sided) effect on profits than voluntary turnover. These results indicate that the significant reductions in revenues stemming from housekeeper turnover exceed the corresponding savings in payroll costs arising from turnover. Accordingly, management should consider ways to either reduce housekeeper turnover or prevent housekeeper turnover from impacting the customer experience. Higher levels of voluntary front desk turnover are associated with marginally significantly ($p < 0.10$, two-sided) higher profits, while involuntary front desk turnover is not significantly associated with profit. As discussed previously, front desk performance appears to have little impact on customer purchase decisions, and hence, revenues. Conversely, voluntary front desk turnover significantly reduces costs, and thus leads to higher profits.

## Robustness Tests

We hypothesize that turnover leads to poor financial performance, but it could be that poor financial performance causes turnover. Financially troubled properties may reduce the hours each housekeeper workers, prompting some workers to leave voluntarily. To investigate this concern, we correlated housekeeping hours with turnover for each property. The correlation between housekeeping hours and turnover is relatively small ($r = 0.11$; $p < 0.01$) and positive, indicating that turnover is actually higher when hours are higher. Thus, there is no evidence that poor financial performance leads to higher voluntary turnover of the housekeeping staff. It is unlikely that poor financial performance leads to involuntary turnover because less than 1% of involuntary turnover arose from lay-offs.

Our study separates voluntary and involuntary turnover because, as mentioned in the introduction, combining the two might mask theoretical or empirical inferences that are specific to either of the two types of turnover. To see if empirical inferences would have been masked in our study, we ran our regressions using total turnover. While the results of our untabulated tests were qualitatively similar, we found that combining voluntary and involuntary turnover for front desk attendants masks competing effects on controllable costs.

Since employee turnover is viewed as a nonfinancial leading indicator of financial results, we tested a lagged model where turnover in year $t$ is used to explain cross-sectional variations in revenue. We ran a two-period lagged model and found no support for a relationship between revenue and housekeeper voluntary turnover, front desk attendant voluntary turnover and front desk attendant involuntary turnover. We did find a persistent lagged effect with housekeeper involuntary turnover and revenue that is consistent with the contemporaneous effect. This lagged effect could stem from these fired housekeepers impacting customers' decisions to book the same hotel in the future.

## CONCLUSION

This study investigates the impact of turnover on revenues, costs, and profits using data from over 527 hotels in a major lodging chain. We find that the relation between turnover and performance differs by turnover type (voluntary vs. involuntary) and category of unskilled worker, reiterating the need to differentiate between turnover type and the importance of context in studying turnover.

We provide evidence that voluntary turnover is associated with both lower service quality and lower costs. Consistent with prior studies on service quality, higher voluntary turnover for both types of employees is associated with more customer complaints; however, only housekeeper quits lead to reduced revenues. This result suggests, as do complaints data, that room cleanliness plays a larger part in customer purchase decisions than the professionalism of front desk personnel. In contrast to prior literature, but consistent with our predictions, voluntary turnover of both housekeepers and front desk attendants significantly lowers costs. In the case of housekeepers, reductions in revenues stemming from voluntary turnover exceed the corresponding savings in costs arising from turnover so that profit falls significantly ($p < 0.05$, two-sided) as voluntary turnover increases. In the case of front desk attendants, the reductions in costs stemming from voluntary turnover lead to marginally significantly ($p < 0.10$, two-sided) higher profits.

Results for involuntary turnover are consistent with those of voluntary turnover for complaints, revenues, and profits, but not costs. As with voluntary turnover, higher involuntary turnover for both types of employees is associated with more customer complaints, but only house-keeper dismissals are associated with lower revenues. Similarly, controllable profit is negatively associated with housekeeper dismissals, suggesting that senior management should refine selection procedures for house-keepers to reduce the number of "bad" hires who will eventually be fired. In contrast to the results for voluntary turnover, controllable costs are positively associated with dismissal rates, and this association is significant ($p < 0.01$, two-tailed) for front desk attendants. Our results are consistent with management's view that involuntary terminations are highly disruptive and very costly.

Our findings expand the literature on three important dimensions. First, we challenge the assumption that voluntary turnover is categorically harmful and our results for front desk attendants support the view that organizations choose turnover levels that maximize performance. Second, we provide new evidence on the effects of involuntary turnover. Contrary to the established notion that dismissing less able employees should improve performance, we find that involuntary turnover has negative consequences. Our results also demonstrate the importance of distinguishing voluntary turnover from involuntary turnover and the need to include both in models predicting turnover's performance effects. Third, by analyzing unskilled jobs requiring little firm-specific knowledge, we can largely attribute turn-over's effects to organizational-level processes, rather than the job performance, human capital, or social capital of the individual workers who separate. Finally, this study examines turnover among unskilled workers who constitute a significant portion of the workforce yet receive little attention from researchers.

Three limitations of this study merit mention. First, the scope of this study is limited to the performance effects of turnover; thus, we make no attempt to understand why the workers separate voluntarily or involuntarily. Second, as in most archival studies, we cannot establish causality. One concern is that poor performing properties reduce the hours of house-keepers, who then leave. Our robustness tests, however, find that turnover is actually higher when hours are higher and thus suggests workers do not quit when their hours are reduced. Third, the decision to study a sample of unskilled workers in the service industry limits the applicability of these findings to skilled workers or other industries. Despite these limitations, this study has important implications for managers in service industries that employ unskilled workers.

# REFERENCES

Abelson, M. A., & Baysinger, B. D. (1984). Optimal and dysfunctional turnover: Toward an organizational level model. *Academy of Management Review, 9*, 331–341.

Alexander, J. A., Bloom, J. R., & Nuchols, B. A. (1994). Nursing turnover and hospital efficiency: An organization level analysis. *Industrial Relations, 33*, 505–520.

Anderson, E. W., Fornell, C., & Mazvancheryl, S. K. (2004). Customer satisfaction and shareholder value. *Journal of Marketing, 68*, 172–185.

Bamberger, P., & Meshoulam, I. (2000). *Human resource strategy*. Thousand Oaks, CA: Sage.

Banker, R. D., Potter, G., & Srinivasan, D. (2000). An empirical investigation of an incentive plan that includes nonfinancial performance measures. *The Accounting Review, 75*(1), 65–92.

Batt, R. (2002). Managing customer services: Human resources practices, quit rates, and sales growth. *Academy of Management Journal, 45*, 587–597.

Batt, R., & Colvin, A. J. S. (2011). An employment systems approach to turnover: HR practices, quits, dismissals, and performance. *Academy of Management Journal, 54*, 695–717.

Becker, G. (1975). *Human capital: A theoretical and empirical analysis, with special reference to education* (2nd ed.). Chicago, IL: University of Chicago Press.

Boudreau, J. W. (1992). Utility analysis for decisions in human resource management. In M. D. Dunnette & L. M. Hough (Eds.), *Handbook of industrial and organizational psychology* (pp. 621–745). Palo Alto, CA: Consulting Psychologists Press.

Bycio, P., Hackett, R., & Alvares, K. (1990). Job performance and turnover: A review and meta-analysis. *Applied Psychology: An International Review, 39*, 47–76.

Cascio, W. F. (1999). *Cost human resources: The financial impact of behavior in organizations* (4th ed.). Boston, MA: South-Western College Publishing.

Dalton, D. R., Todor, W. D., & Krackhardt, D. M. (1982). Turnover overstated: The functional taxonomy. *Academy of Management Review, 7*, 117–123.

Dess, G. G., & Shaw, J. D. (2001). Voluntary turnover, social capital, and organizational performance. *Academy of Management Review, 26*, 446–456.

Eaglen, A., Lashley, C., & Thomas, R. (2000). The benefits of training in leisure retailing: A case study of McDonald's restaurants. *Strategic Change, 9*(6), 333–345.

Fornell, C., Johnson, M. D., Cha, J., & Bryant, B. (1996). The American customer satisfaction index: Description, findings, and implications. *The Journal of Marketing, 60*(October), 7–18.

Gelade, G. A., & Ivery, M. (2003). The impact of human resource management and work climate on organizational performance. *Personnel Psychology, 56*, 383–404.

Glebbeek, A. C., & Bax, E. H. (2004). Is high employee turnover really harmful? An empirical test using company records. *Academy of Management Journal, 47*, 277–286.

Griffeth, R. W., Hom, P. W., & Gaertner, S. (2000). A meta-analysis of antecedents and consequences of employee turnover: Update, moderator tests, and research implications for the next millennium. *Journal of Management, 26*, 463–488.

Gumbus, A., & Johnson, S. D. (2003). The balanced scorecard at Futura industries. *Strategic Finance, 85*(1), 36.

Hatch, N. W., & Dyer, J. H. (2004). Human capital and learning as a source of sustainable competitive advantage. *Strategic Management Journal, 25*, 1155–1178.

Hausknecht, J. P., & Trevor, C. O. (2011). Collective turnover at the group, unit, and organizational levels: Evidence, issues, and implications. *Journal of Management, 37*(1), 352−388.

Heskett, J. L., Jones, T., Loveman, G. W., Sasser, W. E., & Schlesinger, L. A. (1994). Putting the service-profit chain to work. *Harvard Business Review, 72* (March−April), 164−174.

Hinkin, T. R., & Tracey, J. B. (2000). The cost of turnover: Putting a price on the learning curve. *Cornell Hotel and Restaurant Administration Quarterly, 41*(3), 14−21.

Holtom, B. C., Mitchell, T. R., Lee, T. W., & Eberly, M. B. (2008). Turnover and retention research: A glance at the past, a closer review of the present, and a venture into the future. *Academy of Management Annals, 2*, 231−274.

Huselid, M. A. (1995). The impact of human resource management practices on turnover, productivity, and corporate financial performance. *Academy of Management Journal, 38*, 635−672.

Ittner, C. D., & Larcker, D. F. (1998). Are non-financial measures leading indicators of financial performance? An analysis of customer satisfaction. *Journal of Accounting Research, 36*(3), 1−35.

Jackofsky, E. (1984). Turnover and job performance: An integrated process model. *Academy of Management Review, 9*, 74−83.

Jackofsky, E., Ferris, K., & Breckenridge, B. (1986). Evidence for a curvilinear relationship between job performance and turnover. *Journal of Management, 12*, 105−111.

Jovanovic, B. (1979). Job matching and the theory of turnover. *Journal of Political Economy, 87*, 972−990.

Kacmar, K. M., Andrews, M. C., Van Rooy, D. L., Steilberg, R. C., & Cerrone, S. (2006). Sure everyone can be replaced ... but at what cost? Turnover as a predictor of unit-level performance. *Academy of Management Journal, 49*, 133−144.

Koys, D. J. (2001). The effects of employee satisfaction, organizational citizenship behavior, and turnover on organizational effectiveness: A unit-level, longitudinal study. *Personnel Psychology, 54*, 101−114.

Lashley, C. (2001). Costing staff turnover in hospitality service organizations. *Journal of Services Research, 1*(2), 3−25.

Leana, C. R., & Van Buren, H. J. (1999). Organizational social capital and employment practices. *Academy of Management Review, 24*, 538−555.

Malina, M. A., Nørreklit, H. S. O., & Selto, F. H. (2011). Lessons learned: Advantages and disadvantages of mixed methods research. *Qualitative Research in Accounting & Management, 8*(1), 59−71.

McElroy, J. C., Morrow, P. C., & Rude, S. N. (2001). Turnover and organizational performance: A comparative analysis of the effects of voluntary, involuntary, and reduction-in-force turnover. *Journal of Applied Psychology, 86*, 1294−1299.

McEvoy, G., & Cascio, W. (1987). Do good or poor performers leave? A meta-analysis of the relationship between performance and turnover. *Academy of Management Journal, 30*, 744−762.

Morrow, P., & McElroy, J. (2007). Efficiency as a mediator in turnover-organizational performance relations. *Human Relations, 60*, 827−849.

Peterson, S. J., & Luthans, F. (2006). The impact of financial and nonfinancial incentives on business-unit outcomes over time. *Journal of Applied Psychology, 91*, 156−165.

Price, J. L. (1977). *The study of turnover*. Ames, IA: Iowa State University Press.

Riordan, C. M., Vandenberg, R. J., & Richardson, H. A. (2005). Employee involvement climate and organizational effectiveness. *Human Resource Management, 44*, 471–488.

Rust, R., & Zahorik, A. (1993). Customer satisfaction, customer retention, and market share. *Journal of Retailing, 69*(2), 193–216.

Sailors, J. F., & Sylvestre, J. (1994). Reduce the cost of employee turnover. *Journal of Compensation and Benefits, 9*, 32–34.

Salamin, A., & Hom, P. W. (2005). In search of the elusive U-shaped performance-turnover relationship: Are high performing Swiss bankers more liable to quit? *Journal of Applied Psychology, 90*, 1204–1216.

Shaw, J. D., Duffy, M. K., Johnson, J. L., & Lockhart, D. E. (2005). Turnover, social capital losses, and performance. *Academy of Management Journal, 48*, 594–606.

Shaw, J. D., Gupta, N., & Delery, J. E. (2005). Alternative conceptualization of the relationship between voluntary turnover and organizational performance. *Academy of Management Journal, 48*, 50–68.

Siebert, W. S., & Zubanov, N. (2009). Searching for the optimal level of employee turnover: A study of a large UK retail organisation. *Academy of Management Journal, 52*, 294–313.

Simon, H. A., Guetzkow, H., Kozmetsky, G., & Tyndall, G. (1954). *Centralization vs. decentralization in organizing the controller's department.* New York, NY: American Book-Stratford Press, Inc.

Simons, T., & Hinkin, T. (2001). The effect of employee turnover on hotel profits: A test across multiple hotels. *Cornell Hotel and Restaurant Administration Quarterly, 42*, 65–69.

StataCorp. (2011). *Stata: Release 12.* Statistical Software. College Station, TX: StataCorp LP.

Staw, B. M. (1980). The consequences of turnover. *Journal of Occupational Behavior, 1*, 253–273.

Sturman, M. (2003). Searching for the inverted U-shaped relationship between time and performance: Meta-analyses of the experience/performance, tenure/performance, and age/performance relationships. *Journal of Management, 29*, 609–640.

Sturman, M., Shao, L., & Katz, J. (2012). The effect of culture on the curvilinear relationship between performance and turnover. *Journal of Applied Psychology, 97*, 46–62.

Sturman, M., & Trevor, C. (2001). The implications of linking the dynamic performance and employee turnover literatures. *Journal of Applied Psychology, 86*, 684–696.

Subramony, M., & Holtom, B. (2012). The long-term influence of service employee attrition on customer outcomes and profits. *Journal of Service Research, 15*, 460–473.

Thoms, P., Wolper, P., Scott, K. S., & Jones, D. (2001). The relationship between immediate turnover and employee theft in the restaurant industry. *Journal of Business and Psychology, 1*, 561–577.

Ton, Z., & Huckman, R. S. (2008). Managing the impact of employee turnover on performance: The role of process conformance. *Organization Science, 19*, 56–68.

Tracey, J. B., & Hinkin, T. R. (2008). Contextual factors and cost profiles associated with employee turnover. *Cornell Hospitality Quarterly, 49*, 12–27.

Trevor, C., Gerhart, B., & Boudreau, J. (1997). Voluntary turnover and job performance: Curvilinearity and the moderating influences of salary growth and promotions. *Journal of Applied Psychology, 82*, 44–61.

Ulrich, D. (1997). Measuring human resources: An overview of practice and a prescription for results. *Human Resource Management, 36*(3), 303–320.

U.S. Department of Labor, Bureau of Labor Statistics. (2012). News Release USDL-12-2404. Employer Cost for Employee Compensation – September 2012. Retrieved from http://www.bls.gov/news.release/pdf/ecec.pdf

Van Iddekinge, C. H., Ferris, G. R., Perryman, P. L., Blass, F. R., & Heetderks, T. D. (2009). Effects of selection and training on unit-level performance over time: A latent growth modeling approach. *Journal of Applied Psychology, 94*, 829−843.

Williams, T., & Livingstone, L. (1994). Another look at the relationship between performance and voluntary turnover. *Academy of Management Journal, 37*, 269−298.

# THE ASSOCIATION BETWEEN THE USE OF MANAGEMENT ACCOUNTING PRACTICES WITH ORGANIZATIONAL CHANGE AND ORGANIZATIONAL PERFORMANCE

Nuraddeen Abubakar Nuhu, Kevin Baird and Ranjith Appuhami

## ABSTRACT

Purpose — *This study examines the association between the use of a package of contemporary and a package of traditional management accounting practices with organizational change and organizational performance.*

Methodology/approach — *Data were collected based on a mail survey distributed to a sample of 740 public sector organizations.*

Findings — *The findings indicate that while the prevalence of traditional practices is still dominant, such practices were not associated with organizational change or performance. Rather, those organizations that use*

Advances in Management Accounting, Volume 26, 67–98
ISSN: 1474-7871/doi:10.1108/S1474-787120150000026003

*contemporary management accounting practices to a greater extent experienced greater change and stronger performance.*

*Practical implications* — *The findings suggest that contemporary management accounting practices can assist public sector practitioners in improving performance and promoting organizational change.*

*Originality/value* — *The study provides an empirical insight into the use and effectiveness of management accounting practices in the public sector. The study provides the first empirical analysis of the effect of using a package of management accounting practices in the public sector.*

**Keywords:** Contemporary management accounting practices; traditional management accounting practices; organizational change; organizational performance; public sector

# INTRODUCTION

The public sector has experienced many changes following the implementation of public management reforms around the world including New Public Management (NPM) and national legislations such as National Competition Policy (NCP) in the case of Australia; Collaborative Public Management in the United States; the Financial Management Initiative (FMI) in the United Kingdom; and the State Sector and Public Finances Act in New Zealand (Christensen & Lægreid, 2007; Hoque & Moll, 2001). Such reforms have resulted in an increased focus on accountability, efficiency, and effectiveness (Hood, 1995), with many public sector organizations placing greater emphasis on the adoption of private sector management practices in an attempt to achieve these objectives (Farneti & Guthrie, 2008; Hood, 1995; Lapsley, 2009; Parker & Gould, 1999). For example, Lapsley (2009, p. 2) indicates that the NPM draws on 'private sector-derived accounting and management technologies in the pursuit of public sector efficiency'. Similarly, Messner (1999) indicates that the use of financial and management accounting practices is how 'managerial and public accountability is achieved in modern-day organizations' (Robbins & Lapsley, 2015, p. 21). Hence, new management accounting practices are 'advanced as contributing to a better functioning of the public sector' (Van Helden & Northcott, 2010, p. 216).

However, despite the advocacy of management accounting practices, there is sparse empirical evidence regarding the prevalence and success of management accounting practices within public sector organizations. Hence, there are concerns regarding the effectiveness of such practices with both Northcott and Llewellyn (2003) and Ellwood (1996) suggesting that there may be problems associated with introducing 'private sector methods into units lacking the capability, inclination, experience and resources to manage commercially' (Hopper & Bui, 2015, p. 12). Similarly, Broadbent and Guthrie (2008) and Lapsley and Oldfield (2001) indicate concerns regarding the viability of private sector practices due to the unique characteristics of the public sector. Finally, there are concerns regarding the effectiveness of practices which are either forced upon public sector organizations (Jackson & Lapsley, 2003, p. 370) or the adoption of which is 'determined by imitation rather than rational choice' (Newell, Robertson, & Swan, 2001; cited in Modell, 2009).

Accordingly, this study aims to contribute to the public sector literature by providing an empirical insight into the prevalence and effectiveness of management accounting practices. In focusing on the prevalence of such practices, the first objective of the study is to examine the extent to which contemporary and traditional management accounting practices are used in the public sector. While public sector organizations have tended to focus on the use of traditional management accounting practices (Van Helden & Jansen, 2003), which contribute to the bureaucracy and inefficiency in the public sector (Lapsley & Oldfield, 1999), a number of scholars have noted the potential usefulness of contemporary management accounting practices in the achievement of public sector reform objectives (Chia & Koh, 2007; Lapsley & Wright, 2004). In particular, given the purported usefulness of contemporary management accounting practices in the public sector (Lapsley & Wright, 2004), the increased usage of such practices has been advocated in the public sector (Chia & Koh, 2007).

In addition, the study adopts a contingency-based approach to evaluate the effectiveness of management accounting practices by focusing on the impact of both traditional and contemporary management accounting practices on organizational change and performance. While public sector organizations play an important role in every economy (Tyler, 2005), they are often stereotyped as inefficient and ineffective in their operations (Antwi, Analoui, & Nana-Agyekum, 2008). Therefore, there is growing pressure to introduce change and to improve the performance of such organizations (Holmes, Piñeres, & Kiel, 2006; Lapsley, 2009) in order to provide better delivery of public services. The importance of organizational change in public institutions is exacerbated due to the increasing competition associated with privatization, commercialization, managerialism, and the corporatization of the public sector (Durán, Dubois, & Saltman, 2011). Indeed, Lapsley and Oldfield (2001, p. 523) indicate that the 'focus on processual change has been coined the New Public Management by Hood (1991, 1995)'.

Given their tendency to promote the status quo (Kloot, 1997), the usage of traditional management accounting practices has been considered to constrain public sector organizations' ability to undertake change (Lapsley & Oldfield, 1999). Alternatively, the use of contemporary management accounting practices is associated with the introduction of initiatives that promote the addition of value-added activities and/or the deletion of non-value-adding activities (Ittner, Lanen, & Larcker, 2002). Such initiatives may prompt public sector organizations to undertake appropriate changes in their structures, systems, markets and services offerings (Maiga & Jacobs, 2004; Sarkis, 2001). The use of contemporary management accounting practices may also assist public sector organizations to manage costs effectively (Chenhall & Langfield-Smith, 1998b) and to improve the efficiency and effectiveness of their operations (Ashworth, Boyne, & Delbridge, 2009).

Despite the potential for contemporary management accounting practices to promote change and improve performance, there is a dearth of empirical research examining such relationships in the public sector. The extant studies on the role of management accounting practices in promoting organizational change and organizational performance are limited to the context of the private sector. The findings of such studies are inconsistent and inconclusive with 'mixed evidence as to the usefulness and appropriateness of such techniques to organizations' (Jackson & Lapsley, 2003, p. 363). For instance, while studies (e.g. King, Clarkson, & Wallace, 2010; Maiga & Jacobs, 2008; Modell, 2001) have reported a positive association between the use of specific contemporary management accounting practices with organizational change and organizational performances, other studies (e.g. Farragher, Kleiman, & Sahu, 2001; Hoque, 2004; Soin, Seal, & Cullen, 2002) have reported no association. Hence, given the dearth of studies and the inconsistent findings in respect to the impact of contemporary management accounting practices on organizational change and performance, the second objective of this study is to examine the association between the use of contemporary and traditional management accounting practices with organizational change and performance in the public sector.

The majority of previous studies which have examined the effectiveness of management accounting practices have adopted the cartesian approach of contingency fit, examining the effect of specific practices in isolation

(Kennedy & Widener, 2008). This reductionist approach has been criticised in the literature for assuming that the impact of such practices can be evaluated independently (Grabner & Moers, 2013). Accordingly, this study aims to contribute to the literature by employing an alternative approach, the configuration approach of contingency fit (Gerdin & Greve, 2004), whereby the effect of employing a number of management accounting practices is examined. Here, Grabner and Moers (2013, pp. 407–408) refer to management controls (MCs) as a system and as a package. MC as a system occurs when the practices are interdependent and involves 'selecting practices that match the set of contingencies facing the organization'. Alternatively, MC as a package represents the complete set of control practices in place.

Since this study aims to provide an insight into the effectiveness of the management accounting practices used in the public sector, as opposed to hypothesising the impact of specific practices or considering the interdependencies between such practices, we incorporate the use of a package of management accounting practices. In this respect, a package of management accounting practices is regarded as a set or collection of management accounting practices (Malmi & Brown, 2008). This approach is considered appropriate 'as the aim to provide a holistic view of the MC practices in place, not interdependence among them' (p. 409). In addition, this approach is in line with Grabner and Moers (2013, p. 408) argument that 'the contingency approach examines the performance effect of a combination of MC practices' and with real-life whereby multiple management accounting practices are in place at the same time (Malmi & Brown, 2008). In line with Sandelin's (2008) call for internal consistency in MC packages, confirmatory factor analysis was performed to determine the specific practices that were compatible in respect to the package of traditional and contemporary management accounting practices (see the appendix).

There is no study to date which has examined the effect of using management accounting practices as a package in the public sector. Hence, while we acknowledge that previous studies have focused on innovation diffusion processes and/or how such innovations are entwined with organizational actions (e.g. Cavalluzzo & Ittner, 2004; Gosselin, 1997), the purpose of this study is to address the gap in the literature by providing a preliminary insight into whether using management accounting practices as a package explains the association between the use of contemporary and traditional management accounting practices with organizational change and organizational performance in the public sector. In summary, the objectives of the study are to:

- Examine the extent of use of contemporary and traditional management accounting practices in the public sector.
- Explore the association between the use of a package of contemporary and a package of traditional management accounting practices with organizational change and organizational performance in the public sector.

The findings suggest that while public sector organizations still place a greater emphasis on the use of traditional management accounting practices, they are increasingly exposed to pressures to adopt contemporary management accounting practices to facilitate organizational change and improve their performance. While the prevalence of traditional practices is still dominant, such practices are not influencing change or performance. Rather, those organizations that use contemporary management accounting practices to a greater extent experienced greater change and stronger performance. Accordingly, it is recommended that public sector managers should strongly consider adopting novel practices to a greater extent to facilitate performance enhancing changes.

The remainder of this paper is organized as follows. The following section presents an integrated review of the main study constructs and develops relevant hypotheses. The next section then outlines the research methodology. The section 'Results' presents the empirical findings of the study, while the final section discusses the findings and their implications, provides an overview of the limitations of the study and discusses directions for future research.

## LITERATURE REVIEW

### *Management Accounting Practices*

Management accounting practices are organizational information systems that provide an organization with relevant information to add value to its customers and organizations (Langfield-Smith, 2009). They facilitate effective decisions and assist organizations in promoting intended behaviours (Axelsson, Laage-Hellman, & Nilsson, 2002). As discussed in the following sub-section, based on the period of their development and/or their characteristics, management accounting practices are categorised into traditional and contemporary management accounting practices.

*Traditional versus Contemporary Management Accounting Practices*
Kaplan and Johnson (1987) regard traditional management accounting practices as those that were developed before the 1980s including Standard Costing, Variance Analysis, Return on Investment (ROI), Budgeting, and Cost Benefit Analysis (CBA). Traditional management accounting practices are regarded as those management accounting practices that are short-term in focus, and internally and financially oriented (Chenhall & Langfield-Smith, 1998a; Pavlatos & Paggios, 2008). It was considered that most traditional management accounting practices would fail to meet the needs of post-1980 managers due to their arbitrariness in allocating costs (Kaplan & Johnson, 1987). It was also thought that they would promote dysfunctional behaviour such as gaming and compromising long-term capability development at the expense of meeting short-term profitability targets (Sulaiman, Ahmad, & Alwi, 2005). Consequently, the relevance of traditional management accounting practices was questioned and even considered to be lost (Kaplan & Johnson, 1987).

A number of new management accounting practices were subsequently developed to overcome the limitations of traditional management accounting practices and to cater for the demands of the changing business environment (Wu, Boateng, & Drury, 2007). These management accounting practices are referred to as contemporary management accounting practices and interchangeably referred to in the literature as innovative, modern, recently developed, new, advanced or innovative management accounting practices. Contemporary management practices are regarded as those management accounting practices that have the ability to relate operations, processes and/or activities with strategic outcomes (Chenhall & Langfield-Smith, 1998b; Hyvönen, 2005). Specifically, since they aid in implementing strategic priorities, contemporary management accounting practices are regarded as being strategically focused (Chenhall & Langfield-Smith, 1999; Kaplan & Norton, 2001b). They also focus on both historical and future events, and they are inter-organizational in nature (Abdel-Kader & Luther, 2006).

Contemporary costing and cost-management practices are those practices that have the ability to identify sources of cost, manage and reduce costs, and eliminate wasteful activities. They are also process oriented and are focused on identifying and analysing the drivers of costs (Smith, Thorne, & Hilton, 2006). Contemporary budgeting practices are detailed in nature and encompass all activities and departments. Contemporary performance measurement/evaluation practices focus on issues both internal and external to an organization. They are multi-dimensional in nature and cover a wide range of critical success factors (Langfield-Smith, 2009), both financial and

74 NURADDEEN ABUBAKAR NUHU ET AL.

non-financial. They equally emphasise continuous improvement and bench-marking standards against external parties (Smith et al., 2006).

This study focuses on eight contemporary (i.e. Activity-Based Management (ABM), Activity-Based Costing (ABC), The Balanced Scorecard (BSC), Value Chain Analysis (VCA), Total Quality Management (TQM), Key Performance Indicators (KPIs), Supply Chain Management (SCM) and Benchmarking) and seven traditional (i.e. CBA, ROI, Formal Strategic Planning, Budgeting for Planning and Control, Capital Budgeting, Standard Costing and Variance Analysis) management accounting practices. These practices were chosen as there is evidence of their use in the public sector (Jackson & Lapsley, 2003; Van Helden & Jansen, 2003). They include a combination of practices encompassing all management accounting functions including the performance measurement, cost control, budgeting, costing and cost-management functions.

*The Use of Management Accounting Practices in the Public Sector*
Although both traditional and contemporary management accounting practices are private sector innovations (Lapsley & Wright, 2004), these practices have also diffused into the public sector (Jackson & Lapsley, 2003; Van Helden & Jansen, 2003). The development of accounting in the public sector dates back to the late 19th Century, a period that coincides with the transformation of industrialized economies (Goddard, 2002). During this period, public sector accounting was concerned with meeting state regulations rather than achieving efficiency and/or accountability, and hence accounting practices were referred to as coercive controls (Goddard, 2002). From 1920 to 1945, the emphasis on public sector accounting shifted from a legal to a financial accounting emphasis. The use of management accounting practices had become prevalent by around 1945 and this continued during the post-World War II era. Specifically, during this period until the 1970s, rational planning techniques such as strategic planning and budgeting, costing techniques, and other traditional management accounting practices became widely used in the public sector (Goddard, 2002). Finally, from the 1980s onwards, the advent of new managerialism, among other associated doctrines of NPM, has resulted in the restructuring of the public sector in the form of privatized, corporatized and commercialized institutions that search for improvements in efficiency, effectiveness and quality (Parker & Gould, 1999). Accordingly, contemporary management accounting practices have become increasingly relevant in the public sector (Ter Bogt, 2008).

## *Organizational Change*

Organizational change is an important research stream in the organizational literature (Chiang, 2010; Klarner, By, & Diefenbach, 2011). As a broad concept, organizational change is defined in different ways. Simply, it can be regarded as the modification in organizational activities, structure or behaviour (Claiborne, Auerbach, Lawrence, & Schudrich, 2013). Similarly, Gioia and Chittipeddi (1991) define organizational change as deviations from the existing thinking and operations of an organization. In addition to perceiving organizational change as a modification and/or deviation from existing paradigms, it can also be regarded as the adoption of a new idea or behaviour by an organization (Liberatore, Hatchuel, Weil, & Stylianou, 2000).

From the extant organizational change research, some studies define and conceptualize organizational change as a change in strategy (often referred to as strategic change), while others regard it as a change in scope. With respect to organizational change as a change in strategy, some researchers (Abernethy & Brownell, 1999; Naranjo-Gil & Hartmann, 2007) regard it as merely a change in generic strategy. Hence, they define and conceptualize organizational change as a change in the strategic orientation, for example, from a defender to prospector or vice versa. This conceptualization seems more relevant for purely profit-oriented entities. Alternatively, in respect to the operationalization of organizational change as a change of scope, some commentators (Brunninge, Nordqvist, & Wiklund, 2007; Goodstein, Gautam, & Boeker, 2006; Goll, Johnson, & Rasheed, 2007) regard it as the expansion, curtailing or reorganization of operations, activities, products and/or services of an organization. These researchers adopt a more comprehensive view of organizational change capturing the multiple perspectives of organizational change. In response to Abernethy and Brownell's (1999) recommendation that future studies should consider change from a broader perspective, this study operationalizes organizational change in this manner.

## *The Association between the Use of Management Accounting Practices with Organizational Change and Performance*

### *The Association between Contemporary Management Accounting Practices with Organizational Change and Organizational Performance*

Ferreira and Otley (2009) contend that the effective implementation of new strategies and other changes requires the deployment of a package of controls. Specifically, using a number of contemporary management accounting practices as a package is expected to enhance their effect on organizational change, since the usage of a number of contemporary management accounting practices together yield complementary effects (Adler, Everett, & Waldron, 2000). This is supported by the general MCS literature (Malmi & Brown, 2008; Sandelin, 2008) which contends that using a number of controls to a great extent will enable the achievement of organizational goals. Specifically, contemporary practices operate as a total system solution, interacting with one another to produce intended outcomes rather than operating as individual practices in isolation (Ittner et al., 2002). For example, Sarkis (2001) stated that the implementation of Benchmarking is likely to be more effective when supplemented with KPIs. Ittner et al. (2002) also posited that the usage of ABC is more beneficial when it supplements other advanced practices, while the use of TQM is likely to be associated with a reliance on the use of non-financial measures (Kennedy & Widener, 2008).

Furthermore, in a case study, Chenhall and Langfield-Smith (1999) found that the case organization integrated its management accounting system to develop what is known as an integrated advanced cost-management system (ACMS). The integrated system that included ABM, KPIs and Benchmarking was developed to facilitate continuous improvement. Such a finding indicates the potential for using a set of contemporary management accounting practices in promoting change. Accordingly, with innovative practices considered to facilitate organizational change in public sector organizations due to the strategic outlook of such practices (Damanpour & Schneider, 2009), the use of a package of contemporary management accounting practices is expected to promote organizational change in public sector organizations.

**H1:** The extent to which a package of contemporary management accounting practices is used will be positively associated with organizational change.

With respect to organizational performance, while some prior studies have reported no relationship between the use of specific contemporary management accounting practices with organizational performance, others have reported a positive association. Organizations tend to gain greater benefits by using a set of practices together (Kaplan & Norton, 2001b). Specifically, the MCS literature contends that the appropriateness of management accounting practices in achieving organizational outcomes lies in their usage as a package instead of using the practices in isolation

(Sandelin, 2008). In particular, a number of scholars have advanced the potential for contemporary management accounting practices to work together to enhance outcomes. For example, Banker, Bardhan, and Chen (2008) indicated that the ability of Activity-Based Practices to improve quality, efficiency and the cost of processes may require the use of other process improvement initiatives such as TQM. Drew (1997) also stated that the success of Benchmarking is only partial if it is not integrated with other practices. Similarly, the BSC, ABM and ABC are considered complementary to one another, with Activity-Based Practices facilitating the measurement of all four perspectives of the BSC (Maiga & Jacobs, 2003). Finally, activity analysis practices are regarded as the foundation of VCA, with the coordination and improvement in activities across the value chain supported by the information generated by cost driver analysis (Dekker, 2003).

Cooper and Slagmulder (2006) noted that additional cost reductions will be achieved when cost-management programmes/practices are integrated as opposed to using the practices in isolation. Accordingly, with public sector organizations operating under cost pressure (Bowerman, Francis, Ball, & Fry, 2002), using a set of contemporary management accounting practices would enable such organizations to achieve effective cost management. Additionally, Adler et al. (2000) found that while individual contemporary management accounting practices exhibited no effect, when a group of the practices were examined together a positive association with sales was found. Similarly, Chenhall (1997) found that combining TQM with non-financial performance measures resulted in improved performance, because the feedback generated from the non-financial performance measures enhanced the effectiveness of TQM strategies. Accordingly, the use of a combination of contemporary management accounting practices is expected to assist public sector organizations in their search for better performance (Wisniewski & Ólafsson, 2004).

**H2:** The extent to which a package of contemporary management accounting practices is used will be positively associated with organizational performance.

*The Association between Traditional Management Accounting Practices with Organizational Change and Organizational Performance*
As discussed previously, given the changing nature of the operating environment, traditional management accounting practices have been considered to constrain behaviour (Kaplan & Johnson, 1987). Organizational change, which is partly undertaken in response to the changes in the

external environment (Wally & Becerra, 2001), needs to be supported by appropriate information regarding the external environment. However, traditional management accounting practices are unable to serve the needs of the contemporary environment (Kaplan & Johnson, 1987). Rather, such practices encourage stability and maintaining the status quo, and hence inhibit the change that is required to align with the ever-changing nature of the external environment. Accordingly, previous studies (Andersen, 2000; Awerbuch, Dillard, Mouck, & Preston, 1996) have highlighted the constraining effect of using specific traditional management accounting practices with respect to organizational change. While these studies highlight the effect of specific traditional management accounting practices on organizational change, using a combination of such practices may have a greater impact on organizational change.

In practice, organizations tend to use a number of traditional management practices in combination. For instance, Formal Strategic Planning exercises are typically followed by Planning and Control Budgeting as well as Capital Budgeting (Peel & Bridge, 1998). Similarly, Standard Costing and Variance Analysis are complementary. In particular, public sector organizations have been found to adopt a number of traditional management accounting practices such as Operational Budgeting, Capital Budgeting, Planning, and Variance Analysis, with such practices serving the bureaucratic and control orientation of the traditional public sector (Van Helden & Jansen, 2003). However, with the orientation of the public sector transforming towards flexibility and change (Chia & Koh, 2007), the use of a combination of traditional management accounting practices may be detrimental to change efforts. Accordingly, as Menon, Choudhury, and Lucas (2002) found that an organization's ability to initiate change is negatively associated with the use of a number of traditional management accounting practices, the combined use of traditional management accounting practices is also likely to constrain public sector organizations' efforts in introducing changes.

H3: The extent of using traditional management accounting practices as a package is negatively associated with organizational change.

In relation to organizational performance, previous studies examining the effect of specific traditional management accounting practices have reported both positive and negative associations with organizational performance. For instance, traditional Budgeting for Planning and Control, with its role of promoting efficiency by ensuring standards are achieved, leads to improved performance (King et al., 2010), particularly in the short term. Alternatively, the use of traditional budgeting threatens the achievement of long-term organizational performance, as the achievement of budget targets leads to gaming and other dysfunctional behaviour which adversely affects the overall effectiveness of an organization (Jensen, 2001). Similarly, while Standard Costing and Variance Analysis lead to enhanced performance (Modarress, Ansari, & Lockwood, 2005) (due to their cost control function, Cooper & Slagmulder, 2006), their short-term focus and dysfunctional behaviour associated with their use distorts organizational performance (Baines & Langfield-Smith, 2003). Likewise, the use of Capital Budgeting can hinder (Awerbuch et al., 1996) as well as promote (Peel & Bridge, 1998) organizational performance.

Given that traditional management accounting practices represent an established part of organizational systems, organizations are likely to use a number of traditional management accounting practices at the same time. This assertion is supported by the high usage of various traditional management accounting practices reported in previous studies (Badem, Ergin, & Drury, 2013; Chenhall & Langfield-Smith, 1998a; Sulaiman & Mitchell, 2005). In particular, as traditional management accounting practices such as Budgeting, CBA and Variance Analysis are commonly used in the public sector (Van Helden & Jansen, 2003), it is likely that public institutions use a set of such practices. However, since the use of specific traditional management accounting practices has both favourable and adverse effects on organizational performance (Awerbuch et al., 1996; Kaplan & Norton, 2001a; King et al., 2010; Miller & Cardinal, 1994), the effects on organizational performance resulting from the use of a package of such practices can be either positive or negative (Henri, 2006). Therefore, a null hypothesis is developed stating that:

**H4:** The use of a package of traditional management accounting practices is not associated with organizational performance.

# METHOD

Data were collected using the survey approach. Seven hundred and forty questionnaires were distributed to public sector organizations in Australia, including local government councils, government business enterprises, government agencies/departments and other types of public sector organizations. The questionnaires were sent to the heads of the accounting and finance departments or the heads of the organizations/business units, which included Chief Financial Officers (CFOs), Financial Controllers, Chief Executive Officers (CEOs) or similarly titled employees. These executives were chosen because they were deemed to have the awareness, experience, knowledge and/or responsibility for the management accounting practices used by their business units. Business units were used as the level of analysis, since the use of management accounting practices may differ across different business units within the same organization.

To improve the response rate, the survey was designed and administered using Dillman's Tailored Design Method (Dillman, 2000). This resulted in 82 initial responses. Four weeks after the initial distribution, a reminder was sent to non-respondents resulting in another 50 responses. Hence, a total of 132 questionnaires were returned (18%). However, since 5 of these were not usable due to a large amount of missing data, there were 127 usable questionnaires (17.12%). This response rate compares favourably with previous management accounting studies (Banker et al., 2008 (6.5%); Ittner et al., 2002 (11%); King et al., 2010 (14.6%)).

To test for non-response bias, an independent sample $t$-test was carried out to compare the means of the early and late responses with respect to size and the dependent and independent variables. No significant differences were found, and hence, it is concluded that there is no non-response bias. Therefore, the representativeness of the sample is assured.

*Measurement of Variables*

Since confirmatory factor analysis is appropriate in the context of the theoretical base (Verbeeten, 2006), it was used to evaluate the constructs of the study. Accordingly, measurement models in AMOS software were estimated for each of the constructs, and evaluated based on standard-errors, $t$-statistics, modification indices and a number of goodness-of-fit indices (Kaynak, 2003).

*Organizational Change*
The extent of organizational change was measured using a 13-item scale developed following a review of the literature (Dean & Sharfman, 1996; Gimbert, Bisbe, & Mendoza, 2010). Respondents were asked to indicate the extent to which they undertook changes over the last three years on 7-point Likert scales with anchors of 1 "Not at all" to 7 "To a great extent". A period of three years is typically used in the management and

management accounting research as it is considered sufficient for the effect of implementing strategies to be manifested (Chenhall, 1997).

The initial organizational change measurement model did not fit the data well (CMIN/DF = 2.731; GFI = 0.837; CFI = 0.796; AGFI = 0.771). Hence, two items (see the appendix) were removed based on the Modification Indices (MI), with the resultant model fitting the data well (CMIN/DF = 2.103; GFI = 0.893; CFI = 0.894; AGFI = 0.840) and having a variance of 1.306. The scores of the 11 retained items were subsequently aggregated to reflect the extent of organizational change with higher (lower) scores reflecting greater (less) change.

*Use of Contemporary and Traditional Management Accounting Practices*
The extent of usage of contemporary and traditional management accounting practices was measured using an adapted version of a scale developed by Chenhall and Langfield-Smith (1998a). The scale has been used in many management accounting studies (e.g. Al & McLellan, 2011; Joshi, 2001; Wu et al., 2007) and includes eight contemporary (i.e. Benchmarking, ABM, ABC, the BSC, VCA, TQM, KPIs and SCM) and seven traditional management accounting practices (Formal Strategic Planning, Budgeting for Planning and Control, Capital Budgeting, CBA, Standard Costing, Variance Analysis and ROI). Respondents were asked to indicate the extent to which they used each of these practices over the last three years on a 7-point Likert scale anchored from 1 "Not at all" to 7 "to a great extent".

To assess whether the eight specific contemporary practices and the seven specific traditional practices are compatible to be used as a package, confirmatory factor analysis was undertaken. A second-order measurement model with two dimensions was developed, one for the eight contemporary management accounting practices and the other for seven traditional practices. The initial model (CMIN/DF = 3.101; GFI = 0.780; CFI = 0. 649; AGFI = 0.703) did not fit well, and hence based on the Modification Indices, two contemporary practices (ABC and KPIs) and two traditional practices (Variance Analysis and ROI) were removed (see the appendix). The revised model (CMIN/DF = 1.614; GFI = 0.911; CFI = 0.907; AGFI = 0.863) fitted the data adequately, with the variances of the two factors (dimensions) being 0.372 and 0.240, respectively. The remaining six contemporary practices and five traditional practices were aggregated to compute the extent of use of a package of contemporary and traditional management accounting, respectively. This approach was undertaken in line with the recommendation of Sandelin (2008) that studies should determine MC packages based on mechanisms of internal consistency instead of the mere collection of control practices.

*Organizational Performance*

Organizational performance was measured using an instrument developed from a review of the literature (Griffin, Neal, & Parker, 2007; Walker & Boyne, 2006), with the chosen items considered relevant for the assessment of public sector performance. The instrument required respondents to rate their performance over the last three years (using a 7-point Likert scale ranging from 1 "Very Poor" to 7 "Excellent"). The measurement model was estimated using six items (see the appendix) and the model was a good fit with the data (CMIN/DF = 3.808; GFI = 0.915; CFI = 0.911; AGFI = 0.802), with a variance of 0.295.

# RESULTS

## *Reliability and Validity of Constructs*

The descriptive statistics of the study are depicted in Table 1. The retained items used in measuring the four constructs are reported in the appendix. The reliability of the four constructs was assessed, with Table 1 showing that with the exception of the package of traditional management accounting practices (0.67), the Cronbach alphas all exceeded the recommended cut-off of 0.7 (Nunnally, 1978). With the coefficients of each item of the four constructs more than twice their standard errors and the value of the $t$-statistics significant, the convergent validity of all of the constructs was confirmed. Further, based on the correlation matrix and Cronbach alphas, it is evident that the reliability coefficients of each scale are greater than its correlation with other scales. This suggests that the study scales have high discriminant validity. Finally, content validity was also confirmed by pretesting the questionnaire among experts in the field of management accounting and public sector research.

Additionally, tests for both common method bias and multicollinearity were performed. Using Harman's (1967) single factor test, the highest Eigenvalue value accounted for was less than 50% of the variance (22.85%) indicating that common method bias was not of concern (Podsakoff, MacKenzie, Lee, & Podsakoff, 2003). Similarly, the Variance Inflation Factor (1.328) for the two independent variables (package of contemporary and package of traditional management accounting practices) was below the normal cut-off (10) and a more conservative cut-off (4), thereby indicating that multicollinearity was not a problem (O'Brien, 2007).

## The Extent of Use of Management Accounting Practices

Table 1 shows that while the extent of organizational change is modest (mean = 3.37), organizational performance is relatively high (mean = 5.32). Table 1 also shows that the extent of use of the package of traditional management accounting practices (mean = 4.99) is higher than that of contemporary management accounting practices (mean = 3.57).

Table 2 provides a more detailed insight into the use of the traditional and contemporary management accounting practices. In particular, Table 2 shows the extent of use of each of the six contemporary and five traditional management accounting practices. The extent of use is divided into three categories: "non-users" (response point of 1 on the 7-point likert scale); "use to a small extent" (response points 2, 3 and 4) and "use to a great extent" (response points 5, 6 and 7). The majority of organizations are "non-users" or "use to a small extent" four of the contemporary management accounting practices, ABM, the BSC, VCA and TQM. For the other two contemporary practices, 58.4% and 46.83% of respondents used Benchmarking and SCM, respectively, to a great extent. Alternatively, the results show that with the exception of Standard Costing (31.8%), a high proportion of organizations indicated that they used all traditional management accounting practices to a great extent: Budgeting for Planning and Control (95.16%), Formal Strategic Planning (80.95%), Capital Budgeting (77.78%) and CBA (49.21%). Similarly, Table 2 shows that while on average 66.98% of the respondents were using traditional management accounting practices to a great extent, only 35.85% used contemporary management accounting practices to a great extent. Furthermore, while only 4.77% of respondents are not using traditional management accounting practices, 16.42% of the organizations are not using contemporary management accounting practices.

## The Association between the Use of Management Accounting Practices with Organizational Change and Organizational Performance

The association between the extent of use of the package of contemporary and traditional management accounting practices with organizational

*Table 1.* Descriptive Statistics, Cronbach Alphas, and Bivariate Correlations for the Study Constructs.

| Variables | 1 | 2 | 3 | 4 | Mean | Theoretical Range | Actual Range | Cronbach alpha |
|---|---|---|---|---|---|---|---|---|
| 1. Package of contemporary management accounting practices | 1 | | | | 3.57 | 1–7 | 1.17–6.00 | 0.730 |
| 2. Package of traditional management accounting practices | 0.497** | 1 | | | 4.99 | 1–7 | 2.60–7.00 | 0.667 |
| 3. Organizational change | 0.434** | 0.320** | 1 | | 3.37 | 1–7 | 1.45–5.55 | 0.866 |
| 4. Organizational performance | 0.207* | 0.109 | 0.266** | 1 | 5.32 | 1–7 | 2.00–7.00 | 0.842 |

**, * Statistically significant at 1% and 5%, respectively.

*Table 2.* Extent of Use of Specific Management Accounting Practices.

| Management Accounting Practices | Non-Users (1) | Use to a Small Extent (2–4) | Use to a Great Extent (5–7) | Mean |
|---|---|---|---|---|
| *Contemporary practices* | | | | |
| Benchmarking | 4 (3.20%) | 48 (38.40%) | 73 (58.40%) | 4.53 |
| Activity-based management (ABM) | 16 (12.80%) | 60 (48.00%) | 49 (39.20%) | 3.82 |
| The balanced scorecard (BSC) | 28 (22.22%) | 61 (48.41%) | 37 (29.37%) | 3.16 |
| Value chain analysis (VCA) | 42 (33.33%) | 72 (57.14%) | 12 (9.52%) | 2.40 |
| Total quality management (TQM) | 26 (20.63%) | 60 (47.62%) | 40 (31.75%) | 3.35 |
| Strategic cost management (SCM) | 8 (6.35%) | 59 (46.83%) | 59 (46.83%) | 4.16 |
| Average (%) | 16.42 | 47.73 | 35.85 | |
| *Traditional practices* | | | | |
| Budgeting for planning and control | 0 (0%) | 6 (4.84%) | 118 (95.16%) | 6.11 |
| Formal strategic planning | 0 (0%) | 24 (19.05%) | 102 (80.95%) | 5.47 |
| Capital budgeting | 3 (2.38%) | 25 (19.84%) | 98 (77.78%) | 5.33 |
| Cost benefit analysis (CBA) | 5 (3.97%) | 59 (46.83%) | 62 (49.21%) | 4.40 |
| Standard costing | 22 (17.5%) | 64 (50.8%) | 40 (31.8%) | 3.63 |
| Average (%) | 4.77 | 28.27 | 66.98 | |

change and organizational performance was assessed using Structural Equation Modelling (SEM). To account for the non-normality of the data (sample), the model was estimated using the Generalised least square (GLS) estimation approach instead of default (maximum likelihood) estimation. The model was first estimated using a control variable, organizational size. However, given that the control variable was not found to be associated with either organizational change or organizational performance, the variable was removed, with the results reported in Table 3. The results show that the model (CMIN/DF = 4.897; GFI = 0.981; CFI = 0.864; AGFI = 0.806) fitted the data well. As expected a significant positive relationship was found between the use of the package of contemporary management accounting practices with organizational change ($\beta$ = 0.376, $p$ = 0.000) indicating that a higher level of organizational change occurs when the package of contemporary practices is used to a greater extent. Hypothesis 1 is therefore supported. Similarly, the association between the use of the package of contemporary management accounting with organizational performance was significant and in the predicted direction ($\beta$ = 0.210, $p$ = 0.043), indicating that organizational performance is higher when the package of contemporary management accounting practices is used to a greater extent. Therefore, Hypothesis 2 is also supported.

Alternatively, the association between the use of a package of traditional management accounting practices with organizational change was not

***Table 3.*** Structural Equation Model ($n$ = 127) of the Extent of the Use of a Package of Management Accounting Practices with Organizational Change and Performance.

| Description of Path | Path Coefficient | $p$ (Sig) |
|---|---|---|
| Use of package of contemporary management accounting practices→organizational change | 0.376 | 0.000*** |
| Use of package of contemporary management accounting practices→organizational performance | 0.210 | 0.043** |
| Use of package of traditional management accounting practices→organizational change | 0.147 | 0.119 |
| Use of package of traditional management accounting practices→organizational performance | 0.010 | 0.920 |
| Goodness-of-fit indices | CMIN/DF = 4.897 GFI = 0.981 CFI = 0.864 AGFI = 0.806 | |

***, ** Statistically significant at 1% and 5%, respectively.

significant ($\beta = 0.147$, $p = 0.119$), and hence, Hypothesis 3 is not supported. While a negative association was expected, this result indicates that no association exists between the use of a package of traditional management accounting practices and organizational change. Hence, the use of a package of traditional management accounting practices does not have a detrimental impact on change. Similarly, the association between the use of the package of traditional management accounting practices with organizational performance was not significant ($\beta = 0.010$, $p = 0.920$). Hypothesis 4, which was stated as a null hypothesis, is therefore supported.

# DISCUSSION AND CONCLUSION

## Discussion

The first objective of the study was to examine the extent of use of contemporary and traditional management accounting practices in the public sector. The study found that the use of traditional management accounting practices is high. In particular, almost all public sector organizations (95.16%) were using Budgeting for Planning and Control to a great extent, with the majority of organizations also using Formal Strategic Planning, CBA and Capital Budgeting. This is consistent with earlier private sector studies (Sulaiman, Ahmad, & Alwi, 2004; Yalcin, 2012) which have reported a high usage of traditional management accounting practices. A possible explanation for the high use of traditional management accounting practices, despite their limitations in the public sector (Lapsley & Oldfield, 1999), might be attributed to the organizations' lack of awareness and/or expertise in contemporary practices (Sulaiman et al., 2004). Another plausible reason might be attributed to the long-term association that organizations have with traditional management accounting practices (Joshi, 2001), as such practices are consistent with the control objectives of the traditional public sector (Van Helden & Jansen, 2003).

Alternatively, the study found that with the exception of Benchmarking and SCM, the extent of use of the remaining contemporary management accounting practices (ABM, the BSC, VCA and TQM) in the public sector organizations was quite low. Similarly, while the extent of use of the package of traditional management practices was high, the use of the package of contemporary practices was low. This finding is in line with previous public sector studies (Jackson & Lapsley, 2003; Tyler, 2005). A possible explanation for such low usage rates may be the complexity of public sector activities, with internal politics and slow decision-making processes making it difficult for public sector organizations to adopt private sector practices (Baird, 2007; Lapsley & Oldfield, 2001). Similarly, the lack of flexibility and resistance to change which hinders the implementation of new systems (practices) in the public sector (Baird, 2007; Jackson & Lapsley, 2003) may explain the low rates reported.

The second objective of the study was to examine the association between the use of a package of contemporary and traditional management accounting practices with organizational change and organizational performance. Although the extent of use of the package of traditional management accounting practices was high, the use of such practices was not associated with either organizational change or organizational performance. While it appears that focusing on the use of traditional practices does not assist public sector managers attempting to effect change and improve performance (Holmes et al., 2006; Lapsley, 2009), this may be attributed to the measures used in this study. In particular, the aggregated measure of performance used can hide the trade-offs between various performance dimensions. Hence, as recommended by Modell (2012), future studies may explore these relationships further by examining the association between such practices and various performance dimensions which consider the conflicting demands of public sector stakeholders.

Alternatively, the study found that using a package of contemporary management accounting practices was positively associated with organizational change, thereby indicating that public sector practitioners wishing to initiate change can emphasise the use of contemporary management accounting practices. Unlike earlier studies (Modell, 2001; Soin et al., 2002) which have reported mixed findings when examining the effect of specific contemporary practices on organizational change in isolation, the findings of this study reveal that the use of a combination of Benchmarking, SCM, ABM, the BSC, VCA and TQM had a significant positive association with organizational change. Given that the study found that the use of these contemporary management accounting practices as a package was positively associated with organizational performance, public sector practitioners need to consider using a number of contemporary management accounting practices at the same time, rather than specific practices in isolation. Such findings will assist the managers of public sector organizations in realizing the benefits of such practices (Malmi & Brown, 2008).

While contemporary management accounting practices are shown to have a role in promoting organizational change and performance in the public sector, given their low usage rates, there is scope for increasing the use of such practices in the public sector. This can be achieved in a number of ways. First, since employees play a key role in the adoption of new ideas (Iverson, McLeod, & Erwin, 1996), on-going training of public sector employees could be promoted, as through such training employees will become acquainted with the existence and mechanics of contemporary management accounting practices. Participation in professional and trade associations is another medium through which employees could enhance their awareness of contemporary management accounting practices (Midgley, Morrison, & Roberts, 1992).

In addition to employee initiatives, organizational culture also plays an essential role in the implementation of new practices (Schneider, Brief, & Guzzo, 1996). Therefore, since the lack of flexibility and tendency to resist change can hinder public sector organizations from adopting private sector practices (Baird, 2007), there is a need for public sector organizations to embrace a more flexible and empowered organizational culture. This is because flexible organizations have a greater tendency to embrace new practices (Thomke, 1997) while empowered employees are less likely to resist such practices (Gal-Or & Amit, 1998). Finally, as the use of innovations in the public sector organizations is to some extent determined by government influence (Lapsley & Wright, 2004), policy makers could exert coercive measures (Ribeiro & Scapens, 2006) such as directives and legislations to promote the use of contemporary management accounting practices in public sector organizations.

*Conclusion*

The purpose of this study was to examine whether using management accounting practices as a package can explain the association between the use of contemporary and traditional management accounting practices with organizational change and organizational performance in the public sector. The empirical evidence has supported this inquiry in respect to the use of contemporary management accounting practices. The study's findings make a significant contribution to the literature in a number of ways. First, the study provides an insight into the state of diffusion of innovative management practices in the public sector revealing that relative to traditional management accounting practices, the use of contemporary management accounting practices is low. This indicates that traditional management accounting practices are still the dominant management accounting practices employed in the public sector. Hence, despite the increased use of innovative practices propagated by public sector reforms (Chia & Koh, 2007), public sector organizations are lagging in such effort. Secondly, by examining the use of management accounting practices as a package, the study contributes to the literature by resolving the inconsistency reported in previous studies which have examined the management accounting practices in isolation. Specifically, the use of a package of contemporary management accounting practices explains the positive association between such practices with organizational change and performance.

The findings also have a number of practical implications. First, the study informs practitioners that in their effort to improve performance and promote change with the aid of organizational systems and practices, they can consider using a number of contemporary management accounting practices at the same time. Second, while the public sector reforms have encouraged the use of innovative management practices in public sector organizations (Farneti & Guthrie, 2008), given the use of contemporary management accounting practices in such organizations was found to be low, some practical measures were suggested so that practitioners and policy makers could promote the use of such practices in the public sector.

## Limitations and Direction for Further Studies

The study is subject to the typical limitations of the survey approach including the inability to assume causality. Accordingly, future studies could employ a case study and/or longitudinal approach in assessing the effectiveness of management accounting practices. Future studies could also consider using a more rigorous measure of organizational performance which considers the specific performance objectives of the diverse stakeholders of public sector organizations. Furthermore, future studies could provide a more in-depth insight into the impact of management accounting practices by focusing on their diffusion process and/or the impact of organizational factors such as top management support, training, culture and/or information technology on the success of such practices. Also, given the low usage of contemporary management accounting practices reported in this study, future studies could examine the factors that promote their use. Finally, another potential research opportunity is for future studies to examine the effectiveness of management accounting practices and the association between other dimensions of MCSs such as the use of MCSs and the characteristics of MCSs with organizational change and performance.

# REFERENCES

Abdel-Kader, M., & Luther, R. (2006). Management accounting practices in the British food and drinks industry. *British Food Journal, 108*(5), 336–357.

Abernethy, M. A., & Brownell, P. (1999). The role of budgets in organizations facing strategic change: An exploratory study. *Accounting, Organizations and Society, 24*(3), 189–204.

Adler, R., Everett, A. M., & Waldron, M. (2000). Advanced management accounting techniques in manufacturing: Utilization, benefits, and barriers to implementation. Accounting *Forum, 24*(2), 131–150.

Al, S. F. A., & McLellan, J. D. (2011). Management accounting practices in Egypt – A transitional economy country. *Journal of Accounting, Business & Management, 18*(2), 105–120.

Andersen, T. J. (2000). Strategic planning, autonomous actions and corporate performance. *Long Range Planning, 33*(2), 184–200.

Antwi, K., Analoui, F., & Nana-Agyekum, D. (2008). Public sector reform in Sub-Saharan Africa: What can be learnt from the civil service performance improvement programme in Ghana? *Public Administration and Development, 28*(4), 253–264.

Ashworth, R., Boyne, G., & Delbridge, R. (2009). Escape from the iron cage? Organizational change and isomorphic pressures in the public sector. *Journal of Public Administration Research and Theory, 19*(1), 165–187.

Awerbuch, S., Dillard, J., Mouck, T., & Preston, A. (1996). Capital budgeting, technological innovation and the emerging competitive environment of the electric power industry. *Energy Policy, 24*(2), 195–202.

Axelsson, B., Laage-Hellman, J., & Nilsson, U. (2002). Modern management accounting for modern purchasing. *European Journal of Purchasing & Supply Management, 8*(1), 53–62.

Badem, A. C., Ergin, E., & Drury, C. (2013). Is standard costing still used? Evidence from Turkish automotive industry. *International Business Research, 6*(7), 79.

Baines, A., & Langfield-Smith, K. (2003). Antecedents to management accounting change: A structural equation approach. *Accounting, Organizations and Society, 28*(7), 675–698.

Baird, K. (2007). Adoption of activity management practices in public sector organizations. *Accounting & Finance, 47*(4), 551–569.

Baker, W. E., & Sinkula, J. M. (1999). The synergistic effect of market orientation and learning orientation on organizational performance. *Journal of the Academy of Marketing Science, 27*(4), 411–427.

Banker, R. D., Bardhan, I. R., & Chen, T.-Y. (2008). The role of manufacturing practices in mediating the impact of activity-based costing on plant performance. *Accounting, Organizations and Society, 33*(1), 1–19.

Bowerman, M., Francis, G., Ball, A., & Fry, J. (2002). The evolution of benchmarking in UK local authorities. *Benchmarking: An International Journal, 9*(5), 429–449.

Broadbent, J., & Guthrie, J. (2008). Public sector to public services: 20 years of "contextual" accounting research. *Accounting, Auditing & Accountability Journal, 21*(2), 129–169.

Brunninge, O., Nordqvist, M., & Wiklund, J. (2007). Corporate governance and strategic change in SMEs: The effects of ownership, board composition and top management teams. *Small Business Economics, 29*(3), 295–308.

Cavalluzzo, K. S., & Ittner, C. D. (2004). Implementing performance measurement innovations: Evidence from government. *Accounting, Organizations and Society, 29*(3), 243–267.

Chenhall, R. H. (1997). Reliance on manufacturing performance measures, total quality man-agement and organizational performance. *Management Accounting Research, 8*(2), 187–206.

Chenhall, R. H., & Langfield-Smith, K. (1998a). Adoption and benefits of management accounting practices: An Australian study. *Management Accounting Research, 9*(1), 1–19.

Chenhall, R. H., & Langfield-Smith, K. (1998b). The relationship between strategic priorities, management techniques and management accounting: An empirical investigation using a systems approach. *Accounting, Organizations and Society, 23*(3), 243–264.

Chenhall, R. H., & Langfield-Smith, K. (1999). The implementation of innovative manage-ment accounting systems. *Australian Accounting Review, 9*(19), 37–46.

Chia, Y. M., & Koh, H. C. (2007). Organizational culture and the adoption of management accounting practices in the public sector: A Singapore study. *Financial Accountability & Management, 23*(2), 189–213.

Chiang, C. F. (2010). Perceived organizational change in the hotel industry: An implication of change schema. *International Journal of Hospitality Management, 29*(1), 157–167.

Christensen, T., & Lægreid, P. (2007). The whole-of-government approach to public sector reform. *Public Administration Review, 67*(6), 1059–1066.

Claiborne, N., Auerbach, C., Lawrence, C., & Schudrich, W. Z. (2013). Organizational change: The role of climate and job satisfaction in child welfare workers' perception of readiness for change. *Children and Youth Services Review, 35*(12), 2013–2019.

Cooper, R., & Slagmulder, R. (2006). *Contemporary issues in management accounting.* Oxford: Oxford University Press.

Damanpour, F., & Schneider, M. (2009). Characteristics of innovation and innovation adop-tion in public organizations: Assessing the role of managers. *Journal of Public Administration Research and Theory, 19*(3), 495–522.

Dean, J. W., & Sharfman, M. P. (1996). Does decision process matter? A study of strategic decision-making effectiveness. *Academy of Management Journal, 39*(2), 368–392.

Dekker, H. C. (2003). Value chain analysis in interfirm relationships: A field study. *Management Accounting Research, 14*(1), 1–23.

Dillman, D. A. (2000). *Mail and internet surveys: The tailored design method* (Vol. 2). New York, NY: Wiley.

Drew, S. A. (1997). From knowledge to action: The impact of benchmarking on organizational performance. *Long Range Planning, 30*(3), 427–441.

Durán, A., Dubois, H. F., & Saltman, R. B. (2011). The evolving role of hospitals and recent concepts of public sector governance. *Governing Public Hospitals, 25*, 15–33.

Ellwood, S. (1996). Full-cost pricing rules within the national health service internal market-accounting choices and the achievement of productive efficiency. *Management Accounting Research, 7*(1), 25–51.

Farneti, F., & Guthrie, J. (2008). Italian and Australian local governments: Balanced scorecard practices. A research note. *Journal of Human Resource Costing & Accounting, 12*(1), 4–13.

Farragher, E. J., Kleiman, R. T., & Sahu, A. P. (2001). The association between the use of sophisticated capital budgeting practices and corporate performance. *The Engineering Economist, 46*(4), 300–311.

Ferreira, A., & Otley, D. (2009). The design and use of performance management systems: An extended framework for analysis. *Management Accounting Research, 20*(4), 263–282.

Gal-Or, E., & Amit, R. (1998). Does empowerment lead to higher quality and profitability? *Journal of Economic Behavior & Organization, 36*(4), 411–431.

Gerdin, J., & Greve, J. (2004). Forms of contingency fit in management accounting research – A critical review. *Accounting, Organizations and Society, 29*(3), 303–326.

Gimbert, X., Bisbe, J., & Mendoza, X. (2010). The role of performance measurement systems in strategy formulation processes. *Long Range Planning, 43*(4), 477–497.

Gioia, D. A., & Chittipeddi, K. (1991). Sensemaking and sensegiving in strategic change initiation. *Strategic Management Journal, 12*(6), 433–448.

Goddard, A. (2002). Development of the accounting profession and practices in the public sector – A hegemonic analysis. *Accounting, Auditing & Accountability Journal, 15*(5), 655–688.

Goll, I., Johnson, N. B., & Rasheed, A. A. (2007). Knowledge capability, strategic change, and firm performance: The moderating role of the environment. *Management Decision, 45*(2), 161–179.

Goodstein, J., Gautam, K., & Boeker, W. (2006). The effects of board size and diversity on strategic change. *Strategic Management Journal, 15*(3), 241–250.

Gosselin, M. (1997). The effect of strategy and organizational structure on the adoption and implementation of activity-based costing. *Accounting, Organizations and Society, 22*(2), 105–122.

Grabner, I., & Moers, F. (2013). Management control as a system or a package? Conceptual and empirical issues. *Accounting, Organizations and Society, 38*(6), 407–419.

Griffin, M. A., Neal, A., & Parker, S. K. (2007). A new model of work role performance: Positive behavior in uncertain and interdependent contexts. *Academy of Management Journal, 50*(2), 327–347.

Harman, H. (1967). *Modern factor analysis.* Chicago, IL: University of Chicago Press.

Henri, J. F. (2006). Management control systems and strategy: A resource-based perspective. *Accounting, Organizations and Society, 31*(6), 529–558.

Holmes, J. S., Piñeres, S., & Kiel, L. D. (2006). Reforming government agencies internationally: Is there a role for the balanced scorecard? *International Journal of Public Administration, 29*(12), 1125–1145.

Hood, C. (1991). A public management for all seasons. *Public Administration, 69*(1), 3–19.

Hood, C. (1995). The "new public management" in the 1980s: Variations on a theme. *Accounting, Organizations and Society, 20*(2), 93–109.

Hopper, T., & Bui, B. (2015). Has management accounting research been critical? *Management Accounting Research*, forthcoming. doi: 10.1016/j.mar.2015.08.001

Hoque, Z. (2004). A contingency model of the association between strategy, environmental uncertainty and performance measurement: Impact on organizational performance. *International Business Review, 13*(4), 485–502.

Hoque, Z., & Moll, J. (2001). Public sector reform – Implications for accounting, accountability and performance of state-owned entities – An Australian perspective. *International Journal of Public Sector Management, 14*(4), 304–326.

Hyvönen, J. (2005). Adoption and benefits of management accounting systems: Evidence from Finland and Australia. *Advances in International Accounting, 18*, 97–120.

Ittner, C. D., Lanen, W. N., & Larcker, D. F. (2002). The association between activity-based costing and manufacturing performance. *Journal of Accounting Research, 40*(3), 711–726.

Iverson, R. D., McLeod, C. S., & Erwin, P. J. (1996). The role of employee commitment and trust in service relationships. *Marketing Intelligence & Planning, 14*(3), 36−44.

Jackson, A., & Lapsley, I. (2003). The diffusion of accounting practices in the new "managerial" public sector. *International Journal of Public Sector Management, 16*(5), 359−372.

Jensen, M. C. (2001). Corporate budgeting is broken, let's fix it. *Harvard Business Review, 79*(10), 94−101.

Joshi, P. L. (2001). The international diffusion of new management accounting practices: The case of India. *Journal of International Accounting, Auditing and Taxation, 10*(1), 85−109.

Kaplan, R. S., & Johnson, H. T. (1987). *Relevance lost: The rise and fall of management accounting.* Boston, MA: Harvard Business School.

Kaplan, R. S., & Norton, D. P. (2001a). Transforming the balanced scorecard from performance measurement to strategic management: Pt. I. *Accounting Horizons, 15*(1), 87−104.

Kaplan, R. S., & Norton, D. P. (2001b). Transforming the balanced scorecard from performance measurement to strategic management: Pt. II. *Accounting Horizons, 15*(2), 147−160.

Kaynak, H. (2003). The relationship between total quality management practices and their effects on firm performance. *Journal of Operations Management, 21*(4), 405−435.

Kennedy, F. A., & Widener, S. K. (2008). A control framework: Insights from evidence on lean accounting. *Management Accounting Research, 19*(4), 301−323.

King, R., Clarkson, P. M., & Wallace, S. (2010). Budgeting practices and performance in small healthcare businesses. *Management Accounting Research, 21*(1), 40−55.

Klarner, P., By, R. T., & Diefenbach, T. (2011). Employee emotions during organizational change − Towards a new research agenda. *Scandinavian Journal of Management, 27*(3), 332−340.

Kloot, L. (1997). Organizational learning and management control systems: Responding to environmental change. *Management Accounting Research, 8*(1), 47−73.

Langfield-Smith, K. (2009). *Management accounting: Information for creating and managing value.* Sydney: McGraw-Hill Higher Education.

Lapsley, I. (2009). New public management: The cruellest invention of the human spirit? 1. *Abacus, 45*(1), 1−21.

Lapsley, I., & Oldfield, R. (1999). The past is the future: Constructing public sector accountants. *Pacific Accounting Review, 11*(1−2), 137−147.

Lapsley, I., & Oldfield, R. (2001). Transforming the public sector: Management consultants as agents of change. *European Accounting Review, 10*(3), 523−543.

Lapsley, I., & Wright, E. (2004). The diffusion of management accounting innovations in the public sector: A research agenda. *Management Accounting Research, 15*(3), 355−374.

Liberatore, M. J., Hatchuel, A., Weil, B., & Stylianou, A. C. (2000). An organizational change perspective on the value of modeling. *European Journal of Operational Research, 125*(1), 184−194.

Maiga, A. S., & Jacobs, F. A. (2003). Balanced scorecard, activity-based costing and company performance: An empirical analysis. *Journal of Managerial Issues, 15*(3), 283−301.

Maiga, A. S., & Jacobs, F. A. (2004). The association between benchmarking and organizational performance: An empirical investigation. *Managerial Finance, 30*(8), 13−33.

Maiga, A. S., & Jacobs, F. A. (2008). Extent of ABC use and its consequence. *Contemporary Accounting Research, 25*(2), 533−566.

Malmi, T., & Brown, D. A. (2008). Management control systems as a package – Opportunities, challenges and research directions. *Management Accounting Research*, *19*(4), 287–300.

Menon, A., Choudhury, J., & Lucas, B. A. (2002). Antecedents and outcomes of new product development speed. An interdisciplinary conceptual framework. *Industrial Marketing Management*, *32*(4), 314–328.

Messner, M. (1999). The limits of accountability. *Accounting, Organizations and Society*, *34*(8), 918–938.

Midgley, D. F., Morrison, P. D., & Roberts, J. H. (1992). The effect of network structure in industrial diffusion processes. *Research Policy*, *21*(6), 533–552.

Miller, C. C., & Cardinal, L. B. (1994). Strategic planning and firm performance: A synthesis of more than two decades of research. *Academy of Management Journal*, *37*(6), 1649–1665.

Modarress, B., Ansari, A., & Lockwood, D. (2005). Kaizen costing for lean manufacturing: A case study. *International Journal of Production Research*, *43*(9), 1751–1760.

Modell, S. (2001). Performance measurement and institutional processes: A study of managerial responses to public sector reform. *Management Accounting Research*, *12*(4), 437–464.

Modell, S. (2009). Bundling management control innovations: A field study of organisational experimenting with total quality management and the balanced scorecard. *Accounting, Auditing & Accountability Journal*, *22*(1), 59–90.

Modell, S. (2012). The politics of the balanced scorecard. *Journal of Accounting and Organizational Change*, *8*(4), 475–489.

Naranjo-Gil, D., & Hartmann, F. (2007). Management accounting systems, top management team heterogeneity and strategic change. *Accounting, Organizations and Society*, *32*(7), 735–756.

Newell, S., Robertson, M., & Swan, J. (2001). Management fads and fashions. *Organization*, *8*(1), 5–15.

Northcott, D., & Llewellyn, S. (2003). The 'ladder of success' in healthcare: The UK national reference costing index. *Management Accounting Research*, *14*(1), 51–66.

Nunnally, J. C. (1978). *Psychometric theory (2)*. New York, NY: McGraw-Hill.

O'Brien, R. M. (2007). A caution regarding rules of thumb for variance inflation factors. *Quality & Quantity*, *41*(5), 673–690.

Parker, L., & Gould, G. (1999). Changing public sector accountability: Critiquing new directions. *Accounting Forum*, *23*(2), 109–135.

Pavlatos, O., & Paggios, I. (2008). Management accounting practices in the Greek hospitality industry. *Managerial Auditing Journal*, *24*(1), 81–98.

Peel, M. J., & Bridge, J. (1998). How planning and capital budgeting improve SME performance. *Long Range Planning*, *31*(6), 848–856.

Podsakoff, P. M., MacKenzie, S. B., Lee, J.-Y., & Podsakoff, N. P. (2003). Common method biases in behavioral research: A critical review of the literature and recommended remedies. *Journal of Applied Psychology*, *88*(5), 879.

Ribeiro, J. A., & Scapens, R. W. (2006). Institutional theories in management accounting change: Contributions, issues and paths for development. *Qualitative Research in Accounting & Management*, *3*(2), 94–111.

Robbins, G., & Lapsley, I. (2015). From secrecy to transparency: Accounting and the transition from religious charity to publicly-owned hospital. *The British Accounting Review*, *47*(1), 19−32.

Sandelin, M. (2008). Operation of management control practices as a package − A case study on control system variety in a growth firm context. *Management Accounting Research*, *19*(4), 324−343.

Sarkis, J. (2001). Benchmarking for agility. *Benchmarking: An International Journal*, *8*(2), 88−107.

Schneider, B., Brief, A. P., & Guzzo, R. A. (1996). Creating a climate and culture for sustainable organizational change. *Organizational Dynamics*, *24*(4), 7−19.

Smith, K., Thorne, H., & Hilton, R. (2006). *Management accounting 4e information for managing and creating value*. Australia: McGraw-Hill Australia Pty limited.

Soin, K., Seal, W., & Cullen, J. (2002). ABC and organizational change: An institutional perspective. *Management Accounting Research*, *13*(2), 249−271.

Sulaiman, M., Ahmad, N. N. N., & Alwi, N. M. (2004). Is standard costing obsolete? Empirical evidence from Malaysia. *Managerial Auditing Journal*, *20*(2), 109−124.

Sulaiman, M., Ahmad, N. N. N., & Alwi, N. M. (2005). Management accounting practices in selected Asian countries: A review of the literature. *Managerial Auditing Journal*, *19*(4), 493−508.

Sulaiman, S., & Mitchell, F. (2005). Utilising a typology of management accounting change: An empirical analysis. *Management Accounting Research*, *16*(4), 422−437.

Ter Bogt, H. J. (2008). Management accounting change and new public management in local government: A reassessment of ambitions and results − An institutionalist approach to accounting change in the Dutch public sector. *Financial Accountability & Management*, *24*(3), 209−241.

Thomke, S. H. (1997). The role of flexibility in the development of new products: An empirical study. *Research Policy*, *26*(1), 105−119.

Tyler, M. C. (2005). Benchmarking in the non-profit sector in Australia. *Benchmarking: An International Journal*, *12*(3), 219−235.

Van Helden, G. J., & Jansen, E. P. (2003). New public management in Dutch local government. *Local Government Studies*, *29*(2), 68−88.

Van Helden, G. J., & Northcott, D. (2010). Examining the practical relevance of public sector management accounting research. *Financial Accountability & Management*, *26*(2), 213−240.

Verbeeten, F. H. (2006). Do organizations adopt sophisticated capital budgeting practices to deal with uncertainty in the investment decision?: A research note. *Management Accounting Research*, *17*(1), 106−120.

Walker, R. M., & Boyne, G. A. (2006). Public management reform and organizational performance: An empirical assessment of the UK Labour government's public service improvement strategy. *Journal of Policy Analysis and Management*, *25*(2), 371−393.

Wally, S., & Becerra, M. (2001). Top management team characteristics and strategic changes in international diversification: The case of US multinationals in the European community. *Group & Organization Management*, *26*(2), 165−188.

Wisniewski, M., & Ólafsson, S. (2004). Developing balanced scorecards in local authorities: A comparison of experience. *International Journal of Productivity and Performance Management*, *53*(7), 602−610.

Wu, J., Boateng, A., & Drury, C. (2007). An analysis of the adoption, perceived benefits, and expected future emphasis of western management accounting practices in Chinese SOEs and JVs. *The International Journal of Accounting, 42*(2), 171−185.

Yalcin, S. (2012). Adoption and benefits of management accounting practices: An inter-country comparison. *Accounting in Europe, 9*(1), 95−110.

# APPENDIX: QUESTIONNAIRE, ITEMS AND THEIR SOURCES

Those items that have been marked with the symbols (‡) are the retained items after confirmatory factor analysis.

### *Use of Package of Contemporary Management Accounting Practices*

The eight items of this scale were adapted from Chenhall and Langfield-Smith (1998a).

- ‡Benchmarking
- ‡Activity-based management
- Activity-based costing
- ‡The balanced scorecard
- ‡Value chain analysis
- ‡Total quality management
- Key performance indicators
- ‡Strategic cost management

### *Use of Package of Traditional Management Accounting Practices*

All items of this scale were adapted from Chenhall and Langfield-Smith (1998a).

- ‡Formal strategic planning
- ‡Budgeting for planning and control
- ‡Capital budgeting
- ‡Cost benefit analysis
- ‡Standard costing
- Variance analysis
- Return on investment

### *Organizational Change*

All items of this scale were developed from a literature (e.g. Dean & Sharfman, 1996; Gimbert et al., 2010).

- Business unit vision, mission or goals
- Restructuring
- ‡The range of product/service lines provided
- ‡New technology adoption
- ‡Research and development
- ‡Branding and marketing strategies
- ‡Geographic coverage
- ‡Human resources management (e.g. rewards systems, training, recruitment, etc.)
- ‡Product/service quality
- ‡Product/service pricing
- ‡Business partnerships (e.g. strategic alliance, outsourcing relationship, etc.)
- ‡Distribution channels
- ‡Financing operations

*Organizational Performance*

Items 1, 4–6 were adapted from Walker and Boyne (2006), and items 2 and 3 were developed from Griffin et al. (2007) and Baker and Sinkula (1999), respectively.

- ‡The quality of our output (products/services)
- ‡The implementation of new procedures and/or practices
- ‡The introduction of new products/service lines
- ‡The efficiency of our operations
- ‡The effectiveness of our operations
- ‡The level of our customer satisfaction

# HOW MANAGEMENT CONTROL PRACTICES ENABLE STRATEGIC ALIGNMENT DURING THE PRODUCT DEVELOPMENT PROCESS

Chris Akroyd, Sharlene Sheetal Narayan Biswas and Sharon Chuang

## ABSTRACT

Purpose — *This paper examines how the management control practices of organization members enable the alignment of product development projects with potentially conflicting corporate strategies during the product development process.*

Methodology/approach — *Using an ethnomethodology informed research approach, we carry out a case study of an innovative New Zealand food company. Case study data included an internal company document, interviews with organization members, and an external market analysis document.*

Findings — *Our case study company had both sales growth and profit growth corporate strategies which have been argued to cause tensions.*

Advances in Management Accounting, Volume 26, 99–138
ISSN: 1474-7871/doi:10.1108/S1474-787120150000026004

*We found that four management control practices enabled the alignment of product development projects to these strategies. The first management control practice was having the NPD and marketing functions responsible for different corporate strategies. Other management control practices included the involvement of organization members from across multiple functions, the activities they carried out, and the measures used to evaluate project performance during the product development process.*

Research limitations/implications — *These findings add new insights to the management accounting literature by showing how a combination of management control practices can be used by organization members to align projects with potentially conflicting corporate strategies during the product development process.*

Practical implications — *While the alignment of product development projects to corporate strategy is not easy this study shows how it can be enabled through a number of management control practices.*

Originality/value — *We contribute to the management accounting research in this area by extending our understanding of the management control practices used during the product development process.*

**Keywords:** Management control; product development; strategic alignment; corporate strategy; functional strategy; performance measures

# INTRODUCTION

Research has shown that product development[1] is an essential process for the survival and renewal of organizations (Brown & Eisenhardt, 1995; Schoohoven, Eisenhardt, & Lyman, 1990). A review of the product development literature reveals that the alignment of product development projects with corporate strategy is a critical success factor (Acur, Kandemir, & Boer, 2012; Cooper & Edgett, 2001; Edgett, 2013; Ernst, Hoyer, & Rübsaamen, 2010; Khurana & Rosenthal, 1998). Thus, strategy should form the basis for the selection and management of product development projects (Danila, 1989; De Maio, Verganti, & Corso, 1994; Hall & Naudia, 1990; Wheelwright & Clark, 1992).

Creating and maintaining strategic alignment in practice has been shown to be challenging (Simon, Hatch, & Youell, 2008). This is because multiple strategies[2] often compete for managers' attention within an organization (Dodd & Favaro, 2006). Corporate strategies "concerned with the organization-wide decisions that focus on achieving competitive advantage" (Slater, Olson, & Finnegan, 2011, p. 228) need to be linked to functional activities so that strategy can help guide and inform the practice of organization members as they carry out their activities (Hunger & Wheelen, 2010).

Organizations, though, often have corporate strategies that are in conflict with each other. A common tension is that of profit growth versus sales growth. What many organizations find is that "going for more growth damages profitability, and working toward higher profitability slows growth"[3] (Dodd & Favaro, 2006, p. 62). Thus, not only do organization members need to align product development projects with corporate strategy they also need to manage the potential conflicts caused by these strategies.

In this paper, we use an ethnomethodology informed research approach to better understand how organization members can achieve alignment between product development projects and corporate strategies during the product development process. In particular, we aim to show how organization members use management control practices to enable the alignment of product development projects with potentially conflicting corporate strategies. To do this we carry out a case study which examines the practices of five organization members at "FoodCo" (a pseudonym), an innovative New Zealand food manufacturing company.

Our results indicate that organization members at FoodCo used their management control practices to enable strategic alignment by assigning NPD and marketing functions responsibility for different corporate strategies so that a single function did not have to deal with this potential conflict. Organization members then used their management control practices to enable the alignment of projects to these strategies at different product development process stage-gates.[4] This included the involvement of organization members from across multiple functions, a number of formal yet flexible product development activities, and the use of strategy-focused financial and non-financial project performance measures.

The remainder of the paper is organized as follows. The next section introduces our ethnomethodology informed research approach. We then present an overview of the literature which this study builds on. This is followed by an overview of our case study data. We next present our case study findings. The final section discusses our findings and concludes with some limitations and suggestions for future research.

# RESEARCH APPROACH

It has recently been argued that asking "how" questions can add value by providing descriptions of novel contexts to show how organization members get things done in practice (Anteby, Lifshitz, & Tushman, 2014). According to Laurier (2003, p. 1), ethnomethodology informed studies are good at examining "how" questions as they focus on "how things get done by members of particular settings with the resources they have at hand."

In this paper, we use an ethnomethodology informed research approach which focuses on "developing and refining concepts induced from the field" to show how "practices are organized" (Parker, 2012, p. 57). Our ethnomethodology informed approach differs from a traditional ethnography informed approach[5] in a number of important ways. In particular, ethnomethodology does not follow ethnography's "reliance on rules, definitions and meanings to provide causal explanation of order as defined by the analyst" (Pollner & Emerson, 2001, p. 126). Instead ethnomethodology insists that "order and orderliness ... are indigenously produced and appreciated features of social life" (Pollner & Emerson, 2001, p. 126). For this reason, ethnomethodology "is concerned with how members of society go about the task of seeing, describing and explaining order in the world in which they live" (Pollner & Emerson, 2001, p. 126). Thus, this paper is focused on how organization members understand their practices but not on how the practices of organization members can be analyzed using an ethnography informed social theory.

Our ethnomethodology informed approach is based on the writings of Garfinkel (1967, 2002, 2006). Garfinkel developed ethnomethodology through an examination of the role of "accounts" which he learnt about during his undergraduate studies in accounting at the University of Newark (Rawls, 2002). One class in particular "theory of accounts" which "dealt with double entry bookkeeping and cost accounting" inspired his understanding of practice as it showed how order is produced by making things "accountable to superiors and other agencies in a variety of complex ways" (Rawls, 2002, p. 10). For this reason, ethnomethodology focuses on how the practices within particular contexts are organized so as to make them accountable to others (Garfinkel, 2002).

To examine how things are made accountable, ethnomethodology believes in the "objective reality" (Rawls, 2002, p. 2) of social facts, which Garfinkel (2002) argues can only be understood by organization members in their local context. It is important to note that the ethnomethodology meaning of "objectivity" is not defined in terms of a specific set of methods for collecting data but in terms of making sure that the phenomenon is adequately described (Sharrock & Anderson, 2012). For this reason, ethnomethodology "does not have the kind of concern for methods of data collection which are so prominent in the methodological literature" (Sharrock & Anderson, 2012, p. 107).

Following an ethnomethodology informed research approach, we collect data using a case study method focused on the practices of five organization members involved in the development of new products. This provides us with the context-specific knowledge necessary to show how these organization members understand the order created by their management control practices so as to make themselves accountable to other organization members.

The use of an ethnomethodology informed research approach is growing in the management accounting literature. Jönsson and Macintosh (1997) have stated that ethnomethodology could play a valuable role in understanding how practices work in actual organizations. This has led to a number of recent accounting papers using an ethnomethodology informed approach (see, e.g., Akroyd & Maguire, 2011; Balzli & Morard, 2012; O'Grady & Akroyd, 2016).

To gain this perspective, we collect and analyze case study data from an organization which develops many new products each year. Our data includes an external and an internal document as well as interviews with five organization members who were involved in product development activities. Our focus is on how these organization members go about understanding the order created by their management control practices which enabled the alignment of product development projects with potentially conflicting corporate strategies during the product development process.

To connect our ethnomethodology informed research approach to mainstream management accounting discourses, we frame this paper around the management accounting and product development literatures.

## LITERATURE REVIEW

Cooper, Edgett, and Kleinschmidt (1998) argue that the main role of strategy during product development is to guide the actions and efforts of organization members. They show that product development projects need to be "on-strategy," meaning each project should fit with corporate strategy. For example, if the corporate strategy is market share, then the majority of its product development projects should be designed to grow the business.

Management accounting research has shown that management controls can be useful tools in uncertain environments such as product development (Chenhall & Morris, 1986; Dent, 1990; Kren, 1992; Simons, 1987). Uncertainty during the product development process is caused by a lack of control over the outcome—input relationship, market-related uncertainty, technology-related uncertainty, and project scope (Davila, 2000). While many actions and decisions must be made to launch a new product, the profitability of the product and the value and desirability of its features will not be known until it is launched. Thus, complexity in this context arises from the pluralistic requirements of multiple functions which are involved during the product development process (Jørgensen & Messner, 2010).

At a broad organizational level research has shown that firms seek strategic alignment between their corporate strategies and functional activities through the use of various management controls (Simons, 1995, 2000; Tucker, Thorne, & Gurd, 2009). It has been noted that researching management control in a product development setting should not be limited to traditional accounting control practices but needs to include a much broader set of organizational processes (Davila, 2000) which focus on the practices of organization members that take place during the product development processes (Davila, Foster, & Oyon, 2009).

The use of a stage-gate product development process is a common practice in many organizations (Song, Song, & Di Benedetto, 2009). A recent review of "the contemporary art of cost management methods during product development" by Wouters and Morales (2014, p. 259) shows that there have been only six management accounting papers in the 40 journals they surveyed that have been published on the stage-gate process. We aim to extend our understanding of the use of management control in this setting by showing how the involvement of organization members from different functions, the activities they carry out, and the performance measures used to evaluate projects can enable alignment between product development projects and potentially conflicting corporate strategies.

The following sub-sections review the management accounting and product development literatures relating to the involvement of organization members, the activities that they carry out, and project performance measures, which have all been shown to be useful management control practices during product development (Akroyd, Narayan, & Sridharan, 2009; Bonner, Ruekert, & Walker, 2002; Davila, 2000; Hertenstein & Platt, 2000, Poskela & Martinsuo, 2009).

### *Involvement of Organization Members during the Stage-Gate Process*

The involvement of organization members from across multiple functions during the stage-gate process has also been shown to be an important management control practice (Danila, 1989; Hertenstein & Platt, 2000; Souder & Mandakovic, 1986; Taggart & Blaxter, 1992). Hertenstein and Platt (2000) argue that the activities which organization members are involved in during product development can affect both strategy formation and implementation. In order for organization members to fulfill these roles during the stage-gate process, they need to be in a position where information about strategy and strategic change can be easily communicated in a timely manner. Moreover, receiving strategic updates improves resource allocation, as organization members can focus resources on strategically important activities (Danila, 1989).

Jørgensen and Messner (2010) show that the involvement of organization members from across multiple functions was critical to the implementation of strategy set by senior managers. In their case study, organization members from different functions had different perspectives on how to achieve the strategy. Communication between them was critical in clarifying which perspective would be given priority. Once the organization members were clear about the strategic priorities they were able to implement the new strategy. Thus, having organization members from across multiple functions has been argued to help achieve project transparency (Jørgensen & Messner, 2010).

### *Product Development Activities during the Stage-Gate Process*

The product development activities that take place during the stage-gate process are used for guiding products from ideation to launch (Cooper, 1993). Stage activities focus on the development and testing of new product ideas while gate activities involve senior managers using decision criteria to make decisions about which projects are given funding for the next stage (Davila & Wouters, 2007). Firms can choose the stage and gate activities they feel are necessary for the context in which they operate (Akroyd et al., 2009; Product Development Institute Inc., 2012).

Davila (2000) argues that the main role that project activities play during the stage-gate process is to supply the information needed to reduce project uncertainty. Akroyd and Maguire (2011) support and extend this finding by showing that activities at the stages can help reduce uncertainty, while gate activities promote goal congruence.[6] Griffin (1997) found that firms which include strategic activities during their stage-gates have a higher probability of producing successful new products which align with their strategy.

While the activities that take place during the stage-gate process have been shown to be important to provide a structure to organize priorities and establish communication during the product development process, research has shown that flexibility is also important (Jørgensen & Messner, 2009). It has been argued that the flexible use of project activities can help structure the relationship between tasks and provide the basis for specific definitions of what is expected during stage-gates processes (Jørgensen & Messner, 2009). Davila et al. (2009) also discuss how both incremental and radical product innovation need formal stage-gate activities and tools that structure project execution. They argue that activities need to be flexible enough to take advantage of unexpected opportunities that arise but strong enough to maintain the desired direction. Additionally, flexibility is needed to deal with situations when product development projects do not go according to plan (Adler & Borys, 1996). For example, product testing activities may reveal problems with the product design or a competitor may release a similar product necessitating a review of the project to consider if there is still a good market opportunity.

Not all research concerning the use of stage-gate product development activities has shown positive results. Nagji and Tuff (2012), for example, argue that having a stage-gate process may harm radical innovation projects as these projects may get negative reviews at gates before they are properly examined. They argue that organization members should be encouraged to challenge early reviews and experiment with new ideas for radical product innovation to occur (Nagji & Tuff, 2012).

### *Project Performance Measures Used during the Stage-Gate Process*

Simons (2000) discusses the importance of performance measurement for the successful implementation of strategy and shows that effective performance measurement acts to both formalize strategy and as a communication channel to inform employees about strategy. Performance measures can also be used to monitor and provide feedback on strategy implementation (Simons, 2000). During the product development process performance measures help communicate corporate strategy to organization members. Additionally, there is evidence that performance measures also provide feedback on the implementation of strategy (Akroyd & Maguire, 2011; Hertenstein & Platt, 2000; Jørgensen & Messner, 2010).

Jørgensen and Messner (2010) found that companies often create a formal set of rules used at decision gates to assure financial accountability. During the stages the calculation models were seen as problematic so organization members used non-financial measures to refine their understanding of the consequences of their decisions. While a general understanding of the need to be profitable influenced behavior in their case study firm, the limitations of the financial model left room for organization members to have discussions and express different ideas (Jørgensen & Messner, 2010).

Akroyd and Maguire (2011) contribute further insight into project performance measures. Their case company used performance measures to align projects with their sales growth strategy early in the project selection process. For example, the initial idea screen decision gate meeting started with a reminder that potential project ideas needed to be consistent with the corporate sales growth strategy. Later on senior managers used five performance measures to evaluate project ideas in relation to the sales growth corporate strategy. In this way, the firm ensured all its product development projects were aligned with their sales growth strategy from the very start.

Research has also shown that many firms use a combination of both financial and non-financial performance measures (Davila, 2000; Griffin & Page, 1996; Hertenstein & Platt, 1997; Jørgensen & Messner, 2010; Langfield-Smith, 1997; Sjoblom, 1998). Davila (2000) finds evidence that organization members place higher reliance on non-financial measures than financial measures. The logic being that good performance in non-financials can drive good financial performance.

Sjoblom (1998) suggests that while financial measures can be used to identify some problems, they have limited usefulness in operational decision making because financial indicators are lagging measures and therefore not good indicators of future performance. The time lag between costs being incurred to develop product development projects and the launch of products into the market makes it hard to measure the performance of projects in financial terms (Hertenstein & Platt, 1997; Langfield-Smith, 1997). The organization members in the case study by Jørgensen and Messner (2010) acknowledged the limits of the financial quantification of the benefits and costs of projects, due to their inherent uncertainty and complexity. Organization members dealt with this through an iterative process which accounted for both benefits and costs (Jørgensen & Messner, 2010).

The study by Hertenstein and Platt (2000) highlights additional problems with performance measurement used during the product development process. The authors found that most organizations did not have project performance measures which linked to their strategy. This was disconcerting considering prior management accounting literature provides evidence that the best performance measures were those linked to strategy (Kaplan & Norton, 1992; Langfield-Smith, 1997; Nanni, Dixon, & Vollmann, 1992). In their interviews, product development managers believed there should be a greater emphasis on both non-financial and financial performance measures, including measures which linked project performance to strategy (Hertenstein & Platt, 2000). Davila and Wouters (2007) support Hertenstein and Platt's (2000) findings that measuring project performance is challenging and the solutions that have been proposed fall short of fulfilling senior managers' needs. Consequently, Davila and Wouters (2007) highlighted this as an area which would benefit from further research.

*Summary of Literature Review*

In summary, one stream of research has shown the importance of the link between corporate strategy and the actions of organization members. This research argues that the activities that organization members carry out can influence both strategy formation and implementation (Cooper et al., 1998; Hertenstein & Platt, 2000; Jørgensen & Messner, 2010). Another stream of research has shown that a number of management control practices are useful during the product development process. These include the involvement of organization members from across multiple functions, the product development activities they carry out, and the performance measures used to evaluate projects (Akroyd & Maguire, 2011; Davila et al., 2009; Hertenstein & Platt, 2000; Jørgensen & Messner, 2009; Song et al., 2009).

From this review, we have identified a number of open questions. These include: the effect that multiple corporate strategies have on the activities organization members carry out during the product development process; understanding how organization members measure project performance; the link between financial and non-financial performance measurement and strategy during the product development process; and finally the role that organization members from different functions play during the product development process to link product development projects with corporate strategy.

Based on this review, we aim to contribute new insights to these questions through the use of an ethnomethodology informed case study showing how organization members use management control practices (including, the involvement of organization members, the activities they carry out, and the measures used to evaluate project performance) to enable the alignment of product development projects with multiple, potentially conflicting, corporate strategies.

## CASE STUDY DATA

Our case study focuses on the activities of five organization members at "FoodCo" (a pseudonym), an innovative private New Zealand food manufacturing company. At the time of our study, FoodCo had an annual turnover of approximately NZ$145 (US$100) million with assets of NZ$85 (US$57) million so would be classified as a mid-sized company (The Economist, 2012). FoodCo has been operating for over 100 years and is the New Zealand market leader in a highly competitive market where it competes against both large multinational companies and small local companies. FoodCo was selected because it was actively involved in product development and innovation is seen as a critical success factor in the food industry (Winger & Wall, 2006).

Data for this case study (see Table 1 for details) include an external Euromonitor International document which analyzed FoodCo and the market it operates in, an internal FoodCo document as well as interviews with the NPD manager, two NPD technologists, a marketing brand manager and the management accountant which were carried out in August and September 2012. The NPD manager reported directly to the General Manager and had direct day-to-day interactions with NPD members.

*Table 1.* Case Study Data.

| FoodCo Interview Data | 5 hours |
| --- | --- |
| NPD manger | 1 hour |
| First NPD technologist | 1 hour |
| Second NPD technologist | 1 hour |
| Marketing brand manager | 1 hour |
| Management accountant | 1 hour |
| FoodCo document | 12 pages |
| Euromonitor International document | 58 pages |

The management accountant was involved in strategy formulation with the senior management team (see Table 2) and strategy implementation through interacting with NPD technologists during the product development process.

Interviews were semi-structured, guided by a set of questions about the product development process. Open-ended questions were asked which enabled the researchers to adapt the interview to the expertise of each person without diverging from the overall purpose of the study. Furthermore, semi-structured interviews were carried out to avoid the researchers imposing predetermined views on the interviewees and to allow the interviewees to speak freely. During the interviews, additional questions were asked to follow up on comments made by the interviewees or to ask questions about documents shown to us by the interviewees. The recordings were later transcribed in order to better understand what had been said and to gain a more comprehensive view of the practices of these organization members.

Even though we only interviewed five organization members they represent a high percentage of the employees involved in the development of new products at FoodCo and included: the NPD manger, two of the three NPD technologists, one of the three marketing brand managers, and the management accountant. After the interviews were transcribed, the interviewees checked the content of the transcripts and provided us with follow-up information. While we acknowledge that our interview data sample is small, we were able to verify interview data with both an internal FoodCo document and an external document from Euromonitor International. The internal FoodCo document contained information about FoodCo's strategy (shown in Fig. 1) and stage-gate product development process (shown in Fig. 2). The Euromonitor International document contained information about FoodCo's market performance, including market share data for every category between 2010 and 2014.

We used NVivo (version 9) to organize our data around the product development process stage-gates. We used an open coding process which focused on the corporate strategies used at our case study company (Parker, 2012). The analysis revealed a number of strategies which enabled us to check for consistency within the data. The strategies were then compared to the external Euromonitor International document and the internal company document to triangulate the results (Modell, 2009). Finally, the authors followed up with the five organization members we interviewed to see if there were any potential issues. In this way, the researchers were able to check on the internal consistency of the data which we believe improves the credibility and validity of our findings (Denzin, 1978). In the following section, we report on our analysis.

# CASE STUDY FINDINGS

Based on our ethnomethodology informed research approach, this section focuses on how five organization members understand the order created by their management control practices during the stage-gate product development process at FoodCo. We start with a discussion of FoodCo's market conditions to understand the context in which these organization members carried out their activities. We then examine FoodCo's functional and corporate strategies and show how assigning responsibility for different corporate strategies to the NPD and marketing functions was a management control practice. Finally, we show how alignment between product development projects and corporate strategies was enabled through the use of three management control practices: the involvement of organization members from across multiple functions, the activities they carried out, and the performance measures used to evaluate projects (see Table 3 for a summary of the findings).

## *FoodCo's Market Conditions*

According to the Euromonitor International (EI) document, the retail volume and growth rates in FoodCo's main market segment in New Zealand have shown slow growth in recent years. EI explain that while this is partly due to the maturity of the industry the market segment performance was also influenced by growing competition from related niche products. Competition from these products has led a number of companies to expand into related market segments in recent years. EI shows the types of products that competitors have released into the market and explains how FoodCo has taken a different approach to this competitive threat. Instead of just creating new niche products, FoodCo has also used advertising to show consumers how they can make niche type products by mixing FoodCo's current products with other nutritious ingredients. For example, EI explain how FoodCo partnered with leading fruit companies to promote the benefits of eating their products with fruits rich in Vitamin C.

This has enabled FoodCo to continue to lead their market segment with an overall value share of 31% as well as to take the lead in a number of related niche market segments. EI states that FoodCo offers a wide selection of product types and flavor variants under its brand names. According to EI, FoodCo's main brand is an iconic brand in New Zealand and has long been associated with local sports stars. Despite the fact that it is not a typically child-focused brand, it has continued to benefit from advertisements that specifically targets children. This promotional initiative aims to improve the health of children in New Zealand by encouraging them to participate in events held around the country.

EI also tracked FoodCo's new product launches and showed that they helped the firm gain market share in both sales volume and value during the time this study was carried out.

### Corporate Strategies at FoodCo

Given these tough market conditions, FoodCo had just completed a new five-year strategic plan. FoodCo's NPD manager and the management accountant were both members of the strategic planning group that formulated the new plan. The management accountant reported to the commercial manager (CFO) while the NPD managers reported directly to FoodCo's General Manager (GM) (see Table 2).

According to the NPD manager:

> I report to the GM … the GM looks at the big overall [strategic] measures. We have our [NPD strategy] and I liaise with marketing in terms of their [marketing strategy] expectations so we know what the parameters are for this year.

The NPD manager explained that the corporate strategy focused on four main areas:

> Sales growth, profit growth, supply chain excellence and delighting our customers and consumers. They are the four main things. We have performance measures for these areas.

***Table 2.*** The Management Reporting Structure of FoodCo.

| Senior Management Team | Functional Members |
| --- | --- |
| General manager (GM) | |
| NPD manager | NPD technologists |
| Marketing manager | Marketing brand managers |
| Commercial (finance) manager (CFO) | Management accountant |
| Product category manager | |
| Sales manager | |

*Source*: FoodCo document.

Each of these corporate strategies (except "supply chain excellence") was then linked into either the NPD function strategy or the marketing function strategy (see Fig. 1).

The short-term corporate strategy was set by the senior management team based on the new five-year strategic plan for the company. The aim was for functions to be guided by their own strategies so as to help the organization achieve its overall corporate strategy.

NPD aimed "to launch financially viable new products on time and within scope" (*FoodCo document*). The "time" and "scope" parts of the strategy linked to the corporate strategy of delighting customers (retailers) and end-consumers. This shows how important it was for new products, which generated about 25% of FoodCo's turnover (*FoodCo document*), to fit consumers' tastes and be delivered to customers (retailers) on time while at the same time being financially viable. As discussed in the following sections, being on time was critical as one of FoodCo's main customers only introduced new products twice a year, so hitting those dates was critical to getting products to end-consumers.

The NPD manager was part of the senior management team. Being part of this team meant that the NPD manager was always up-to-date with changes in the firm's corporate strategy. This was important as she was responsible for all the product development projects and worked closely

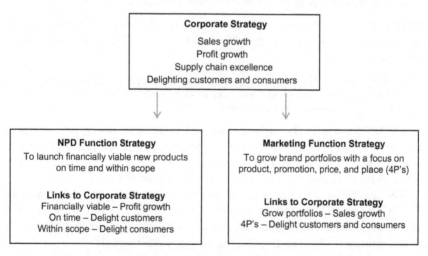

*Fig. 1.* Corporate and Functional Strategies at FoodCo. *Sources*: Based on information collected from the FoodCo document and Interview data.

with marketing to keep informed of any changes in the market or new product launches of their competitors which affected their product strategies.

> I work really really closely with marketing to make sure what product development are doing is really aligned in terms of vision for the brands. So it falls into the strategy and the brand portfolio and then the products really and then the individual projects. (NPD manager)

To increase the flow of information, the NPD manager held progress meetings with the NPD technologists which enabled the communication of strategic changes to NPD members. Even though the NPD manager was part of the senior management team – which facilitated opportunities for communication between NPD and senior management – the communication of strategy was still seen as an area that needed improvement in FoodCo. According to the NPD manager;

> I will put my hand on my heart and say it is something we could do better ... people know what they are doing but it is making sure the bigger picture is communicated. That is a hard thing to do ... it takes time.

To support the increased need for information flow between the senior management team and NPD technologists, the management accountant had been invited to play a larger role in the company.

> There are a lot of big things happening. And [senior managers] need to get our advice on what impact it is going to have on the business. (Management accountant)

During the new five-year strategic planning meetings, the management accountant was asked to give his input to the GM and other senior managers.

> We had a five year high level strategy meeting for the company ... It was mainly just the GMs and senior people, so I was lucky to sit in on that. It largely affects us so it was quite good. (Management accountant)

While NPD's role in the organization was to develop new products which delighted customers and consumers, and contributed to profit growth, it was the marketing's role to find new opportunities in the market place. Thus, marketing had their own strategy which guided their activities.

The marketing strategy focused on supporting the portfolio growth of FoodCo's brands as well as the 4Ps – product, promotion, price, and place. Marketing then built this strategy into their marketing plans and brand strategies. As stated by the marketing brand manager:

> So in terms of our marketing process. We go through a brand planning process, every financial year we will sit down and write our brand plan, that's starting at the top line

strategy and then falls into your 4P's so what you want to do on a product, promotion, price and place or distribution. And from there your yearly activity falls out of it, so specifically what you do ... launch a new product ... Whatever I do with my brands I have to support the growth of our wider portfolios.

The marketing strategy of portfolio growth was linked to the sales growth element of FoodCo's corporate strategy. According to the marketing brand manager:

Growth, sales growth is definitely I would say one of the bigger ones, I mean the brand is doing well if it is growing.

As FoodCo delivered its product to end-users through distribution channels such as supermarkets, it continuously engaged in the promotion of their brands in order to keep a high level of interest in FoodCo's products and maintain shelf-space. Failure to achieve shelf-space levels at supermarkets would lead to a drop in sales and market share as the end-consumers would not have access to FoodCo's products.

In summary, this section showed that marketing and NPD members focused on different parts of FoodCo's corporate strategy. This division of potentially conflicting corporate strategies could be seen as the first management control practice organization members used to enable strategic alignment. The following sub-section examines the stage-gate product development process to show how organization members used other management control practices to align product development projects with potentially conflicting corporate strategies.

### Management Control Practices during the Stage-Gate Product Development Process

The stage-gate product development process provided the guidelines for how new products were developed at FoodCo (see Fig. 2). However, the amount of time spent at each stage-gate varied significantly between projects, as it depended on the type of project being developed.

We have got three [stage-gate] processes, there is a full process which is all of these (points to the stage-gate process — Fig. 2) and that is for (radical) step-change. The light [process] tends to be a concept brief, a development brief and a business case ... there is even an express [process] which is basically just do your business case. You make the call. Most of them [projects] sit in the light process, which is the concept, development and business case. (NPD manager)

The full stage-gate process was only used for radical step-change innovation, which used emerging technologies, the design of a new brand, or entry into a new market. These projects had more novel elements and thus had greater uncertainty and challenges with potentially significant investments.

The light stage-gate process was for incremental innovation, which were mainly line extensions of existing brands that used existing factory facilities. There was also an express stage-gate process. These projects included small changes in product formulation or packaging, which only required the completion of a business case which was carried out during the "Development Stage" and evaluated at Gate 4 (see Fig. 2). The NPD manager explained that while the stage-gate process at FoodCo was controlled manually, they had templates with pre-defined project performance measures that the senior management team used at decision gates to make resource allocation decisions.

As outlined by the NPD manager:

> We always review the market opportunity to make sure it is still valid, the strategic fit and importance, the competitive rationale, technical feasibility, financial reward versus costs, the legal review and obvious show stoppers ... and the timeline.

The following sub-sections review each of the stage-gates that made up FoodCo's product development process. We describe the management control practices of organization members which include the organization members involved, the activities they carried out, and the performance measures used to evaluate projects at decision gates. At the end of each sub-section, we summarize the findings to show how these management control practices enabled the alignment of product development projects with potentially conflicting corporate strategies.

### The Scoping Stage-Gate

FoodCo separated this stage-gate from the other stage-gates by a dotted line in Fig. 2 as only radical step-change product development projects originated here. During the "Scoping Stage," marketing brand managers and NPD technologists carried out activities focused on examining new technical ideas and new market opportunities. According to a marketing brand manager:

> We initiate new product development [at this stage]. Depending on the strategy of our brands and what we want to do with it [NPD technologists] will play a part in it, especially with my brands. I do a lot of [radical step-change] innovation work.

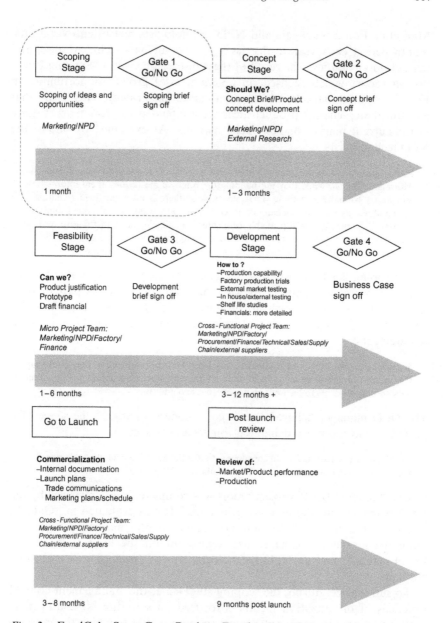

*Fig. 2.* FoodCo's Stage-Gate Product Development Process. *Source*: FoodCo document.

Marketing brand managers and NPD technologists met often over a one-month period each year to discuss a number of new technical ideas and market opportunities. The result of these discussions was a "Scoping Brief" project report which focused on potential sales growth opportunities in FoodCo's target markets, which was a marketing strategy. This meant that all radical step-change product ideas were intended to grow market share in the current market or new niche markets. As explained by one of the NPD technologists,

> In the formulation of the [scoping] brief itself we will already start to have discussions with marketing, so while they are building the brief we are feeding them information and we try to make something workable. Because there is no point them giving us a brief and we say hey look we can't do it. Or if you really want us to do this I think we need new equipment, it will probably be a three year timeline kind of thing so we like that upfront, rather than for them to write a [scoping] brief that's not very useful. So by the time the [scoping] brief is being issued it's more or less ready for sign off.

The "Scoping Brief" project report also contained information about nutritional scope requirements. This was important for NPD as part of their strategic focus was to deliver products "within scope." According to an NPD technologist, scope at this stage involved mainly nutritional requirements:

> So, marketing might say we want to have a heart tick endorsement or they might say they want it to deliver so many % of dietary fibre, any nutritional aspect, or they want only natural products to be used, no preservatives no additives.

The NPD manager believed that a good understanding of the scope of a project was necessary to delight customers and consumers.

> … delighting our customers and consumers, that is the most important [at this stage]. If you do not do that, then the others do not follow. (NPD manager)

Once a "Scoping Brief" project report was complete, it was reviewed by the NPD manager and the marketing manager. It was evaluated at "Gate 1" where a "Go/No Go" decision was made by the marketing manager. Once the marketing manager had signed off on the brief, a marketing brand manager and an NPD technologist started developing new product concepts.

To summarize, during the scoping stage-gate, the management control practices of organization members focused on selecting NPD and marketing members to carry out project scoping activities which the marketing manager evaluated. These management control practices enabled strategic alignment by focusing attention on different corporate strategies:

Marketing, which focused on sales growth opportunities, and NPD, which focused on delivering specific nutritional scope requirements. Since NPD did not carry out product costing activities at this stage-gate, there was no tension between their profit growth strategy and marketing's sales growth strategy.

### The Concept Stage-Gate

All radical step-change and light product development projects went through this stage-gate. During the "Concept Stage," marketing brand managers and NPD technologists carried out activities which were focused on developing different product concepts. These were then written into a "Concept Brief" project report which at this stage was quite broad. As explained by a marketing brand manager,

> It can include the big strategic insight and the concept but you would not go as specific as saying I want this pack size and this flavour variant.

Marketing brand managers and NPD technologists worked together to develop concepts. According to the NPD manager:

> We work really closely with marketing. We have a plan so we know what we are working on is based on the marketing strategy.

At this stage project scope was evaluated by an external research firm to get consumer feedback about the product attributes.

> It's a consumer check, to make sure we should be going down this road ... It's insight driven, we do it through an external agency we may do strategic brainstorming days and then we will take those concepts. If the insight doesn't resonate then you won't get your consumer interest in buying. (NPD manager)

The final "Concept Brief" project reports were written by marketing brand managers. These reports included information about market growth opportunities (a marketing strategy) and project scope (an NPD strategy) which was based on the external research results. The focus on sales growth opportunities and project scope was still important as this was the first stage for light product development projects and the first opportunity for radical step-change projects to get external research.

Once a "Concept Brief" project report was complete, it was reviewed by the NPD manager and the marketing manager. It was then evaluated at "Gate 2" where a "Go/No Go" decision was made by the marketing manager. Once the marketing manager had signed off on the brief, it was given to an NPD technologist who started to work on the product feasibility stage. According to the marketing brand manager:

> Assuming that the [concept] brief is then approved it will go to someone from (NPD). They would then start picking the brief apart and using their knowledge and their skills and their insights to come up with some different flavour ideas or format ideas.

To summarize, during the concept stage-gate the management control practices of organization members focused on selecting NPD and marketing members to carry out project concept activities which the marketing manager evaluated. These management control practices enabled strategic alignment by focusing attention on different corporate strategies: Marketing, which focused on sales growth opportunities, and NPD, which focused on delivering the required product scope attributes to consumers. Since NPD did not carry out product costing activities at this stage-gate there was still no tension between their profit growth strategy and marketing's sales growth strategy.

### The Feasibility Stage-Gate

Radical step-change and light product development projects went through the feasibility stage-gate. The activities carried out during the "Feasibility Stage" were focused on justifying the product concept. This was done using a "Micro Project Team" which included organization members from NPD, marketing, the factory, and finance (represented by the management accountant). The output of this group was a "Development Brief" project report. Depending on the product, it took one to six months for projects to go through feasibility.

NPD activities focused on building product prototypes that were then tested by marketing. According to the marketing brand manager:

> We would say (to NPD) yes we like that, that and that. And then they will go to the lab and make up different samples. And that's when they come back to us again and we try them and say what we think.

Since marketing and NPD had developed the "Concept Brief" together, NPD could be assured that the brief was aligned with their scope strategy and marketing's sales growth strategy. Thus, when the NPD technologists received a "Concept Brief," they would immediately start developing a number of new product concepts. During this process, the marketing member of the project team started to work on the 4Ps of each project to make sure the new product could compete in its market segment.

The management accountant was also a member of the project team and represented the finance function. According to the NPD manager:

> There has got to be some financial viability so accounting is brought in quite early on [at this stage].

A stretch gross profit (GP) margin target had been set for new and existing products by the senior management team. This was a new initiative which had come from the new five-year strategic plan (*FoodCo document*). The senior management team thus gave a lot of attention to GP margin when they evaluated projects at the feasibility gate. According to one of the NPD technologists:

> Our [performance] measurement of course is to deliver to the brief [at feasibility], that's how we are measured. So if the brief says, deliver to that GP (margin) … we are monitoring waste, we are monitoring that it delivers to the formulation, to the bill of materials. Delivering to the hours, to flow rates, all those things that are put in the costing, we must make sure it achieves. Or otherwise GP (margin) shifts.

The activities of the management accountant focused on working with the NPD technologists at this stage on product costings:

> When it comes to costings, it is usually with (NPD technologists) because they are actually doing the recipe. So usually we will deal with them. But often (the NPD manager) gets involved, especially if they have questions, (the NPD manager) will come along to the meetings, and ask those questions too. Often it gets discussed within the weekly product development meeting too, which brings together all parts of the business really, so it is quite cross-functional. (Management accountant)

The NPD technologists knew that for projects to be successful they needed to have strong financials so they valued the interactions with the management accountant. These interactions gave the management accountant a broad understanding of product development projects. This enabled the management accountant to communicate ideas that had been discussed during project team meetings with the senior management team, thus enabling another communication channel between product development activities and senior managers.

For light product development projects, the management accountant would start off by looking at the costing of a similar product and then would work with NPD, marketing, and factory team members to gain an understanding of the new product requirements. The management accountant would then adapt the costing to reflect the required amount of ingredients, the time needed for production and the subsequent overhead allocation. The expected revenue would be estimated by marketing who would base their estimates off past experience and observations of current market trends. Research would need to be carried out by members of the project team if new raw materials or equipment was required, in order to get an idea of the cost involved.

The factory used the product prototypes to determine machine specifications which the management accountant then used to make draft financials. Marketing then used these new product prototypes to carry out market research such as taste testing and focus groups. While the price that marketing set for the product (one of their 4Ps) had an effect on the GP margin calculation, it did not seem to cause tension between the NPD and marketing functions as marketing also knew that GP margin was a key project performance measure. According to one brand manager,

> I am not measured on it specifically but I am not allowed to launch anything that is not over the [GP margin] target.

Once a "Development Brief" project report had been completed it was presented to the senior management team at "Gate 3" where they would make a "Go/No Go" decision. The senior management team included the GM along with the marketing, product category, commercial, NPD and sales managers. The performance measure used by the senior management team at this gate was GP margin (an NPD strategy) but they also reviewed marketing's 4Ps. According to the management accountant:

> Largely it is GP (margin). That is what it really seems to come down to.

If a project did not have a high-enough GP margin, the senior management team would send the project back to the project team. The management accountant understood there was a problem with evaluating products based on the GP margin without considering capacity and stated that:

> You are going to miss out on a lot of opportunities, especially when our factory at the moment is not at full capacity. And why not take on things that are going to give you money towards overheads anyway.

The management accountant recognized that if new products did not get approved when the factory had spare capacity these fixed costs would just get allocated to other products.

> If we've got capacity why not use it … especially with a new product (understanding) what kind of impact that will have on the factory in terms of fixed overheads — they are fixed anyway.

The project team then worked together to come up with ways to improve the GP margin. According to an NPD technologist:

> I think [senior managers] look at GP (margin), we need to send a message to our accountants. Because our bosses are not interested in how we arrive at the GP, they just look at GP. So we need to bring the factory boss and the accountants to come aboard and see what they can do to give a variable GP. If it cannot be done it cannot be done but usually if they look hard enough it can be done.

This shows that while the GP margin was an important measure for evaluating product development projects, organization members at FoodCo understand that it was not a perfect measure so they worked together to make sure that good projects would have a high-enough GP margin to get approved. The "Development Briefs" that were approved by the senior management team at the gate were passed onto NPD where NPD technologists started working on the development of new products.

To summarize, during the feasibility stage-gate, the management control practices of organization members focused on forming micro project teams, determining the activities for them to carry out, and the performance measures used to evaluate projects. Micro project teams were cross-functional and included organization members from NPD, marketing, the factory, and finance (the management accountant). The project team members focused on building product prototypes and justifying product concepts. The senior management team then evaluated projects based mainly on their GP margin. These management control practices enabled strategic alignment by keeping attention focused on different corporate strategies: Marketing, which focused on the 4Ps, and NPD, which focused on profit growth (GP margin). Since both product price and cost are necessary to calculate GP margin there was the potential for tension between marketing (who managed the price) and NPD (who managed the cost) at this stage. This was managed by not allowing marketing to launch new products that did not meet the GP margin target set by senior managers.

*The Development Stage-Gate*
All three types of product development projects (radical step-change, light, and express) went through the development stage-gate. The activities that took place during the "Development Stage" were focused on determining the design features of a new product. This was done with a "Cross-Functional Project Team" which included organization members from NPD, marketing, the factory, procurement, technical, sales, supply

chain, external suppliers, and finance (represented by the management accountant). The output of the activities carried out by this group was a "Business Case" project report which was evaluated by the senior management team at "Gate 4" who made the "Go/No Go" decision. Depending on the project, it took 3–12 months for projects to go through the development stage-gate.

This was the only stage that "Express" projects went through. The activities carried out for these projects were focused on ingredient or packaging changes concerned with decreasing product cost. According to the NPD manager:

> Sometimes there are cost down projects that are quite important. I know it is not really NPD but it does involve a fair amount of formulation review and process review in the factory to see if we can get costs out. For example, testing another ingredient, a cheaper replacement that tastes the same and does the same thing and has the same quality – at all times the sensory cannot be compromised, that's the critical one. You cannot compromise on a sensory platform.

Once a product design had been developed, NPD worked closely with the factory to run production trials for radical step-change and light product development projects. At the same time, marketing activities focused on external market sensory tests for all project types to prove the design. NPD and sales also carried out shelf life studies, while the management accountant did more detailed financial analysis.

During the development stage, project teams continually checked the key project performance measures. While the senior management team had set a GP margin target of XX%, no recent product development projects had actually been able to hit the new target. According to the management accountant:

> None of the costings I have done so far [this year] have hit XX% and [some projects] still seem to go through just because with the complexity of a product like (A), it's almost impossible, unless they are going to cut back to just core components. There's going to be a bigger focus [later] this year on getting NPD to see how they can improve the manufacturing process; things like cutting out intermediates, reducing labor and overheads. Mainly labor as they produce the product, coming up with different ways to do that.

Once the "Business Case" project report had been completed, it was presented at a senior management team gate meeting. We found a greater number of performance measures used by the senior management team at this gate. Financial measures again focused on GP margin (NPD strategy) but also included payback period which provided another view on profit growth. According to the NPD manager:

> Here at [FoodCo] they (new products) have to breakeven by the end of year one. Depending on how innovative it is the payback period is going to be longer.

Payback period was especially important for getting new capital expenditure approved as senior managers wanted to know if it could be paid back within a year. Non-financial measures included timeliness to market (NPD strategy), project scope (NPD strategy), and market-focused sensory results (marketing strategy). Thus, while GP margin and payback period were still important measures, non-financial measures such as delivering on time and within scope (NPD strategies) were also critical decision factors.

> [At this gate its] about timeliness to market. Because we do have these review dates and you have to make sure that you meet them as best you can. So the key is meeting the dates ... and you have to make sure it is within scope. (NPD manager)

Delivering on time was important as one of FoodCo's main customers (a retail chain) only took new products twice a year. For this reason, project team members constantly monitored the progress of their projects against the timelines to ensure they were going to meet these launch dates as they did not want to miss these windows.

> Timings on the process can vary significantly dependent on the project scope. Trade (retail chain) buy-in is essential early on because we have a great new product ... retailers may not think it is that great and you really have to have the retailers on board because they are your access to the consumer. (NPD manager)

Consumer sensory results (a marketing strategy) were also a key non-financial performance measure as delighting customers and consumers was a corporate strategy. This was carried out by an external sensory provider. Each project had to reach a specified result, "for example more than 60% of the consumers surveyed must have selected either liked very much or extremely liked the product" (*marketing brand manager*). If the sensory hurdle was not met, the project team had to go back and review or re-formulate the product.

> Delivering the sensory experience whilst maintaining high nutritional credibility is really important for [FoodCo]. We really try and make sure that everything we do tastes great. It is all about whole food and natural minimally processed. (NPD manager)

These financial and non-financial performance measures provided checks and balances for the project team during the development of new products and ensured that the senior management team evaluated the projects based on factors that were deemed important for achieving corporate strategy as well as helping to reduce the uncertainty and risk associated with developing new products. According to the NPD manager:

> The process does mitigate risk. Launching a new product is really expensive. By the time you add up all the trials and the marketing investment, it can cost over $2 million to launch something and you have to be pretty sure it is going to work.

When a "Business Case" was approved by senior managers at the gate meeting it was given to the project team to prepare the product for launch.

To summarize, during the development stage-gate, the management control practices of organization members focused on forming cross-functional project teams, determining the activities for them to carry out, and the performance measures used to evaluate projects. These cross-functional teams included organization members from NPD, marketing, the factory, procurement, technical, sales, supply chain, external suppliers, and finance (represented by the management accountant). These members carried out activities to determine the design features of new products. The senior management team evaluated projects based on financial measures (GP margin and payback period) as well as non-financial measures (timeliness to market and project scope) and reviewed the 4Ps with a particular focus on the sensory results. These management control practices focused attention on different corporate strategies: Marketing, which focused on the 4Ps, and NPD, which focused on profit growth (GP margin and payback period) as well as timeliness to market and project scope. While the price that marketing set for new products had an effect on the GP margin calculation it did not seem to cause tensions between the NPD and marketing functions during this stage-gate.

*Go to Launch*
This stage was focused on preparing the required factory, sales and marketing plans to launch new products. This could take anywhere from three to eight months and was carried out by the same cross-functional project team which carried out the product development activities during the development stage. We did not examine this part of the stage-gate process as organization members did not need to justify these projects in relation to corporate strategies.

# DISCUSSION AND CONCLUSIONS

The literature has shown that a stage-gate product development process plays an important role during the development of new products (see, e.g., Akroyd & Maguire, 2011; Davila, 2000; Davila et al., 2009; Griffin, 1997; Hertenstein & Platt, 2000; Jørgensen & Messner, 2009, 2010; Song et al., 2009; Wouters & Morales, 2014). In this paper, we use an ethnomethodology informed research approach to build on these studies by examining how five organization members used management control practices to align product development projects with potentially conflicting corporate strategies during the stage-gate process at FoodCo.

The following discussion of our case study findings focuses on: (1) How potential conflict was managed and strategic alignment enabled through assigning functional responsibility for different corporate strategies during the state-gate process; (2) How organization member involvement enabled strategic alignment during the stage-gate process; (3) How the activities that organization members carried out and the reports they produced enabled strategic alignment during the stage-gate process; (4) How performance measures enabled strategic alignment during the stage-gate process. We then summarize these findings by showing how these four management control practices changed during the stage-gate process from a focus on the sales growth corporate strategy during the first half of the stage-gate process (scoping and concept stage-gates) to the profit growth corporate strategy during the second half of the stage-gate process (feasibility and development stage-gates) to enable strategic alignment between product development projects and corporate strategy. Finally, we conclude with the limitations of the study and suggestions for future research.

## Functional Responsibilities and Corporate Strategies

Strategic alignment was first enabled by assigning marketing and NPD functions responsibility for different corporate strategies (see the "Functional Responsibilities and Corporate Strategies" column in Table 3). This can be seen as a management control practice as it enabled managers at FoodCo to influence the activities of NPD and marketing members and got them to focus on activities that were important for the success of the company.

It has been argued in the literature that having both sales growth and profit growth corporate strategies can cause tensions (Dodd & Favaro,

2006). At FoodCo, this was managed by making the NPD function responsible for the profit growth strategy and the marketing function responsible
for sales growth strategy. This created both a separation between the two
strategies and also a link between the corporate and functional strategies
(Hunger & Wheelen, 2010). While the sales growth and profit growth strategies were separated into the functional strategies of NPD and marketing,
the corporate strategy that focused on "delighting customers and consumers" was integrated into both the NPD and marketing functional strategies, each with a slightly different focus. Marketing focused on the 4Ps and
sensory experience of consumers while NPD focused on delivering products
"on time" and "within scope."

### Organization Member Involvement

While the involvement of NPD and marketing members as well as cross-
functional project teams during the stage-gate process was expected, the
high level of involvement by the management accountant in both corporate
strategy planning activities as well as product development activities during
the stage-gate process was a surprise (see the "Organization Member
Involvement" column in Table 3).

Our findings show that the involvement of the management accountant
during the feasibility and development stage-gates enabled strategic alignment through the influence they had on both strategy formulation and
strategy implementation. Thus, the management accountant was able to
facilitate product development activities in a clear, timely manner so that
the other project members could implement the corporate strategies
through their product development activities.

In addition to this, the management accountants' position in the organization enabled the flow of feedback about strategy implementation back to
the senior management team. This feedback was influenced by the involvement of the management accountant during the feasibility and development
stage-gates which Hertenstein and Platt (1998) have argued could play an
important role during the stage-gate process.

### Organization Activities and Project Reports

The activities that organization members carried out and the project reports
they produced also enabled strategic alignment during the stage-gate

**Table 3.** Summary of Findings.

Four Management Controls Used by Organization Members at FoodCo

| Stage-Gate Product Development Process (Project Process Time) | Functional Responsibilities and Corporate Strategies | Organization Member Involvement | Organization Activities and Project Reports | Project Performance Measurement | Strategic Alignment Enabled by |
|---|---|---|---|---|---|
| Scoping stage-gate (1 month) | Marketing (sales growth) NPD (within scope) | Involved NPD and marketing members | NPD and Marketing focused on finding new technologies and market opportunities (Scoping Brief Reports) which were evaluated by the marketing manager | The marketing manager evaluated projects for their potential for sales growth and fit with nutritional scope requirements | Focusing on sales growth opportunities which fit specific product scope requirements |
| Concept stage-gate (1–3 months) | Marketing (sales growth) NPD (within scope) | Involved NPD and marketing members | NPD and Marketing developed and tested product concepts and carried out external consumer research (Concept Brief Reports) which were evaluated by the marketing manager | The marketing manager evaluated projects for their potential for sales growth and fit with consumer-focused product scope attributes | Focusing on sales growth opportunities which fit consumer-focused product scope attributes |
| Feasibility stage-gate (1–6 months) | Marketing (4Ps) NPD (profit growth) | Involved micro project team members who came from NPD, marketing, the factory and also included management accountant | Micro project teams carried out product feasibility activities which included draft financials (Development Brief Reports) which were evaluated by the senior management team | The senior management team evaluated projects based mainly on a financial measure (GP margin) | Focusing on profit growth measured by GP margin |

## Table 3. (Continued)

Four Management Controls Used by Organization Members at FoodCo

| Stage-Gate Product Development Process (Project Process Time) | Functional Responsibilities and Corporate Strategies | Organization Member Involvement | Organization Activities and Project Reports | Project Performance Measurement | Strategic Alignment Enabled by |
|---|---|---|---|---|---|
| Development stage-gate (3–12 months) | Marketing (4Ps) NPD (profit growth) NPD (within scope) NPD (on time) | Involved cross-functional project teams members who came from NPD, marketing, the factory, procurement, technical, sales, supply chain, external suppliers and also included the management accountant | Cross-functional project teams carried out development activities which included financial and non-financial information (Business Case Reports) which were evaluated by the senior management team | The senior management team evaluated projects based on financial measures (GP margin and payback period) and non-financial measures (timeliness to market, project scope, and sensory results). | Focusing on profit growth measured by GP margin and payback period with specified timeliness to market, project scope, and sensory results |

process (see the "Organization Activities and Project Reports" column in Table 3).

At the scoping and concept stage-gates, the activities organization members carried out and the reports they produced focused on finding new technologies and market opportunities. This involved marketing and NPD activities which focused on scoping ideas and opportunities which resulted in product concepts that had a chance to grow sales (a marketing strategy) while being delivered within scope (an NPD strategy). Once the marketing manager felt that a project was capable of delivering sales growth and was within scope, the project then went on to the feasibility and development stage-gates. Since FoodCo considered only radical step-change projects at the scoping stage, this may have encouraged organization members to experiment more with new ideas which could counteract the negative influence that Nagji and Tuff (2012) argue could be a limitation of using a stage-gate process.

At the feasibility and development stage-gates, organization members from multiple functions came together to form project teams. The activities that these project teams carried out first focused on building prototypes and drafting financial information at the feasibility stage then examining production issues, market reactions, and making detailed financial reports at the development stage. Project reports were then sent to the senior management team who evaluated projects based on a number of key performance measures.

### Project Performance Measurement

Project performance measurement was another management control practice used by organization members during the stage-gate process. These performance measures helped both senior managers and project teams maintain strategic alignment of product development projects with corporate strategy throughout their development (see the "Project Performance Measurement" column in Table 3).

As proposed by Simons (2000), the performance measures in FoodCo were used to inform project teams about corporate strategies. Because of this, the details of strategy did not need to be communicated to organization members as strategically aligned performance measures enabled their activities to stay aligned with corporate strategies.

The project performance measures also provided senior managers with feedback on the performance of product development projects, which they used to assist them in their project evaluations at the decision gates. The financial measures used to evaluate product development projects were GP margin at the feasibility gate and GP margin and payback period at the development gate; while the non-financial performance measures used were timeliness to market, delivering within project scope, and the sensory results. This contributes to the call by Davila and Wouters (2007) for additional research on performance measures in product development which fulfills organization members' needs and adds to our knowledge about the role of accounting during the stage-gate process (Wouters & Morales, 2014).

### Strategic Alignment Enabled by

In summary, the four management control practices at FoodCo enabled strategic alignment and managed potential tensions by influencing the focus of organization members on different corporate strategies at different stage-gates of the product development process (see the "Strategic Alignment Enabled By" column in Table 3).

While sales growth was a marketing strategy, organization members only focused on it during the scoping and concept stages. During the feasibility and development stages, marketing focused on the sensory data and the 4Ps to support the profit growth strategy. NPD, on the other hand, focused on delivering products within scope during the scoping and concept stages to support the sales growth strategy but changed their focus to the profit growth strategy during the feasibility and development stages. By doing this, organization members were able to concentrate on corporate strategies which would otherwise have been in conflict with each other (Dodd & Favaro, 2006).

For this reason, limiting the potential for tension at FoodCo did not stop with assigning different corporate strategies to the NPD and marketing functions. These functions would have found it difficult to work together during the stage-gate process if they were simultaneously trying to achieve different strategies. Thus, in addition to assigning functional responsibility to different corporate strategies, the involvement of organization members, the activities they carried out and the project reports they produced, as well as the performance measures used to evaluate projects were management control practices that helped organization members focus on different strategies during each stage-gate which enabled the strategic alignment of product development projects with multiple corporate strategies during the stage-gate product development process.

## Conclusions and Future Research

In conclusion, we show how management control practices at FoodCo were used to enable strategic alignment between product development projects and multiple strategies, some of which had potential conflicts. In particular, this paper contributes to the literature by extending our understanding about how strategic alignment can be achieved during product development when there is tension between corporate strategies.

As this study presents insights at an operational level it is relevant to practitioners, especially management accountants involved in the stage-gate product development process, NPD managers, members of product development project teams, and senior managers involved in evaluating product development projects. This case study could also help management accountants and managers gain new understandings about the use of management control practices and how they can enable the alignment of product development projects with corporate strategies.

In particular, our findings show that organization members from across multiple functions carried out product development activities during the stage-gate process. At FoodCo, the corporate strategy was divided between the NPD and marketing functions which enabled these organization members to focus on different strategies at different process stage-gates. This helped them to avoid tensions between strategies and build alignment between product development projects and corporate strategies.

As with all research, this study has limitations. One of our main limitations was access to data. Since FoodCo was a private company, we were only able to get one company document and interviews with five organization members. We were able to supplement this internal company data with an external document from Euromonitor International which had information about FoodCo's strategy and its market performance. We believe, though, that the management control practices of the five organization members we interviewed at FoodCo provide new insights as to how organization members deal with multiple strategies. Moreover, it gave us a unique context in which to examine how management control practices enable the alignment of product development projects with corporate strategies during the stage-gate process.

Future studies could investigate how senior managers view this issue and how they allocate resources to product development projects during the stage-gate process. This would extend our understanding of the ways in which project budgets as well as other operational management control practices are carried out and would lead to additional insights into how management control practices enable strategic alignment in this context. Another area of future research could be to examine strategic alignment when an organization changes its strategies or goes through a restructuring. There might also be opportunities to use an ethnomethodology informed research approach to look at strategic alignment in other contexts such as the sustainability practices of organization members.

## NOTES

1. Product development has been defined as "ideas and policies leading to the development and launch of new products and services" (Kahn, Barczak, Nicholas, Ledwith, & Perks, 2012, p. 182).

2. Corporate strategy has been defined as "how a company creates value by differentiating its products or services from its competitors" (Simons, 1992, p. 44).

3. A recent example of this is General Motors who according to Nagesh and Stoll (2015, p. B1) are focused "on improving profit margins, not chasing market share."

4. Stage-Gate® is the registered trademark of Stage-Gate Inc. We use the term "stage-gate" in a generic way to signify the different stages and gates of our case companies' product development process.

5. For a comprehensive review of the differences between ethnomethodology and ethnography see Pollner and Emerson (2001).

6. Goal congruence has been defined as effectively aligning employees' self-interest with the organization's interests, so that employees work towards organization goals (Flamholtz, 1983).

## ACKNOWLEDGMENTS

The authors would like to thank the employees of FoodCo who participated in this research project. The authors acknowledge the valuable comments from Mary Malina (Editor) and the feedback and suggestions from the two anonymous reviewers.

## REFERENCES

Acur, N., Kandemir, D., & Boer, H. (2012). Strategic alignment and new product development: Drivers and performance effects. *Journal of Product Innovation Management*, 29(2), 304–318.

Adler, P., & Borys, B. (1996). Two types of bureaucracy: Enabling and coercive. *Administrative Science Quarterly*, 41(1), 61–89.

Akroyd, C., & Maguire, W. (2011). The roles of management control in a product development setting. *Qualitative Research in Accounting & Management, 8*(3), 212–237.

Akroyd, C., Narayan, S. S., & Sridharan, V. G. (2009). The use of control systems in new product development innovation: Advancing the 'help or hinder' debate. *IUP Journal of Knowledge Management, 7*(5–6), 70–91.

Anteby, M., Lifshitz, H., & Tushman, M. (2014). *Using qualitative research for "how" questions.* Retrieved from http://strategicmanagement.net/pdfs/qualitative-research-in-strategic-management.pdf

Balzli, C. E., & Morard, B. (2012). The impact of an integrated financial system implementation on accounting profiles in a public administration: An ethnographic approach. *Journal of Accounting & Organizational Change, 8*(3), 364–385.

Bonner, J. M., Ruekert, R. W., & Walker, O. C. (2002). Upper management control of new product development projects and project performance. *The Journal of Product Innovation Management, 19*(3), 233–245.

Brown, S. L., & Eisenhardt, K. M. (1995). Product development: Past research, present findings, and future directions. *The Academy of Management Review, 20*(2), 343–378.

Chenhall, R. H., & Morris, D. (1986). The impact of structure, environment, and interdependence on the perceived usefulness of management accounting systems. *The Accounting Review, 61*(1), 16–35.

Cooper, R. (1993). *Winning at new products: Accelerating the process from idea to launch.* Reading, MA: Addison Wesley Publishing.

Cooper, R., & Edgett, S. (2001). *Portfolio management for new product: Picking the winners.* Working Paper No. 11. Ontario, Canada: Product Development Institute.

Cooper, R., Edgett, S., & Kleinschmidt, E. (1998). *Portfolio management for new products.* Reading, MA: Addison Wesley Publishing.

Danila, N. (1989). Strategic evaluation and selection of R&D projects. *R&D Management, 19*(1), 47–62.

Davila, A. (2000). An empirical study on the drivers of management control systems' design in new product development. *Accounting, Organizations and Society, 25*(4–5), 383–409.

Davila, A., Foster, G., & Oyon, D. (2009). Accounting and control, entrepreneurship and innovation: Venturing into new research opportunities. *European Accounting Review, 18*(2), 281–311.

Davila, A., & Wouters, M. (2007). Management accounting in the manufacturing sector: Managing costs at the design and production stages. In C. S. Chapman, A. G. Hopwood, & M. D. Shields (Eds.), *Handbook of Management Accounting Research* (Vol. 2, pp. 831–858). Oxford: Elsevier.

De Maio, A., Verganti, R., & Corso, M. (1994). A multi-project management framework for new product development. *European Journal of Operational Research, 78*(2), 178–191.

Dent, J. F. (1990). Strategy, organization and control: Some possibilities for accounting research. *Accounting, Organizations and Society, 15*(1–2), 3–25.

Denzin, N. K. (1978). *The research act: A theoretical introduction to sociological methods.* New York, NY: McGraw-Hill.

Dodd, D., & Favaro, K. (2006). Managing the right tension. *Harvard Business Review, 84*(12), 62–74.

Edgett, S. J. (2013). Portfolio management for product innovation. In K. B. Kahn (Ed.), *The PDMA handbook of new product development* (3rd ed., pp. 154–166). Hoboken, NJ: Wiley.

Ernst, H., Hoyer, W. D., & Rübsaamen, C. (2010). Sales, marketing, and research-and-development cooperation across new product development stages: Implications for success. *Journal of Marketing, 74*(5), 80–92.

Flamholtz, E. (1983). Accounting, budgeting and control systems in their organizational context: Theoretical and empirical perspectives. *Accounting, Organizations and Society*, *8*(2–3), 153–169.

Garfinkel, H. (1967). *Studies in ethnomethodology*. Upper Saddle River, NJ: Prentice Hall.

Garfinkel, H. (2002). *Ethnomethodology's program: Working out Durkheim's aphorism*. Lanham, MD: Rowman & Littlefield Publishers.

Garfinkel, H. (2006). *Seeing sociologically: The routine grounds of social action*. London: Paradigm Publishers.

Griffin, A. (1997). *Drivers of new product success: The 1997 PDMA report*. Chicago, IL: Product Development and Management Association.

Griffin, A., & Page, A. L. (1996). PDMA success measurement project: Recommended measures for product development success and failure. *Journal of Product Innovation Management*, *13*(6), 478–496.

Hall, D., & Naudia, A. (1990). An interactive approach for selecting IR&D projects. *IEEE Transactions on Engineering Management*, *37*(2), 126–133.

Hertenstein, J. H., & Platt, M. B. (1997). Developing a strategic design culture. *Design Management Journal*, *8*(2), 10–19.

Hertenstein, J. H., & Platt, M. B. (1998). Why product development teams need management accountants. *Strategic Finance*, *79*(10), 50–55.

Hertenstein, J. H., & Platt, M. B. (2000). Performance measures and management control in new product development. *Accounting Horizons*, *14*(3), 303–323.

Hunger, J., & Wheelen, T. (2010). *Essentials of strategic management* (5th ed.). Upper Saddle River, NJ: Prentice Hall.

Jönsson, S., & Macintosh, N. B. (1997). Cats, rats, and ears: Making the case for ethnographic accounting research. *Accounting, Organizations and Society*, *22*(3–4), 367–386.

Jørgensen, B., & Messner, M. (2009). Management control in new product development: The dynamics of managing flexibility and efficiency. *Journal of Management Accounting Research*, *21*, 99–124.

Jørgensen, B., & Messner, M. (2010). Accounting and strategising: A case study from new product development. *Accounting, Organizations and Society*, *35*(2), 184–204.

Kahn, K. B., Barczak, G., Nicholas, J., Ledwith, A., & Perks, H. (2012). An examination of new product development best practice. *Journal of Product Innovation Management*, *29*(2), 180–192.

Kaplan, R. S., & Norton, D. P. (1992). The balanced scorecard: Measures that drive performance. *Harvard Business Review*, *70*(1), 71–79.

Khurana, A., & Rosenthal, S. R. (1998). Towards holistic 'front ends' in new product development. *Journal of Product Innovation Management*, *15*(1), 57–74.

Kren, L. (1992). Budgetary participation and managerial performance: The impact of information and environmental volatility. *The Accounting Review*, *67*(3), 511–526.

Langfield-Smith, K. (1997). Management control systems and strategy: A critical review. *Accounting, Organizations and Society*, *22*(2), 207–252.

Laurier, E. (2003). Guest editorial — Technology and mobility. *Environment and Planning*, *35*(9), 1521–1527.

Modell, S. (2009). In defence of triangulation: A critical realist approach to mixed methods research in management accounting. *Management Accounting Research*, *20*(3), 208–221.

Nagesh, G., & Stoll, J. D. (2015). GM CEO: Focus on margins is paying off. *Wall Street Journal*, September 25, pp. B1-B2.

Nagji, B., & Tuff, G. (2012). Managing your innovation portfolio. *Harvard Business Review*, *90*(5), 66–74.

Nanni, A. J., Dixon, J. R., & Vollmann, T. E. (1992). Integrated performance measurement: Management accounting to support the new manufacturing realities. *Journal of Management Accounting Research*, *4*, 1–19.

O'Grady, W., & Akroyd, C. (2016). The MCS package in a non-budgeting organisation: A case study of Mainfreight. *Qualitative Research in Accounting & Management*, *13*(1), forthcoming.

Parker, L. D. (2012). Qualitative management accounting research: Assessing deliverables and relevance. *Critical Perspectives on Accounting*, *23*(1), 54–70.

Pollner, M., & Emerson, R. M. (2001). Ethnomethodology and ethnography. In P. Atkinson, A. Coffey, S. Delamont, J. Lofland, & L. Lofland (Eds.), *Handbook of ethnography* (pp. 118–135). London: Sage.

Poskela, J., & Martinsuo, M. (2009). Management control and strategic renewal in the front end of innovation. *Journal of Product Innovation Management*, *26*(6), 671–684.

Product Development Institute Inc. (2012). *Stage-Gate® – Your roadmap for new product development*. Retrieved from http://www.prod-dev.com/stage-gate.php. Accessed on July 3, 2015.

Rawls, A. W. (2002). Introduction. In W. A. Rawls (Ed.), *Ethnomethodology's program: Working out Durkheim's aphorism*. Lanham, MD: Rowman & Littlefield Publishers.

Schoohoven, C. B., Eisenhardt, K. M., & Lyman, K. (1990). Speeding products to market: Waiting time to first product introduction in new firms. *Administrative Science Quarterly*, *35*(1), 177–207.

Sharrock, W. W., & Anderson, B. (2012). *The ethnomethodologists*. New York, NY: Routledge.

Simon, G., Hatch, T., & Youell, N. (2008). *The challenge of strategic alignment: The role of scorecards & dashboards in strategy execution*. Borehamwood: FSN Publishing Limited.

Simons, R. (1987). Accounting control systems and business strategy: An empirical analysis. *Accounting, Organizations and Society*, *12*(4), 357–374.

Simons, R. (1992). The strategy of control. *CA Magazine*, *125*(3), 44–50.

Simons, R. (1995). *Levers of control: How managers use innovative control systems to drive strategic renewal*. Boston, MA: Harvard Business School Press.

Simons, R. (2000). Basics for successful strategy. In A. Todd (Ed.), *Performance measurement & control systems for implementing strategy*. Upper Saddle River, NJ: Prentice Hall.

Sjoblom, L. (1998). Financial information and quality management – Is there a role for accountants? *Accounting Horizons*, *12*(4), 363–373.

Slater, S. F., Olson, E. M., & Finnegan, C. (2011). Business strategy, marketing organization culture, and performance. *Marketing Letters*, *22*(3), 227–242.

Song, L. Z., Song, M., & Di Benedetto, C. A. (2009). A staged service innovation model. *Decision Sciences*, *40*(3), 571–599.

Souder, W. E., & Mandakovic, T. (1986). R&D project selection models. *Research Management*, *29*(4), 36–42.

Taggart, J. H., & Blaxter, T. J. (1992). Strategy in pharmaceutical R&D: A portfolio risk matrix. *R&D Management*, *22*(3), 241–254.

The Economist. (2012). The mighty middle: Medium-sized firms are the unsung heroes of America's economy. *The Economist*, October 20.

Tucker, B., Thorne, H., & Gurd, B. (2009). Management control systems and strategy: What's been happening? *Journal of Accounting Literature*, *28*, 123–163.

Wheelwright, S. C., & Clark, K. B. (1992). Creating project plans to focus product develop-
    ment. *Harvard Business Review, 70*(2), 70–82.
Winger, R., & Wall, G. (2006). *Food product innovation: A background paper*. Rome: Food and
    Agriculture Organization of the United Nations.
Wouters, M., & Morales, S. (2014). The contemporary art of cost management methods
    during product development. *Advances in Management Accounting, 24*, 259–346.

# METHODS FOR COST MANAGEMENT DURING PRODUCT DEVELOPMENT: A REVIEW AND COMPARISON OF DIFFERENT LITERATURES

Marc Wouters, Susana Morales, Sven Grollmuss and Michael Scheer

## ABSTRACT

Purpose — *The paper provides an overview of research published in the innovation and operations management (IOM) literature on 15 methods for cost management in new product development, and it provides a comparison to an earlier review of the management accounting (MA) literature (Wouters & Morales, 2014).*

Methodology/approach — *This structured literature search covers papers published in 23 journals in IOM in the period 1990–2014.*

Findings — *The search yielded a sample of 208 unique papers with 275 results (one paper could refer to multiple cost management methods). The top 3 methods are modular design, component commonality, and*

Advances in Management Accounting, Volume 26, 139–274
ISSN: 1474-7871/doi:10.1108/S1474-787120150000026005

*product platforms, with 115 results (42%) together. In the MA litera-*
*ture, these three methods accounted for 29%, but target costing was the*
*most researched cost management method by far (26%). Simulation is*
*the most frequently used research method in the IOM literature, whereas*
*this was averagely used in the MA literature; qualitative studies were the*
*most frequently used research method in the MA literature, whereas this*
*was averagely used in the IOM literature. We found a lot of papers pre-*
*senting practical approaches or decision models as a further development*
*of a particular cost management method, which is a clear difference from*
*the MA literature.*

Research limitations/implications – *This review focused on the same*
*cost management methods, and future research could also consider other*
*cost management methods which are likely to be more important in the*
*IOM literature compared to the MA literature. Future research could*
*also investigate innovative cost management practices in more detail*
*through longitudinal case studies.*

Originality/value – *This review of research on methods for cost manage-*
*ment published outside the MA literature provides an overview for MA*
*researchers. It highlights key differences between both literatures in their*
*research of the same cost management methods.*

**Keywords:** Innovation and operations management (IOM);
new product development (NPD); target costing; modular design;
product platforms; component commonality

# INTRODUCTION

Since many costs of a product are determined during new product development (NPD), this phase of the product life-cycle is an obvious lever for
managing costs. During NPD, key product design decisions are made for
the technical realization of a new product or service, for example, decisions
on the functionality and performance of the product, the basic architecture
of the product, selection of technologies, technical standards, components,
and materials. There are many degrees of freedom for making such decisions during NPD, whereas they are difficult to change later in the product
life-cycle, and the possibilities for managing costs become narrower. For
example, realizing cost reduction through material substitution during the
manufacturing stage of the product will be difficult if that means other

design elements will have to be changed as well, with implications for production processes, suppliers, specifications, etc.

This paper reviews literature reporting research on cost management methods during NPD. These are methods for managing the costs of new products and services through influencing the decisions that are made during their development stage. In other words, these cost management methods are the formalized procedures and systems for planning of and reporting on organizational activities for NPD.

Target costing is the typical topic in the management accounting (MA) literature when it comes to cost managing during NPD (Ansari, Bell, & Okano, 2006; Caglio & Ditillo, 2008; Cooper & Slagmulder, 1999, 2004). Wouters and Morales (2014) reviewed the MA literature on methods for cost management during NPD and found that target costing has received by far the most attention in the publications in their sample. However, there is much more, in the sense of *other methods* for cost management during NPD, as well as *other literatures* besides accounting that address cost management during NPD. In particular, a considerable literature in innovation management, technology management, marketing, and operations management addresses this topic. For brevity, we will call this the innovation and operations management (IOM) literature. This literature largely talks about the same topics, such as target costing, modularity, and component commonality (Labro, 2004). Table 1 provides definitions of such methods for cost management during NPD.

The objective of the current literature review is to find out more about what has been published in the IOM literature concerning the same cost management methods as reviewed by Wouters and Morales (2014) and to compare the findings to that earlier review. The main research questions are: What has been published in the IOM literature on methods for cost management during NPD? What are the differences and similarities between the MA and the IOM literature on cost management during NPD? How could these different literatures complement each other? We investigated the distribution of research across 15 cost management methods (see Table 1), 23 journals (listed in Table 2), and 10 research methods. We adopted a similar research method as that of Wouters and Morales (2014), in terms of search process and content analysis, so it would be possible to compare the results.

Similar to Wouters and Morales (2014), the focus of the present review is to organize the literature around specific *methods* for cost management during product development. Other reviews of literature on MA in NPD (such as Anderson & Dekker, 2009; Davila, Foster, & Oyon, 2009) did not

*Table 1.*   Short Descriptions of Various Methods for Managing Costs during NPD, Based on Wouters and Morales (2014) and Slightly Modified.

| | |
|---|---|
| Target costing[a] | Before the NPD project, the allowable manufacturing costs of a product and of its components are determined, starting with the sales price of the product for end users and subtracting target profit margins and nonmanufacturing costs at various stages in the supply chain. During several stages of the NPD project, the manufacturing costs are estimated to assess if these do not exceed their allowable cost targets, which would require redesign. |
| Value engineering | Product cost structures are analyzed to identify changes of the product design which enable it to be manufactured at its target cost. |
| Quality function deployment (QFD) | The priorities of customer requirements are translated into the importance of the technical attributes or functions of the product, which, in turn, guides the allocation of the total allowable cost to the different parts of the product. QFD uses matrices to show the relationships between requirements, functions, and parts. |
| Functional cost analysis (FCA) | Cost structures of products or services are evaluated to find ways for improving either the product design or the production process in order to reduce the cost of providing the required functionality and performance. |
| Kaizen costing | Efforts are made to ensure a continuous cost reduction process during the manufacturing phase of a product at a prespecified amount or rate. |
| Life-cycle costing (LCC) | Cost estimations and measurements are extended from manufacturing costs to also include nonmanufacturing costs, which may be incurred at different stages of the life-cycle of a product (e.g., waste and disposal). |
| Total cost of ownership (TCO) | Cost accounting is used to support purchasing decisions makers to combine price and value for their sourcing decisions. This involves monetary quantification of all costs incurred by the customer as a result of acquiring and using supplier offerings. |
| Stage-gate reviews | After completion of each NPD stage, the design is reviewed on a wide variety of aspects, for which targets have been formulated at the start of the NPD project (such as unit manufacturing cost, other unit costs, cost and lead time of the NPD project, functionality, and performance of the product). The outcomes of these reviews may lead to revisions of the product design or adjustments of the targets. |
| Funnels | A selection process for product development, in which the number of alternatives that a firm is considering gradually decreases as the development process moves toward completion. |
| Design for manufacturing/ assembly (DFM/DFA) | NPD teams are provided with guidelines and constraints which help them to improve their product designs such that these can be manufactured at a low cost. |

***Table 1.***   (*Continued*)

| | |
|---|---|
| Design for X (DFX) | NPD teams are provided with guidelines and constraints which help them to improve their product designs such that costs can be kept low on a wide range of aspects, for example, logistics, disposal, environment, and service. |
| Component commonality | Restricted sets of allowed materials, parts, components, packaging, etc. are defined, which act as constraints during NPD, in order to share these materials, parts, components, packaging, etc. across a wide range of final products. |
| Modular design | Products are designed in such a way, that a wide variety of final products can be produced using a limited number of modules that are adjusted and/or combined with different parts and other modules. |
| Product platform | A product platform concerns the basic architecture of a product by describing the physical implementation of a functional design, and this becomes the basis for a series of derivative products. |
| Technology roadmap | A technology roadmap describes candidate technologies and the levels of specification and required performance in a particular industry that are planned to be reached at different points in the future. |

[a]Target costing was split into two methods in Wouters and Morales (2014), related to setting cost targets and early cost estimation. The current paper considers both aspects under target costing.

center on cost management methods, but were structured around *theoretical themes*, such as interactive control, knowledge management, creativity, uncertainty, strategy, trust, dependency, or organizational boundaries. That is understandable, because studies often look at theoretical explanations for the use of particular MA methods. For example, Wouters, Anderson, and Wynstra (2005) found purchasing orientation and value analysis experience as explanations for the adoption of total cost of ownership (TCO); Dunk (2004) identified competitive advantage and quality of information as explanations for the adoption of life-cycle costing. Moreover, many studies do not focus on a particular MA methods as such, but investigate antecedents and consequences of certain types or attributes of MA methods. Strategic MA (Cadez & Guilding, 2008), advanced MA practices (Baines & Langfield-Smith, 2003), interactive control systems (Bisbe & Malagueño, 2009), and interorganizational cost management (Fayard, Lee, Leitch, & Kettinger, 2012); are examples of such more generally defined types of MA systems, although not in the context of NPD. Cost information precision for designers (Booker, Drake, & Heitger, 2007) and cost goal specificity in

***Table 2.***   List of Journals Included in the Present Literature Review
and Their Research Focus.

| | |
|---|---|
| 1. *Academy of Management Journal* | *AMJ* |
| 2. *Academy of Management Review* | *AMR* |
| 3. *California Management Review* | *CMR* |
| 4. *IEEE Transactions on Engineering Management* | *IEEE-EM* |
| 5. *IIE Transactions* | *IIE* |
| 6. *Industrial Marketing Management* | *IMM* |
| 7. *Interfaces* | *Interf* |
| 8. *International Journal of Operations & Production Management* | *IJOPM* |
| 9. *International Journal of Production Economics* | *IJPE* |
| 10. *International Journal of Production Research* | *IJPR* |
| 11. *International Journal of Technology Management* | *IJTM* |
| 12. *Journal of Engineering and Technology Management* | *JETM* |
| 13. *Journal of Marketing* | *JM* |
| 14. *Journal of Marketing Research* | *JMR* |
| 15. *Journal of Operations Management* | *JOM* |
| 16. *Journal of Product Innovation Management* | *JPIM* |
| 17. *Manufacturing and Service Operations Management* | *MSOM* |
| 18. *MIT Sloan Management Review* | *MIT SMR* |
| 19. *R&D Management* | *RADMA* |
| 20. *Research Policy* | *ResPol* |
| 21. *Research-Technology Management* | *RTM* |
| 22. *Strategic Management Journal* | *SMJ* |
| 23. *Technovation* | *Techn* |

target costing (Gopalakrishnan, Libby, Samuels, & Swenson, 2015) are examples of theoretical attributes of accounting information in NPD. Other studies investigated the wider context of MA in NPD through case studies, such as Jørgensen and Messner (2009) and Taipaleenmäki (2014).

However, the focus on cost management *methods* provides a suitable basis for reviewing the literature, because our objective is to review descriptions and explanations of cost management practices in various literatures. A focus on methods provided an intuitive starting point for reviewing what is known about what firms do for managing costs during NPD, how they do it, and why. This focus also helped to get an understanding of the diversity of cost management methods that are relevant for NPD outside the MA literature. It enabled identifying and incorporating studies that had everything to do with cost management in NPD, but that included perhaps different theoretical constructs than usual in MA research.

The search identified a sample of 208 unique papers. Many contained information about more than one method, yielding 275 research results related to specific cost management methods. Some of the key findings are:

- The distribution of the number of results is very unequal across journals, with the top 4 journals accounting for 172 results (63% of 275 results). The coefficient of variation (CV) of the number of results per journal is 1.29 for the IOM sample, comparable to 1.32 for the MA sample in Wouters and Morales (2014).
- The distribution of the number of results is less unequal across cost management methods. The top 3 methods are modular design, component commonality, and product platforms, with 115 results (42%) together. Results for the MA literature were more uneven, with the top 2 methods (target costing and modular design) accounting for 39% of the results. The CV of the number of results per cost management method is 0.73 for the IOM literature and it was 0.95 for the MA literature.
- Although simulation is the most frequently used research method in the IOM literature, it was averagely used in the MA literature; although qualitative study was the most frequently used research method in the MA literature, it is averagely used in the IOM literature.
- The journals *Decision Sciences* and *Management Science* were included in the review of the MA literature. However, they also meet the inclusion criteria for the IOM literature, so we also compared the IOM literature *with DS* and *MS* to the MA literature *without* these two journals. This shows that the profile of the papers in these two journals is much more alike the IOM literature than the MA literature. As a result, shifting these journals makes the differences between both literatures even more pronounced.
- Results include many papers presenting practical approaches or decision models for the development of a particular cost management method. Some provide empirical support by implementing the proposed approach or decision model in a case study, without making it a real field experiment. Many studies rely on numerical simulation, analysis of mathematical models, or only conceptual argumentation as support for these approaches or decision models.
- In addition to the results mentioned earlier, we found many papers that focused on at least one of the 15 methods but lacked emphasis on cost management and/or did not consider the context of NPD. We clustered these papers in 12 categories and did not review them in detail. Finding

these categories suggest the IOM literature has looked at a wide range of issues around cost management methods during NPD.

The remainder of this paper is structured as follows. The next section describes the various cost management methods in NPD and how these are related. Definitions of these methods are provided in Table 1, and we also refer to Wouters and Morales (2014) for more extensive consideration of these various methods. The "Research Method" section explains how papers have been identified, selected, and analyzed. After that follows a section with the overall results from the IOM literature and comparison to the MA literature. In the section after that, we zoom-in on more specific results for each cost management method. Conclusions are the final section.

## COST MANAGEMENT METHODS IN NEW PRODUCT DEVELOPMENT (NPD)

In MA there is much attention for *target costing*. It is actually much more elaborate than the often-quoted rule "maximum allowable cost price = attainable selling price − required profit margin" (Dekker & Smidt, 2003, p. 295). The starting point is to consider what kind of product will be offered, at what sales price, and how this compares to the kinds of competitors' products that are expected to be available, and the assumed sales prices of those. So the targets do not only relate to sales prices and cost targets derived from those but also to the whole spectrum of functionality and performance of the product. Clearly, there are trade-offs to be made among these various kinds of targets. Furthermore, the starting point for target costing requires looking ahead, at least beyond the development time of the new product. Car companies, for example, need to consider these targets for several years into the future. As a result, target costing is surrounded with considerable uncertainty. Moreover, if product development requires significant resources and lead time, there will also be targets for the cost and lead time of that NPD project. Car companies, for example, may spend more than a billion Euros during several years on the development of a new model. The budget for this NPD project will be broken down into several stages and cost categories.

Next, starting with the sales price, the various costs, taxes, import duties, profit margins, etc. at several stages in the supply chain (e.g., retailer, distributor, and importer) will have to be deducted to arrive at the sales price which the manufacturing company will receive for the product. With multiple models of the product, multiple sales channels, price erosion, and learning curves, these kinds of analyses involve approximations, such as weighted-average sales prices and costs and, moreover, will be dynamic (i.e., defined for several points in time). Deducing the target profit margin gives the *allowable total unit cost* for the manufacturer, from which the costs for marketing, sales, distribution, warranty, service, and other non-manufacturing costs need to be deducted to get to the *allowable manufacturing unit cost*. This allocable cost can be broken down to obtain target costs for the major components of the product. *Quality function deployment* can be used as part of this, because it is a method to better understand customer requirements and to support the disaggregation of the overall cost target.

Target costing can also be extended toward suppliers. The target cost of a component provides the maximum purchase price for the manufacturer. If the manufacturer and supplier also talk about the supplier's detailed cost breakdown for manufacturing the component, this is called open-book accounting.

So far, we described only the planning part of target costing at the start of the NPD project. During the NPD project, the growing design of the new product is reviewed after completion of each development phase. This is shown in Fig. 1. A design review is a milestone within a product development process whereby a design is evaluated against its requirements in order to verify the outcomes of previous activities and identify issues before committing to — and possibly re-prioritize — further work. The manufacturing cost of the product and the components will be estimated, based on what is known about the semi-finished design. However, "does the estimated product cost meet the target cost?" is not the only question during

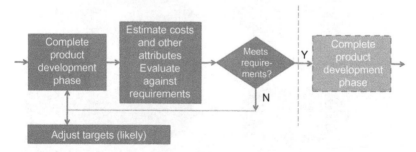

*Fig. 1.* Target Costing as Part of a Stage-Gate System with Design Reviews.

these reviews. Similarly, the proposed design will be examined in terms of the other targets for functionality and performance. For example, a car design must also meet targets for speed, engine power and torque, emissions, interior noise, weight, safety, aerodynamics, and include the specified features. Moreover, the cost and progress of the NPD project as such will be reviewed. Therefore, target costing should be seen in the wider context of *stage-gate reviews* (Hertenstein & Platt, 2000) or *funnels*.

If the product and project fall significantly short on such targets – the allowable cost being only one, but often important criterion of these – redesign is needed. Finding such improvements for the design of the product is also the objective of *value engineering* and *functional cost analysis*, so these can be used within the context of target costing.

Moreover, adjustment of targets may be called for. This is more subtle than the simple question whether the target cost can be exceeded – a violation of the "cardinal rule" (Cooper & Slagmulder, 1999). Many more trade-offs are involved, as also shown in Fig. 2.

- Targets for functionality and performance could be abated in order to save costs and meet the target for the product cost (a). Yet, this may likely impact the sales price and volume (b), which also needs to be considered for the impact of such adjustments on the total profitability of the new product.

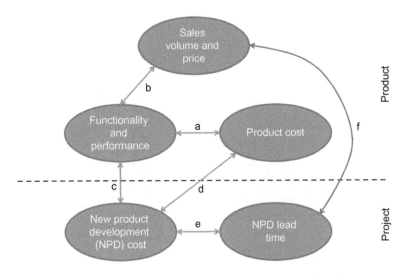

*Fig. 2.*    Trade-Offs among Different Targets during New Product Development.

- The product development efforts and costs could be increased in order to find ingenious solutions for achieving the targets for functionality and performance (c) or for achieving the cost targets (d). However, the effect of the additional NPD cost on the total profitability of the new product should be considered.
- If putting more emphasis on NPD activities would increase the NPD lead time (e), the new product might be on the market at a later point in time (f). This may also impact the sales price and volume, which again has to be part of the overall tradeoff when making these kinds of adjustments during design reviews. *Kaizen Costing* is a focus on cost management after the NPD activities when the product is on the market.

Target costing and the other methods mentioned earlier mainly focus on the manufacturing costs and the NPD cost of one type of product. However, when a company is producing and selling a large number of different products and serving a large number of different customers, some costs can hardly be addressed within the scope of the NPD project for only one product type (Davila & Wouters, 2007). Structural cost management is required, considering organizational design, product design, and process design, to create a supply chain cost structure that is with firm strategy (Anderson & Dekker, 2009). For example, the costs of logistics are often assumed to be driven by the number of different stock-keeping units (SKUs). Managing these costs means reducing the number of SKUs across the firm's portfolio of products, and that requires coordination of design decisions among multiple NPD projects. Similarly, the total R&D costs of the firm may be driven by the number of different parts, modules, designs, patterns, or versions. Managing R&D costs involves coordination of product design decisions. Or, purchasing transaction costs may be driven by the number of different suppliers the firm is doing business with, purchase prices may be affected by the number of units purchased per part, and manufacturing costs may be affected by the number of units purchased per part and the opportunities for realizing opportunities of scale. More refined costing methods, such as *total cost of ownership* and *life-cycle costing* provide insight into the role of these kinds of cost drivers that have to do with variety and complexity.

"Attacking" these kinds of costs drivers and the associated complexity-based costs requires additional cost management methods besides target costing. That is the focus of methods such as *component commonality, modular design, product platforms*, and *technology roadmaps*. For example, component commonality may reduce NPD costs, because fewer components need to be designed. However, designing components that must be suitable for several different products may be more complex and increase the development cost per component. Using common components may lead to higher variable costs per unit if the component is overspecified for lower-end products, or it may lead to negative reactions from customers if the component is underspecified for higher-end products. Commonality may reduce manufacturing costs due to economies of scale in production and in purchasing, and it may reduce inventory costs due to risk-pooling. Furthermore, the design guidelines which are central to *design for manufacturing* and *design for X* may be addressing coordinated choices across different products, although these guidelines may also provide ways to "simply" reduce the costs of individual products.

To conclude, the methods that will be reviewed in this paper aim to help managing costs during NPD in various ways. Clearly, many of these cost management methods are not only, or even primarily, of interest to researchers and practitioners in accounting, but also in marketing and in operations, innovation, and technology management. We will review what these literatures have to offer concerning these various cost management methods and compare that to the earlier findings of Wouters and Morales (2014) for the same methods in the MA literature.

# RESEARCH METHOD

In this section, we will describe the research method for identifying, selecting, and analyzing the papers that comprise the basis for this review of the IOM literature on cost management methods in NPD. As explained earlier, since this is intended to be a follow-up and comparison to the review by Wouters and Morales (2014), the research method is in several ways quite similar. We will be brief on the overlapping parts and more complete on the disparate parts of the method, namely the selection of journals and the introduction of subcategories for particular topics.

## Selection of Journals

In order to gain an overview of relevant journals in the IOM literature covering cost management practices during NPD, we compared six different rankings and analyses of journals in this area. These are listed in Table 3

***Table 3.*** Six Literature Rankings Used as the Basis for Compiling the Journal List for the Current Literature Review.

| Source | [a] | Selection Approach | Description |
|---|---|---|---|
| Linton and Thongpapanl (2004) | 50 | Citation analysis of journals | The top 50 journals in technology and innovation management were identified, which was based on how frequently journals were cited by a set of base journals in the field (see their Table 4, p. 127). |
| Stonebraker et al. (2012) | 30 | Journal impact factors | Collectively, 14 previous studies identified, rated and/or ranked 173 academic operations management journals. Further selection based on the availability of data on impact factors reduced the list to 30 journals (see their Table 2, p. 30). |
| Page and Schirr (2008) | 10 | Expert judgement | Ten journals in marketing, management, and R&D were identified as the leading journals publishing many papers on NPD (see their Table 2, p. 235). |
| Gorman and Kanet (2005) | 27 | Author affiliation index | A ranking of 27 operations management journals was created with the Author Affiliation Index, which is based on the percentage of a journal's U.S. academic authors that comes from a set of 60 top U.S. business research universities (see their Table 3, p. 10). |
| Durisin et al. (2010) | 11 | References in papers published in *JPIM* | The papers and books cited most in *JPIM* from 1984 to 2004 were identified (16 books and 28 papers). These papers were published in 11 different journals (see their appendix, pp. 450–451). |
| Martin et al. (2012) | 20 | Journals with the most citations to a core set of STS publications | All 9,579 non-identical references in 136 chapters in five handbooks of science and technology studies (STS) were listed. Citation analysis within these references identified a set of 155 core contributions. This analysis reflects the relative importance of these references to authors of the handbook chapters, who are experts *within* the field of STS. Next, all citations in Web of Science to these core contributions were listed, showing which 20 journals included the most citations to the STS core (see their Table 6, p. 1189). |

[a]The second column indicates the number of journals included in that particular ranking and used for journal selection in the current literature review. The total number of *different* journals included in all six rankings together is 94.

(Durisin, Calabretta, & Parmeggiani, 2010; Gorman & Kanet, 2005; Linton & Thongpapanl, 2004; Martin, Nightingale, & Yegros-Yegros, 2012; Page & Schirr, 2008; Stonebraker, Gil, Kirkwood, & Handfield, 2012). These rankings are based on citations of papers, journal impact factors, and expert judgment. Collectively, these rankings contained 94 different journals.

Starting with this longlist, we created the specific journal selection (containing 23 journals) for the current review in several steps. First, the journals already included in Wouters and Morales (2014) were excluded (i.e., *Administrative Science Quarterly, Decision Sciences, Harvard Business Review*, and *Management Science*).

Next, we prioritized those journals that were included in at least three of the rankings mentioned in Table 3, assuming these were likely the most relevant journals in IOM. This pertained to the following eight journals: *Academy of Management Review (AMR), IEEE Transactions on Engineering Management (IEEE-EM), Industrial Marketing Management (IMM), International Journal of Operations & Production Management (IJOPM), Journal of Marketing (JM), Journal of Product Innovation Management (JPIM), Research Policy (ResPol)*, and *Strategic Management Journal (SMJ)*.

We also decided that all 10 journals identified by Page and Schirr (2008) needed to be included anyhow in the current review, as we considered their selection the most focused and applicable set of journals in NPD. This criterion added the following four journals to the selection thus far: *Academy of Management Journal (AMJ), Journal of Marketing Research (JMR), R&D Management (RADMA)*, and *Research Technology Management (RTM)*.

Furthermore, based on our familiarity with the literature, we included journals from the longlist that we expected to have published research that would be relevant for the current review. This pertained to the following eleven journals: *California Management Review (CMR), International Journal of Technology Management (IJTM), Journal of Engineering and Technology Management (JETM), MIT Sloan Management Review (MIT SMR), Technovation (Techn), IIE Transactions (IIE), Interfaces (Interf), International Journal of Production Economics (IJPE), International Journal of Production Research (IJPR), Journal of Operations Management (JOM)*, and *Manufacturing and Service Operations Management (MSOM)*. The resulting selection of 23 journals is listed in Table 2.

## Search and First Selection of Literature

In a next step, we used Google Scholar to search for papers. In addition to the 38 search terms for the 15 cost management methods defined by Wouters and Morales (2014), we added 21 new spelling variations of these search terms. For example, singular and plural variants for all terms, writing words together or separately, and including both "cost" and "costing." The number of different terms and spelling variations varied across the cost management methods. For target costing, only "target costing" was used, because we did not expect broad and general terms such as "cost target" or "target cost" would help identifying additional papers reporting research on target costing. For life-cycle costing, functional cost analysis, or component commonality, various specific terms exist that we could use for identifying research related to those cost management methods.

The search covered the period 1990–2014, whereas Wouters and Morales (2014) included 1990–2013. We included papers that were available online to be published after 2014. The 1,357 search requests in Google Scholar combining search terms and journals yielded almost 5,700 results. These were not unique papers, because a paper could be included in multiple search requests.

The next step involved a quick assessment of each paper to check its relevance. This was focused on excluding papers that were obviously not relevant for the current review. Reasons to exclude papers were similar to Wouters and Morales (2014), so we will only mention a few examples here:

- The method was only mentioned briefly in the paper (sometimes even only in the list of references, an author biography, or a footnote) but the content of the paper was clearly misaligned with the scope of our research.
- The method was mentioned in the paper, but it had a different meaning or it was mentioned in an entirely different context.
- The method was not mentioned at all in the paper. For example, the paper was retrieved, because the search term occurred as a result of the ending of a sentence and the beginning of the following sentence, or due to other language-related circumstances. Or, the abbreviation of the costing method had a different meaning.
- We excluded book reviews, as the actual contribution to research is found in the book which was being reviewed. For example, Cole (2000) is a review of Kolarik (1995).

When papers were not available to us in full text, only the abstract or the available excerpt was scanned as the basis to exclude or not to exclude the respective paper. We made sure to obtain the paper if it was kept for the next step. At this stage in the literature selection process, and after the removal of duplicates, we had a preliminary list of 1,082 papers.

## Further Selection

Further selection of papers required a more in-depth assessment of each paper, to understand if it included research findings on at least one of the 15 cost management methods. These did not have to be the most important findings, and the relevant parts could be only a small part of the entire paper. We also found that some papers did report such research findings, but they considered the methods only indirectly with respect to cost management or to NPD. For example, several papers discuss metrics for quantifying the extent of component commonality. This illustrates how some papers are, indeed, focusing on one of methods, but are also not addressing the cost management aspect of the method. These papers were also retained at this stage. Major reasons for excluding papers based on the more in-depth assessment were:

- The method is part of the research, but neither cost management nor NPD are in focus. For example, the relationship between component commonality and the customer service level is assessed in Yeung, Wong, Ma, and Law (1999), but neither cost management nor NPD are covered in the research.
- The method was mentioned in the paper; however, it had a different meaning which was not linked to cost management during NPD or was in an entirely different context. For example, Karim (2006) deals with modularity in the organizational structure and specifically explores the reconfiguration of business units.
- The paper is a predecessor of another paper and included the same or less information relevant for our research. For example, we excluded Bard and Sousk (1990), whereas Bard (1992) is part of this present literature review as the more recent and more comprehensive paper.
- The paper was an introduction to other papers (e.g., presenting a special issue of a particular journal) and merely consisted of a brief literature review and a summary of the subsequent papers. For example, Mäkinen, Seppänen, and Ortt (2014) is an introduction to the *Journal of Product*

*Innovation Management Special Issue: Platforms, Contingencies and New Product Development.*

After this further assessment and selection, the set included 728 papers.

### Identification of Categories

Many of the retained papers did actually focus on at least one of the 15 MA methods (that is why they have been kept) but they were still not fitting the current literature review. This is because a paper lacked emphasis on the application of the MA method for the purpose of *cost management* and/or the paper did not consider the context of *NPD*. For example, the paper looked more broadly at the anteceding conditions that are associated with the adoption of a particular method, such as competition and uncertainty (Ax, Greve, & Nilsson, 2008). Or, a paper addressed consequences and implications of the implementation of a method for the organization, such as the impact on development time (Danese & Filippini, 2013). Sometimes a paper addressed particular aspects as part of the method that had little do with costs, such measuring the level of component commonality based on technical characteristics of a product (Blecker & Abdelkafi, 2007). The notion of cost management motivates why the paper looks at a particular method, but then the actual focus of the paper is on something else and not concerned in any detail with the cost management aspect of the method. In other words, the link to one of our 15 methods means the paper has something to do with managing costs, but only in the background.

We decided to not include these papers in the content analysis of the IOM literature, but to cluster these papers in categories as to provide an overview or impression of this part of the IOM literature. The categories are listed in Table 4. Arriving at these twelve categories was an inductive process. We first coded the papers very specifically and without worrying too much about overlaps into 68 very specific categories, such as "Design for Six Sigma," "Influence of modular design and IT on supply chain responsiveness," "Measuring modular design/component commonality/ product platforms," and "Nuclear plant." We then looked for related categories and more abstract topics to cluster the papers into more generally formulated categories. After a few iterations, this resulted in the final list of categories. One paper could be assigned to several categories.

Of course, many topics in this classification may indirectly lead to cost reduction or cost reduction potential (e.g., papers on reducing development

***Table 4.*** Categories Defined for Literature Which Are Not
Included in Detail.

| Category Description | a | Examples |
|---|---|---|
| *Adoption:* Papers investigating which organizations or industries apply particular cost management methods, the distinctive characteristics of these organizations or industries, and their reasons for adoption. Some of these papers merely include descriptive statistics measuring the rate of adoption of the methods. Other papers investigate antecedents, preconditions and motives leading to the adoption of particular cost management methods. Most studies are based on survey data. | 58 | Ax et al. (2008) Ettlie and Trygg (1995) Lichtenthaler (2004) |
| *Outcomes of application:* Papers describing estimated or measured effects of the application of particular cost management methods (without explicitly addressing effects on costs) and the preconditions for these. Examples are reduction in development or manufacturing cycle times. These effects are derived from analytical models or empirical research. Moreover, it is demonstrated that the application of the methods may lead to broader organizational consequences (e.g., changing the organizational structure of a company). Benefits, identified potentials, disadvantages, and limitations of cost management methods may occur within a company and may also affect suppliers, customers, or other external parties. | 121 | Danese and Filippini (2013) Lau, Yam, and Tang (2011) Sethi and Iqbal (2008) |
| *Technology projecting:* Papers dealing with technology roadmapping within a company. Different facets and managerial challenges around the application of technology roadmapping are examined (e.g., improvements, extensions, and adaptions of the concept or the acquisition of relevant data and knowledge). Furthermore, open innovation as well as technology acquisition and exploitation are considered. In some papers, the role and impact of cross-company roadmaps (e.g., within the semiconductor industry) is discussed. | 37 | Cosner et al. (2007) Lichtenthaler (2008) Müller-Seitz (2012) |
| *External collaboration on the supply side:* "Supply chain collaboration occurs when two or more companies share the responsibility of exchanging common planning, management, execution and performance measurement information" (Anthony, 2003, p. 41). These papers investigate if and how cost management | 44 | Lau (2014) Lawson, Petersen, Cousins, and Handfield (2009) |

### *Table 4.* *(Continued)*

| Category Description | [a] | Examples |
| --- | --- | --- |
| methods are applied and in which way they influence the integration of suppliers in NPD. Antecedents are identified, the degree to which suppliers are given responsibility is assessed, and it is evaluated whether the integration of suppliers in NPD has benefits for the buyer (and which benefits). | | |
| *External collaboration on the demand side:* Papers focusing on the application of particular cost management methods to incorporate the wishes and requirements of customers into NPD projects. This often involves the combination of several concepts, frameworks, and methods. The vast majority of these papers look at QFD. Many papers deal with the prioritization of customer requirements. | 56 | Armacost, Componation, Mullens, and Swart (1994) Matzler and Hinterhuber (1998) |
| *External collaboration—strategic alliances and other partnerships:* Papers dealing with how companies can work together with external parties, such as strategic alliances and other types of partnerships. Challenges and managerial issues in communicating and exchanging information as well as the placing trust in partners are assessed. Furthermore, aspects of open innovation and technology acquisition are discussed. | 8 | Badir and O'Connor (2015) |
| *Internal collaboration and coordination:* Papers addressing how different functions, departments, locations, etc. within a company can work together cooperatively, and how concerns and decisions can be handled jointly. Cross-functional teams, design for manufacturing, and concurrent engineering are emblematic topics. Also, these papers discuss how information and knowledge are created, used, transferred and maintained across different interfaces and globally distributed locations within a company. | 65 | Goffin and Micheli (2010) Kerr, Phaal, and Probert (2012) Zeschky, Daiber, Widenmayer, and Gassmann (2014) |
| *Protection and management of intellectual property (IP):* Papers about the application of management practices for the protection of IP, the exploitation of technologies (e.g., through licensing) and patent planning. | 11 | Quan and Chesbrough (2010) |
| *Product architecture and variety:* Papers that deal with the efficient management of product variety by adjusting the architecture of products and by optimizing processes in R&D, manufacturing, and in | 77 | Blecker and Abdelkafi (2007) Settanni, Newnes, Thenent, Parry, and Goh (2014) Swaminathan (2001) |

***Table 4.***   (*Continued*)

| Category Description | [a] | Examples |
|---|---|---|
| the supply chain. Common components and modules, platforms, postponement, and targeted individualization are enablers for mass customization. Papers on measures for modularity and other quantitative assessments of product architectures also play a central role. Moreover, effects on manufacturing operations, purchasing, and warehousing are considered. | | |
| *Stage-gate processes:* Papers that focus on the management, the implementation (set-up) and the usage of stage-gate processes in NPD. These papers primarily show insights in companies' practices and their approach in managing stage-gate systems. Also, adaptations, extensions and enhancement of Robert Cooper's initial stage-gate approach (Cooper, 1988, 1990; Cooper & Kleinschmidt, 1991) are presented. | 45 | Jenkins, Forbes, and Durrani (1997) Cooper (1994) Cooper (2014) |
| *Success factors:* Papers describing challenges and managerial issues in the application of particular cost management methods and proposing how these challenges can be overcome. The papers suggest success factors and guiding principles, which facilitate the implementation, use and application of these methods. Often, these factors rely on the practical experience of the authors and reflect their view on the specific method or, alternatively, the authors look in several companies and provide insight into their way of implementing the cost management methods. | 82 | Davidson, Clamen, and Karol (1999) O'Connor (1994) Tatikonda (1999) |
| *Others:* In this category, we consolidate remaining papers that deal with specific topics that did not fit the categories listed earlier. | 9 | Demeester, Eichler, and Loch (2004) McGrath and Young (2002) |

[a]The second column provides the number of results included in this category, 613 in total. The number of unique papers was 389 because a paper may be included multiple times if it addresses several categories.

cycle time). However, there is no direct focus on cost management in these papers. Nevertheless, a paper would be included if only parts of the paper deal with cost management methods in NPD focusing on costs, even if the largest part of the paper would fit very well into one of the categories in Table 4.

We believe these subcategories are interesting to mention in this review for two reasons. First, these categories give an impression of what research is conducted around MA methods in the IOM literature. This is a substantial amount of research, looking at a broad range of issues concerning MA topics. This may be surprising for MA researchers and it may provide further opportunities for drawing upon relevant research and perhaps contributing to research outside accounting. Second, finding many papers about these methods in the IOM literature, but with a (very) different emphasis than cost management in NPD is, by itself, also an interesting difference between the IOM and MA literature. Wouters and Morales (2014) do not report running into many papers that focused on a variety of issues around their selected MA methods. The IOM literature seems broader when it comes to research on specific management methods that are also part of MA.

In the process of reviewing papers in more detail and forming these categories, an additional 131 papers were found not to be relevant for this review, for similar reasons as mentioned above, yielding a sample of 597 papers. Of these, 389 unique papers were related to the categories (as indicated in Table 4) and 208 papers from the IOM literature were included in this literature review for further detailed analysis.

*Content Analysis*

The content analysis was done in a comparable way as Wouters and Morales (2014). We distilled some information from every paper in tables, such as which cost management method the paper addressed, the journal, the industry, a summary, and the kind of research. This summary information exclusively focused on the cost management method, so it was not intended to necessarily summarize all, or even the main results of the paper.

We distinguished several types of non-empirical and empirical research (based on the kinds of data):

- *Theoretical*: The study motivates research topics, develops theory, proposes ideas for a cost management method, or formulates hypotheses for future research.
- *Analytical*: The study makes inferences on the basis of mathematical analyses and proofs of a formal model.
- *Simulation study*: The study is similar to an analytical study in that it is based on a formal model, but relationships in the formal model are investigated with numerical simulation.

- *Experimental*: The data are generated under fully controlled circumstances or through a field experiment.
- *Market*: Based on data on market transactions (such as stock prices).
- *Archival*: Proprietary archival firm data (e.g., on costs or project lead times).
- *Observations*: Measurements and estimates initiated for the research, generating the kind of data that, by their nature, could have existed as objective, archival data, but that did not exist or were not available to the researcher.
- *Survey*: Based on data gathered through responses to a questionnaire by research participants.
- *Qualitative*: Based on data that are not expressed as numbers; for example, interview notes or transcripts, photos, company documents with descriptions, and exhibits.
- *Mixed data*: In the sense that the study relied on both quantitative and qualitative data.

In so far as empirical studies involved field work, which we understand as a substantive interaction of the researchers with actual organizations to inform the research, we differentiated between particular "flavors" of field work (in the second column in the tables):

- *Case study*: The study generated new theoretical insights based on in-depth information (qualitative and/or quantitative data) from one or a few organizations.
- *Engineering*: The study presented detailed new methods and calculation models for solving or optimizing particular problems ("how to"), and these were tried out on realistic settings in actual organizations (as a "proof of concept").
- *Management practice*: The study offered pragmatic ideas for management practices based on eclectic observations of practices, "sensible" reasoning, and frameworks.

## OVERAL RESULTS FROM THE IOM LITERATURE AND COMPARISON TO THE MA LITERATURE

The final sample from the IOM literature includes 208 papers reporting research on the 15 cost management methods, leading to 275 results because one paper may address multiple cost management methods.

Tables 5 and 6 provide overviews of the distribution of the results across the journals and the research methods.

With 15 methods, equally distributed results would mean 6.7% (i.e., 18.3 results) per method. Table 5 shows three cost management methods that are clearly above this average: modular design (16%), component commonality (13%), and product platforms (12%); four cost managements provide only 1−2% per method; and the remaining eight cost management methods are between 3% and 11% per method. The results for the MA literature are also included in Table 5. Two cost management methods already had 26% and 13% of the results (target costing and modular design). For both literatures, we calculated the standard deviation of the number of results per cost management method relative to the average number of results, that is, the coefficient of variation (CV) (standard deviation/average). This is 0.95 for the MA literature and 0.73 for the IOM literature, supporting the impression that the distribution of the results across the cost management methods is more unequal for the MA literature.

## Results for the Journals

Results for the different journals are shown vertically in Table 5. Note, first of all, that results are provided for 20 of the 23 journals, because our final sample did not include any papers from *Academy of Management Review*, *California Management Review*, and *Strategic Management Journal*.

The distribution of the number of results across the journals is very uneven, as Table 5 illustrates. With 20 journals, equally distributed results would mean 5.0% per journal, and four journals have far more results than that, namely *International Journal of Production Research* (*IJPR*) (27%), *Journal of Product Innovation Management* (*JPIM*) (14%), *International Journal of Production Economics* (*IJPE*) (12%), and *IEEE Transactions on Engineering Management* (*IEEE-EM*) (9%); the next two journals are closer to the average number of results, namely *IIE Transactions* (*IIE*) (7%) and *Research-Technology Management* (*RTM*) (5%), and the remaining 15 journals have far below-average numbers of references (0.4−3%).

The results of Wouters and Morales (2014) for the MA literature are not included in Table 6, but they were comparably heterogeneous across journals. Three journals had by far the greatest number of results, namely *Management Science*, *Management Accounting Research*, and *Accounting, Organizations and Society*. The other journals were around the average, or they accounted for only a very few results. Indeed, the CV of the number

**Table 5.** Number of References per Cost Management Method and per Journal.

*Results IOM Literature*

| Journals[a] | % | Target Costing | Value Engineering | Quality Function Deployment | Functional Cost Analysis | Kaizen Costing | Life-Cycle Costing | Total Cost of Ownership | Stage-Gate Reviews | Funnels | Design for Manufacturing | Design for X | Component Commonality | Modular Design | Product Platforms | Technology Roadmap | Total |
|---|---|---|---|---|---|---|---|---|---|---|---|---|---|---|---|---|---|
| | | 18 / 7% | 11 / 4% | 29 / 11% | 2 / 1% | 3 / 1% | 19 / 7% | 6 / 2% | 24 / 9% | 3 / 1% | 21 / 8% | 17 / 6% | 37 / 13% | 45 / 16% | 33 / 12% | 7 / 3% | 275 / 100% |
| 1. AMJ | 0.4% | | | | | | | | 1 | | | | | | | | 1 |
| 2. IEEE-EM | 9% | 1 | 1 | 2 | | | 5 | 1 | 1 | | 2 | 2 | 3 | 6 | 1 | 1 | 26 |
| 3. IIE | 7% | | | 1 | | | 4 | | | | 3 | 1 | 4 | 2 | 3 | | 18 |
| 4. IMM | 1% | 1 | | | | | | 1 | 2 | | | | | | | | 4 |
| 5. Interf | 0.4% | | | | | | | | | | | | | | | 1 | 1 |
| 6. IJOPM | 3% | 1 | | 1 | | | | | 1 | | 1 | 1 | 1 | 3 | | | 9 |
| 7. IJPE | 12% | 7 | 3 | 2 | 1 | | 2 | | | | 2 | 2 | 4 | 8 | 3 | | 34 |
| 8. IJPR | 27% | 2 | 3 | 17 | 1 | 1 | 5 | 1 | 1 | | 6 | 5 | 13 | 8 | 11 | | 74 |
| 9. IJTM | 1% | | | | | | 1 | | | | | | | 1 | | | 2 |
| 10. JETM | 3% | 1 | 1 | 1 | | 1 | | | | | 1 | 1 | 1 | 1 | 1 | | 9 |
| 11. JM | 2% | | | | | | | | | | | | 1 | 2 | 2 | | 5 |
| 12. JMR | 0.4% | | | 1 | | | | | | | | | | | | | 1 |
| 13. JOM | 2% | | | | | | | 1 | | | 1 | | 1 | 2 | | | 5 |
| 14. JPIM | 14% | 1 | 2 | 3 | | | | 1 | 8 | | 4 | 3 | 2 | 4 | 8 | 2 | 38 |
| 15. MSOM | 3% | | | | | | | | | | | | 4 | 2 | 1 | | 7 |

| # / Category | 1 | 2 | 3 | 4 | 5 | 6 | 7 | 8 | 9 | 10 | 11 | 12 | 13 | 14 | 15 | Total |
|---|---|---|---|---|---|---|---|---|---|---|---|---|---|---|---|---|
| 16. *MIT SMR* | 2 | | | | | | | | | | | 1 | 1 | | 1 | 5 / 2% |
| 17. *RADMA* | | | | | | 3 | | | | 1 | | 1 | 1 | 1 | 2 | 9 / 3% |
| 18. *ResPol* | 1 | | 1 | | | | | | | 1 | | 2 | 3 | 1 | | 7 / 3% |
| 19. *RTM* | 1 | | | | | | | | 2 | 6 | | 1 | 1 | 3 | 1 | 15 / 5% |
| 20. *Techn* | 1 | | | | | | | | 1 | 1 | 1 | | 1 | | | 5 / 2% |
| **Total** | | | | | | | | | | | | | | | | 275 / 100% |

*Results MA literature*

| Category | 1 | 2 | 3 | 4 | 5 | 6 | 7 | 8 | 9 | 10 | 11 | 12 | 13 | 14 | 15 | Total |
|---|---|---|---|---|---|---|---|---|---|---|---|---|---|---|---|---|
| | 38 / 26% | 10 / 7% | 4 / 3% | 2 / 1% | 11 / 7% | 14 / 9% | 6 / 4% | 6 / 4% | 1 / 1% | 8 / 5% | 1 / 1% | 14 / 9% | 20 / 13% | 9 / 6% | 5 / 3% | 149 / 100% |
| *Decision Sciences* | 1 | | 1 | | | 1 | | | | 1 | | 3 | 4 | 1 | | 12 / 100% |
| *Management Science* | | | 3 | | | 3 | | 1 | 1 | 6 | 1 | 10 | 9 | 5 | 1 | 40 / 100% |
| IOM with *DS* and *MS* | 19 / 6% | 11 / 3% | 33 / 10% | 2 / 1% | 3 / 1% | 23 / 7% | 6 / 2% | 25 / 8% | 4 / 1% | 28 / 9% | 18 / 6% | 50 / 15% | 58 / 18% | 39 / 12% | 8 / 2% | 327 / 100% |
| MA without *DS* and *MS* | 37 / 38% | 10 / 10% | 0 / 0% | 2 / 2% | 11 / 11% | 10 / 10% | 6 / 6% | 5 / 5% | 0 / 0% | 1 / 1% | 0 / 0% | 1 / 1% | 7 / 7% | 3 / 3% | 4 / 4% | 97 / 100% |

aThe final sample did not contain results from *AMR*, *CMR*, and *SMJ*.

**Table 6.** Number of References per Cost Management Method and Research Method.

| Results IOM Literature | Total | % | Target Costing | Value Engineering | Quality Function Deployment | Functional Cost Analysis | Kaizen Costing | Life-Cycle Costing | Total Cost of Ownership | Stage-Gate Reviews | Funnels | Design for Manufacturing | Design for X | Component Commonality | Modular Design | Product Platforms | Technology Roadmap | Results MA literature | % | Decision Sciences | Management Science | IOM with DS and MS | % | MA without DS and MS | % |
|---|---|---|---|---|---|---|---|---|---|---|---|---|---|---|---|---|---|---|---|---|---|---|---|---|---|
| Total | 275 | 100% | 18 | 11 | 29 | 2 | 3 | 19 | 6 | 24 | 3 | 21 | 17 | 37 | 45 | 33 | 7 | 149 | 100% | 12 | 40 | 327 | 100% | 97 | 100% |
| Non-Empirical: theoretical | 24 | 9% |  |  | 2 |  |  | 2 |  | 2 |  | 1 | 3 | 3 | 3 | 4 | 4 | 24 | 16% | 3 | 1 | 28 | 9% | 20 | 21% |
| Non-Empirical: analytical | 21 | 8% | 1 |  | 2 |  |  | 4 |  |  |  |  |  | 5 | 8 | 1 |  | 13 | 9% |  | 10 | 31 | 9% | 3 | 3% |
| Non-Empirical: simulation | 67 | 24% | 2 | 2 | 12 | 1 |  | 5 | 2 |  |  | 4 | 3 | 16 | 11 | 9 |  | 14 | 9% | 4 | 9 | 80 | 24% | 1 | 1% |
| Empirical: experimental | 2 | 1% | 1 |  |  |  |  |  |  |  |  |  |  |  |  | 1 |  | 3 | 2% |  | 2 | 4 | 1% | 1 | 1% |
| Empirical: market | 0 | 0% |  |  |  |  |  |  |  |  |  |  |  |  |  |  |  | 0 | 0% |  |  | 0 | 0% | 0 | 0% |
| Empirical: archival | 16 | 6% | 3 | 1 | 5 |  | 1 | 4 |  | 2 |  | 2 | 1 | 3 | 1 | 2 |  | 9 | 6% |  | 7 | 23 | 7% | 2 | 2% |
| Empirical: observations | 32 | 12% | 6 | 2 | 4 |  |  |  |  | 4 | 2 | 4 | 2 | 3 | 1 | 4 | 1 | 4 | 3% |  | 4 | 36 | 11% | 0 | 0% |
| Empirical: survey | 41 | 15% | 4 | 4 | 1 |  | 1 | 1 | 1 | 9 |  | 8 | 1 | 4 | 5 | 1 |  | 24 | 16% | 5 | 1 | 47 | 14% | 18 | 19% |
| Empirical: qualitative | 29 | 11% | 1 | 1 |  |  | 1 | 1 | 2 | 4 | 1 | 1 | 6 | 3 | 4 | 4 | 1 | 32 | 21% |  |  | 29 | 9% | 32 | 33% |
| Empirical: mix (QQ) | 43 | 16% |  | 1 | 3 | 1 |  | 2 | 1 | 3 |  | 1 | 1 |  | 12 | 7 | 1 | 26 | 17% |  | 6 | 49 | 15% | 20 | 21% |
| Total | 275 | 100% |  |  |  |  |  |  |  |  |  |  |  |  |  |  |  | 149 | 100% | 12 | 40 | 327 | 100% | 97 | 100% |

of results per journal is 1.29 for the IOM literature and 1.32 for the MA literature, supporting the impression that the results for both literatures are about equally uneven.

## Results for the Research Methods

Table 6 presents the results for the 10 different research methods, so uniformly distributed results would mean 10% for every research method. The distribution of the actual number of results is quite uneven, with three research methods having a far above-average numbers of results: simulation (24%), mixed research methods (16%), and surveys (15%). The CV of the number of results per research method is 0.73. Overall, 59% of the results (163) are based on empirical methods, which is comparable to the 66% (98) Wouters and Morales (2014) found for the MA literature. Target costing, value engineering, stage-gate systems, and design for manufacturing are far more often based on empirical research, with 83%, 82%, 92%, and 76%, respectively. With 35%, component commonality has the lowest percentage of results based on empirical methods.

The results for the MA literature are also shown in Table 6. Four research methods have far above-average number of results: qualitative studies (21%), mixed research methods (17%), surveys (16%), and theoretical papers (16%). The CV of the number of results per research method in the MA literature was 0.74, so almost identical to the IOM literature. However, the emphasis on research methods is quite different: Simulation is the most frequently used research method in the IOM literature, but it is averagely used in the MA literature; qualitative study was the most frequently used research method in the MA literature, but it is averagely used in the IOM literature. Note one striking similarity between both these literatures: Both did not include any studies based on market data.

## Sensitivity Analysis: The Impact of the Journals Decision Sciences and Management Science

The earlier literature review by Wouters and Morales (2014) of the MA literature included the journals *Decision Sciences* and *Management Science*. Those authors based their journal selection on the list of 37 journals in the review by Bonner, Hesford, Van der Stede, and Young (2006) on the most influential journals in academic accounting, which included those two journals. For that reason, we have excluded *Decision Sciences* and *Management Science* thus far from the current review, as explained in the "Research Method" section. However, these journals also meet the selection criteria for the sample of IOM journals, because both were part of at least three of the lists of journals shown in Table 3 that formed the basis for defining the sample of IOM journals. Therefore, this section includes a sensitivity analysis, in the sense of comparing the results for both literatures when both journals are excluded from the MA literature and included in the IOM literature. Another reason for conducting this analysis is that the results for the MA literature were strongly influenced by *Decision Sciences* and *Management Science*, because research on design for manufacturing, component commonality, modular design, and product platforms was mainly published in only these two journals.

The results in Table 5 for the IOM literature remain largely the same. The same three cost management methods have the largest number of results: modular design (from 16% to 18%), component commonality (from 13% to 15%), and product platforms (remains 12%). The CV increases slightly from 0.73 to 0.80. The results for the MA literature change much more strongly. Before, target costing attracted by far the largest number of results with 26%, and this even becomes 38%. Modular design had 13% of the results, but now the number of results is only average with 7%; component commonality is reduced from 9% to 1%. The CV increases from 0.95 to 1.43, supporting the impression that the results are strongly affected by this change in journal selection.

The existing differences between both literatures become much more articulated in terms of attention for different research methods. As summarized in Table 7, the three methods of component commonality, modular design, and product platforms were already much more important in the IOM literature (together 42% vs. 29%), and this differences becomes much larger (45% vs. 11%). Target costing was already much more pronounced in the MA literature (26% vs. 7%), and this difference becomes even larger (38% vs. 6%).

The number of results per research method is in Table 6. Moving *Decision Sciences* and *Management Science* from the MA sample to the IOM sample does not have much impact on the results for the IOM literature, and the CV remains almost unchanged (from 0.73 to 0.70). In the MA literature, the results become more centered on the same four research methods, and the CV, indeed, increases from 0.74 to 1.20.

**Table 7.**   Impact on Percentages of References for Selected Cost Management Methods When *Decision Sciences* and *Management Science* Are Shifted from MA Literature to IOM Literature.

| | DS and MS in MA Literature | | DS and MS Shifted to IOM Literature | |
|---|---|---|---|---|
| | CMP[a] | Target costing | CMP | Target costing |
| IOM literature | 42% | 7% | 45% | 6% |
| MA literature | 29% | 26% | 11% | 38% |

Rounding creates some differences between percentages given in Tables 5 and 7.
[a]Component commonality, modular design, and product platform.

**Table 8.**   Impact on Percentages of References for Selected Research Methods When *DS* and *MS* Are Shifted from MA Literature to IOM Literature.

| | DS and MS in MA Literature | | DS and MS Shifted to IOM Literature | |
|---|---|---|---|---|
| | Simulation | Qualitative | Simulation | Qualitative |
| IOM literature | 24% | 11% | 24% | 9% |
| MA literature | 9% | 21% | 1% | 33% |

Here we also see that the differences between both literatures become more pronounced. As summarized in Table 8, simulation is a much more important research method in the IOM literature compared to the MA literature (24% vs. 9%) and this difference increases (24% vs. 1%), because almost all simulation results (13 out of 14) disappear from the MA literature. Qualitative studies were more important in the MA literature (21% vs. 11%) and this difference also becomes larger (33% vs. 9%), because all these qualitative studies remain in the MA sample relative to a lower total number of studies.

In sum, the IOM and MA literature were already quite different in terms of their attention for certain cost management methods and their use of particular research methods. The papers in our sample from the journals *Decision Sciences* and *Management Science* are much more alike the IOM literature than the MA literature. Therefore, when including these two journals in the IOM literature instead of in the MA literature, the differences between both literatures become even more pronounced.


# RESULTS FROM THE IOM LITERATURE FOR EACH COST MANAGEMENT METHOD

In this section, we will summarize for each cost management method the main results, drawing on the information in Tables 5–23. The latter present the detailed results per cost management method, whereby each row in these tables provides information for one paper: the author(s) and journal, the cost management method(s) addressed, the industry, a summary of the paper regarding the focal cost management method(s), the type of data, and the type of field work. We will not try to further "summarize the summaries" but we refer to Tables 9–23 for the specific information in the papers.

In each of the following sections, we characterize the research on a cost management method, draw a comparison with the earlier review of the MA literature, and highlight a few of the results in the table. We will not discuss the cost management method itself in any detail. In the section "Cost Management Methods in New Product Development" and in Table 1 we briefly describe the methods, and Wouters and Morales (2014) provide more complete discussions of these various cost management methods.


*Target Costing*

The results for target costing are shown Tables 5 and 6 and in more detail in Table 9. There are 18 results across many journals with 1–2 results, except for *IJPE* with 7 results. Most results represent empirical research (15 of 18). Surveys and qualitative research are the mostly used research method, with six and four results. Furthermore, different kinds of field studies are shown in Table 9. Almost all studies were done in the manufacturing industry.

Target costing is often researched in combination with other methods, such as value engineering, Kaizen costing, and QFD. Target costing is most often studied in the context of various manufacturing industries. These observations are quite similar to the results presented by Wouters

**Table 9.** Results for Target Costing.

| Author (Date) Journal | Cost Management Method(s) | Industry | Summary (Regarding the Focal Cost Management Method) | Type of Data | Field Work |
|---|---|---|---|---|---|
| Afonso et al. (2008) *IJPE* | Target costing | Manufacturing | This paper investigated the influence of TC and Time-to-Market (TtM) on NPD success. It is based on 82 responses to a survey among Portuguese manufacturing SMEs. TC was not always related to NPD success. Only firms which applied TC on a product level seemed to have a significant advantage, unlike the firms which used TC on a component level. Another finding was even when TC and TtM both had a positive impact on NPD success, they did not significantly correlate with each other. | Empirical: Survey | None |
| Albright and Kappel (2003) *RTM* | Target costing Technology roadmaps | Telecommunication industry (Lucent Technologies) | See Table 23. | Empirical: mix | Management practice |
| Onofrei et al. (2004) *MIT SMR* | Target costing | Diverse | The intention of the paper is to give managers a roadmap for implementing TC systems. An in-depth case study among seven big Japanese companies was conducted. | Empirical: qualitative | Management practice |
| Cooper and Slagmulder (2004) *MIT SMR* | Target costing Kaizen costing | Technology and telecommunication | The paper focused on how Olympus Optical Co. Ltd achieves sustainable cost reductions through the complete life-cycle of their products. Therefore, the authors made in-depth observations at the consumer products division of Olympus Optical focusing on the new Stylus Zoom camera. TC and Kaizen Costing (general and product-specific) were three of five methods observed. One conclusion is that considering multiple costing methods will be more beneficial in most cases than focusing on just one. | Empirical: qualitative | Management practice |
| Cooper and Yoshikawa (1994) *IJPE* | Target costing Value engineering | Automotive | Interviews with managers and engineers were conducted to investigate the interorganizational cost management system of three companies in one supply chain in the automotive industry. Results show that TC in combination with value engineering can be used to spread the competitive pressure and pass on consumers' demands along the value chain. | Empirical: qualitative | Case study |

**Table 9.** (Continued)

| Author (Date) Journal | Cost Management Method(s) | Industry | Summary (Regarding the Focal Cost Management Method) | Type of Data | Field Work |
|---|---|---|---|---|---|
| Everaert and Bruggeman (2002) *IJOPM* | Target costing | Consumer goods | Considering cost targets and time pressure, this paper examines their impact on NPD. Experiments are used to simulate a real design process. The interaction of cost targets and time pressure indicates that the use of cost targets is not always beneficial. Cost targets are helpful when no time pressure is given, so they can direct to cost improvements without adverse impact on design quality. On the other hand, if time pressure exists, cost targets may even lead to an increase in development time without achieving a reduction in costs. | Empirical: experimental | None |
| Filomena et al. (2009) *IJPE* | Target costing | Automotive | The paper describes an experience with developing early-stage cost parameters for a specific product development process effort at a mid-sized Brazilian manufacturing company. A model for the application of TC is proposed and applied, which should help operationalizing the method during NPD. TC is split in four stages. In stage 1 the product is divided into parts, features and common elements. Stage 2 focuses on the unitary target PD costs, which are the target cost per unit product related to the costs incurred to develop a product. The objective of stage 3 is the actual product target cost. Stage 4 defines "Insertion Target Costs," "Insertion Target Cost Breakdown into Parts," and "Insertion Target Cost Breakdown into Features." | Empirical: observations | Engineering, "how to" |
| Hoque et al. (2005) *IJPR* | Target costing QFD | Technology and telecommunication | To encourage concurrent engineering, this paper presents a model that represents a simple solution for the integration of different functions and departments within an organization. It is applied in a fictional case of a cellular phone development. The authors integrate the methods QFD and TC in their approach in order to consider customer needs (QFD) and develop an economically feasible product (TC). | Non-empirical: analytical | None |

| Reference | Keywords | Setting | Description | Method | Theory |
|---|---|---|---|---|---|
| Ibusuki and Kaminski (2007) *IJPE* | Target costing Value engineering QFD | Automotive | This research proposes a method for the product development process in an automotive company. It is tried out in a case study: the development of a pneumatic engine-starter. VE is split in three steps: "Concept VE," "Project VE" and "Validation VE." Within this framework, QFD and TC are applied to integrate customer desires and financial aspects in the design process. For the purpose of reducing costs, other methods like DFM or modular design are briefly discussed. | Empirical: observations | Engineering, "how to" |
| Kee (2010) *IJPE* | Target costing | Not specified | The paper argues that the lack of cost of capital in most TC approaches can lead to wrong decisions during the design stage of a product. A numerical example demonstrates that a traditional TC model can lead to accepting products that have a negative net present value, while rejecting products that have a positive net present value. | Non-empirical: simulation | None |
| Li, Wang, Yin, Kull, and Choi (2012) *IJPE* | Target costing | Not specified | Two different approaches of target pricing (demand side and supply side) are analyzed in the paper. Using a general oligopoly and Cournot duopoly model, the authors characterize the equilibrium and optimal policy for each approach under various conditions. They find that sharing cost-reduction expenses allows the manufacturer using the supply-side approach to attain competitive advantage in the form of increased market share and higher profit, particularly in industrial conditions where margins are thin and price sensitivities are high. | Non-empirical: simulation | None |
| Liker et al. (1996) *ResPol* | Target costing Value engineering | Automotive component suppliers (Japan, the United States) | Based on a survey, this paper investigates the differences in supplier design involvement between Japanese and U.S. component suppliers and their largest customers. Value engineering was used much by subsystem suppliers in both countries, yet even more in Japan (92% and 70% of U.S. subsystem suppliers). In both countries, value engineering was more widespread among subsystem suppliers than among lower-tier suppliers. Value engineering resulted in financial advantages, as subsystem suppliers reported an average of 17% cost savings in Japan and 15% in the United States. Target pricing was common for almost all Japanese subsystem suppliers and also substantial for their U.S. counterparts. | Empirical: survey | None |

**Table 9.** (Continued)

| Author (Date) Journal | Cost Management Method(s) | Industry | Summary (Regarding the Focal Cost Management Method) | Type of Data | Field Work |
|---|---|---|---|---|---|
| Petersen et al. (2003) *JPIM* | Target costing | Multiple industries | This paper develops a model to assess supplier integration into NPD to identify critical activities for successful integration. Sharing information on technology and costs was positively associated with supplier involvement in decision-making and with project outcomes. Even though not particularly in focus, TC objectives motivated buyers and suppliers to jointly work on alternative technical solutions. | Empirical: survey | None |
| Plank and Ferrin (2002) *IMM* | Target costing TCO | Mainly manufacturing industries | By conducting an exploratory survey among purchasing agents, this paper discusses the use and application of different methods and ways in which industrial companies value purchase offerings. Total cost of ownership was frequently used, especially among manufactured parts, yet respondents saw potential for further development. They viewed their firms' capability to effectively identify cost drivers for total cost of ownership purchase offering valuation only to be mediocre on average. The use of varying cost drivers for different kinds of offerings was medium. Target pricing was used in half the purchases reported. | Empirical: survey | None |
| Rabino (2001) *JETM* | Target costing Value engineering Kaizen costing | Multiple industries | Based on a survey among managers affiliated with NPD teams, this paper examines if NPD teams wanted to employ U.S. and Japanese accounting information and if accountants were increasingly considered in cross-functional NPD teams. Japanese accounting practices employed methods such as Kaizen costing, TC, and value engineering. Activity-based costing (ABC) is presented as a typical U.S. accounting method. The outcome suggests that both Japanese and U.S. methods were increasingly asked for. Remarkably, accounting was consistently ranked as the least important functional team member and accountants were part of only 34% of the respondents' teams. | Empirical: survey | None |

| Ro et al. (2007) *IEEE-EM* | Target costing Modular design | Automotive original equipment manufacturers (OEMs) and suppliers (the United States) | The purpose of this paper is to better understand the process and consequences of moving toward modularity as part of a mass customization strategy, using automotive as a case example. Modularity had considerable effects on product development, outsourcing, and supply chain coordination. The ineffective implementation of target pricing was seen as an impediment toward modularity among U.S. suppliers, and more generally, suppliers felt that their additional cost incurred through modularity were not sufficiently reflected in the OEMs' cost assessments. U.S. automotive companies seemed to outsource modules to suppliers for cost-reduction purposes, rather than to satisfy customers. | Empirical: qualitative | Management practice |
|---|---|---|---|---|---|
| Yazdifar and Askarany (2012) *IJPE* | Target costing | Manufacturing | This paper researches the adoption and implementation of TC. A survey among selected members of the Chartered Institute of Management Accountants (CIMA) was conducted. The 584 responses identify the "ability to get the job/service done quicker" (p. 390) and "being able to try the technique before deciding to implement it (or not)" (p. 390) as the main attributes for implementing TC. | Empirical: survey | None |
| Zengin and Ada (2010) *IJPR* | Target costing Value engineering QFD Kaizen costing | Manufacturing | The study investigates an implementation of TC combined with QFD analysis and value engineering in a small manufacturing company, and it develops a TC module that will encourage its use in SMEs. Additionally, Kaizen costing is introduced as a tool for continuous improvement after the actual NPD process. The company was able to significantly reduce its cost without sacrificing quality and functionality. Other results are that the introduced QFD-TC process is very reliant on cross-functional integration and that QFD-TC can be a suitable solution for SMEs to manage their NPD process. | Empirical: observations | Case study |

and Morales (2014) for the MA literature. As discussed earlier, in terms of the "size" of the topic, the IOM and MA literatures are quite different regarding target costing. This cost management method had by far the largest number of results in the MA literature, but this is only average in the IOM literature.

Several surveys investigate the antecedents or consequences (Afonso, Nunes, Paisana, & Braga, 2008; Liker, Kamath, Wasti, & Nagamachi, 1996; Petersen, Handfield, & Ragatz, 2003; Plank & Ferrin, 2002; Rabino, 2001; Yazdifar & Askarany, 2012) of target costing or related cost management methods.

Other studies adopted case studies to better understand target costing practices (Cooper & Yoshikawa, 1994; Zengin & Ada, 2010) or to provide pragmatic ideas for the use of target costing (Cooper & Slagmulder, 2004; Filomena, Neto, & Duffey, 2009; Ibusuki & Kaminski, 2007; Onofrei, Hunt, Siemienczuk, Touchette, & Middleton, 2004; Ro, Liker, & Fixson, 2007).

One of the few experimental papers in our entire sample from the IOM literature investigates the effect of time pressure on development time and cost improvements (Everaert & Bruggeman, 2002).

Integration is an important theme in these studies on target costing: cross-functional integration within the organization (Rabino, 2001; Zengin & Ada, 2010) and interorganizational toward suppliers (Liker et al., 1996; Petersen et al., 2003; Ro et al., 2007), or with customers (Hoque, Akter, & Monden, 2005; Ibusuki & Kaminski, 2007; Plank & Ferrin, 2002).

*Value Engineering*

The findings for value engineering are quite comparable to target costing: the results are mainly empirical (9 of 11), and surveys is the mostly used method for these (4 of 9). The two non-empirical methods are based on simulation. Most results have been found in *IJPE* (as was also the case for target costing) and *IJPR* (which was under-represented for target costing), with three results in each journal. Value engineering, again as target costing, is often studied in combination with other methods (for 8 of 11 results), and mostly together with target costing (5 results).

These observations on the use of research methods and the study of value engineering in combination with other methods are quite similar to the findings for the MA literature. In both the IOM and the MA literature, value engineering is not a particularly important topic, with 4% and 7% of total results, respectively.

More detailed results for research on value engineering are shown in Table 10. Several papers provide guidelines or tools for the use of value engineering (Chung, Syachrani, Jeong, & Kwak, 2009; Romano, Formentini, Bandera, & Tomasella, 2010; Wang & Che, 2008; Yoshikawa, Innes, & Mitchell, 1994) in addition to similar kind of papers already mentioned earlier that included both value engineering and target costing.

### Quality Function Deployment

Quality function deployment (QFD) is an important cost management method in the IOM literature (with 29 results representing 11% of all results), whereas QFD was a marginal topic in the MA literature with only 4 results (3%). (Note also that those were all published in either *Decision Sciences* or *Management Science*, so when shifting those journals to the IOM literature sample, the topic vanishes completely from the MA literature.) QFD is also an "outspoken" topic in the IOM literature. The vast majority of results (17 of 29) has been published in *IJPR*, and simulation is the most often used research method (12 results).

More detailed results for research on QFD are shown in Table 11, indicating in 20 of the results QFD is the sole cost management being investigated. This pattern provides a clear contrast to the research for target costing and value engineering described earlier.

Many studies present methodological refinements of the QFD method (e.g., Brad, 2009; Chaudhuri & Bhattacharyya, 2009; Hoyle & Chen, 2009; Iranmanesh & Thomson, 2008; Ji, Jin, Wang, & Chen, 2014), often by developing ways for using fuzzy logic in combination with QFD (e.g., Bai & Kwong, 2003; Chen, Fung, & Tang, 2005; Chen & Ngai, 2008; Fung, Tang, Tu, & Wang, 2002; Karsak, 2004). These studies are typically based on simulation of results and perhaps showing an illustrative example application. Some studies include a real-life case study for trying out the proposed method (Bovea & Wang, 2007; Delice & Güngör, 2011, 2013; Lee, Kang, Yang, & Lin, 2010; Olhager & West, 2002; Romli, Prickett, Setchi, & Soe, 2014).

A few case studies (Fargnoli, De Minicis, & Tronci, 2013; Griffin, 1992) or surveys (Cristiano, Liker, & White, 2000; Heim, Mallick, & Peng, 2012; Ittner & Larcker, 1997; Trygg, 1993) are more aimed at understanding the use of QFD rather than "improving" the method. Most of these studies

**Table 10.** Results for Value Engineering.

| Author (Date) Journal | Cost Management Method(s) | Industry | Summary (Regarding the Focal Cost Management Method) | Type of Data | Field Work |
|---|---|---|---|---|---|
| Chung et al. (2009) *IEEE-EM* | Value engineering | Construction industry | This paper presents a process simulation VE model. It attempts to quantify experts' estimations on cost and time savings of different alternatives while at the same time aiming at minimizing the level of subjectivity involved. The monetary value of different functions is compared to the estimated actual cost. This enables the engineers to make effective decisions for different design alternatives. In an empirical case study on one specific construction activity of a hospital building project, the different phases of the model are explained and demonstrated in detail. Also when considering the implementation cost, the execution of the model achieved cost savings. The authors estimate that applying the model generates a return on investment between 1,200 and 2,200%. | Empirical: archival | Engineering, "how to" |
| Cooper and Yoshikawa (1994) *IJPE* | Target costing Value engineering | Automotive | See Table 9. | Empirical: qualitative | Case study |
| Ibusuki and Kaminski (2007) *IJPE* | Target costing Value engineering QFD | Automotive | See Table 9. | Empirical: observations | Engineering, "how to" |
| Liker et al. (1996) *ResPol* | Target costing Value engineering | Automotive component suppliers (Japan, the United States) | See Table 9. | Empirical: survey | None |

| Reference | Techniques | Industry/Context | Description | Method | |
|---|---|---|---|---|---|
| Loch, Stein, and Terwiesch (1996) *JPIM* | Value engineering DFM/A Design for X | Electronics industry | This paper presents a model to measure NPD output performance as the driver of business success and applies it to a sample of 95 companies within the electronics industry. Various antecedent and consequential relationships between variables describing the development process (e.g., DFM, VE), their outputs (e.g., design-to-cost) and business success are established, often with reference to specific branches within the electronics industry. On this basis, particularities of the different electronics branches are determined, and managerial implications are derived. | Empirical: survey | None |
| Martínez Sánchez and Pérez (2003) *JPIM* | Value engineering DFM/A | Automotive suppliers (Spain) | This paper shows the results of a survey of 63 Spanish automotive suppliers to test the moderation effect of cooperation in the relationship between the use of NPD firm practices and the company's NPD time and cost minimization abilities. The application of NPD practices was found to be more widespread among high-cooperation companies, allowing them to be better able to reduce NPD time and cost. The results suggest that cross-functional design (including value analysis) and the design-manufacturing interface (including DFM) are explanatory factors for this perceived time and cost minimization ability. The posited moderation effect of cooperation was supported. | Empirical: survey | None |
| Rabino (2001) *JETM* | Target costing Value engineering Kaizen costing | Multiple industries | See Table 9. | Empirical: survey | None |

**Table 10.** (Continued)

| Author (Date) Journal | Cost Management Method(s) | Industry | Summary (Regarding the Focal Cost Management Method) | Type of Data | Field Work |
|---|---|---|---|---|---|
| Romano et al. (2010) *IJPR* | Value engineering | Cruise ship building | The authors developed and implemented in an Italian company an original decision support tool, based on value analysis, which designers can use to document and formalize their choices. This tool helped to cut costs and supported the selection of the most valuable solution by means of objective parameters. | Empirical: mix | Engineering, "how to" |
| Wang and Che (2008) *IJPR* | Value engineering | Technology and telecommunication | This paper focusses on the problems that come along with changing parts of a product. To overcome these problems during the redesign of a product, a theoretical model is proposed and supported by an illustrative example. VE is part of the second step in the model (out of three). It is shown how the method can be used for the evaluation of suppliers. | Non-empirical: Simulation | None |
| Yoshikawa et al. (1994) *IJPE* | Functional cost analysis Value engineering | Manufacturing | This paper explores the nature and impact of functional cost analysis as it is used in VE. Based on numerical examples, a guideline for the application of FCA in different manufacturing areas is given. It is concluded that FCA is not just limited to physical products but it is also applicable to overhead services and business processes. | Non-empirical: Simulation | None |
| Zengin and Ada (2010) *IJPR* | Target costing Value engineering QFD Kaizen costing | Manufacturing | See Table 9. | Empirical: observations | Case study |

**Table 11.** Results for Quality Function Deployment.

| Author (Date) Journal | Cost Management Method(s) | Industry | Summary (Regarding the Focal Cost Management Method) | Type of Data | Field Work |
|---|---|---|---|---|---|
| Bai and Kwong (2003) *IJPR* | QFD | Automotive | Typically, in the early design stage of a product no precise information about final specifications can be given. The paper introduces a fuzzy optimization approach to support decision-making within QFD in this early stage. The proposed model is able to generate a set of solutions depending on different design scenarios and engineering requirements. Costs are seen as one possible design requirement. The model is demonstrated with a numerical example. | Non-empirical: simulation | None |
| Bovea and Wang (2007) *IJPR* | Life-cycle costing QFD | Consumer goods | This paper presents a redesign approach that allows integrating environmental requirements in product development, taking into account cost and customer preferences. The proposed method allows the identification of environmental improvement options and assessment of the effect of incorporating these. Through QFD combined with LCC and some other methods, it was found that for the case of office furniture products, 50% of the customers are willing to pay 14% more for an environmental friendlier product. | Empirical: mix | Case study |
| Brad (2009) *IJPR* | QFD Design for X | Consumer goods | QFD is a major part of the concurrent multifunction deployment (CMFD) method presented in the paper. The model can be seen as an advanced form of QFD that integrates concepts of concurrent engineering for planning product development with multi-objective functions. | Non-empirical: simulation | None |

**Table 11.** (Continued)

| Author (Date) Journal | Cost Management Method(s) | Industry | Summary (Regarding the Focal Cost Management Method) | Type of Data | Field Work |
|---|---|---|---|---|---|
| Chaudhuri and Bhattacharyya (2009) *IJPR* | QFD | Automotive | Starting point of this research is the idea that QFD and Conjoint Analysis (CA) both cannot be used sole to guaranty successful NPD, but connected they can. So in the suggested model QFD is used to determine the required product profiles including the needed technical characteristics, and CA is afterward applied to maximize customer utility. To promote this model an illustrative numerical example with hypothetical data is presented. | Non-empirical: simulation | None |
| Chen and Ngai (2008) *IJPR* | QFD | Automotive | The paper argues that today's QFD approaches cannot handle complex product planning (CPP), multiple engineering requirements, and uncertainty simultaneously. Therefore, fuzzy set theory is embedded in a QFD framework and a novel fuzzy QFD program modeling approach to CPP is proposed to optimize the values of engineering characteristics by taking into account design uncertainty and financial considerations. | Non-empirical: simulation | None |
| Chen et al. (2005) *IJPR* | QFD | Automotive | A novel fuzzy expected value operator approach is proposed to model the QFD process in a fuzzy environment, and two fuzzy expected value models are used to determine the target values of engineering characteristics in handling different practical design scenarios. The illustrated example of a quality improvement problem of a motor car shows that the proposed approach can model the QFD process effectively in a fuzzy environment by taking into account competition requirements, technical feasibility and financial factors. | Non-empirical: simulation | None |

| Reference | Method | Industry | Description | Study type | Contribution |
|---|---|---|---|---|---|
| Cristiano et al. (2000) *JPIM* | QFD | Multiple industries | This paper provides a study on QFD, in particular by comparing its adoption and several other aspects between Japan and the U.S. Cost deployment is found to be scarcely used both in Japan and the United States Notably decreased manufacturing costs as an impact of QFD are reported by 14.3% of the Japanese and 23.8% of the U.S. companies. | Empirical: survey | None |
| Delice and Güngör (2011) *IJPR* | QFD | Consumer goods | This paper uses a mixed-integer linear programming strategy and a mixed-integer goal programming model to manage discrete values of design requirements. The results should deliver the best solution for the product design, by incorporating customer satisfaction, cost and technical issues. The model is tested in the case of a washing machine development. | Non-empirical: simulation | None |
| Delice and Güngör (2013) *IJPR* | QFD | Consumer Goods | This paper refines the model mentioned in the row above by implementing a fuzzy mixed-integer goal programming procedure. The change is made to take into account imprecise information and uncertainty about the future environment during product development. The proposed model was tried out for the Turkish white goods industry. | Empirical: observations | Engineering, "how to" |
| Fargnoli et al. (2013) *JETM* | QFD Design for X | Gardening equipment firm (Italy) | Conducting a case study, this paper investigates how to integrate environmental aspects in NPD considering other aspects, such as the user-product relationship and cost (called Design Management for Sustainability). Relying on Bovea and Wang (2007), a Green-QFD approach is employed to address different aspects of the products in various QFD-houses. Costs are considered in the cost house, distinguishing between internal costs (such as materials, manufacturing, and waste management) | Empirical: mix | Case study |

**Table 11.** (Continued)

| Author (Date) Journal | Cost Management Method(s) | Industry | Summary (Regarding the Focal Cost Management Method) | Type of Data | Field Work |
|---|---|---|---|---|---|
| | | | and external costs (social consequences during the product's life-cycle). | | |
| Fung et al. (2002) *IJPR* | QFD | Consumer goods | The proposed model tries to maximize the benefit from used resources for future products. This research focuses on the correlation between individual technical attributes and how they can influence each other. A nonlinear fuzzy model connected to either a parametric optimization method or a hybrid genetic algorithm is applied to receive an optimal solution. The model is demonstrated using the hypothetical development of a pencil as an example. | Non-empirical: simulation | None |
| Griffin (1992) *JPIM* | QFD | Multiple industries | A field-based, scientific study of U.S. firms' efforts to implement QFD methods. Based on a study of 35 projects, the author found that QFD provided only minor, short-term, measurable impacts on product development performance. For two physical goods projects and five service projects out of 35 projects observed, QFD resulted in increased performance at the same product cost. Time or cost to commercialization was reduced for these two physical goods projects. | Empirical: observations | Case study |
| Heim et al. (2012) *IEEE-EM* | QFD DFM/A | Manufacturing industries | This paper investigates the use and impact of NPD practices (DFM, QFD and rapid prototyping) and software tools (e.g., computer-aided design, product data management) among manufacturing industries through an international survey. The results suggest that the NPD practices have a positive on (1) cost control (2) responsiveness (3) product conformance | Empirical: survey | None |

| Source | Methods | Industry | Description | Research type | Contribution |
|---|---|---|---|---|---|
| Hoque et al. (2005) *IJPR* | Target costing QFD | Technology and telecommunication | quality (4) product performance quality (5) time to market. Of these performance metrics, cost control, time to market, and performance quality showed evidence to drive market success. See Table 9. | Non-empirical: analytical | None |
| Hoyle and Chen (2009) *IEEE-EM* | QFD | Not specified | Addressing the notion that QFD is biased toward fulfilling customer requirements and lacks consideration of costs, this paper presents a new design tool as a replacement of QFD. The method is used to select the preferred design concept, set target levels of engineering performance, and set engineering priorities and thereby aims to maximize enterprise utility. It incorporates estimates on costs, such as manufacturing and material costs. In an example, the suggested tool yielded significantly higher profits and lower unit costs than the QFD method. | Non-empirical: simulation | None |
| Ibusuki and Kaminski (2007) *IJPE* | Target costing Value engineering QFD | Automotive | See Table 9. | Empirical: observations | Engineering, "how to" |
| Iranmanesh and Thomson (2008) *IJPE* | QFD | Technology and telecommunication | A cost-design parameter method that optimizes cost and design characteristics simultaneously during product development is presented. The method is based on QFD, which relates desired product attributes to design characteristics. The method works at three levels: strategic, tactical and operational. This model is validated through use in an example, where customer satisfaction versus new expenditure on the product is calculated. | Non-empirical: simulation | None |

**Table 11.** (Continued)

| Author (Date) Journal | Cost Management Method(s) | Industry | Summary (Regarding the Focal Cost Management Method) | Type of Data | Field Work |
|---|---|---|---|---|---|
| Ittner and Larcker (1997) *JMR* | QFD | Automotive and computer industry (Canada, Germany, Japan, the United States) | The authors develop and test a simple conceptual model linking product development cycle time to organizational performance. They find faster cycle time alone is not associated with higher accounting returns, sales growth, or perceived overall performance. Tools like QFD, failure mode and effects analysis and design of experiments moderate the relationship between cycle time and organizational performance and increase return on assets and return on sales in the computer industry. | Empirical: survey | None |
| Ji et al. (2014) *IJPR* | QFD | Technology and telecommunication | This paper integrates an existing model on customer requirements with QFD. A mixed non-linear integer programming model is formulated to maximize customer satisfaction under cost and technical constraints. An illustrative example regarding the design of notebook computers is presented to demonstrate the availability of the proposed approach. | Non-empirical: simulation | None |
| Karsak (2004) *IJPR* | QFD | Consumer goods | This paper presents a fuzzy multiple objective programming approach that incorporates imprecise and subjective information in the QFD planning process to determine the level of fulfilment of design requirements. Linguistic variables are used to represent the imprecise design information and the importance of each design objective. The fuzzy Delphi method is utilized to achieve consensus of customers in determining the importance of customer needs. A pencil design example illustrates the | Non-empirical: simulation | None |

| Study | Method | Industry | Description | Type | Contribution |
|---|---|---|---|---|---|
| Lager (2005) *RADMA* | QFD | Not specified (multiple empirical studies) | application of the multiple objective decision analysis. This paper provides a literature review and analysis on QFD, assessing its industrial usability and, in particular, identifying best practices and success factors in its introduction and use. Evidence of QFD lowering manufacturing costs was scarce (only two out of nine studies reviewed showed weak support), lower design costs were not reported at all. | Non-empirical: theoretical | None |
| Lee et al. (2010) *IJPR* | QFD | Metals and electronics | The paper presents a framework for the selection of engineering characteristics (ECs) for product design. In the first phase, QFD is incorporated with the supermatrix approach of analytic network process (ANP) and the fuzzy set theory to calculate the priorities of ECs. In the second phase, a multi-choice goal programming model is constructed based on the outcome of the first phase and other goals, such as NPD cost and manufacturability, in order to select the most suitable ECs. A case study of the product design process of backlight unit in thin film transistor liquid crystal display industry in Taiwan is carried out to verify the practicality of the proposed framework. | Empirical: mix | Engineering, "how to" |
| Olhager and West (2002) *IJOPM* | QFD | Technology and telecommunication | The paper applies the QFD approach to manufacturing flexibility. It proposes an approach to deploy flexibility-related customer needs into manufacturing system features regarding costs, quality, innovativeness and more. The suggested method is successfully applied in the case of a mobile phone manufacturer. | Empirical: qualitative | Case study |

*Table 11.* (*Continued*)

| Author (Date) Journal | Cost Management Method(s) | Industry | Summary (Regarding the Focal Cost Management Method) | Type of Data | Field Work |
|---|---|---|---|---|---|
| Romli et al. (2014) *IJPR* | QFD | Health and pharmaceuticals | This paper presents an integrated eco-design decision-making method using three stages: life-cycle assessment, an eco-design process model and an enhanced eco-design QFD process. An application of the approach is presented in a case study of the redesign of a single-use medical forceps. | Empirical: observations | Engineering, "how to" |
| Trygg (1993) *JPIM* | QFD DFM/A | Manufacturing industry (Sweden) | Based on a survey among Swedish manufacturing companies, this paper investigates how these companies employ concurrent engineering methods to improve their speed to market. Design for manufacturing and assembly (DFMA) was found to be significantly more applied among the successful companies, which have achieved shorter lead times in their product development. This also applies to the use of QFD, yet less distinctly. For QFD, there was only a marginal effect on development lead time (56% yes, 44% no) and on development cost (52% yes, 48% no). | Empirical: survey | None |
| Vanegas and Labib (2001) *IJPR* | QFD | Automotive | This paper proposes a novel method for determining optimum targets in QFD. Fuzzy numbers are used to represent the imprecise nature of the relationships between engineering characteristics and customer attributes. Constraints such as cost, technical difficulty and market position are considered. An example of a car door is presented to show the application of the method. | Non-empirical: simulation | None |

| | | | | | |
|---|---|---|---|---|---|
| Wasserman (1993) *IIE* | QFD | Not specified | This paper presents a mathematical decision framework to prioritize design requirements during QFD. In an example, it is shown that cost considerations can influence the designers' decisions considerably, if the importance of certain design requirements is set in relation to cost instead of employing it as sole decision criterion. Ranking the design requirements based on the importance/cost ratio is recommended to assign resources. | Non-empirical: analytical | None |
| Zengin and Ada (2010) *IJPR* | Target costing<br>Value engineering<br>QFD<br>Kaizen costing | Manufacturing | See Table 9. | Empirical: observations | Case study |
| Zhang (1999) *IJPR* | QFD<br>Life-cycle costing | Automotive | Green Quality Function Deployment-II (GQFD-II) is introduced in this paper. By integrating Life-Cycle Costing (LCC) into QFD matrices and deploying quality, environmental and cost requirements throughout the entire product development process it is possible to design products with focus on quality and cost as well as environmental issues. An illustrative example (engine filters) is used to demonstrate the concept of GQFD-II. | Non-empirical: simulation | None |

reported beneficial effects of using QFD. However, Griffin (1992) remarks that only about one quarter of the projects observed in her study were successful in the sense of product or process improvements, increased sales or lower product costs. Furthermore, Trygg (1993) surveyed Swedish manufacturing companies and only a little more than half of these reported a positive impact on development cost or lead time.

## Functional Cost Analysis

For functional cost analysis, we found only very few results, comparable to the MA literature, with 1% in both studies. Detailed information is provided in Table 12.

## Kaizen Costing

Only 3 results for Kaizen costing are included in this literature review (1%), whereas the 11 results (7%) in the MA literature was quite average. As indicated in Table 13, the three studies were all empirical and all in combination with at least target costing. That is understandable, because Kaizen costing is seen as a key example of a Japanese cost accounting approach, strongly related to target costing, value engineering and QFD. However, whereas the latter three focus on cost reduction for new products, Kaizen costing is concerned with cost reduction for existing products.

## Life-Cycle Costing

The 19 results (7%) is quite average in our sample of the IOM literature, comparable to the 9% of the results in the sample of the MA literature in Wouters and Morales (2014). The journals *IEEE-EM* and *IIE* have together published nine results (47%), which is much more than would be expected, as these journals together have published 16% of all results. Furthermore, *IJPR* published five results (26%), which is in line with what would be expected based on the overall 27% of results published in this journal.

Also, an above expected number of results was found for analytical methods (four results) and archival data (four results). Simulation was used

***Table 12.*** Results for Functional Cost Analysis.

| Author (Date) Journal | Cost Management Method(s) | Industry | Summary (Regarding the Focal Cost Management Method) | Type of Data | Field Work |
|---|---|---|---|---|---|
| Roy, Souchoroukov, and Griggs (2008) *IJPR* | Functional cost analysis | Diverse | This paper presents a function-based cost estimating (FUCE) framework to link the commercial and engineering departments in the conceptual design stage. The objective of FUCE is to translate the un-quantified terminology and requests regarding product specifications that are used by cost estimators with a *commercial* background into a medium that cost estimators with an *engineering* background can process. FUCE is developed using a detailed case study on an automotive exhaust system. The method is then validated using two case studies from the automotive and aerospace industries. | Empirical: mix | Case study |
| Yoshikawa et al. (1994) *IJPE* | Functional cost analysis Value engineering | Manufacturing | See Table 10. | Non-empirical: simulation | None |

*Table 13.* Results for Kaizen Costing.

| Author (Date) Journal | Cost Management Method(s) | Industry | Summary (Regarding the Focal Cost Management Method) | Type of Data | Field Work |
|---|---|---|---|---|---|
| Cooper and Slagmulder (2004) *MIT SMR* | Target costing Kaizen costing | Technology and telecommunication | See Table 9. | Empirical: qualitative | Management practice |
| Rabino (2001) *JETM* | Target costing Value engineering Kaizen costing | Multiple industries | See Table 9. | Empirical: survey | None |
| Zengin and Ada (2010) *IJPR* | Target costing Value engineering QFD Kaizen costing | Manufacturing | See Table 9. | Empirical: observations | Case study |

often (five results) but that is not unexpected given the overall large adoption of simulation as research method.

Detailed results are shown in Table 14. Quite a few studies report further development of approaches and decision models for life-cycle costing, mostly without empirical support (Grote, Jones, Blount, Goodyer, & Shayler, 2007; Hatch & Badinelli, 1999; Hegde, 1994; Johnson & Wang, 1995; Kleyner & Sandborn, 2008; Mangun & Thurston, 2002; Neto, Walther, Bloemhof, van Nunen, & Spengler, 2010; Riggs & Jones, 1990; Usher & Whitfield, 1993), although some studies tried out the proposed approach or model in a real-life case study (Bard, 1992; Elimam & Dodin, 1994; Goffin, 2000) or based on archival data (Folgado, Peças, & Henriques, 2010).

Some of the studies on life-cycle costing explicitly consider environmental and ecological aspects, such as energy usage, emissions, or recycling of materials (Elimam & Dodin, 1994; Grote et al., 2007; Johnson & Wang, 1995; Mangun & Thurston, 2002; Neto et al., 2010).

*Total Cost of Ownership*

TCO is a small topic in our sample of IOM studies, with only six results (2%). This is not so different from the MA literature with six results, representing 4%.

Detailed information on the six TCO studies is provided in Table 15. Some empirical research focusses on how TCO may be used for decision-making during NPD. Goffin (1998, 2000) addresses the evaluation of product support requirements during the design stage (design for supportability). He found that 45% of the companies surveyed would consider TCO in their product support planning, and about the same percentage of respondents confirmed that quantitative goals for this product support cost figure would exist at the design stage (Goffin, 1998). The case study at Hewlett-Packard's medical and healthcare division illustrated that ensuring the easy upgradeability of a medical device already at its design stage could lower the total costs of ownership for hospitals. Goffin (2000) provides further ideas on design for supportability and the importance of considering lifetime costs instead of only development and production costs. However, Wouters, Anderson, Narus, and Wynstra (2009) remark that although TCO is beneficial in principle, it is very difficult to be applied during the design process due to large data needed and it being time-consuming.

**Table 14.** Results for Life-Cycle Costing.

| Author (Date) | Cost Management Method(s) | Industry | Summary (Regarding the Focal Cost Management Method) | Type of Data | Field Work |
|---|---|---|---|---|---|
| Bard (1992) *IIE* | Life-cycle costing | U.S. Army | Extending Bard and Sousk (1990), this paper reports a case study dealing with two different methods to assess technological alternatives of rough terrain cargo handlers for the U.S. Army. Life-cycle costs were used as scaling constant for both methods. The case study group believed that a full assessment of life-cycle costs would provide more supportive data, yet the effort required was considered to be considerable. | Empirical: mix | Case study |
| Bovea and Wang (2007) *IJPR* | Life-cycle costing QFD | Consumer goods | See Table 11. | Empirical: mix | Case study |
| Dutta and Lawson (2008) *IJTM* | Life-cycle costing | High-technology industries | This paper investigates how accounting standards and their financial effects influence firms' decisions to invest internally in "sustaining technology" and through joint ventures or research partnerships in "disruptive technologies." Even though the method of LCC is not particularly in focus, the paper depicts the distribution of costs and profits over the products' lifetime for comparing sustainable and disruptive technologies. | Empirical: archival | Case study |
| Elimam and Dodin (1994) *IIE* | Life-cycle costing | Wastewater treatment plants | This paper examines the selection of sludge dewatering processes and operation modes for wastewater treatment. It applies an infinite-horizon LCC model and a mathematical programming model. The model considers operations, maintenance, cost of capital, transportation, and use of polymers (for sludge treatment). The models were applied in two wastewater treatment plants in Kuwait. | Empirical: archival | Engineering, "how to" |

| Reference | Topics | Industry | Description | Research type | |
|---|---|---|---|---|---|
| Folgado et al. (2010) *IJPE* | Life-cycle costing | Manufacturing | The topic of this paper is the selection of the best technology alternative for the manufacturing of injection molds in the product development stage through LCC. The proposed model is verified by a case study with archival data. For the life-cycle costs, in this example the critical variable was the targeted production volume. | Empirical: archival | None |
| Goffin (2000) *RTM* | Life-cycle costing TCO Design for X | Multiple industries | By giving many practical examples, the author suggests that supportability concerns are not sufficiently considered by many companies, yet inspiring cases exist. It is proposed to incorporate aspects of product support early in the design stage to achieve cost savings (which may be measured with total cost of ownership or LCC approaches). The author also presents a simple way to classify companies' design for support activities. | Empirical: qualitative | Management practice |
| Goh, Newnes, Mileham, McMahon, and Saravi (2010) *IEEE-EM* | Life-cycle costing | Not specified | This paper presents a review of the uncertainty classification in the engineering literature and the nature of uncertainty in life-cycle cost estimation. Based on the review, the paper presents a critique of the current uncertainty modeling approaches in cost estimation and suggests requirements for a different approach to handling uncertainty in life-cycle cost estimation. | Non-empirical: theoretical | None |
| Grote et al. (2007) *IJPR* | Design for X Life-cycle costing | Consumer Goods | In this paper a model for the development of "energy using products" is presented. The model comprises DFX and LCC elements. It pays attention to economic as well as ecological design requirements. A fictitious case study for a small household item is conducted. The results indicate a reduction of $CO_2$ emissions and energy costs. | Non-empirical: simulation | None |
| Hatch and Badinelli (1999) *IEEE-EM* | Life-cycle costing TCO | Not specified (tests with typical data from military logistics support) | This paper presents a model-based approach to coordinate concurrent engineering and to support decision-making among cross-functional design-team members. The model uses dynamic programming to minimize life-cycle costs/total costs of ownership while attempting to achieve a good level of product availability. The model | Non-empirical: analytical | None |

**Table 14.** (*Continued*)

| Author (Date) | Cost Management Method(s) | Industry | Summary (Regarding the Focal Cost Management Method) | Type of Data | Field Work |
|---|---|---|---|---|---|
| | | | includes an algorithm that selects the best combination of options and computes the resulting product availability and LCC. The model is tested with several samples of realistic input parameters regarding military logistics support. | | |
| Hegde (1994) *IIE* | Life-cycle costing | Durable goods industry | This paper presents a model to estimate LCC for a durable product (e.g., a computer) by considering failure cost data, which engineers may obtain from field support. The model is illustrated with a numerical example, which suggests that considering failure cost may be critical for selecting design alternatives. The authors further stress the need for improved cost information sharing between engineering and the field support function. | Non-empirical: analytical | None |
| Johnson and Wang (1995) *IJPR* | Design for X Life-cycle costing | Technology & Telecommunication | The disassembly of products is the prime issue in this research. A model is developed to support and improve material recovery. Besides the opportunity to reuse some materials at the end of a product's life, LCC of a product were also considered. This was accomplished through a DFX approach, supported by LCC. An example is provided that demonstrates the approach. | Non-empirical: simulation | None |
| Kleyner and Sandborn (2008) *IJPE* | Life-cycle costing | Automotive | This paper investigates the relationship between the reliability of a product and its life-cycle costs. The model creates different scenarios through a Monte Carlo simulation to estimate the trade-off. To testify its applicability, the model is illustrated in an example in the automotive industry. Findings indicate that the regularly requested +99% in reliability may be not the optimum when considering the life-cycle cost. | Non-empirical: simulation | None |

| Study | Method | Industry | Description | Type | Classification |
|---|---|---|---|---|---|
| Mangun and Thurston (2002) *IEEE-EM* | Life-cycle costing Design for X | Not specified (example from personal computer industry) | This paper develops a model for incorporating long-range planning for component reuse in product design. The model employs a product portfolio approach based on market segmentation, rather than a single product. The model is embedded in a decision tool for when a product should be taken back, and which components should be reused, recycled, or disposed. A case study of a line of personal computers (PCs) demonstrates an implementation of the model. It uses cost information on product take-back and disassembly and therefore represents a form of LCC, even though LCC is not literally mentioned in the paper. One important finding is that allowing the possibility of reuse, remanufacture, or recycling actually improved cost, environmental impact and customer satisfaction when a company was exposed to product take-back legislation. | Empirical: archival | Engineering, "how to" |
| Mildenberger and Khare (2000) *Techn* | Life-cycle costing | Automotive | The paper focusses on the environmental issues in the automobile industry and the environmental impact presently associated with the automobile's life-cycle. The paper reviews existing tools and opportunities for reducing these burdens in the future through decision-making by the industry and other stakeholders. LCC tools are briefly introduced and related to the automotive industry. | Non-empirical: theoretical | None |
| Neto et al. (2010) *IJPR* | Life-cycle costing | Metals & Electronics | This paper researches the sustainability of closed loop supply chains (CLSCs). A fictional case study is presented. In this model for CLSCs, LCC is addressed as a method to manage costs, and life-cycle assessment is seen as a method to get an overview of the environmental impacts. The model can be used for the development of sustainable products. | Non-empirical: simulation | None |

**Table 14.** (*Continued*)

| Author (Date) | Cost Management Method(s) | Industry | Summary (Regarding the Focal Cost Management Method) | Type of Data | Field Work |
|---|---|---|---|---|---|
| Riggs and Jones (1990) *IEEE-EM* | Life-cycle costing | Not specified | Using a hypothetical example of a radar system, this paper presents a graphical representation technique, called a flow graph, illustrating the interrelationships between the variables and functions to conduct LCC analyses. Advantages include computational solvability, the graphical representation, which makes logical errors more evident, as well as reduced time necessary for someone to comprehend the cost system. | Non-empirical: analytical | None |
| Tubigand Abetti (1990) *IEEE-EM* | Life-cycle costing | U.S. Defense | Conducting a survey, this paper assesses the effects of various factors on defense R&D contractor performance. The authors give advice on which type of contract to choose for major development programs and whether to initiate competition between several contractors. LCC is recommended to ensure cost-effectiveness. | Empirical: survey | None |
| Usher and Whitfield (1993) *IIE* | Life-cycle costing | Not specified | This paper proposes a model for estimating the total life of each component in a used, multi-component system through the use of fuzzy set theory and linguistic variables. The resulting component life estimates provide the times at which a cost for component replacement is incurred. Based on this assessment, a cost model is set up to estimate the annual costs for owning and operating the system. This enables selecting the least expensive system. The model is demonstrated with a hypothetical example. | Non-empirical: analytical | None |
| Zhang (1999) *IJPR* | QFD Life-cycle costing | Automotive | See Table 11. | Non-empirical: simulation | None |

**Table 15.** Results for Total Cost of Ownership.

| Author (Date) Journal | Cost Management Method(s) | Industry | Summary (Regarding the Focal Cost Management Method) | Type of Data | Field Work |
|---|---|---|---|---|---|
| Goffin (1998) *JPIM* | TCO Design for X | High-technology companies (+ case study at Hewlett-Packard) | Based on a survey, this paper investigates how companies assess product support requirements within the design stage. Additionally, a case study was undertaken, and evidence suggests that by considering a variety of these requirements in design, reducing the complexity of the product may save costs. For instance, facilitating software upgrades of the product (termed Design for Upgradability) resulted in considerable cost savings, also in terms of cost of ownership for the company's customers. | Empirical: mix | Case study |
| Goffin (2000) *RTM* | Life-cycle costing TCO Design for X | Multiple industries | See Table 14. | Empirical: qualitative | Management practice |
| Heilala, Helin, and Montonen (2006) *IJPR* | TCO | Manufacturing | A TCO analysis tool is introduced to improve the design of modular assembly systems. It is based on selected industrial standards and the authors' own experience of assembly system design and simulation. The TCO method is claimed to be useful in system-supplier and end-user communication, and helps in trade-off analyses of system concepts. A fictitious case study illustrates the use of the TCO method. | Non-empirical: simulation | None |
| Plank and Ferrin (2002) *IMM* | Target costing TCO | Mainly manufacturing industries | See Table 9. | Empirical: survey | None |

**Table 15.** (*Continued*)

| Author (Date) Journal | Cost Management Method(s) | Industry | Summary (Regarding the Focal Cost Management Method) | Type of Data | Field Work |
|---|---|---|---|---|---|
| Sohn and Kim (2011) *IEEE-EM* | TCO | Not specified | This paper applied an adapted cost of ownership model (Kim, Kim, Jeon, & Sohn, 2009) to address the international standardization of related technologies. The model helped to identify the most promising projects and enabled their joint, effective development under consideration of budget constraints. Joint development might lead to higher benefits while at the same time lowering costs. The model was applied in an example of radio-frequency identification (RFID) technology development. | Non-empirical: simulation | None |
| Wouters et al. (2009) *JOM* | TCO | Diverse | The subject of the paper is monetary quantification of points of difference. Interviews and a survey are conducted to investigate the use of such information during NPD projects. TCO, although beneficial in principle, is very hard to implement in the design process. The need for information is too large and it takes too much time for most NPD projects. | Empirical: qualitative | None |

## Stage-Gate Reviews

Stage-gate reviews is a considerable topic in the IOM literature with 24 results (9%). In contrast, this was quite an unimportant topic in the MA literature with six results (4%). Most research published in two journals, namely *JPIM* with eight results and *RTM* with six results. The number of results is not only high in absolute terms but it is also much larger than the expected number of results. Surveys represent the most used research method for stage-gate reviews, with nine results. This is large both in absolute terms and compared to the expected number.

More detailed results are in Table 16. Research on development of stage-gate systems has been stimulated by Robert G. Cooper's observations of management practice since the late 1970s. Stage-gate reviews, stage-gate systems, or stage-gate processes provide a common engineering model according to which a product development process can be organized. As a conceptual and operational management tool, it is intended to structure the process from a new product idea to the final product's launch, to increase both its effectiveness and efficiency (Cooper & Kleinschmidt, 1991). Cooper analyzed many products from different companies, identifying several numbers of factors that lead to financial success, and he proposed the stage-gate process as a formal, systematic development process. Five papers that Cooper authored or coauthored are incorporated in this literature review. Many papers propose pragmatic ideas about stage-gate systems, sometimes only conceptually (e.g., Boer, 2003; Bremser & Barsky, 2004), sometimes with empirical support based on real-life case studies (e.g., Baker & Bourne, 2014; Boardman & Clegg, 2001; Coldrick, Longhurst, Ivey, & Hannis, 2005; Kumar & Wellbrock, 2009; Reitzig, 2011).

Stage-gate reviews are almost never researched in combination with another cost management method. Of the nine survey-based papers, six have been published in *JPIM*. The survey-based research mostly focuses on the antecedents and consequences of using stage-gate systems, but some of the qualitative and mixed studies also investigate factors around the use of this method (e.g., Harmancioglu, McNally, Calantone, & Durmusoglu, 2007; Stevens, Burley, & Divine, 1999; Van Oorschot, Akkermans, Sengupta, & Van Wassenhove, 2013; Van Oorschot, Sengupta, Akkermans, & Van Wassenhove, 2010).

**Table 16.** Results for Stage-Gate Reviews.

| Author (Date) Journal | Cost Management Method(s) | Industry | Summary (Regarding the Focal Cost Management Method) | Type of Data | Field Work |
|---|---|---|---|---|---|
| Baker and Bourne (2014) *RTM* | Stage-gate reviews | Footwear and apparel industry | This paper proposes a governance framework to be applied during stage-gate processes, specifically to assist managers at gate-decisions. Through feedforward control, this framework gives signals to managers to consider a reassessment of the current product portfolio. The application in a footwear and apparel company resulted in scaled down product portfolios, improved productivity and increased profit. | Empirical: observations | Engineering, "how to" |
| Boardman and Clegg (2001) *IJOPM* | Stage-gate reviews | Aerospace | The paper investigates the product development process for aerospace products and an extended enterprise. These products are usually too complex for a single company. A framework for structuring and synchronizing phases and stage-gates is proposed as solution for several problems, including the coordination of different companies within the NPD process. Benefits from the stage-gate process are pointed out as maximum return on substantial investments. | Empirical: observations | Case study |
| Boer (2003) *RTM* | Stage-gate reviews | Not specified | This paper proposes a method to value projects adjusting for high risk, by applying discounted cash flows, decision trees and real options. The method is presented in a fictive business case using extensive calculations and explanations. The stage-gate concept is not specifically emphasized, yet the author recommends applying this method in stage-gate management systems. He sees benefits for decision-making in cases where projects yield zero or slightly negative net present values. | Non-empirical: theoretical | None |

| Source | Tool/method | Industry | Description | Empirical status | Contribution |
|---|---|---|---|---|---|
| Bremser and Barsky (2004) *RADMA* | Stage-gate reviews | Not specified | Building on the notion that R&D is a determining factor in strategy implementation, this paper proposes the integration of the stage-gate approach with the balanced scorecard. This aim is to link resource commitments with strategic objectives through a balanced mix of financial and non-financial metrics in R&D. In a theoretical example, the authors illustrate how R&D- and stage-gate-related metrics can be mapped to strategic indicators in the balanced scorecard. This integrated scorecard is to be cascaded top-down to achieve agreement across several management levels. | Non-empirical: theoretical | None |
| Chai, Wang, Song, Halman, and Brombacher (2012) *JPIM* | Stage-gate reviews Product platforms | Multiple non-service industries (the United States) | See Table 22. | Empirical: survey | None |
| Coldrick et al. (2005) *Techn* | Stage-gate reviews | Not specified | This paper applies an earlier model (Lockwood, 1999) to a sample of projects. The model includes scoring models, a risk assessment, a cost-benefit analysis and discounted cash flows. The model aims to make the project selection process more transparent and to support decision-making. The authors suggest incorporating the model in stage-gate systems as a method for go/kill-decisions. | Empirical: mix | Engineering, "how to" |
| Cooper (2006) *RTM* | Stage-gate reviews | Multiple industries | This paper describes how a selection of companies has approached fundamental research or technology management projects with adapted stage-gate processes. Cost management is not specifically in focus, but the author criticizes the excessive use of financial tools and data. Because of the highly uncertain nature of the projects, numerical estimates of expected sales, costs, investment, and profits are likely to be very inaccurate. Instead, the author suggests a predominantly qualitative scorecard method to support decision-making at gates. | Empirical: qualitative | Management practice |

**Table 16.** (Continued)

| Author (Date) Journal | Cost Management Method(s) | Industry | Summary (Regarding the Focal Cost Management Method) | Type of Data | Field Work |
|---|---|---|---|---|---|
| Cooper (2013) *RTM* | Stage-gate reviews | Multiple industries | This paper addresses the question how to manage and foster breakthrough innovations. The author draws on models and tools used in leading companies to show different approaches to portfolio management. For the stage-gate model, the use of scoring models instead of sophisticated financial metrics at early stages, and an option-based investment model at later stages are proposed. The overall intent is to guard venturesome, but promising projects against kill-decisions during early stages. | Empirical: qualitative | Management practice |
| Cooper and Kleinschmidt (1991) *IMM* | Stage-gate reviews | Multiple industries | This paper reports the impact on performance achieved by five different companies after implementing stage-gate and other new product processes. Improved product success rates, higher customer satisfaction and meeting time, quality and cost objectives were the most frequently cited areas of positive impact. Furthermore, other aspects of new product processes are explored (e.g., deficiencies, suggested improvements, and the motivation for implementing the process). | Empirical: qualitative | Case study |
| Cooper and Kleinschmidt (1995) *JPIM* | Stage-gate reviews | Multiple industries | This paper is based on a benchmarking study among 135 companies active in product development. The study included 10 different performance metrics (e.g., on sales, profits, etc.), which were reduced to two underlying performance dimensions and illustrated on a "new product performance map." Four groups of firms were identified, associated with distinct success factors in NPD. The authors concluded among that successful firms employ well-executed, thorough and flexible NPD processes. | Empirical: survey | None |

| Reference | Focus | Industry/Context | Description | Method | Framework |
|---|---|---|---|---|---|
| Cooper and Kleinschmidt (2007) *RTM* | Stage-gate reviews | Multiple industries | This is a reprint of an earlier paper (Cooper & Kleinschmidt, 1996) with reflections of the authors. They comment that their research has led them to develop a "performance diamond," intended to represent the four key success drivers of NPD. | Empirical: survey | None |
| Ettlie and Elsenbach (2007) *JPIM* | Stage-gate reviews | Automotive industry (assemblers and suppliers) | Conducting a survey among 72 automotive engineering managers supervising the NPD process of assemblers and suppliers, this study addresses various aspects of (modified) stage-gate processes. The study suggests that companies optimize trade-offs between cost and quality after they graduate from more typical stage-process management to modified regimes. This modified stage-gate was significantly related to NPD process improvement and superiority of commercialization. | Empirical: survey | None |
| Harmancioglu et al. (2007) *RADMA* | Stage-gate reviews | Building materials industry | In an exploratory case study of three companies in the building materials industry, this paper investigates how the NPD processes differ across companies with a strategic objective of innovation-induced growth. Relying on in-depth interviews with managers and engineers, it is proposed the use of formal stage-gate processes is negatively related to innovation performance. This also applies to senior-level involvement, because projects with low risk and short-term rewards may more likely be selected instead of breakthrough products. | Empirical: qualitative | Case study |
| Hart, Hultink, Tzokas, and Commandeur (2003) *JPIM* | Stage-gate reviews | Industrial goods companies (the Netherlands and the United Kingdom) | This paper presents the results of a study on the evaluation criteria that companies use at several gates in the NPD process. The findings from 166 managers suggest that companies use different criteria at different NPD evaluation gates. While such criteria as technical feasibility, intuition and market potential are stressed in the early screening gates of the NPD process, a focus on product performance, quality, and staying within the development budget are | Empirical: survey | None |

**Table 16.** (Continued)

| Author (Date) Journal | Cost Management Method(s) | Industry | Summary (Regarding the Focal Cost Management Method) | Type of Data | Field Work |
|---|---|---|---|---|---|
| | | | considered of paramount importance after the product has been developed. The financial dimension emerges prominently in the business analysis gate and gains importance in the short- and long-term performance evaluation after launch. | | |
| Jägle (1999) *RADMA* | Stage-gate reviews | Technology-intensive companies | The paper proposes a binomial valuation framework which links the NPD process with real options. The different phases in this process are regarded as real options on the next phase in order to model uncertainty and quantify flexibility and risk. Stage-gate is presented as an emblematic sequential NPD process, which allows for the application of the valuation framework. In two numerical examples, the results of the framework are compared those of the discounted cash flow tree. The application of the framework is also demonstrated in a case study, dealing with the options-based valuation for the initial public offering of a biotech company. | Empirical: archival | Engineering, "how to" |
| Kleinschmidt, De Brentani, and Salomo (2007) *JPIM* | Stage-gate reviews | Multiple industries (business-to-business; North America, Europe) | The paper tests a model of the impact of organizational resources (e.g., top management involvement, NPD process formality) on global NPD program performance, mediated by global NPD process capabilities. While stage-gate processes were not in focus, NPD process formality (as applicable in stage-gate systems) did not exhibit a direct, significant impact on financial performance. Evidence suggests that a more formal process permits the effective deployment of NPD process capabilities that significantly impact global NPD program outcome. However, for very | Empirical: survey | None |

| Author (Year) Journal | Industry | Type | Description | | |
|---|---|---|---|---|---|
| | | | innovative or entrepreneurial projects it may impede the access to new markets, products, and technological arenas. | | |
| Kumar and Wellbrock (2009) *IJPR* | Metals and electronics | Stage-gate reviews | Based on observations in a company, the paper suggests a new way to manage the product introduction process. The model is based on Cooper's Stage-gate process with some modifications regarding the different stages. Cost savings are expressed in time reductions. These are reduction of design engineer's time, CAD service time, and general development time. | Empirical: observations | Case study |
| Ozer and Cebeci (2010) *IEEE-EM* | Multiple industries (Chinese Hong Kong firms) | Stage-gate reviews | This study investigates the relationship between the development of new products with a global market focus and the performance of NPD programs, and investigates various organizational, procedural, and operational conditions that may moderate this relationship. Using a stage-gate process was found to be of high importance in global R&D. It was positively related to financial performance and it had a positive moderating role in the relationship between a firm's global market focus in its NPD and the financial performance of its NPD programs. | Empirical: survey | None |
| Schultz, Salomo, De Brentani, and Kleinschmidt (2013) *JPIM* | Manufactured goods and services companies (Austria and Denmark) | Stage-gate reviews | This paper evaluates NPD programs in terms of formal control mechanisms, their immediate outcomes and the influence of the degree of NPD innovativeness. Stage-gate systems did not directly impact NPD program performance, yet transparent decision-making emerged as a mediator. The results suggest that this mediated relationship also holds when the degree of innovativeness of the NPD program is high. It is also found that when firms are involved in more innovative NPD programs, project management control systems should be combined with higher organizational level stage-gate-type processes. | Empirical: survey | None |
| Stevens et al. (1999) *JPIM* | Chemical industry | Stage-gate reviews | This paper investigates the role of individual creativity in effectively analyzing early-stage NPD project ideas. All NPD analysts taking part in the research were extensively trained | Empirical: mix | Case study |

**Table 16.** (*Continued*)

| Author (Date) Journal | Cost Management Method(s) | Industry | Summary (Regarding the Focal Cost Management Method) | Type of Data | Field Work |
|---|---|---|---|---|---|
| | | | in stage-gate business discipline. It was found that having creative analysts in the early stages and a high-quality NPD system increased profitability. The average profit achieved by "creative" NPD analysts exceeded that of analysts with a low creativity-measure by a factor of 12.5. | | |
| Tzokas, Hultink, and Hart (2004) *IMM* | Stage-gate reviews | Industrial and consumer goods industries (the United Kingdom and the Netherlands) | This study presents empirical evidence of the evaluative criteria used by experienced NPD managers from the United Kingdom and the Netherlands to control performance at different gates of the NPD process. Findings show that financial criteria (profit objectives, the internal rate of return, ROI, etc.) were predominantly applied at the business analysis gate. In contrast to previous research, financial criteria were used less frequently than market-based criteria (except for the business analysis gate). | Empirical: survey | None |
| Van Oorschot et al. (2013) *AMJ* | Stage-gate reviews | Automotive | This paper investigates failures of NPD projects. A stage-gate managed project is used as real case example. The findings suggest that teams in complex dynamic environments characterized by delays are subject to multiple "information filters" that blur their perception of actual project performance. Consequently, teams do not realize their projects are in trouble and repeatedly fall into a "decision trap" in which they stretch current project stages at the expense of future stages. This slowly and gradually reduces the likelihood of project success. However, because of the information filters, teams fail to notice what is happening until it is too late. | Empirical: observations | Case study |

| | | | | | |
|---|---|---|---|---|---|
| Van Oorschot et al. (2010) *JPIM* | Stage-gate reviews | Semiconductor industry | This paper seeks to examine whether using stage-gates may lead companies also to abandon some "right" projects (that could have become successful). This was tested by applying a system dynamics model on an exemplary NPD project. The simulation results suggest that when faced with asymmetrical uncertainty, relaxing constraints set up by stage-gate may save projects and ensure the timely completion within budget. Further managerial implications are derived. | Empirical: mix | Case study |
| Walwyn, Taylor, and Brickhill (2002) *RTM* | Stage-gate reviews | Chemical and pharmaceutical industry | Relying on the theory of bond pricing, this paper puts forth a calculation method to compute a risk-adjusted internal rate of return for research projects. The method can be applied at every stage in a stage-gate process and aims to improve the returns from R&D by ensuring that a portfolio of research projects achieves across time the cost of capital. | Empirical: archival | Engineering, "how to" |

*Funnels*

For funnels, we found only very few results (3), comparable to Wouters and Morales (2014), with 1% in both studies. Detailed information on both studies is provided in Table 17. One remarkable pattern is that all three studies aim at providing very pragmatic guidance, which we have labeled "management practice research," and focus only on funnels, so not in combination with any other cost management method.

*Design for Manufacturing/Assembly (DFM/DFA) and*
*Design for X (DFX)*

Because both topics are closely related, we will discuss these together. The number of results in the IOM literature is 21 and 17, together 14% of all results, so quite average. In contrast, the MA literature included only nine results for both methods together (6%) and these had all but one been published in *Decision Sciences* or *Management Science*. So, when moving these journals to the IOM sample, the topic disappears from the MA literature.

*IJPR* and *JPIM* published most of the results for both methods, but this is not higher than would be expected based on the overall share of results in these two journals. In terms of research methods, DFM/A was most often researched with surveys and DFX based on mixed data, and these methods were also used considerably more often than what would be expected. Empirical methods in general are used in the majority of studies of both cost management methods.

More detailed results are in Tables 18 and 19. Several studies provide refinements of the methods for DFM/A and DFX. Some provide indications of the effects of these based on numerical simulation (Curran et al., 2007; Das & Kanchanapiboon, 2011; Madan, Rao, & Kundra, 2007; Taylor, 1997), whereas other studies provide empirical support for such refinements (Bevilacqua, Ciarapica, & Giacchetta, 2007; Boer & Logendran, 1999; Chan & Lewis, 2000; Dowlatshahi, 1995; Ijomah, McMahon, Hammond, & Newman, 2007; Lin, Lee, & Bohez, 2012; Lu & Wood, 2006; Pullan, Bhasi, & Madhu, 2012).

Several studies based on surveys focus on explaining the antecedents and consequences of the use of DFM/A or DFX (Kessler, 2000; Liker, Collins, & Hull, 1999; Marion & Meyer, 2011; Rusinko, 1999; Swink & Nair, 2007). One study with a similar objective is based on archival data of a limited number of cases (Wang & Trolio, 2001). A special kind of study is the

**Table 17.** Results for Funnels.

| Author (Date) Journal | Cost Management Method(s) | Industry | Summary (Regarding the Focal Cost Management Method) | Type of Data | Field Work |
|---|---|---|---|---|---|
| Mathews (2010) *RTM* | Funnels | Aerospace and defense company (Boeing) | This paper presents a multi-phase innovation portfolio process at Boeing to address enhanced customer requirements and competition. It is set up to effectively funnel more and higher-quality ideas and concepts into the project portfolio for development and execution, based on quantitative assessments. The innovation portfolio was supported by management and represented a more methodical approach than the company's former way of concept selection. | Empirical: observations | Management practice |
| Mathews (2011) *RTM* | Funnels | Aerospace and defense company (Boeing) | Building on Mathews (2010), this paper provides insight in how a business unit at Boeing values, assesses and selects concepts and ideas before full investment is made for their development. A multi-phase innovation portfolio process is presented for focusing the stream of ideas and shaping the project portfolio. The author describes attributes and metrics used by this business unit for their decision-making. | Empirical: observations | Management practice |
| Reitzig (2011) *MIT SMR* | Funnels | Not specified | The paper deals with an improved way for selecting ideas for new products or other improvements related to the company. It is based on analysis of thousands of idea proposals as well as observations within a company. Problems are outlined and a framework for a customized selection funnel is proposed to save money and time for the organization. | Empirical: mix | Management practice |

**Table 18.** Results for Design for Manufacturing/Assembly.

| Author (Date) Journal | Cost Management Method(s) | Industry | Summary (Regarding the Focal Cost Management Method) | Type of Data | Field Work |
|---|---|---|---|---|---|
| Boer and Logendran (1999) *IIE* | DFM/A | Electromechanical assemblies company (the United States) | This paper puts forth a "how to" method for empirical research on the effects of product development characteristics on project/product success (i.e., cost and time). The authors suggest using variables that address DFM issues, especially if the company is interested in understanding the associations with cost. The method was applied at a manufacturing company in the United States. The approach is explained in detail and practical advice is given. In the example, it is found that cost increased, as the number of parts in a product and the number of assembly processes increased. | Empirical: archival | Engineering, "how to" |
| Chan and Lewis (2000) *IJPR* | DFM/A | Metals and electronics | The paper introduces a computerized DFM tool for small to medium-sized enterprises for integrating information about costs and manufacturability during product development. The tool has been developed together with six companies, but actual applications are not reported in any detail. | Empirical: qualitative | None |
| Curran et al. (2007) *IJPE* | DFM/A | Not specified | The main contribution of the work is to present a method that facilitates the integration of design and manufacturing modeling at the concept design stage, including cost. The paper presents an illustration of the application of this method to the fuselage of a commercial regional jet. | Non-empirical: simulation | None |
| Das and Kanchanapiboon (2011) *IJPR* | DFM/A | Consumer goods | Pro-DFM, a multi-criteria model for manufacturability analysis that identifies cost-reduction opportunities is presented. Pro-DFM assumes the NPD team has a baseline estimate of production costs, and it evaluates how DFM issues will affect the expected unit production cost. The Pro-DFM model analyses a new design on three factors: part procurement and handling, product assembly | Non-empirical: simulation | None |

| Reference | Method | Industry | Description | Type | |
|---|---|---|---|---|---|
| | | | fabrication processes, and inventory costs. A numerical example demonstrates the DFM evaluation process. | | |
| Dowlatshahi (1995) *IJPE* | DFM/A | Metals and electronics | This paper details a real-life proposal that describes a design of self-contained, integrated manufacturing and assembly for pipe valves. It presents a detailed and comprehensive analysis of part design, manufacturing operations, and manufacturing system design. The part design is subjected to a set of DFM/DFA tests and it has been significantly revised and upgraded. These revisions or improvements provide for ease as well as economical manufacture and assembly operations. | Empirical: observations | None |
| Heim et al. (2012) *IEEE-EM* | QFD DFM/A | Manufacturing industries | See Table 11. | Empirical: survey | None |
| Kessler (2000) *JETM* | DFM/A | Multiple industries | This paper presents the results of a survey among large companies in multiple industries and assesses the impact of various methods on NPD costs. A significant relationship between DFM and development costs was not found. However, the study examines several other methods which are linked to this present literature review in a broader sense (e.g., team autonomy, process overlap, etc.), which is why this paper is included. | Empirical: survey | None |
| Liker et al. (1999) *JPIM* | DFM/A | Multiple industries | This paper proposes and tests a contingency model of system integration of product design and manufacturing (DMSI) among producers of goods involving tooling development. The model predicts which combinations of organizational and technical practices will be most effective under conditions of high and low design newness. DMSI is operationalized as a combination of DFM and flexible manufacturing capability. As one result, it was found that DMSI has a strong, direct effect on manufacturing time and cost. | Empirical: survey | None |

**Table 18.** (Continued)

| Author (Date) Journal | Cost Management Method(s) | Industry | Summary (Regarding the Focal Cost Management Method) | Type of Data | Field Work |
|---|---|---|---|---|---|
| Lin et al. (2012) *IJPR* | DFM/A | Metals and electronics | This paper describes an integrated model to estimate the manufacturing cost and production system performance at the conceptual design stage. A fully automated conceptual framework for DFM is developed. The model was incorporated in a computer program and tested for the design of helicopter rotor blades. | Empirical: observations | Engineering, "how to" |
| Loch et al. (1996) *JPIM* | Value engineering DFM/A Design for X | Electronics industry | See Table 10. | Empirical: survey | None |
| Lu and Wood (2006) *IJOPM* | DFM/A Design for X | Metals and electronics | Starting point of this paper is the argumentation that DFM moves in the product realization chain from product design to the process execution, ignoring the process design stage. To overcome this issue, DFM is refined and split in diverse "design for" elements. The findings suggest a positive impact on the performance of product realization (especially time to market) and thus operational competitiveness. | Empirical: observations | Case study |
| Madan et al. (2007) *IJPR* | DFM/A | Manufacturing | A computer-aided system for early cost estimation, feature-cost sensitivity and optimal machine loading for die-casting is presented. It can be used both as a DFM as well as an early cost-estimation tool for preparing quotations. The system suggests a minimum cost to manufacture a part, accounting for the possibility of using of multi-cavity dies and with available resources, namely die-casting machines. | Non-empirical: simulation | None |
| Martínez Sánchez and Pérez (2003) *JPIM* | Value engineering DFM/A DFM/A | Automotive suppliers (Spain) | See Table 10. | Empirical: survey | None |

| Reference | DFX | Industry | Description | Research type | Contribution |
|---|---|---|---|---|---|
| Pullan et al. (2012) *IJPR* | | Metals and electronics | This paper describes an integrated manufacturing framework to link the design stage to the other stages in the manufacturing systems. A model is developed using object oriented technology, based on the fundamental elements necessary for modeling of manufacturing, process planning, and collaborative design of machine tools. | Empirical: observations | Engineering, "how to" |
| Rusinko (1999) *IEEE-EM* | DFM/A | Manufacturing companies (the United States) | This paper reports results of a quantitative study of design-manufacturing integration (DMI) practices to facilitate effective new product development (NPD). Some of the DMI practices assessed are related to DFM (i.e., using manufacturability guidelines in design). The use of manufacturability guidelines was found to be positively associated with effective NPD, whereas the effect of the applicability of these guidelines (which means they are applicable to more than one project) was negative. | Empirical: survey | None |
| Ray and Ray (2011) *Techn* | DFM/A Design for X Modular design | Automotive (Tata Motors) | The "Nano" of Tata Motors is one of the cheapest cars in the world. This paper investigates how Tata Motors' choices regarding the use of technology, product design and organizational practices for NPD enabled it to meet the challenge of innovation for India's masses. It is shown that the Nano is systematically optimized for cost (e.g., using less components, less material). Even though DFM and "design for cost" as a form of DFX are not explicitly mentioned, the paper in its entirety makes it evident that these methods have been employed. Moreover, a modular product architecture was used to lower assembly and logistics costs. | Empirical: mix | Case study |
| Sik Oh, O'Grady, and Young (1995) *IIE* | DFM/A | Not specified | Product design is subject to constraints, which may be interconnected, forming a constraint network. A DFA system is developed and programmed as a constraint network in order to support the designer. The program provides the designer with the total assembly cost and may suggest changes to the design, if a lower cost is desired. | Non-empirical: theoretical | None |

**Table 18.** (*Continued*)

| Author (Date) Journal | Cost Management Method(s) | Industry | Summary (Regarding the Focal Cost Management Method) | Type of Data | Field Work |
|---|---|---|---|---|---|
| Swink and Nair (2007) *JOM* | DFM/A | Manufacturing | This paper describes and tests a theory of complementarities between design-manufacturing integration (DMI) and usage of advanced manufacturing technologies (AMT). The study focusses on aspects of DMI such as concurrent engineering and DFM/A. The authors analyze data from 224 manufacturing plants in order to test the hypotheses that DMI moderates the relationships between AMT usage and manufacturing performance. Regression analysis results indicate that DMI plays the role of complementary asset to AMT usage when quality, delivery and process flexibility are considered. A complementary role is not observed for cost efficiency and new product flexibility. In fact, the results suggest that combined high levels of DMI and AMT usage can be costly. | Empirical: survey | None |
| Taylor (1997) *IIE* | DFM/A Design for X | Not specified | This paper provides a mathematical model for design for global manufacturing and assembly (DFGMA) to assist designers in making optimal sourcing, capital procurement, and market timing decisions in a multi-facility, global environment. The DFGMA model incorporates various kinds of costs (e.g., design costs, inventory costs, etc.) and has the objective to minimize the sum of all of these costs. It is designed to make product sourcing decisions during the design stage. It may also help in designing products in a way to exploit existing tooling capabilities at multiple facilities. | Non-empirical: simulation | None |

| | | | | | |
|---|---|---|---|---|---|
| Trygg (1993) *JPIM* | QFD DFM/A | Manufacturing industry (Sweden) | See Table 11. | Empirical: survey | None |
| Wang and Trolio (2001) *IJPR* | DFM/A | Diverse | This paper studies the benefits of DFA. It investigates 12 product cases that employed DFA method for redesign and it was found that DFA benefits correlate with product assembly properties. These were measured using manual handling and insertion assembly elements. Two sets of correlation models for estimating potential DFA benefits were developed. An example is provided to illustrate the estimation procedure and its result. | Empirical: archival | None |

**Table 19.** Results for Design for X.

| Author (Date) Journal | Cost Management Method(s) | Industry | Summary (Regarding the Focal Cost Management Method) | Type of Data | Field Work |
|---|---|---|---|---|---|
| Bevilacqua et al. (2007) *IJPR* | Design for X | Metals and electronics | The paper proposes a new way for combining environmental and economic considerations with sustainable development. It is based on integrating Design for Environment method and the life-cycle assessment technique. A case study of an electrical distribution board manufacturer demonstrated how environmental expertise can be integrated into the design process without much extra effort. For cost management an environmental/economical break-even point was calculated. | Empirical: observations | Engineering, "how to" |
| Bordoloi and Guerrero (2008) *IJPE* | Design for X | Not specified | The paper introduces "Design for Control" (DFC) to manage the costs associated with the introduction of new products to the manufacturing control system. | Non-empirical: theoretical | None |
| Brad (2009) *IJPR* | QFD Design for X | Consumer goods | See Table 11. | Non-empirical: simulation | None |
| Elgh and Cederfeldt (2007) *IJPE* | Design for X | Manufacturing | The paper introduces a cost-estimation tool in NPD. The tool is aligned with principles of DFP (Design for Producibility), a method close to DFM. It can serve as a decisions tool that enables the evaluation of different courses of action in the early stages in the development of product variants. The tool was applied and realized through a software implementation in the case of the design of heavy welded steel structures. | Empirical: mix | Engineering, "how to" |

| Reference | Method(s) | Industry/Context | Notes | Empirical type | Approach |
|---|---|---|---|---|---|
| Fargnoli et al. (2013) *JETM* | QFD, Design for X | Gardening equipment firm (Italy) | See Table 11. | Empirical: mix | Case study |
| Goffin (1998) *JPIM* | TCO, Design for X | High-technology companies | See Table 15. | Empirical: mix | Case study |
| Goffin (2000) *RTM* | Life-cycle costing, TCO, Design for X | Multiple industries | See Table 14. | Empirical: qualitative | Management practice |
| Grote et al. (2007) *IJPR* | Life-cycle costing, Design for X | Consumer goods | See Table 14. | Non-empirical: simulation | None |
| Ijomah et al. (2007) *IJPR* | Design for X | Diverse | The aim of this paper is the development of design-for-remanufacturing guidelines to support the development of green products. Multiple case studies in the mechanical and electromechanical sector of the United Kingdom are used as a foundation. Findings suggest environmental issues are not the first reason to implement such a method, more likely the economic benefits are a major driver followed by the desire to have a green image. | Empirical: mix | Case study |
| Johnson and Wang (1995) *IJPR* | Life-cycle costing, Design for X | Technology and telecommunication | See Table 14. | Non-empirical: simulation | None |
| Loch et al. (1996) *JPIM* | Value engineering, DFM/A, Design for X | Electronics industry | See Table 10. | Empirical: survey | None |
| Lu and Wood (2006) *IJOPM* | DFM/A, Design for X | Metals and electronics | See Table 18. | Empirical: observations | Case study |
| Mangun and Thurston (2002) *IEEE-EM* | Life-cycle costing, Design for X | Not specified (example from personal computer industry). | See Table 14. | Empirical: archival | Engineering, "how to" |

**Table 19.** (*Continued*)

| Author (Date) Journal | Cost Management Method(s) | Industry | Summary (Regarding the Focal Cost Management Method) | Type of Data | Field Work |
|---|---|---|---|---|---|
| Marion and Meyer (2011) *JPIM* | Design for X | Physical assembled products where design plays a role, less than 10 years old. | Using a survey and subsequent in-depth interviews, this study investigates the impact of industrial design and cost engineering (which we consider as a particular form of DFX) activities on NPD and business performance in early-stage firms. Cost engineering showed to have negative effects on product development cost, time and project break-even timing, yet a positive impact on cumulative sales and product margins. When intensively applied jointly with industrial design, cost engineering showed positive effects in terms of product development cost and time as well as project breakeven time. | Empirical: mix | Case study |
| Murthy and Blischke (2000) *IEEE-EM* | Design for X | Manufacturing | This paper provides a life-cycle framework which can be used to formulate a warranty strategy. Warranty costs can be influenced in the design stage of a product. Therefore, this paper puts particular emphasis on several pre-launch stages (e.g., pre-design phase, design phase, etc.). It is described how warranty costs may be influenced before product launch and which cost-trade-offs exist. We consider this DFX, although "design for warranty" is not explicitly mentioned. | Non-empirical: theoretical | None |
| Ray and Ray (2011) *Techn* | DFM/A Design for X Modular design | Automotive (Tata Motors) | See Table 18. | Empirical: mix | Case study |
| Taylor (1997) *IIE* | DFM/A Design for X | Not specified | See Table 18. | Non-empirical: simulation | None |

in-depth descriptive case study of the development of the Nano by Tata Motors and the intense focus on cost targets (Ray & Ray, 2011).

## Component Commonality

In this review, we understand component commonality in an encompassing context, which includes the sharing of parts, materials, modules, tools or packaging. These shared between different products in the sense of product variants in a product family or across subsequent product generations. Within the context of a large company, such sharing may encompass within advanced engineering projects, between corporate departments and organizational units or levels, between suppliers or between globally located institutions (Nobelius & Sundgren, 2002).

Component commonality is a very significant topic in this sample of IOM studies, with 37 results (13%), mostly published in *IJPR* (13 results, although that is not much more than what would be expected based on the overall share of publications in *IJPR*). Simulation is by far the most research method for studying component commonality: 16 results, so around 43% of all results, whereas simulation was used in 24% of all the results. Moreover, component commonality is the topic with the least empirical research methods, namely only 35% (compared to 59% overall). Component commonality is, thus, a very pronounced topic.

Component commonality is strongly related to modular design and product platforms. Indeed, Tables 20–22 with the detailed results for these three methods include many cross references. These three topics are also clearly the most important topics in the IOM literature and together represent 115 results, so about 42%. In contrast, in the IOM literature these topics represented around 28% and most of these had been published in the journals *Decision Sciences* and *Management Science*. When these two journals are shifted to the IOM sample, the contrast becomes very stark, with 45% versus 11% of all results in the IOM literature versus the MA literature for these three cost management methods together.

The more detailed results for component commonality are shown in Table 20. There is much attention to the impact of component commonality on inventory levels, because of the effect of risk-pooling. When components are used for a greater number of products, the fluctuation of demand for these different products may somewhat cancel out and reduce the fluctuation of demand for the components. This inventory risk-pooling effect reduces the inventory level that is required for achieving a particular service

**Table 20.** Results for Component Commonality.

| Author (Date) Journal | Cost Management Method(s) | Industry | Summary (Regarding the Focal Cost Management Method) | Type of Data | Field Work |
|---|---|---|---|---|---|
| Agrawal, Sao, Fernandes, Tiwari, and Kim (2013) *IJPR* | Modular design Component com. Product platforms | Not specified | The paper presents a decision model for the application of modular design and component commonality. The model is tested through numerical simulation with realistic but fictitious data. In most scenarios the combination of both methods is most beneficial. | Non-empirical: simulation | None |
| Caux et al. (2006) *IJPR* | Component com. | Manufacturing | This paper studies the implementation of delayed product differentiation in batch process industries by adding an intermediate stock with highly standardized components. The authors implement their approach as a linear programming model and apply it to the aluminum-conversion industry. In the case the introduction of an intermediate stock was beneficial, because reducing the number of slab types from 100 to 8 enabled the implementation of a make-to-stock strategy at a reasonable cost. | Empirical: observations | Case study |
| Chakravarty (1994) *IIE* | Component com. | Small electromechanical parts assembly | This paper provides a quantitative analysis of flexible assembly capacity, resulting from the choice between either product-specific assembly systems or more expensive flexible assembly systems. Higher component commonality among the parts to be assembled leads to lower fixed and operational costs. | Non-empirical: analytical | None |
| Davila and Wouters (2007) *IJPR* | Component com. | Technology and telecommunication | The paper evaluates the benefits of a postponement strategy on inventory, services and costs. The authors analyze empirical data of a disk drive manufacturer that had redesigned its supply chain by implementing a postponement strategy. An increase in the percentage of generic products had a positive impact on on-time delivery as well as on operational costs but not on | Empirical: archival | Case study |

| Reference | Commonality type | Industry | Description | Method | |
|---|---|---|---|---|---|
| | | | inventory turns. Postponement can be used for improving customer service or reducing inventory. | | |
| DeCroix et al. (2009) *MSOM* | Component com. | Not specified | The paper considers a multiproduct assemble-to-order system with a focus on the impact of returns of components. The value of component commonality depends on how much and which components are recoverable. In most scenarios, component commonality yields cost improvements due to risk-pooling. | Non-empirical: simulation | None |
| Eynan and Rosenblatt (1996) *IIE* | Component com. | Not specified | This paper employs a mathematical single-period model to examine how component commonality affects inventory cost. The optimal inventory level depends on the desired service level. Furthermore, component commonality results in lower inventory cost. However, it is not advisable when the common component is much more expensive. | Non-empirical: analytical | None |
| Farrell and Simpson (2010) *IJPR* | Product platforms Component com. Modular design | Metals and electronics | This paper examines how commonality within the redesign of an existing product line can be improved to achieve cost savings. The method considers manufacturing as well as implementation costs for the choice between a modular or a scaled strategy. The proposed four-step product platform portfolio optimization method shows promise for creating a product platform portfolio from a set of candidate component platforms that is most cost-effective within an existing product line. | Non-empirical: simulation | None |
| Gupta and Benjaafar (2004) *IIE* | Component com. Product platforms | Not specified | This paper presents several mathematical models to examine various aspects of delayed product differentiation (e.g., costs, benefits) of a platform in series production. In one situation, it is determined whether it is more cost-effective to employ several semi-differentiated platforms for different products than a single one. | Non-empirical: simulation | None |

**Table 20.** (*Continued*)

| Author (Date) Journal | Cost Management Method(s) | Industry | Summary (Regarding the Focal Cost Management Method) | Type of Data | Field Work |
|---|---|---|---|---|---|
| Halman et al. (2003) *JPIM* | Component com. Modular design | Multiple industries (OEMs; case studies at ASML, Skil, SDI). | Based on case studies in three technology-driven companies, this paper investigates how and why companies are adopting, developing, implementing, and monitoring platform and product family concepts in practice. Cost benefits were expected, for example through part or component reuse, or modular design. However, most companies mentioned increased development times, costs and complexity of the initial platform as a risk of product family development. | Empirical: qualitative | Case study |
| Heese and Swaminathan (2006) *MSOM* | Component com. | Not specified | This paper discusses the benefits of component commonality when a manufacturer designs a product line consisting of two products sold in two market segments with different valuations of quality. The authors develop a model and analyze the outcomes of cost-reduction efforts. The paper shows that the common assumption commonality leads to cost savings and loss of product differentiation always leads to less attractive product lines and reduced revenues was not supported. An optimally designed product line involving common components might be more attractive and yield higher revenues than a product line based on different variants. | Non-empirical: analytical | None |
| Hillier (2000) *IIE* | Component com. | Not specified | This paper applies a mathematical multi-period model to investigate the impact of component commonality on costs. Component commonality may not be beneficial, in particular if the purchasing or production cost of a common component is even slightly higher than the cost of the respective conventional component which is to be | Non-empirical: simulation | None |

| Reference | Commonality / approach | Context | Description | Method | Study type |
|---|---|---|---|---|---|
| | | | replaced. Savings on inventory costs may not be sufficient to outweigh the additional cost of the common component. Numerical experiments are used to test the benefits of component commonality under varying conditions. | Empirical: mix | Case study |
| Ismail et al. (2007) *IEEE-EM* | Component com. Modular design Product platforms | Small and medium-sized enterprises (SMEs) | This paper introduces and demonstrates, through two case studies, how the principles of mass customization have been adopted by SMEs n the context of manufacturing agility and product flexibility. The paper explores the issues of product configuration, component similarity, and tools and measures of performance to steer the implementation process of mass customization. The authors find that SMEs generally lack the internal costing structures that enable them to clearly quantify the benefits of product rationalization or mass customization. | | |
| Izui et al. (2010) *IJPR* | Component com. | Metals and electronics | The paper analyzes the trade-off among inventory level, delivery lead time and product performance when applying a component commonality approach. The analysis is based on a multi-objective component commonality design optimization problem. The use of component commonality in a fictitious switchgear design case shows inventory cost reductions as well as a reduction of product delivery lead times. | Non-empirical: simulation | None |
| Johnson and Kirchain (2009) *IJPE* | Component com. Product platforms | Automotive | The selection of alternative materials and the use of platform strategy for the design of new products are linked and discussed in this paper. A process-based cost model was applied in a case study in the automotive industry. Results indicated the cost-saving effects of component commonality can be greater than under a product strategy with a focus on cost savings through alternative materials. | Empirical: observations | Case study |

**Table 20.** (*Continued*)

| Author (Date) Journal | Cost Management Method(s) | Industry | Summary (Regarding the Focal Cost Management Method) | Type of Data | Field Work |
|---|---|---|---|---|---|
| Johnson and Kirchain (2010) *IEEE-EM* | Component com. | Automotive OEMs (the United States) | Based on cases of two automotive instrument panel part families and applying a process-based cost-model, this study scrutinizes the relationship between component commonality and cost. Various commonality metrics are assessed to determine how they correlate with cost savings. In both case studies, component commonality resulted in considerable savings, mainly from reductions in assembly and development costs. | Empirical: archival | Engineering, "how to" |
| Liu et al. (2010) *IJPR* | Component com. Modular design Product platforms | Metals and electronics | This paper presents a systematic framework to assist implementing modularity and commonality in platform development. A tractable optimization method is used to capture and resolve the trade-off between commonality configuration and individual product performance. A family of power tool designs is used to demonstrate the potential and feasibility of the proposed framework. | Empirical: observations | Engineering, "how to" |
| Marion et al. (2007) *IJPR* | Component com. Product platforms | Diverse | Two examples involving two consumer product companies and their product lines are presented. Product family components and estimated tooling costs are analyzed, as well as development time and profit margins to demonstrate why companies are moving away from product platforms in certain types of consumer products. A novel method relating component commonality decisions to major cost drivers is introduced and applied to both examples. There were fewer financial or functional benefits to develop product platforms that share common components or subsystems when these products are being manufactured offshore. | Empirical: archival | Case study |

| Meyer and Dalal (2002) *JPIM* | Component com. Product platforms | Non-assembled products | By conducting a case study in three companies, this paper investigates management of platform architectures for non-assembled products. Two methods for measuring platform efficiency and platform reuse are proposed and tested. In a case study of an electronics manufacturer, a platform-centric product line with greater reuse achieved better performance (e.g., in terms of lower average product development cost, higher revenue, higher ROI) compared to the product line with less reuse. | Empirical: mix | Case study |
| Meyer and Mugge (2001) *RTM* | Component com. Product platforms | Computer hardware industry (IBM) | This paper describes guidance principles and success factors when implementing and managing product platforms, also considering component commonality. Particular emphasis is put on the case of IBM's hardware business, where platforms are employed extensively. Applied concurrently with other initiatives, platform management resulted in performance improvement in various aspects (e.g., 42% less NPD spending from 1994 to 1997, yet revenues were increased; less abandoned projects; shorter time-to-market). Moreover, cost considerations of product platforms in general are discussed. | Empirical: qualitative | Management practice |
| Nobelius and Sundgren (2002) *JETM* | Component com. Product platforms | Manufacturing industry (Sweden) | The aim of this case study is to explore the managerial difficulties associated with the parts sharing process. Six manufacturing companies in four different industries are investigated. Managerial difficulties are divided into four categories: organizational, strategic, technology and cost related, and support-system related issues. In one case, the promotion of parts sharing led to repeated redesigns of platform elements, causing a cost/ performance ratio increase of more than 30%, and the time-schedule was exceeded by more than 40%. In another case, parts that were to be transferred from the | Empirical: mix | Case study |

**Table 20.** (Continued)

| Author (Date) Journal | Cost Management Method(s) | Industry | Summary (Regarding the Focal Cost Management Method) | Type of Data | Field Work |
|---|---|---|---|---|---|
| | | | most expensive model to the remaining models were found too expensive, considering the remaining models' cost strategy. | | |
| Park and Simpson (2005) *IJPR* | Component com. | Metals and electronics | A production cost-estimation framework to support product family design is presented and illustrated with the example of a family of cordless electric power screwdrivers considering sharing various components. Using this framework enabled designers to investigate a production system and product structure for product family design, estimate production costs, and analyze the activities generated in the production system to find resources to be shared, selected, reduced, and eliminated. | Non-empirical: simulation | None |
| Park and Simpson (2008) *IJPR* | Component com. Product platforms | Metals and electronics | Two cases are studied to investigate the cost effects of product family design. The first case investigates the cost effects of commonality in terms of cost allocations of overhead costs on each product. The second case investigates an architectural solution to a platform and its cost effects. As a result, an activity-based costing model is presented to support the design of cost-efficient product families. | Non-empirical: simulation | None |
| Perera, Nagarur, and Tabucanon (1999) *IJPE* | Component com. | Not specified | The paper studies the effect of component part standardization on life-cycle costs. Therefore the life-cycle phases of product development, manufacturing, distribution, usage and disposal are analyzed and possible effects of standardization are identified. Possible benefits and disadvantages of component part standardization are discussed. | Non-empirical: theoretical | None |

| | | | | | |
|---|---|---|---|---|---|
| Perlman (2012) *IJPR* | Component com. | Automotive | The paper analyzes the effect of risk on product family design for uncertain consumer segments. A model is used to analyze whether the producer's risk level affects the decision of implementing common components. The case of an automotive product family shows that common components are preferred under high market uncertainty while companies prefer unique configurations under low uncertainty. | Non-empirical: simulation | None |
| Ramdas, Fisher, and Ulrich (2003) *MSOM* | Component com. | Automotive | This paper presents a method for determining which versions of a set of related components should be offered to support a defined finished product portfolio. Coordinated projects, project-by-project, and a hybrid partially coordinated projects are three different organizational approaches to component sharing. It is examined how the gain from the coordinated projects approach relative to the project-by-project approach varies with the number of component versions in consideration, warranty costs, complexity costs, and demand variability. | Non-empirical: simulation | None |
| Salvador et al. (2007) *IJOPM* | Component com. | Automotive | This paper investigates the factors enabling or hindering the simultaneous pursuit of volume flexibility and mix flexibility within a supply chain. through the lens of a manufacturing plant seeking to implement a build-to-order strategy. An in-depth case study of a manufacturing plant and its supply chain was conducted. The results suggest that volume flexibility and mix flexibility may be achieved synergistically, as initiatives such as component standardization or component-process interface standardization would improve both volume flexibility and mix flexibility. | Empirical: qualitative | Case study |

**Table 20.** (Continued)

| Author (Date) Journal | Cost Management Method(s) | Industry | Summary (Regarding the Focal Cost Management Method) | Type of Data | Field Work |
|---|---|---|---|---|---|
| Sanchez (1999) *JM* | Component com. Modular design Product platforms | Not specified | This paper broadly discusses a multitude of aspects of modular product architectures. Several properties as well as effects, benefits and opportunities enabled by modularity are described, with special emphasis on the changes it will bring to marketing strategy and processes. The author also discusses how modularity can achieve cost reductions in product creation and realization (e.g., savings enabled through common components). | Non-empirical: theoretical | None |
| Song and Zhao (2009) *MSOM* | Component com. | Not specified | The value of component commonality in a dynamic inventory system with lead times is the research topic of this paper. A numerical simulation is used to analyze the benefits of component commonality for different inventory systems. The results can be used to evaluate the implementation of component commonality during the product design process. | Non-empirical: simulation | None |
| Ulrich (1995) *ResPol* | Component com. Modular design | Not specified | This paper defines product architecture, provides a typology of product architectures, and articulates the potential linkages between the architecture of the product and five areas of managerial importance: (1) product change (2) product variety (3) component standardization (4) product performance, and (5) product development management. The author notes that standardized components usually cost less and have a higher performance compared to specifically-designed components. | Non-empirical: theoretical | None |
| Vakharia et al. (1996) *JOM* | Component com. | Not specified | The effects of component commonality on manufacturing firms which use a material requirements planning system | Non-empirical: simulation | None |

| Reference | Commonality type | Industry | Description | Method | |
|---|---|---|---|---|---|
| Wu, De Matta, and Lowe (2009) *IEEE-EM* | Component com. Modular design | Not specified | are the focus of this paper. Results are based on two simulated MRP systems with different lot sizing methods. Mostly positive, as well as some negative impacts are discussed. This paper employs an analytical model to examine when and how to update modular products, considering the possibility to carry over parts to the next generation. Conditions are provided when updating every component or only some components or continuing selling the old product may be most effective in terms of cost management or profit contribution. | Non-empirical: analytical | None |
| Xu, Ong, and Nee (2007) *IJPR* | Component com. | Technology and telecommunication | Within the evaluation of a proposed model for product family design reuse, the paper discovers a relation between cost-effectiveness of product family design and component commonality. The results of a simulated scenario indicate a positive correlation for the use of commonality and lower costs. | Non-empirical: simulation | None |
| Yura et al. (2000) *IJPR* | Component com. | Not specified | This research provides a model to evaluate the trade-off between specialized and common parts for a set of end products. The financial basis for the evaluation are manufacturing and recycle costs. A numerical example with different demand scenarios is used to demonstrate the application. | Non-empirical: simulation | None |
| Zhang and Huang (2010) *IJPR* | Component com. Product platforms Modular design | Manufacturing | This paper discusses optimizing decision variables for simultaneously configuring not only platform-based product variants but also their supply chain. The authors developed a mixed-integer programming model that integrates both platform product design and material purchase decisions based on cost drivers related to commonality and modularity. A numerical example is presented to illustrate how manufacturers strive to dynamically adjust their product design strategies in | Non-empirical: simulation | None |

**Table 20.** (Continued)

| Author (Date) Journal | Cost Management Method(s) | Industry | Summary (Regarding the Focal Cost Management Method) | Type of Data | Field Work |
|---|---|---|---|---|---|
| | | | response to changes in the market demands and/or supply base. | | |
| Zhang, Huang, and Rungtusanatham (2008) *IJPE* | Component com. Product platforms Modular design | Manufacturing | Based on earlier research (Zhang & Huang, 2010), a game-theoretic approach is applied to work out maximal profit over the entire supply chain. Findings suggest that if a platform strategy (regardless of whether focused on modular design or component commonality) is used for the product design, all companies in a supply chain will be better off. | Non-empirical: simulation | None |
| Zhou and Grubbström (2004) *IJPE* | Component com. | Not specified | This paper focuses on the effect of commonality in multi-level production-inventory systems, especially assembly systems. The basic balance equations of MRP, and input-output analysis together with the Laplace transform, are used for comparing the cases with and without commonality. Applying the net present value as the objective function, conclusions are derived in the form of conditions for when commonality is recommended, and when not. | Non-empirical: simulation | None |
| Zwerink et al. (2007) *RADMA* | Component com. Modular design | Electronics industry (Philips) | This paper provides a matrix framework which relates decisions about product architecture characteristics (e.g., reuse, component commonality, modularity) with product architecture capabilities, performance at the organizational level and performance at the business unit level (e.g., sales, cost of goods sold). The framework is intended to be used and discussed during a workshop to provide a structured learning experience about product architecture implications, and to generate recommendations about future product architecture decisions for similar products. | Empirical: qualitative | Engineering, "how to" |

level. Some studies investigate this effect based on numerical simulation of a model (e.g., DeCroix, Song, & Zipkin, 2009; Gupta & Benjaafar, 2004; Hillier, 2000; Izui et al., 2010; Song & Zhao, 2009; Vakharia, Parmenter, & Sanchez, 1996) or analytical solutions for a mathematical model (Eynan & Rosenblatt, 1996). Other studies also conduct empirical studies of the effects of component commonality on inventory costs (Caux, David, & Pierreval, 2006; Davila & Wouters, 2007).

Other economic effects of component commonality that have been investigated, also through case studies, concern R&D costs (Halman, Hofer, & Van Vuuren, 2003), material and manufacturing costs (Chakravarty, 1994; Farrell & Simpson, 2010; Johnson & Kirchain, 2009; Park & Simpson, 2008; Yura, Ishikura, & Hitomi, 2000), and revenues, because of how component commonalty may negatively affect product differentiation (Heese & Swaminathan, 2006; Liu, Wong, & Lee, 2010).

Some studies have looked more broadly and the managerial and implementation issues of component commonality, typically in combination with product platforms and modular designs (Halman et al., 2003; Ismail, Reid, Mooney, Poolton, & Arokiam, 2007; Marion, Thevenot, & Simpson, 2007; Meyer & Dalal, 2002; Meyer & Mugge, 2001; Nobelius & Sundgren, 2002; Salvador, Rungtusanatham, Forza, & Trentin, 2007; Sanchez, 1999; Zwerink, Wouters, Hissel, & Kerssens-van Drongelen, 2007).

### *Modular Design*

Modular design is a cost management method for efficiently offering a large product variety, so a great number of different end products and possibilities for customization. The idea is reduce internal variety and complexity reduction through the design of architectures (e.g., manufactured product architectures or software architectures). "A modular architecture includes a one-to-one mapping from functional elements in the function structure to the physical components of the product, and specifies decoupled interfaces between components" (Ulrich, 1995, p. 422). Modularity involves building a complex product or process from smaller subsystems that can be designed independently yet function together as a whole. The subsystems (or modules) are designed and tested independently, and the interfaces among components are standardized, so multiple products can be configured by mixing and matching from a base set of modules and components to introduce or configure new products (Baldwin & Clark, 1997). In this review, modular design is understood as a design method which enables the cost-effective production of a wide variety of products with a limited set of modules that are adjusted and/or combined with different parts and other modules.

Modular designs may save development cost (fewer different modules need to be developed in total, although each one may be more complex and costly to develop compared to when no explicit modular design strategy is used) and it may save manufacturing costs (each module is produced in a greater quantity and economies of scale can be used, but for some products the modules used may be "overspecified" which increases cost). Modular designs may increase sales prices or sales volumes by offering more differentiated or even customized products (however, having to work with modules may involve compromises, so "underspecification" instead of "overspecification," and customers may be less willing to pay premium prices if product differentiation is less). Thus, trade-offs must be made.

As mentioned earlier, modular design is the topic with the greatest number of results in this sample of studies in the IOM literature: 45 results. These have been published in many different journals and not one of these stands out in terms of publishing an unexpectedly high number of studies on this topic. In terms of research methods applied, the 12 results based on mixed data are unexpectedly high (27% for modular design, but only 16% overall) and the 8 results for analytical studies (18% for modular design, but only 8% overall).

Detailed results are in Table 21. Many studies investigate the impact, either theoretically or empirically, of modular design on manufacturing costs (Agard & Bassetto, 2013; Agard & Penz, 2009; Thyssen, Israelsen, & Jørgensen, 2006), development costs (Chakravarty & Balakrishnan, 2001; Sanderson, 1991), cost of returns (Chang & Yeh, 2013; Das & Chowdhury, 2012; Mukhopadhyay & Setoputro, 2005), or pricing and revenues (Chakravarty & Balakrishnan, 2001; Hopp & Xu, 2005).

Several case studies investigate the use of modular designs in depth in one or a few organizations (Garud & Munir, 2008; Gil, 2009; Magnusson & Pasche, 2014; Ray & Ray, 2010; Sanderson & Uzumeri, 1995; Sundgren, 1999; Uskonen & Tenhiälä, 2012; Zhang & Huang, 2010) sometimes with an emphasis on pragmatic approaches for how to develop and implement modularity (Jiao, 2012; Kaski & Heikkila, 2002; Wouters, Workum, & Hissel, 2011).

**Table 21.** Results for Modular Design.

| Author (Date) Journal | Cost Management Method(s) | Industry | Summary (Regarding the Focal Cost Management Method) | Type of Data | Field Work |
|---|---|---|---|---|---|
| Agard and Bassetto (2013) *IJPR* | Modular design | Metals and electronics | The paper introduces a model for selecting a set of modules that allows the constraints of each product to be satisfied, while minimizing the total production cost for the product family. An example of the modular design of headlamp devices is presented for illustrating and analyzing the model. | Non-empirical: simulation | None |
| Agard and Penz (2009) *IJPE* | Modular design | Automotive | The paper presents a method for modular design which helps to generate a bill of materials for large products families at minimum cost, depending on the maximum assembly time of a product and the number of functions of a modular unit. Computational experiments are conducted to demonstrate the effectiveness of the model. | Non-empirical: simulation | None |
| Agrawal et al. (2013) *IJPR* | Modular design Component com. Product platforms | Not specified | See Table 20. | Non-empirical: simulation | None |
| Chakravarty and Balakrishnan (2001) *IIE* | Modular design | OEMs | This paper presents a mathematical approach to show how the choice of module-options affects product variety, total sales, product development cost, and hence, the firm's profit, in settings where modules can be self-developed (by wholly-owned subsidiary suppliers) or bought from independent suppliers. It is demonstrated how to develop or buy the optimal number and type of module-options. | Non-empirical: analytical | None |
| Chang and Yeh (2013) *IJPR* | Modular design | Not specified | The authors investigate the effects of the manufacturer's refund for the retailer's unsold products and product modularity under the decentralized and the centralized strategies. The order quantity and customer's return probability both affect the optimal modularity level of the product, and the optimal modularity level is related to the refund policy. | Non-empirical: analytical | None |

**Table 21.** (*Continued*)

| Author (Date) Journal | Cost Management Method(s) | Industry | Summary (Regarding the Focal Cost Management Method) | Type of Data | Field Work |
|---|---|---|---|---|---|
| Das and Chowdhury (2012) *IJPE* | Modular design | Not specified | This study proposes an integrated, reverse logistics supply chain planning process with modular product design that produces and markets products at different quality levels. A mixed-integer programming model formulates the overall planning process required to maximize profit by considering the collection of returned products, the recovery of modules, and the proportion of the product mix at different quality levels. This study uses a total supply-chain view that considers the production, transportation and distribution of products to customers. A numerical example illustrates the applicability of the models. | Non-empirical: simulation | None |
| Farrell and Simpson (2010) *IJPR* | Product platforms Component com. Modular design | Metals and electronics | See Table 20. | Non-empirical: simulation | None |
| Garud and Munir (2008) *ResPol* | Modular design | Photography equipment (Polaroid) | Studying the case of a Polaroid camera, this paper examines the transformation costs that arise when competencies across a production network are reorganized because of design changes. These costs may exceed the anticipated benefits, when only transaction costs are considered for decision-making. Especially for radical, modular design changes and in- or outsourcing considerations that come with it, considering the transformation costs is advised. | Empirical: mix | Case study |
| Gil (2009) *IEEE-EM* | Modular design | Airport industry | This study defines safeguard as the design and physical development work for ensuring, or enhancing, the embedment of an option in the project outcome. An option to change the design can be exercised if environmental uncertainties resolve favorably in the future. An example of a | Empirical: mix | Case study |

| Reference | Topic | Industry | Description | Method | Application |
|---|---|---|---|---|---|
| Halman et al. (2003) *JPIM* | Component com. Modular design Product platforms | Multiple industries | safeguard is additional space in a master plan. The paper includes a case study of an airport expansion program. A lower degree of modularity of the architecture of the infrastructure made investments in safeguards more attractive. See Table 20. | Empirical: qualitative | Case study |
| He and Kusiak (1996) *IJPR* | Modular design | Not specified | This paper studies the impact of modular product designs on the performance of a manufacturing system. The performance of product designs is measured by the makespan of the corresponding schedule. Three design rules for the improvement of performance of product designs are developed. The selection problem of modular designs is formulated as an integer programming model. The problem can be solved by an existing heuristic algorithm. Examples illustrate the model. | Non-empirical: simulation | None |
| Hopp and Xu (2005) *MSOM* | Modular design | Not specified | This paper addresses the strategic impact of modular design on the optimal length and price of a differentiated product line. Two crucial aspects can be derived from the model: First, the potential of modular design is not only reduction of development cost, but also enlargement of product variety, higher market share and the possibility to charge higher prices. Second, clear differentiation of products is needed for success of modularity. | Non-empirical: analytical | None |
| Huang, Stewart, and Chen (2010) *IJOPM* | Modular design | Metals and electronics | This paper investigates the relationships between integrated supplier management, new product development, knowledge sharing practices and the business performance of company. A survey and semi-structured interviews in the Taiwanese electronics manufacturing industry were conducted. Findings show that the implementation of modular design had great positive influence on manufacturing performance and consequently on business performance. | Empirical: mix | Case study |

**Table 21.** (Continued)

| Author (Date) Journal | Cost Management Method(s) | Industry | Summary (Regarding the Focal Cost Management Method) | Type of Data | Field Work |
|---|---|---|---|---|---|
| Ismail et al. (2007) *IEEE-EM* | Component com. Modular design Product platforms | Small and medium-sized enterprises (SMEs) | See Table 20. | Empirical: mix | Case study |
| Jacobs, Vickery, and Droge (2007) *IJOPM* | Modular design | Automotive | This paper examines the effects of product modularity on four aspects of competitive performance: cost, quality, flexibility, and cycle time, based on a survey of the automotive sector. The relationships between product modularity and performance are tested with three different integration strategies as mediators. Modularity positively and directly influences each aspect of competitive performance for each integration strategy tested. Indirect effects were found for each integration strategy for cost and flexibility; and for manufacturing integration and cycle time. | Empirical: survey | None |
| Jacobs, Droge, Vickery, and Calantone (2011) *JPIM* | Modular design | Automotive suppliers (the United States) | By conducting a survey among first-tier automotive suppliers in the United States, this study assesses the effects of product and process modularity on firm growth performance (includes measures such as ROI, ROS, and market share) and manufacturing agility. Several models with different assumed relationships are tested. The results suggest that product modularity directly and positively influences process modularity, firm growth performance and manufacturing agility. Product modularity did not influence firm growth performance indirectly through manufacturing agility. | Empirical: survey | None |
| Jiao (2012) *IIE* | Modular design Product platforms | Not specified (framework tested in an electronics company) | This paper provides a mathematical real-options framework, which integrates financial and engineering analysis. The framework supports product platform planning by evaluating the flexibility within product platforms. | Empirical: archival | Engineering, "how to" |

| | | | | | |
|---|---|---|---|---|---|
| | | | The proposed approach has been applied in an electronics company. | Non-empirical: theoretical | None |
| John, Weiss, and Dutta (1999) *JM* | Modular design Product platforms | Companies in technology-intensive markets | This paper examines technology-intensive markets (e.g., semiconductors) from a marketing perspective. The decision to decide between platform products and tailored products is briefly discussed. It is suggested to align the platform to high-end users to recover development costs first, in order to be able to offer lower-price platform products for little incremental cost at a later stage. Furthermore, the decision to choose between integral and modular designs is discussed. | Non-empirical: theoretical | None |
| Kamrad, Schmidt, and Ülkü (2013) *IEEE-EM* | Modular design | Not specified | This paper applies an economic model to determine under which conditions it may be advantageous for a firm to employ modularly upgradeable product architecture, while particularly considering technological change. Different conditions are investigated to understand when a modular, upgradeable product is more beneficial or profitable than an integral product. In particular, these are: (1) market scale is small; (2) the firm's cost of redesigning an integral product is high; (3) production costs are high; (4) the firm's pricing power is limited; (5) the components evolve at very different rates; (6) the performance loss due to modularity is low; and (7) user integration costs are low. | Non-empirical: analytical | None |
| Kaski and Heikkila (2002) *IJTM* | Modular design | Cellular network industry | This paper investigates a way to improve supply-chain efficiency based on a case study of a cellular network base station. Different product structure alternatives are compared using two design metrics, and simulation methods (an inventory value model and an activity-based costing model) are applied to estimate the inventory and operating costs of the alternative structures. The simulation results indicate that operating costs are closely linked to the number of physical modules and the dependencies within the product structure. As for inventory costs, both metrics have an effect, yet only if both are improved jointly. | Empirical: mix | Engineering, "how to" |

**Table 21.** (Continued)

| Author (Date) Journal | Cost Management Method(s) | Industry | Summary (Regarding the Focal Cost Management Method) | Type of Data | Field Work |
|---|---|---|---|---|---|
| Lau, Yam, and Tang (2007) *IJPE* | Modular design | Manufacturing | The impact of modular design on product performance is examined, based on a survey with 251 participants from the plastics, electronics and toys industries in Hong Kong. Results indicate that product modularity influences the capabilities of delivery, flexibility and customer service, and the capabilities of delivery and flexibility positively relate to product performance. These findings show that modular product design cannot improve each capability simultaneously, as existing literature suggests. | Empirical: survey | None |
| Lau, Yam, and Tang (2010) *IJOPM* | Modular design | Manufacturing | The paper examines the relationship between supply chain integration (SCI) and modular product design, as well as their impact on product performance. Survey data from 251 manufacturers in Hong Kong are analyzed with structural equation modeling. Results show that information sharing, product co-development and organizational coordination are crucial organizational processes within SCI. Companies that have high levels of product modularity appear to be good at product co-development and organizational coordination directly and at information sharing indirectly. Furthermore, companies that have high levels of product co-development or product modularity appear to have better product performance. | Empirical: survey | None |
| Liu et al. (2010) *IJPR* | Component com. Modular design Product platforms | Metals and electronics | See Table 20. | Empirical: observations | Engineering, "how to" |

| Reference | Topic | Context | Description | Empirical type | Method |
|---|---|---|---|---|---|
| Magnusson and Pasche (2014) *JPIM* | Modular design Product platforms | Manufacturing industry (Sweden) | The paper investigates contingencies influencing the applicability of modularization and product platforms. Moreover, the paper addresses how different organizing solutions are interrelated with the use of modularization and product platform approaches. The case study shows that platforms were applied for products where the speed of change is low and cost-efficient functionality is demanded, whereas modularity was employed for products which are subject to frequent changes and which should be customizable. Also, modularity was perceived to reduce coordination costs for integrating components. | Empirical: qualitative | Case study |
| Mukhopadhyay and Setoputro (2005) *JOM* | Modular design | Not specified | This paper introduces a model to increase profits on built-to-order markets. A numerical simulation shows how to find a proper level of modularity and suitable return policy to manage the trade-off between increasing sales and revenues and growing costs of returned goods and development. In addition the paper includes a number of managerial guidelines. | Non-empirical: simulation | None |
| Nepal, Monplaisir, and Singh (2005) *IJPE* | Modular design | Consumer goods | This paper presents a formal method for optimizing the performance attributes of prospective modules while modularizing the product architecture early in the concept development phase. Although the paper illustrates the procedure for minimizing the cost of modular architecture, the method can also be used for optimization of other attributes such as quality, reliability, manufacturability, etc. A case example is presented to demonstrate the proposed method. | Non-empirical: simimulation | None |
| Ray and Ray (2010) *IEEE-EM* | Modular design | Indian telecommunication industry | This paper assesses the case of an Indian telecommunication company in order to investigate what kind of innovation models effectively suit the needs of emerging markets. A modular design strategy enabled the case company to achieve savings in terms of costs of innovation, R&D and materials. Further positive effects were observed (e.g., facilitation of the training of operators). | Empirical: mix | Case study |

**Table 21.** (*Continued*)

| Author (Date) Journal | Cost Management Method(s) | Industry | Summary (Regarding the Focal Cost Management Method) | Type of Data | Field Work |
|---|---|---|---|---|---|
| Patel and Jayaram (2014) *JOM* | Modular design | Not specified | This research focuses on the antecedents and consequences of product variety in new ventures. As one result of a survey among 141 new ventures from the United States, modular design was underlined as relevant driver for more product variety. The study also gave some practical implications on what must be considered with the introduction of modular design. | Empirical: survey | None |
| Rai and Allada (2003) *IJPR* | Product platforms Modular design | Metals and electronics | This paper provides a two-step approach to tackle the modular product family design problem. The first step performs a multi-objective optimization using a multi-agent framework to determine the Pareto design solutions for a given module set. The second step performs post-optimization analysis that includes a novel application of the quality loss function to determine the optimal platform level for a related set of product families and their variants. The proposed method is applied to a product family design example to demonstrate its validity and effectiveness. | Non-empirical: simulation | None |
| Ramachandran and Krishnan (2008) *MSOM* | Modular design | Technology and telecommunication | The challenges for markets with short innovation cycles are studied, comparing integrated and modular design architectures. Modular design is an efficient method to keep pace of innovation and ensuring constant profitability. Further the paper distinguishes between proprietary and nonproprietary approaches for the design of modular products. Recommendations for the appropriate use of modular design in different scenarios are given. | Non-empirical: analytical | None |

| Reference | Topics | Industry/Context | Description | Research type | Method |
|---|---|---|---|---|---|
| Ro et al. (2007) *IEEE-EM* | Target costing Modular design | Automotive OEMs and suppliers (the United States) | See Table 9. | Empirical: qualitative | Management practice |
| Ray and **Ray** (2011) *Techn* | DFM/A Design for X Modular design | Automotive industry (Tata Motors) | See Table 18. | Empirical: mix | Case study |
| Sanchez (1999) *JM* | Component com. Modular design Product platforms | Not specified | See Table 20. | Non-empirical: theoretical | None |
| Sanderson (1991) *JETM* | Modular design | Example from television industry | This paper identifies and evaluates the cost implications of two complementary approaches to information management in the design of new products: virtual design and modular design. An analytical model is developed to show the dependence of product development cost on the design management strategy, characterized by investment in tools and infrastructure for virtual design and modular technology methods. Modular design through group technology is considered to reduce costs for designing and manufacturing standard parts. | Non-empirical: analytical | None |
| Sanderson and Uzumeri (1995) *ResPol* | Modular design Product platforms | Consumer electronics (Sony) | This paper represents an in-depth study of the case of the Sony Walkman product family and seeks to investigate what led to the Walkman's worldwide success. Modular designs and the use of platforms enabled Sony to achieve low costs while ensuring high quality for a wide range of models. | Empirical: mix | Case study |
| Sundgren (1999) *JPIM* | Modular design Product platforms | Manufacturing industry (Sweden) | By conducting a longitudinal case study among two Swedish manufacturing companies, this paper investigates how interface management is practically managed in new platform development. In one case, a product cost reduction of 30% was achieved among a product family through a highly configured platform, however, to the disadvantage of extended development time. | Empirical: mix | Case study |

**Table 21.** (Continued)

| Author (Date) Journal | Cost Management Method(s) | Industry | Summary (Regarding the Focal Cost Management Method) | Type of Data | Field Work |
|---|---|---|---|---|---|
| Thyssen et al. (2006) *IJPE* | Modular design | Diverse | The paper reports an activity-based costing (ABC) analysis supporting decision-making about product modularity. The ABC analysis is communicated to decision-makers by telling how much higher the variable cost of the multi-purpose module can be compared to the average variable cost for the product-unique modules that it substitutes to break even in total cost. Three general rules of cost efficiency of modularization are formulated. | Empirical: mix | Engineering, "how to" |
| Ulrich (1995) *ResPol* | Component com. Modular design | Not specified | See Table 20. | Non-empirical: theoretical | None |
| Uskonen and Tenhiälä (2012) *IJPE* | Modular design | Consumer goods | This paper shows how change orders in the make-to-order manufacturing industry can be handled cost efficiently. The production of refrigeration machineries and remotely refrigerated display cabinets are the topic of a case study. A mix of empirical data was used to show, for example, that modularity in many cases can reduce the costs of a change order. | Empirical: mix | Case study |
| Wouters et al. (2011) *RADMA* | Modular design | Medical equipment industry (Philips) | This paper presents an approach to financially assess the product architecture decision about the incorporation of a product feature. The case company employed modularity to prepare their product for the easy incorporation of a product feature at a later stage quickly and at low cost, if customers desired this feature. However, the case results suggest that preparing for the product feature was expensive, and would pay off only if demand for the feature came up shortly after product launch. | Empirical: mix | Case study |

| Reference | Research themes | Industry | Description | Method | Theory |
|---|---|---|---|---|---|
| Wu et al. (2009) *IEEE-EM* | Component com. Modular design | Not specified | See Table 20. | Non-empirical: analytical | None |
| Xu, Lu, and Li (2012) *IJPE* | Modular design | Not specified | This paper introduces a model for the optimal employment of modular design under the constraints of a volatile market. The model is based on real-options theory and was applied in a fictitious case study. The results show that when market is more volatile, it is optimal for a firm to postpone modularization; when a firm's investment efficiency at the preparation stage is higher, the firm can start modular production earlier with relatively low product modularity. An increase in market uncertainty will stimulate the firm to improve its product modularity. Comparing the predictions from the net present value method (NPV) to the results from the real-options model shows that traditional NPV method underestimates a firm's value for modular production and might mislead a firm to modularize earlier. | Non-empirical: simulation | None |
| Zhang and Huang (2010) *IJPE* | Component com. Product platforms Modular design | Manufacturing | See Table 20. | Non-empirical: simulation | None |
| Zhang et al. (2008) *IJPR* | Component com. Product platforms Modular design | Manufacturing | See Table 20. | Non-empirical: simulation | None |
| Zwerink et al. (2007) *RADMA* | Component com. Modular design | Electronics industry (Philips) | See Table 20. | Empirical: qualitative | Engineering, "how to" |

### Product Platform

With 33 results (12%), product platforms comes in third regarding the number of results in this sample of studies in the IOM literature. As for modular design, these results have been published in many different journals, and mainly in *IJPR* and *JPIM*, but no journal published an unexpectedly high number of studies on this topic. In terms of research methods applied, simulation and mixed data are used most frequently, but this is line with the overall results.

Product platforms go yet further in shaping the architecture of products and influencing product costs during product development (Robertson & Ulrich, 1998). Beyond having only design guidelines or common parts and even modules, product platforms imply that the product architecture is fundamentally developed to facilitate a range of different end products and several generations of those. Product platforms provide a common technical foundation and physical implementation for a family of products on the basis of constant parameters, features and/or components (Simpson, Maier, & Mistree, 2001). In other words, a product platforms is "a set of subsystems and interfaces intentionally planned and developed to form a common structure from which a stream of derivative products can be efficiently developed and produced" (Muffatto & Roveda, 2000, p. 619). It means that whole set of resources will be shared across products, ranging from components to production processes, and so component commonality, modular design and product platforms are closely related among each other.

Detailed results are in Table 22. Several studies used numerical simulation for investigating the impact of modular design on costs (Ben-Arieh, Easton, & Choubey, 2009; Bhandare & Allada, 2009) or on sales revenues (Kang, Hong, & Huh, 2012). A few case studies have developed approaches for modular designs and tried these out in real companies (Cao, Luo, Kwong, & Tang, 2014; Hauser, 2001; Krishnan, Singh, & Tirupati, 1999; Luo, Kwong, Tang, Deng, & Gong, 2011; Moore, Louviere, & Verma, 1999; Muffatto, 1999).

### Technology Roadmap

For technology roadmaps, we found only very few results (seven), comparable to the MA literature with five results, and these numbers represent 3% in both studies. Detailed information on both studies is provided in Table 23.

**Table 22.** Results for Product Platform.

| Author (Date) Journal | Cost Management Method(s) | Industry | Summary (Regarding the Focal Cost Management Method) | Type of Data | Field Work |
|---|---|---|---|---|---|
| Agrawal et al. (2013) *IJPR* | Modular design Component com. Product platforms | Not specified | See Table 20. | Non-empirical: simulation | None |
| Ben-Arieh et al. (2009) *IJPR* | Product platforms | Metals and electronics | A method for selecting one or multiple platforms for a product family is proposed. It minimizes production costs of the products, which include the costs of components, costs of mass assembly, and costs for adding/removing components from the individual products, while considering the individual demand for each product type. A numerical example shows the effectiveness of the algorithm and indicates it can be advantageous to use more than one platform for a product family. | Non-empirical: simulation | None |
| Bhandare and Allada (2009) *IJPR* | Product platforms | Metals and electronics | A method is proposed to determine the minimum number of scalable platforms needed for creating known product variants by considering the tradeoff between cost-effectiveness and performance degradation. The method also provides values of several design variables for each platform. The objective function is based on the total cost of providing each variant, which is a function of the cost of each product variant and the cost associated with performance loss owing to platforming. The method is demonstrated using the example of a family of axial piston pumps. | Non-empirical: simulation | None |

**Table 22.** (*Continued*)

| Author (Date) Journal | Cost Management Method(s) | Industry | Summary (Regarding the Focal Cost Management Method) | Type of Data | Field Work |
|---|---|---|---|---|---|
| Cao et al. (2014) *IJPR* | Product platforms | Metals and electronics | A supplier pre-selection method for platform-based products is proposed to obtain the minimal overall outsourcing cost and supply risk probability from the perspective of whole product, to help engineers evaluate and improve early product designs, and to reduce the probability of design change at the stage of production. Analytic hierarchy process and reliability matrix are applied to evaluate the supply risk of candidate suppliers, and a genetic algorithm is adopted to solve the optimization model. A case study is provided to illustrate the effectiveness of the model and algorithm. | Empirical: experimental | Engineering, "how to" |
| Chai et al. (2012) *JPIM* | Stage-gate reviews Product platforms | Multiple non-service industries (the United States) | This paper investigates platform-based product development. It is found that product platform extensibility is positively linked to platform development cycle time and cost efficiency. Factors that have a significant effect on platform development cost are statistically different from those that have a significant effect on platform development time. For example, a formalized development process positively affected cycle time, but not development cost. See Table 20. | Empirical: survey | None |
| Farrell and Simpson (2010) *IJPR* | Product platforms Component com. Modular design | Metals and electronics | | Non-empirical: simulation | None |
| Guiltinan (2011) *JPIM* | Product platforms | Not specified | This paper provides a literature review about models and empirical evidence on product line pricing, and referring to platform-based development, cost and profit issues seem to be especially problematic. | Non-empirical: theoretical | None |

| Reference | Topic(s) | Industry/context | Findings | Method | Type |
|---|---|---|---|---|---|
| Gupta and Benjaafar (2004) *IIE* | Component com. Product platforms | Not specified | See Table 20. | Non-empirical: simulation | None |
| Halman et al. (2003) *JPIM* | Component com. Modular design Product platforms | Multiple industries | See Table 20. | Empirical: qualitative | Case study |
| Hauser (2001) *JPIM* | Product platforms | Office equipment industry | This paper provides recommendation on how much relative importance to attach to various performance metrics (e.g., customer satisfaction, time to market, etc.). The proposed method was applied in an office equipment company, which used platform reuse as a performance metric. It was found the case company put too much emphasis on platform reuse and thereby lost focus on customer satisfaction, thus hindering innovation. Decreasing focus on reuse would increase profits. | Empirical: mix | Engineering, "how to" |
| Ismail et al. (2007) *IEEE-EM* | Component com. Modular design Product platforms | Small and medium-sized enterprises | See Table 20. | Empirical: mix | Case study |
| Jiao (2012) *IIE* | Modular design Product platforms | Not specified | See Table 21. | Empirical: archival | Engineering, "how to" |
| John et al. (1999) *JM* | Modular design Product platforms | Companies n technology-intensive markets | See Table 21. | Non-empirical: theoretical | None |
| Johnson and Kirchain (2009) *IJPE* | Component com. Product platforms | Automotive | See Table 20. | Empirical: observations | Case study |
| Kang et al. (2012) *IIE* | Product platforms | Not specified | The paper presents a model to determine the optimal lifetime of platforms by trading-off the cost efficiency of platform development and lost sales due to obsolete technologies. A numerical study is conducted to assess a platform's economic value over its life. A multitude of results and implications are attained, such as companies with low platform development costs should replace platforms in short intervals. | Non-empirical: simulation | None |

## Table 22. (Continued)

| Author (Date) Journal | Cost Management Method(s) | Industry | Summary (Regarding the Focal Cost Management Method) | Type of Data | Field Work |
|---|---|---|---|---|---|
| Krishnan et al. (1999) *MSOM* | Product platforms | Metals and electronics | A model for the design of a product family, sharing a common platform, is presented. The model balances development cost including feasible investments against the financial benefits in the production stage, in order to determine the optimal level of commonality. The model is tried in a real case application with encouraging results. However the authors mention reliable information as the major difficulty for its use. | Empirical: mix | Engineering, "how to" |
| Liu et al. (2010) *IJPR* | Component com. Modular design Product platforms | Metals and electronics | See Table 20. | Empirical: observations | Engineering, "how to" |
| Luo et al. (2011) *IJPR* | Product platforms | Metals and electronics | This research considers the joint optimization of component selection and supplier selection for a platform-based product family. Components of a product platform can have various functionalities or features to satisfy diversified customer requirements. The goal is to determine optimal configurations of individual product variants offered in a product family while considering the products revenue in a multiple-segment market and outsourcing-related cost. A mixed-integer nonlinear programming model with the objective of maximizing the total product family profit is formulated and a genetic algorithm and a tabu search algorithm are proposed to solve the model. | Empirical: observations | Engineering, "how to" |

| Reference | Concept | Context | Description | Method | Study type |
|---|---|---|---|---|---|
| Magnusson and Pasche (2014) *JPIM* | Modular design Product platforms | Manufacturing industry (Sweden) | See Table 21. | Empirical: qualitative | Case study |
| Marion et al. (2007) *IJPR* | Component com. Product platforms | Diverse | See Table 20. | Empirical: archival | Case study |
| Meyer and Dalal (2002) *JPIM* | Component com. Product platforms | Non-assembled products | See Table 20. | Empirical: mix | Case study |
| Meyer and Mugge (2001) *RTM* | Component com. Product platforms | Computer hardware industry (**IBM**) | See Table 20. | Empirical: qualitative | Management practice |
| Moore et al. (1999) *JPIM* | Product platforms | Electronic test equipment company | This paper applies conjoint analyses in order to gain relevant data for product platform design decisions. In the case study, it is shown that introducing a product platform for two products would yield a profit six times greater than when launching only one product (the second one would have been unprofitable, if it had been developed fully independently). Also, products can be equipped with more features (to better meet customer requirements), if the necessary fixed costs (e.g., for engineering) are shared among several products. | Empirical: observations | Case study |
| Muffatto (1999) *IJPE* | Product platforms | Automotive | The paper analyses the introduction of a platform strategy in new product development with an application in the automobile industry. A definition of platform and associated core concepts, such as product architecture, modularization and standardization is given. The implication and benefits of a platform strategy are then discussed both from the technical and organizational points of view. | Empirical: qualitative | Case study |
| Nobelius and Sundgren (2002) *JETM* | Component com. Product platforms | Manufacturing industry (Sweden) | See Table 20. | Empirical: mix | Case study |

*Table 22.* (*Continued*)

| Author (Date) Journal | Cost Management Method(s) | Industry | Summary (Regarding the Focal Cost Management Method) | Type of Data | Field Work |
|---|---|---|---|---|---|
| Park and Simpson (2008) *IJPR* | Component com. Product platforms | Metals and electronics | See Table 20. | Non-empirical: simulation | None |
| Rai and Allada (2003) *IJPR* | Product platforms Modular design | Metals and electronics | See Table 21. | Non-empirical: simulation | None |
| Robertson and Ulrich (1998) *MIT SMR* | Product platforms | Diverse | This paper covers fundamentals, challenges as well as benefits of product platforms. The importance of sound balance between commonality and uniqueness is underlined and practical advocacies on the implementation are given. | Non-empirical: theoretical | None |
| Sanchez (1999) *JM* | Component com. Modular design Product platforms | Not specified | See Table 20. | Non-empirical: theoretical | None |
| Sanderson and Uzumeri (1995) *ResPol* | Modular design Product platforms | Consumer electronics (Sony) | See Table 21. | Empirical: mix | Case study |
| Sundgren (1999) *JPIM* | Modular design Product platforms | Manufacturing industry (Sweden) | See Table 21. | Empirical: mix | Case study |
| Zhang and Huang (2010) *IJPE* | Component com. Product platforms Modular design | Manufacturing | See Table 20. | Non-empirical: simulation | None |
| Zhang et al. (2008) *IJPR* | Component com. Product platforms Modular design | Manufacturing | See Table 20. | Non-empirical: simulation | None |

**Table 23.** Results for Technology Roadmap.

| Author (Date) Journal | Cost Management Method(s) | Industry | Summary (Regarding the Focal Cost Management Method) | Type of Data | Field Work |
|---|---|---|---|---|---|
| Albright and Kappel (2003) *RTM* | Target costing Technology roadmaps | Telecommunication industry (Lucent Technologies) | This paper describes the structure and the set-up of technology roadmaps at a telecommunication company. Detailed, practitioner-oriented explanations are given and success factors in crafting and implementing roadmaps, and benefits are outlined. For the hardware industry, it is suggested to apply experience curves to provide support in setting price and cost targets. | Empirical: mix | Management practice |
| Choi, Kim, Yoon, Kim, and Lee (2013) *RADMA* | Technology roadmaps | Not specified | This paper builds on the notion that conventional technology roadmap creation is costly, because it requires a lot of information and expert involvement. A semi-automatic text-mining approach is presented. Complex interrelationships between technology, functions (the development purpose of technologies) and products are extracted from text-based patent information in order to develop a particular technology roadmap. This approach facilitates decision-making in technology projecting by reducing time and costs involved in crafting technology roadmaps. | Non-empirical: theoretical | None |
| Kostoff and Schaller (2001) *IEEE-EM* | Technology roadmaps | Science and industries (not specified) | This intends to bring some common definition to roadmapping practices and display the underlying unity of seemingly fragmented roadmap approaches. Many different practices and aspects of roadmapping are presented, and guiding principles for successful and effective roadmaps are explained. The major cost of crafting a roadmap is the time of all the individuals involved in developing and reviewing it. | Non-empirical: theoretical | None |

**Table 23.** (Continued)

| Author (Date) Journal | Cost Management Method(s) | Industry | Summary (Regarding the Focal Cost Management Method) | Type of Data | Field Work |
|---|---|---|---|---|---|
| Lee, Lee, Seol, and Park (2008) *RADMA* | Technology roadmaps | Not specified | This paper provides a keyword-based text-mining approach to extract relevant information from broadly distributed patents to create technology roadmaps for incremental innovation. This enabled experts to save on the time and costs of retrieving and understanding all the patents from related technical fields. | Non-empirical: theoretical | None |
| Perdue, McAllister, King, and Berkey (1999) *Interf* | Technology roadmaps | Public sector | The paper focusses on the valuation of R&D projects using options pricing and decision analysis models. Within this valuation process, technology roadmaps are used for better communication. They serve as the ultimate plan, so if milestones are not reached in time the entire project is canceled. This strict line is advocated to maintain an effective utilization of scarce scientific talent. | Empirical: observations | Engineering, "how to" |
| Sarangee, Woolley, Schmidt, and Long (2014) *JPIM* | Technology roadmaps | High-technology companies | This study seeks to identify mechanisms that prevent managers from carrying on (and thereby assigning further budget to) projects, which have become unlikely to produce satisfactory results. Monitoring the roadmap and comparing it with those of other companies or with the competitive landscape in general was among these de-escalation mechanisms. | Empirical: qualitative | Case study |
| Simonse, Hultink, and Buijs (2014) *JPIM* | Technology roadmaps | Multiple industries | This paper assesses 12 practitioner-cases in the literature in order to examine innovation roadmapping and its impact on innovation performance. Based on the case assessment, it is hypothesized that the application of roadmapping improves the competitive timing of market entry. | Non-empirical: theoretical | None |

# CONCLUSIONS

This literature review focused on 15 different methods for cost management during NPD and reviewed the literature on these methods in 23 different journals in IOM. The search process identified 208 unique papers with 275 results, whereby one paper could be included multiple times if it referred to several of the cost management methods. The purpose of this review was to provide an overview of what has been published in the IOM literature concerning these cost management methods during NPD and to compare the results for the IOM literature with the results of a similar kind of review of research published in the MA literature (Wouters & Morales, 2014).

We found results in 20 of the 23 journals. Four journals have the largest number of results, namely *IJPR, JPIM, IJPE*, and *IEEE-EM*. This top 4 accounts for 63% of all results. The distribution of the results was comparably unequal across journals in the MA literature: The CV of the number of results per journal is 1.29 for the IOM literature and 1.32 for the MA literature.

Three cost management methods clearly receive most results: modular design, component commonality, and product platforms, together 42% of all results. In the MA literature, results were even more unequal across cost management methods: the CV of the number of results per cost management method is 0.73 for the IOM literature and 0.95 for the MA literature. In that literature, target costing was by far the mostly researched cost management method (26%).

We distinguished 10 research methods. Three research methods have the largest number of results: simulation (24%), mixed research methods (16%), and surveys (15%). The coefficient of variation of the results across research methods is 0.73. This was 0.74, so almost identical, for the MA literature. The emphasis on research methods is quite different: Simulation is the most frequently used research method in the IOM literature, but it was averagely used in the MA literature; qualitative study was the most frequently used research method in the MA literature, but it is averagely used in the IOM literature.

We also investigated the effect of shifting the journals *Decision Sciences* and *Management Science* from the MA to the IOM set of journals, because these two journals also meet the criteria for including them in the IOM sample. These journals are much more alike the IOM literature than the MA literature: They included many results on component commonality, modular design, and product platform, but only one result on target costing; they often used simulation, but no qualitative studies. Therefore, when including these two journals in the IOM literature instead of in the MA literature, the differences between both literatures become more pronounced and the profiles of both literatures are intensified. What disappeared from the MA literature are 34 of the 43 results for component commonality, modular design, and product platform, and 13 of the 14 simulation studies; however, all but one target costing result and all qualitative studies are kept in the MA literature.

Furthermore, we found many papers that actually focused on at least one of the 15 MA methods but that were still not fitting the current literature review. This was because a paper lacked emphasis on the application of the MA method for the purpose of cost management and/or the paper did not consider the context of NPD. We clustered these papers in 12 categories (listed in Table 4) to provide an impression of what research is going conducted around cost management methods in the IOM literature. This was a substantial amount of research, looking at a broad range of issues concerning MA topics. This may provide MA researchers with further opportunities for drawing upon relevant research and perhaps contributing to research outside accounting. Second, finding many papers about these methods in the IOM literature, albeit with a (very) different emphasis than cost management in NPD is a significant difference between the IOM and MA literature. It suggests the IOM literature has looked at a wide range of issues around these cost management methods.

Rather characteristic for the IOM literature − this is a marked difference from the MA literature − is that we found a lot of papers presenting practical approaches or decision models as further development of a particular cost management method. For example, different stages for target costing are described, target costing is combined with QFD, fuzzy logic is used to extend QFD approaches, cost-estimation methods for life-cycle costing and TCO are developed, managerial and pragmatic studies suggest how to implement stage-gate systems, DFA/M guidelines for reducing costs are extended, and models for trade-offs around component commonality and modular are presented. Some of these studies provide empirical support by implementing their proposed approach or decision model in a case study, without making it a real field experiment. Many studies rely on numerical simulation, analysis of mathematical models, or only conceptual argumentation as support for these approaches or decision models. Compared to the MA literature in the sample of studies presented by Wouters and Morales (2014), this sample of the IOM literature has more attention for development of methods with the aim of supporting their practical application − with an "engineering flavor." Of course, there are also many studies looking at these methods as phenomena in organizations, using surveys and case studies. But such a research focused at "explaining" is not as predominant as it was in the MA literature.

A limitation of the present literature review is that the set of cost management methods considered was limited to the same 15 as in the review of the MA literature by Wouters and Morales (2014). Future research could also consider other cost management methods which are likely to be more important in the IOM literature compared to the MA literature, such as concurrent engineering, delayed product differentiation, six sigma, lean NPD, failure mode and effect analysis, and rapid prototyping. Another limitation is that the cost management method of "Design for X" has not been explored more comprehensively. Future research could search for specific "Xs," like "design for serviceability," "design for sustainability," or "design for green products." Furthermore, we have limited the comparison between the IOM and MA literatures to a descriptive level. The current study verifies the impression one gets from reading both literatures. We believe this descriptive evidence is a worthwhile contribution because as far as we are aware of, it is the first systematic comparison between MA and IOM of published research on cost management in NPD. Future research could look for theoretically founded explanations as why MA and IOM research in this area has developed so differently.

Future research could also study the actual *use* of the various methods for supporting the management of costs in the development stage. Such a study could help to better understand which cost management methods are used in combination. The present literature review has shown that they are often studied in combination and it seems likely that the methods would also be adopted in combination, but we lack empirical evidence.

Future research could also provide in-depth descriptions of innovative cost management practices. Many companies in the automotive industry, consumer electronics, semiconductors, medical devices, drug development, or aerospace industry spend billions of Dollars or Euros every year on NPD. For example, Volkswagen Group, which includes Audi, Seat, Skoda, Bently, Porsche, and Lamborghini, aims to become the largest automotive company in the world. To support this strategic growth objective, it offers a very wide variety of brands and car models. Managing an enormous diversity and complexity in combination with controlling costs is a key challenge. Modular design of cars is therefore of strategic importance: To enable the configuration of many different end products but still allowing economies of scale in development, engineering, purchasing, and manufacturing. Volkswagen's MQB platform is one of the main product platforms

(Rücker, Jaenicke, & Hofer, 2014; Szengel, Middendorf, Möller, & Bennecke, 2012). This has required an investment of several billions of Euros, and it is considered one of the best examples of modular design not only from an engineering point of view but also from a cost management and marketing perspective. However, there is hardly any information about this in the academic literature. Therefore, "simply" documenting and analyzing inspiring examples of innovative management practices could also constitute valuable contributions to the literature. Although these practices may not work everywhere and may not necessarily classify as "best practices," they can provide useful inspiration for both researchers and practitioners.

# REFERENCES

Afonso, P., Nunes, M., Paisana, A., & Braga, A. (2008). The influence of time-to-market and target costing in the new product development success. *International Journal of Production Economics*, *115*(2), 559−568. Retrieved from http://doi.org/10.1016/j.ijpe. 2008.07.003

Agard, B., & Bassetto, S. (2013). Modular design of product families for quality and cost. *International Journal of Production Research*, *51*(6), 1648−1667. Retrieved from http://doi.org/10.1080/00207543.2012.693963

Agard, B., & Penz, B. (2009). A simulated annealing method based on a clustering approach to determine bills of materials for a large product family. *International Journal of Production Economics*, *117*(2), 389−401. Retrieved from http://doi.org/10.1016/j.ijpe. 2008.12.004

Agrawal, T., Sao, A., Fernandes, K. J., Tiwari, M. K., & Kim, D. Y. (2013). A hybrid model of component sharing and platform modularity for optimal product family design. *International Journal of Production Research*, *51*(2), 614−625. Retrieved from http://doi.org/10.1080/00207543.2012.663106

Albright, R. E., & Kappel, T. A. (2003). Technology roadmapping: Roadmapping the corporation. *Research-Technology Management*, *46*(2), 31−40.

Anderson, S. W., & Dekker, H. C. (2009). Strategic cost management in supply chains. Part 1: Structural cost management. *Accounting Horizons*, *23*(2), 201−220. Retrieved from http://doi.org/10.2308/acch.2009.23.2.201

Ansari, S., Bell, J., & Okano, H. (2006). Target costing: Uncharted research territory. In C. S. Chapman, A. G. Hopwood, & M. D. Shields (Eds.), *Handbooks of management accounting research* (Vol. 2, pp. 507−530). Oxford: Elsevier. Retrieved from http://doi. org/10.1016/S1751-3243(06)02002-5

Anthony, T. (2003). Supply chain collaboration: Success in the new internet economy. In A. Wharton & N. Mulani (Eds.), *Achieving supply chain excellence through technology* (2nd ed., pp. 41−44). San Francisco, CA: B. Jacobs & N. Smith.

Armacost, R. L., Componation, P. J., Mullens, M. A., & Swart, W. W. (1994). An AHP framework for prioritizing customer requirements in QFD: An industrialized housing application. *IIE Transactions*, *26*(4), 72–79. Retrieved from http://doi.org/10.1080/07408179408966620

Ax, C., Greve, J., & Nilsson, U. (2008). The impact of competition and uncertainty on the adoption of target costing. *International Journal of Production Economics*, *115*(1), 92–103. Retrieved from http://doi.org/10.1016/j.ijpe.2008.04.010

Badir, Y. F., & O'Connor, G. C. (2015). The formation of tie strength in a strategic alliance's first new product development project: The influence of project and partners' characteristics. *Journal of Product Innovation Management*, *32*(1), 154–169. Retrieved from http://doi.org/10.1111/jpim.12222

Bai, H., & Kwong, C. K. (2003). Inexact genetic algorithm approach to target values setting of engineering requirements in QFD. *International Journal of Production Research*, *41*(16), 3861–3881. Retrieved from http://doi.org/10.1080/0020754031000138367

Baines, A., & Langfield-Smith, K. (2003). Antecedents to management accounting change: A structural equation approach. *Accounting, Organizations and Society*, *28*(7–8), 675–698. Retrieved from http://doi.org/10.1016/S0361-3682(02)00102-2

Baker, M., & Bourne, M. (2014). A governance framework for the idea-to-launch process: Development and application of a governance framework for new product development. *Research-Technology Management*, *57*(1), 42–49. Retrieved from http://doi.org/10.5437/08956308X5701105

Baldwin, C. Y., & Clark, K. B. (1997). Managing in an age of modularity. *Harvard Business Review*, *75*(5), 84–93.

Bard, J. F. (1992). A comparison of the analytic hierarchy process with multiattribute utility theory: A case study. *IIE Transactions*, *24*(5), 111–121. Retrieved from http://doi.org/10.1080/07408179208964251

Bard, J. F., & Sousk, S. F. (1990). A tradeoff analysis for rough terrain cargo handlers using the AHP: An example of group decision making. *IEEE Transactions on Engineering Management*, *37*(3), 222–228. Retrieved from http://doi.org/10.1109/17.104292

Ben-Arieh, D., Easton, T., & Choubey, a. M. (2009). Solving the multiple platforms configuration problem. *International Journal of Production Research*, *47*(7), 1969–1988. Retrieved from http://doi.org/10.1080/00207540701561520

Bevilacqua, M., Ciarapica, F. E., & Giacchetta, G. (2007). Development of a sustainable product lifecycle in manufacturing firms: A case study. *International Journal of Production Research*, *45*(18–19), 4073–4098. Retrieved from http://doi.org/10.1080/00207540701439941

Bhandare, S., & Allada, V. (2009). Scalable product family design: Case study of axial piston pumps. *International Journal of Production Research*, *47*(3), 585–620. Retrieved from http://doi.org/10.1080/00207540701441913

Bisbe, J., & Malagueño, R. (2009). The choice of interactive control systems under different innovation management modes. *European Accounting Review*, *18*. Retrieved from http://doi.org/10.1080/09638180902863803

Blecker, T., & Abdelkafi, N. (2007). The development of a component commonality metric for mass customization. *IEEE Transactions on Engineering Management*, *54*(1), 70–85. Retrieved from http://doi.org/10.1109/TEM.2006.889068

Boardman, J. T., & Clegg, B. T. (2001). Structured engagement in the extended enterprise. *International Journal of Operations & Production Management*, *21*(5/6), 795–811. Retrieved from http://doi.org/10.1108/01443570110390471

Boer, F. P. (2003). Risk-adjusted valuation of R&D projects. *Research-Technology Management*, *46*(5), 50–58.

Boer, M., & Logendran, R. (1999). A methodology for quantifying the effects of product development on cost and time. *IIE Transactions*, *31*(4), 365–378. Retrieved from http://doi.org/10.1023/A:1007621616823

Bonner, S. E., Hesford, J. W., Van der Stede, W. a., & Young, S. M. (2006). The most influential journals in academic accounting. *Accounting, Organizations and Society*, *31*(7), 663–685. Retrieved from http://doi.org/10.1016/j.aos.2005.06.003

Booker, D. M., Drake, A. R., & Heitger, D. L. (2007). New product development: How cost information precision affects designer focus and behavior in a multiple objective setting. *Behavioral Research in Accounting*, *19*(1), 19–41. Retrieved from http://doi.org/10.2308/bria.2007.19.1.19

Bordoloi, S., & Guerrero, H. H. (2008). Design for control: A new perspective on process and product innovation. *International Journal of Production Economics*, *113*(1), 346–358. Retrieved from http://doi.org/10.1016/j.ijpe.2007.02.043

Bovea, M. D., & Wang, B. (2007). Redesign methodology for developing environmentally conscious products. *International Journal of Production Research*, *45*(18-19), 4057–4072. Retrieved from http://doi.org/10.1080/00207540701472678

Brad, S. (2009). Concurrent Multifunction Deployment (CMFD). *International Journal of Production Research*, *47*(19), 5343–5376. Retrieved from http://doi.org/10.1080/00207540701564599

Bremser, W. G., & Barsky, N. P. (2004). Utilizing the balanced scorecard for R&D performance measurement. *R&D Management*, *34*(3), 229–238. Retrieved from http://doi.org/10.1111/j.1467-9310.2004.00335.x

Cadez, S., & Guilding, C. (2008). An exploratory investigation of an integrated contingency model of strategic management accounting. *Accounting, Organizations and Society*, *33*(7–8), 836–863. Retrieved from http://doi.org/10.1016/j.aos.2008.01.003

Caglio, A., & Ditillo, A. (2008). A review and discussion of management control in inter-firm relationships: Achievements and future directions. *Accounting, Organizations and Society*, *33*. Retrieved from http://doi.org/10.1016/j.aos.2008.08.001

Cao, Y., Luo, X., Kwong, C. K., & Tang, J. (2014). Supplier pre-selection for platform-based products: A multi-objective approach. *International Journal of Production Research*, *52*(1), 1–19. Retrieved from http://doi.org/10.1080/00207543.2013.807376

Caux, C., David, F., & Pierreval, H. (2006). Implementation of delayed differentiation in batch process industries: A standardization problem. *International Journal of Production Research*, *44*(16), 3243–3255. Retrieved from http://doi.org/10.1080/00207540500521543

Chai, K. H., Wang, Q., Song, M., Halman, J. I. M., & Brombacher, A. C. (2012). Understanding competencies in platform-based product development: Antecedents and outcomes. *Journal of Product Innovation Management*, *29*(3), 452–472. Retrieved from http://doi.org/10.1111/j.1540-5885.2012.00917.x

Chakravarty, A. K. (1994). Assembly capacity mix planning with product-flexible technology and fixtures. *IIE Transactions*, *26*(4), 19–35. Retrieved from http://doi.org/10.1080/07408179408966616

Chakravarty, A. K., & Balakrishnan, N. (2001). Achieving product variety through optimal choice of module variations. *IIE Transactions*, *33*(7), 587–598. Retrieved from http://doi.org/10.1080/07408170108936856

Chan, D. S. K., & Lewis, W. P. (2000). The integration of manufacturing and cost information into the engineering design process. *International Journal of Production Research*, *38*(17), 4413–4427. Retrieved from http://doi.org/10.1080/00207540050205190

Chang, S.-Y., & Yeh, T.-Y. (2013). Optimal order quantity and product modularity for a two-echelon returnable supply chain. *International Journal of Production Research, 51*(17), 5210–5220. Retrieved from http://doi.org/10.1080/00207543.2013.802051

Chaudhuri, A., & Bhattacharyya, M. (2009). A combined QFD and Fuzzy integer programming framework to determine attribute levels for conjoint study. *International Journal of Production Research, 47*(23), 6633–6649. Retrieved from http://doi.org/10.1007/978-90-481-2860-0_13

Chen, Y. Z., Fung, R. Y. K., & Tang, J. (2005). Fuzzy expected value modelling approach for determining target values of engineering characteristics in QFD. *International Journal of Production Research, 43*(17), 3583–3604. Retrieved from http://doi.org/10.1080/00207540500032046

Chen, Y. Z., & Ngai, E. W. T. (2008). A fuzzy QFD program modelling approach using the method of imprecision. *International Journal of Production Research, 46*(24), 6823–6840. Retrieved from http://doi.org/10.1080/00207540701463297

Choi, S., Kim, H., Yoon, J., Kim, K., & Lee, J. Y. (2013). An SAO-based text-mining approach for technology roadmapping using patent information. *R&D Management, 43*(1), 52–74. Retrieved from http://doi.org/10.1111/j.1467-9310.2012.00702.x

Chung, B. Y., Syachrani, S., Jeong, H. S., & Kwak, Y. H. (2009). Applying process simulation technique to value engineering model: A case study of hospital building project. *IEEE Transactions on Engineering Management, 56*(3), 549–559. Retrieved from http://doi.org/10.1109/TEM.2009.2013831

Coldrick, S., Longhurst, P., Ivey, P., & Hannis, J. (2005). An R&D options selection model for investment decisions. *Technovation, 25*(3), 185–193. Retrieved from http://doi.org/10.1016/S0166-4972(03)00099-3

Cole, M. H. (2000). Review of: "Creating Quality" William J. Kolarik McGraw-Hill, Inc., 1995, 925 pp., ISBN 0-07-035217-8. *IIE Transactions, 32*(6), 570–570. Retrieved from http://doi.org/10.1080/07408170008963940

Cooper, R. G. (1988). The new product process: A decision guide for management. *Journal of Marketing Management, 3*(3), 238–255. Retrieved from http://doi.org/10.1080/0267257X.1988.9964044

Cooper, R. G. (1990). Stage-gate systems: A new tool for managing new products. *Business Horizons, 33*(3), 44–54. Retrieved from http://doi.org/10.1016/0007-6813(90)90040-I

Cooper, R. G. (1994). Third-generation new product processes. *Journal of Product Innovation Management, 11*(1), 3–14. Retrieved from http://doi.org/10.1111/1540-5885.1110003

Cooper, R. G. (2006). Managing technology development projects. *Research-Technology Management, 49*(6), 23–31.

Cooper, R. G. (2013). Invited article: Where are all the breakthrough new products?: Using portfolio management to boost innovation. *Research-Technology Management, 56*(5), 25–33. Retrieved from http://doi.org/10.5437/08956308X5605123

Cooper, R. G. (2014). Invited article: What's next?: After stage-gate. *Research-Technology Management, 57*(1), 20–31. Retrieved from http://doi.org/10.5437/08956308X5606963

Cooper, R. G., & Kleinschmidt, E. J. (1991). New product processes at leading industrial firms. *Industrial Marketing Management, 20*(2), 137–147. Retrieved from http://doi.org/10.1016/0019-8501(91)90032-B

Cooper, R. G., & Kleinschmidt, E. J. (1995). Benchmarking the firm's critical success factors in new product development. *Journal of Product Innovation Management, 12*(5), 374–391. Retrieved from http://doi.org/10.1111/1540-5885.1250374

Cooper, R. G., & Kleinschmidt, E. J. (1996). Winning businesses in product development: The critical success factors. *Research-Technology Management, 39*(4). Cited in Cooper & Kleinschmidt (2007).

Cooper, R. G., & Kleinschmidt, E. J. (2007). Winning businesses in product development: The critical success factors. *Research-Technology Management, 50*(3), 52–66.

Cooper, R., & Slagmulder, R. (1999). Develop profitable new products with target costing. *Sloan Management Review, 40*(4), 23–33.

Cooper, R., & Slagmulder, R. (2004). Achieving full cycle cost management – Five techniques. *MIT Sloan Management Review, 46*(1), 45–52.

Cooper, R., & Yoshikawa, T. (1994). Inter-organizational cost management systems: The case of the Tokyo-Yokohama-Kamakura supplier chain. *International Journal of Production Economics, 37*(1), 51–62.

Cosner, R. R., Hynds, E. J., Fusfeld, A. R., Loweth, C. V., Scouten, C., & Albright, R. E. (2007). Integrating roadmapping into technical planning. *Research-Technology Management, 50*(6), 31–48.

Cristiano, J. J., Liker, J. K., & White, C. C. (2000). Customer-driven product development through quality function deployment in the U.S. and Japan. *Journal of Product Innovation Management, 17*(4), 286–308. Retrieved from http://doi.org/10.1016/S0737-6782(00)00047-3

Curran, R., Gomis, G., Castagne, S., Butterfield, J., Edgar, T., Higgins, C., & McKeever, C. (2007). Integrated digital design for manufacture for reduced life cycle cost. *International Journal of Production Economics, 109*(1–2), 27–40. Retrieved from http://doi.org/10.1016/j.ijpe.2006.11.010

Danese, P., & Filippini, R. (2013). Direct and mediated effects of product modularity on development time and product performance. *IEEE Transactions on Engineering Management, 60*(2), 260–271. Retrieved from http://doi.org/10.1109/TEM.2012.2208268

Das, K., & Chowdhury, A. H. (2012). Designing a reverse logistics network for optimal collection, recovery and quality-based product-mix planning. *International Journal of Production Economics, 135*(1), 209–221. Retrieved from http://doi.org/10.1016/j.ijpe.2011.07.010

Das, S., & Kanchanapiboon, A. (2011). A multi-criteria model for evaluating design for manufacturability. *International Journal of Production Research, 49*(4), 1197–1217. Retrieved from http://doi.org/10.1080/00207540903505267

Davidson, J. M., Clamen, A., & Karol, R. A. (1999). Learning from the best new product developers. *Research-Technology Management, 42*(4), 12–18.

Davila, A., Foster, G., & Oyon, D. (2009). Accounting and control, entrepreneurship and innovation: Venturing into new research opportunities. *European Accounting Review, 18*. Retrieved from http://doi.org/10.1080/09638180902731455

Davila, A., & Wouters, M. J. F. (2007). An empirical test of inventory, service and cost benefits from a postponement strategy. *International Journal of Production Research, 45*(10), 2245–2267. Retrieved from http://doi.org/10.1080/00207540600725002

DeCroix, G. a., Song, J.-S., & Zipkin, P. H. (2009). Managing an assemble-to-order system with returns. *Manufacturing & Service Operations Management, 11*(1), 144–159. Retrieved from http://doi.org/10.1287/msom.1070.0209

Dekker, H. C., & Smidt, P. (2003). A survey of the adoption and use of target costing in Dutch firms. *International Journal of Production Economics, 84*(3), 293–305. Retrieved from http://doi.org/10.1016/S0925-5273(02)00450-4

Delice, E. K., & Güngör, Z. (2011). A mixed integer goal programming model for discrete values of design requirements in QFD. *International Journal of Production Research*, *49*(10), 2941–2957. Retrieved from http://doi.org/10.1080/00207541003720343

Delice, E. K., & Güngör, Z. (2013). Determining design requirements in QFD using fuzzy mixed-integer goal programming: Application of a decision support system. *International Journal of Production Research*, *51*(21), 6378–6396. Retrieved from http://doi.org/10.1080/00207543.2013.803625

Demeester, L., Eichler, K., & Loch, C. H. (2004). Organic production systems: What the biological cell can teach us about manufacturing. *Manufacturing & Service Operations Management*, *6*(2), 115–132. Retrieved from http://doi.org/10.1287/msom.1030.0033

Dowlatshahi, S. (1995). An integrated manufacturing system design: An applied approach. *International Journal of Production Economics*, *42*(2), 187–199.

Dunk, A. S. (2004). Product life cycle cost analysis: The impact of customer profiling, competitive advantage, and quality of IS information. *Management Accounting Research*, *15*(4), 401–414. Retrieved from http://doi.org/10.1016/j.mar.2004.04.001

Durisin, B., Calabretta, G., & Parmeggiani, V. (2010). The intellectual structure of product innovation research: A bibliometric study of the journal of product innovation management, 1984–2004. *Journal of Product Innovation Management*, *27*(3), 437–451. Retrieved from http://doi.org/10.1111/j.1540-5885.2010.00726.x

Dutta, S. K., & Lawson, R. A. (2008). A tale of two technologies: The financial chapter. *International Journal of Technology Management*, *42*(3), 205–225. Retrieved from http://doi.org/10.1504/IJTM.2008.018104

Elgh, F., & Cederfeldt, M. (2007). Concurrent cost estimation as a tool for enhanced producibility: System development and applicability for producibility studies. *International Journal of Production Economics*, *109*(1–2), 12–26. Retrieved from http://doi.org/10.1016/j.ijpe.2006.11.007

Elimam, A. A., & Dodin, B. (1994). Optimum selection and operation of Sludge dewatering processes. *IIE Transactions*, *26*(3), 89–100. Retrieved from http://doi.org/10.1080/07408179408966611

Ettlie, J. E., & Elsenbach, J. M. (2007). Modified Stage-Gate® regimes in new product development. *Journal of Product Innovation Management*, *24*(1), 20–33. Retrieved from http://doi.org/10.1111/j.1540-5885.2006.00230.x

Ettlie, J. E., & Trygg, L. D. (1995). Design-manufacturing practice in the US and Sweden. *IEEE Transactions on Engineering Management*, *42*(1), 74–81. Retrieved from http://doi.org/10.1109/17.366407

Everaert, P., & Bruggeman, W. (2002). Cost targets and time pressure during new product development. *International Journal of Operations & Production Management*, *22*(12), 1339–1353. Retrieved from http://doi.org/10.1108/01443570210452039

Eynan, A., & Rosenblatt, M. J. (1996). Component commonality effects on inventory costs. *IIE Transactions*, *28*(2), 93–104. Retrieved from http://doi.org/10.1080/07408179608966255

Fargnoli, M., De Minicis, M., & Tronci, M. (2013). Design management for sustainability: An integrated approach for the development of sustainable products. *Journal of Engineering and Technology Management*, *34*, 29–45. Retrieved from http://doi.org/10.1016/j.jengtecman.2013.09.005

Farrell, R. S., & Simpson, T. W. (2010). Improving cost effectiveness in an existing product line using component product platforms. *International Journal of Production Research*, *48*(11), 3299–3317. Retrieved from http://doi.org/10.1080/00207540802620753

Fayard, D., Lee, L. S., Leitch, R. a., & Kettinger, W. J. (2012). Effect of internal cost management, information systems integration, and absorptive capacity on inter-organizational cost management in supply chains. *Accounting, Organizations and Society, 37*(3), 168–187. Retrieved from http://doi.org/10.1016/j.aos.2012.02.001

Filomena, T. P., Neto, F. J. K., & Duffey, M. R. (2009). Target costing operationalization during product development: Model and application. *International Journal of Production Economics, 118*(2), 398–409. Retrieved from http://doi.org/10.1016/j.ijpe.2008.12.007

Folgado, R., Peças, P., & Henriques, E. (2010). Life cycle cost for technology selection: A case study in the manufacturing of injection moulds. *International Journal of Production Economics, 128*(1), 368–378. Retrieved from http://doi.org/10.1016/j.ijpe.2010.07.036

Fung, R. Y. K., Tang, J., Tu, Y., & Wang, D. (2002). Product design resources optimization using a non-linear fuzzy quality function deployment model. *International Journal of Production Research, 40*(3), 585–599. Retrieved from http://doi.org/10.1080/00207540110061634

Garud, R., & Munir, K. (2008). From transaction to transformation costs: The case of Polaroid's SX-70 camera. *Research Policy, 37*(4), 690–705. Retrieved from http://doi.org/10.1016/j.respol.2007.12.010

Gil, N. (2009). Project safeguards: Operationalizing option-like strategic thinking in infrastructure development. *IEEE Transactions on Engineering Management, 56*(2), 257–270. Retrieved from http://doi.org/10.1109/TEM.2009.2016063

Goffin, K. (1998). Evaluating customer support during new product development – An exploratory study. *Journal of Product Innovation Management, 15*(1), 42–56.

Goffin, K. (2000). Design for supportability: Essential component of new product development. *Research-Technology Management, 43*(2), 40–47.

Goffin, K., & Micheli, P. (2010). Maximizing the value of industrial design in new product development. *Research-Technology Management, 53*(5), 29–37.

Goh, Y. M., Newnes, L. B., Mileham, A. R., McMahon, C. A., & Saravi, M. E. (2010). Uncertainty in through-life costing-review and perspectives. *IEEE Transactions on Engineering Management, 57*(4), 689–701. Retrieved from http://doi.org/10.1109/TEM.2010.2040745

Gopalakrishnan, M., Libby, T., Samuels, J. a., & Swenson, D. (2015). The effect of cost goal specificity and new product development process on cost reduction performance. *Accounting, Organizations and Society, 42*, 1–11. Retrieved from http://doi.org/10.1016/j.aos.2015.01.003

Gorman, M. F., & Kanet, J. J. (2005). Evaluating operations management-related journals via the author affiliation index. *Manufacturing & Service Operations Management, 7*(1), 3–19. Retrieved from http://doi.org/10.1287/msom.1040.0062

Griffin, A. (1992). Evaluating QFD's use in US firms as a process for developing products. *Journal of Product Innovation Management, 9*(3), 171–187. Retrieved from http://doi.org/10.1111/1540-5885.930171

Grote, C., Jones, R., Blount, G., Goodyer, J., & Shayler, M. (2007). An approach to the EuP directive and the application of the economic eco-design for complex products. *International Journal of Production Research, 45*(18–19), 4099–4117. Retrieved from http://doi.org/10.1080/00207540701450088

Guiltinan, J. (2011). Progress and challenges in product line pricing. *Journal of Product Innovation Management, 28*, 744–756. Retrieved from http://doi.org/10.1111/j.1540-5885.2011.00837.x

Gupta, D., & Benjaafar, S. (2004). Make-to-order, make-to-stock, or delay product differentiation? A common framework for modeling and analysis. *IIE Transactions, 36*(6), 529–546. Retrieved from http://doi.org/10.1080/07408170490438519

Halman, J. I. M., Hofer, A. P., & Van Vuuren, W. (2003). Platform-driven development of product families: Linking theory with practice. *Journal of Product Innovation Management, 20*(2), 149–162. Retrieved from http://doi.org/10.1111/1540-5885.2002007

Harmancioglu, N., McNally, R. C., Calantone, R. J., & Durmusoglu, S. S. (2007). Your New Product Development (NPD) is only as good as your process: An exploratory analysis of new NPD process design and implementation. *R&D Management, 37*(5), 399–424. Retrieved from http://doi.org/10.1111/j.1467-9310.2007.00486.x

Hart, S., Hultink, E. J., Tzokas, N., & Commandeur, H. R. (2003). Industrial companies' evaluation criteria in new product development gates. *Journal of Product Innovation Management, 20*(1), 22–36. Retrieved from http://doi.org/10.1111/1540-5885.201003

Hatch, M., & Badinelli, R. D. (1999). A concurrent optimization methodology for concurrent engineering. *IEEE Transactions on Engineering Management, 46*(1), 72–86. Retrieved from http://doi.org/10.1109/17.740039

Hauser, J. R. (2001). Metrics thermostat. *Journal of Product Innovation Management, 18*(3), 134–153. Retrieved from http://doi.org/10.1111/1540-5885.1830134

He, D. W., & Kusiak, a. (1996). Performance analysis of modular products. *International Journal of Production Research, 34*(1), 253–272. Retrieved from http://doi.org/10.1080/00207549608904900

Heese, H. S., & Swaminathan, J. M. (2006). Product line design with component commonality and cost-reduction effort. *Manufacturing & Service Operations Management, 8*(2), 206–219. Retrieved from http://doi.org/10.1287/msom.1060.0103

Hegde, G. G. (1994). Life cycle cost: A model and applications. *IIE Transactions, 26*(6), 56–62. Retrieved from http://doi.org/10.1080/07408179408966638

Heilala, J., Helin, K., & Montonen, J. (2006). Total cost of ownership analysis for modular final assembly systems. *International Journal of Production Research, 44*(18–19), 3967–3988. Retrieved from http://doi.org/10.1080/00207540600806448

Heim, G. R., Mallick, D. N., & Peng, X. (2012). Antecedents and consequences of new product development practices and software tools: An exploratory study. *IEEE Transactions on Engineering Management, 59*(3), 428–442. Retrieved from http://doi.org/10.1109/TEM.2011.2172608

Hertenstein, J. H., & Platt, M. B. (2000). Performance measures and management control in new product development. *Accounting Horizons, 14*(3), 303–323. Retrieved from http://doi.org/10.2308/acch.2000.14.3.303

Hillier, M. S. (2000). Component commonality in multiple-period, assemble-to-order systems. *IIE Transactions, 32*(8), 755–766. Retrieved from http://doi.org/10.1080/07408170008967433

Hopp, W. J., & Xu, X. (2005). Product line selection and pricing with modularity in design. *Manufacturing & Service Operations Management, 7*(3), 15. Retrieved from http://doi.org/10.1287/msom.1050.0077

Hoque, M., Akter, M., & Monden, Y. (2005). Concurrent engineering: A compromising approach to develop a feasible and customer-pleasing product. *International Journal of Production Research, 43*(8), 1607–1624. Retrieved from http://doi.org/10.1080/00207540412331320490

Hoyle, C. J., & Chen, W. (2009). Product Attribute Function Deployment (PAFD) for deci-
sion-based conceptual design. *IEEE Transactions on Engineering Management*, *56*(2),
271–284. Retrieved from http://doi.org/10.1109/TEM.2008.927787

Huang, T.-T. A., Stewart, R. A., & Chen, L. (2010). Identifying key enablers to improve business performance in Taiwanese electronic manufacturing companies. *International
Journal of Operations & Production Management*, *30*(2), 155–180. Retrieved from
http://doi.org/10.1108/01443571011018699

Ibusuki, U., & Kaminski, P. C. (2007). Product development process with focus on value engineering and target-costing: A case study in an automotive company. *International
Journal of Production Economics*, *105*(2), 459–474. Retrieved from http://doi.org/10.
1016/j.ijpe.2005.08.009

Ijomah, W. L., McMahon, C. A., Hammond, G. P., & Newman, S. T. (2007). Development of
robust design-for-remanufacturing guidelines to further the aims of sustainable development. *International Journal of Production Research*, *45*(18–19), 4513–4536. Retrieved
from http://doi.org/10.1080/00207540701450138

Iranmanesh, H., & Thomson, V. (2008). Competitive advantage by adjusting design characteristics to satisfy cost targets. *International Journal of Production Economics*, *115*(1),
64–71. Retrieved from http://doi.org/10.1016/j.ijpe.2008.05.006

Ismail, H., Reid, I., Mooney, J., Poolton, J., & Arokiam, I. (2007). How small and medium
enterprises effectively participate in the mass customization game. *IEEE Transactions
on Engineering Management*, *54*(1), 86–97. Retrieved from http://doi.org/10.1109/
TEM.2006.889069

Ittner, C. D., & Larcker, D. F. (1997). Product development cycle time and organizational performance. *Journal of Marketing Research*, *34*(1), 13–23. Retrieved from http://doi.org/
10.2307/3152061

Izui, K., Nishiwaki, S., Yoshimura, M., Kariya, H., Ogihara, Y., & Hayashi, S. (2010).
Switchgear component commonality design based on trade-off analysis among inventory level, delivery lead-time and product performance. *International Journal of
Production Research*, *48*(10), 2821–2840. Retrieved from http://doi.org/10.1080/
00207540902791868

Jacobs, M., Droge, C., Vickery, S. K., & Calantone, R. (2011). Product and process modularity's effects on manufacturing agility and firm growth performance. *Journal of Product
Innovation Management*, *28*(1), 123–137. Retrieved from http://doi.org/10.1111/j.1540-
5885.2010.00785.x

Jacobs, M., Vickery, S. K., & Droge, C. (2007). The effects of product modularity on competitive performance: Do integration strategies mediate the relationship? *International
Journal of Operations & Production Management*, *27*(10), 1046–1068. Retrieved from
http://doi.org/10.1108/01443570710820620

Jägle, A. J. (1999). Shareholder value, real options, and innovation in technology-intensive
companies. *R&D Management*, *29*(3), 271–288. Retrieved from http://doi.org/10.1111/
1467-9310.00136

Jenkins, S., Forbes, S., & Durrani, T. S. (1997). Managing the product development process.
Part I: An assessment. *International Journal of Technology Management*, *13*(4),
359–378.

Ji, P., Jin, J., Wang, T., & Chen, Y. (2014). Quantification and integration of Kano's model
into QFD for optimising product design. *International Journal of Production Research*,
*52*(21), 6335–6348. Retrieved from http://doi.org/10.1080/00207543.2014.939777

Jiao, J. (Roger). (2012). Product platform flexibility planning by hybrid real options analysis. *IIE Transactions*, *44*(6), 431–445. Retrieved from http://doi.org/10.1080/0740817X.2011.609874

John, G., Weiss, A. M., & Dutta, S. (1999). Marketing in technology-intensive markets: Toward a conceptual framework. *Journal of Marketing*, *63*, 78–91. Retrieved from http://doi.org/10.2307/1252103

Johnson, M. D., & Kirchain, R. E. (2009). Quantifying the effects of product family decisions on material selection: A process-based costing approach. *International Journal of Production Economics*, *120*(2), 653–668. Retrieved from http://doi.org/10.1016/j.ijpe.2009.04.014

Johnson, M. D., & Kirchain, R. E. (2010). Developing and assessing commonality metrics for product families: A process-based cost-modeling approach. *IEEE Transactions on Engineering Management*, *57*(4), 634–648. Retrieved from http://doi.org/10.1109/TEM.2009.2034642

Johnson, M. R., & Wang, M. H. (1995). Planning product disassembly for material recovery opportunities. *International Journal of Production Research*, *33*(11), 3119–3142. Retrieved from http://doi.org/10.1080/00207549508904864

Jørgensen, B., & Messner, M. (2009). Management control in new product development: The dynamics of managing flexibility and efficiency. *Journal of Management Accounting Research*, *21*(1), 99–124. Retrieved from http://doi.org/10.2308/jmar.2009.21.1.99

Kamrad, B., Schmidt, G. M., & Ülkü, S. (2013). Analyzing product architecture under technological change: Modular upgradeability tradeoffs. *IEEE Transactions on Engineering Management*, *60*(2), 289–300. Retrieved from http://doi.org/10.1109/TEM.2012.2211362

Kang, C. M., Hong, Y. S., & Huh, W. T. (2012). Platform replacement planning for management of product family obsolescence. *IIE Transactions*, *44*(12), 1115–1131. Retrieved from http://doi.org/10.1080/0740817X.2012.672791

Karim, S. (2006). Modularity in organizational structure: The reconfiguration of internally developed and acquired business units. *Strategic Management Journal*, *27*, 799–823. Retrieved from http://doi.org/10.1002/smj.547

Karsak, E. E. (2004). Fuzzy multiple objective decision making approach to prioritize design requirements in quality function deployment. *International Journal of Production Research*, *42*(18), 3957–3974. Retrieved from http://doi.org/10.1080/00207540410001703998

Kaski, T., & Heikkila, J. (2002). Measuring product structures to improve demand-supply chain efficiency. *International Journal of Technology Management*, *23*(6), 578. Retrieved from http://doi.org/10.1504/IJTM.2002.003027

Kee, R. (2010). The sufficiency of target costing for evaluating production-related decisions. *International Journal of Production Economics*, *126*(2), 204–211. Retrieved from http://doi.org/10.1016/j.ijpe.2010.03.008

Kerr, C., Phaal, R., & Probert, D. (2012). Cogitate, articulate, communicate: The psychosocial reality of technology roadmapping and roadmaps. *R&D Management*, *42*(1), 1–13. Retrieved from http://doi.org/10.1111/j.1467-9310.2011.00658.x

Kessler, E. H. (2000). Tightening the belt: Methods for reducing development costs associated with new product innovation. *Journal of Engineering and Technology Management*, *17*(1), 59–92. Retrieved from http://doi.org/10.1016/S0923-4748(99)00020-X

Kim, Y., Kim, H. S., Jeon, H., & Sohn, S. Y. (2009). Economic evaluation model for international standardization of technology. *IEEE Transactions on Instrumentation and Measurement*, *58*(3), 657–665. Retrieved from http://doi.org/10.1109/TIM.2008.2005555

Kleinschmidt, E. J., De Brentani, U., & Salomo, S. (2007). Performance of global new product development programs: A resource-based view. *Journal of Product Innovation Management, 24*(5), 419–441.

Kleyner, A., & Sandborn, P. (2008). Minimizing life cycle cost by managing product reliability via validation plan and warranty return cost. *International Journal of Production Economics, 112*(2), 796–807. Retrieved from http://doi.org/10.1016/j.ijpe.2007.07.001

Kolarik, W. J. (1995). *Creating quality.* New York: McGraw-Hill, Inc.

Kostoff, R. N., & Schaller, R. R. (2001). Science and technology roadmaps. *IEEE Transactions on Engineering Management, 48*(2), 132–143. Retrieved from http://doi.org/10.1109/17.922473

Krishnan, V., Singh, R., & Tirupati, D. (1999). A model-based approach for planning and developing a family of technology-based products. *Manufacturing & Service Operations Management, 1*(2), 132–156. Retrieved from http://doi.org/10.1287/msom.1.2.132

Kumar, S., & Wellbrock, J. (2009). Improved new product development through enhanced design architecture for engineer-to-order companies. *International Journal of Production Research, 47*(15), 4235–4254. Retrieved from http://doi.org/10.1080/00207540801939030

Labro, E. (2004). The cost effects of component commonality: A literature review through a management-accounting lens. *Manufacturing & Service Operations Management, 6*(4), 358–367. Retrieved from http://doi.org/10.1287/msom.1040.0047

Lager, T. (2005). The industrial usability of quality function deployment: A literature review and synthesis on a meta-level. *R&D Management, 35*(4), 409–426. Retrieved from http://doi.org/10.1111/j.1467-9310.2005.00398.x

Lau, A. K. W. (2014). Influence of contingent factors on the perceived level of supplier integration: A contingency perspective. *Journal of Engineering and Technology Management, 33*, 210–242. Retrieved from http://doi.org/10.1016/j.jengtecman.2014.07.002

Lau, A. K. W., Yam, R. C. M., & Tang, E. (2007). The impacts of product modularity on competitive capabilities and performance: An empirical study. *International Journal of Production Economics, 105*(1), 1–20. Retrieved from http://doi.org/10.1016/j.ijpe.2006.02.002

Lau, A. K. W., Yam, R. C. M., & Tang, E. (2011). The impact of product modularity on new product performance: Mediation by product innovativeness. *Journal of Product Innovation Management, 28*(2), 270–284. Retrieved from http://doi.org/10.1111/j.1540-5885.2011.00796.x

Lau, A. K. W., Yam, R. C. M., & Tang, E. P. Y. (2010). Supply chain integration and product modularity. *International Journal of Operations & Production Management, 30*(1), 20–56. Retrieved from http://doi.org/10.1108/01443571011012361

Lawson, B., Petersen, K. J., Cousins, P. D., & Handfield, R. B. (2009). Knowledge sharing in interorganizational product development teams: The effect of formal and informal socialization mechanisms. *Journal of Product Innovation Management, 26*(2), 156–172. Retrieved from http://doi.org/10.1111/j.1540-5885.2009.00343.x

Lee, A. H. I., Kang, H.-Y., Yang, C.-Y., & Lin, C.-Y. (2010). An evaluation framework for product planning using FANP, QFD and multi-choice goal programming. *International Journal of Production Research, 48*(13), 3977–3997. Retrieved from http://doi.org/10.1080/00207540902950845

Lee, S., Lee, S., Seol, H., & Park, Y. (2008). Using patent information for designing new product and technology: Keyword based technology roadmapping. *R&D Management, 38*(2), 169–188. Retrieved from http://doi.org/10.1111/j.1467-9310.2008.00509.x

Li, H., Wang, Y., Yin, R., Kull, T. J., & Choi, T. Y. (2012). Target pricing: Demand-side versus supply-side approaches. *International Journal of Production Economics, 136*(1), 172–184. Retrieved from http://doi.org/10.1016/j.ijpe.2011.10.002

Lichtenthaler, E. (2004). Technology intelligence processes in leading European and North American multinationals. *R&D Management, 34*(2), 121–135. Retrieved from http://doi.org/10.1111/j.1467-9310.2004.00328.x

Lichtenthaler, U. (2008). Integrated roadmaps for open innovation. *Research-Technology Management, 51*(3), 45–49.

Liker, J. K., Collins, P. D., & Hull, F. M. (1999). Flexibility and standardization: Test of a contingency model of product design-manufacturing integration. *Journal of Product Innovation Management, 16*(3), 248–267. Retrieved from http://doi.org/10.1016/S0737-6782(98)00049-6

Liker, J. K., Kamath, R. R., Wasti, S. N., & Nagamachi, M. (1996). Supplier involvement in automotive component design: Are there really large US Japan differences? *Research Policy, 25*(1), 59–89. Retrieved from http://doi.org/10.1016/0048-7333(95)00826-8

Lin, T., Lee, J.-W., & Bohez, E. L. J. (2012). New integrated model to estimate the manufacturing cost and production system performance at the conceptual design stage of helicopter blade assembly. *International Journal of Production Research, 50*(24), 7210–7228. Retrieved from http://doi.org/10.1080/00207543.2011.644818

Linton, J. D., & Thongpapanl, N. (Tek). (2004). Perspective: Ranking the technology innovation management journals. *Journal of Product Innovation Management, 21*(2), 123–139. Retrieved from http://doi.org/10.1111/j.0737-6782.2004.00062.x

Liu, Z., Wong, Y. S., & Lee, K. S. (2010). Modularity analysis and commonality design: A framework for the top-down platform and product family design. *International Journal of Production Research, 48*(12), 3657–3680. Retrieved from http://doi.org/10.1080/00207540902902598

Loch, C., Stein, L., & Terwiesch, C. (1996). Measuring development performance in the electronics industry. *Journal of Product Innovation Management, 13*(1), 3–20. Retrieved from http://doi.org/10.1016/0737-6782(95)00089-5

Lockwood, C. (1999). *Comparison of average-passage equation closures through simulation of single and multi-row axial compressors; the limitations of using a commercial CFD code.* Ph.D. Thesis, Cranfield University. Cited in Coldrick et al. (2005).

Lu, Q., & Wood, L. (2006). The refinement of design for manufacture: Inclusion of process design. *International Journal of Operations & Production Management, 26*(10), 1123–1145. Retrieved from http://doi.org/10.1108/01443570610691102

Luo, X. G., Kwong, C. K., Tang, J. F., Deng, S. F., & Gong, J. (2011). Integrating supplier selection in optimal product family design. *International Journal of Production Research, 49*(14), 4195–4222. Retrieved from http://doi.org/10.1080/00207543.2010.544337

Madan, J., Rao, P. V. M., & Kundra, T. K. (2007). System for early cost estimation of diecast parts. *International Journal of Production Research, 45*(20), 4823–4847. Retrieved from http://doi.org/10.1080/00207540600789016

Magnusson, M., & Pasche, M. (2014). A contingency-based approach to the use of product platforms and modules in new product development. *Journal of Product Innovation Management, 31*(3), 434–450. Retrieved from http://doi.org/10.1111/jpim.12106

Mäkinen, S. J., Seppänen, M., & Ortt, J. R. (2014). Introduction to the special issue: Platforms, contingencies and new product development. *Journal of Product Innovation Management, 31*(3), 412–416. Retrieved from http://doi.org/10.1111/jpim.12104

Mangun, D., & Thurston, D. L. (2002). Incorporating component reuse, remanufacture, and recycle into product portfolio design. *IEEE Transactions on Engineering Management*, *49*(4), 479–490. Retrieved from http://doi.org/10.1109/TEM.2002.807292

Marion, T. J., & Meyer, M. H. (2011). Applying industrial design and cost engineering to new product development in early-stage firms. *Journal of Product Innovation Management*, *28*, 773–786. Retrieved from http://doi.org/10.1111/j.1540-5885.2011.00839.x

Marion, T. J., Thevenot, H. J., & Simpson, T. W. (2007). A cost-based methodology for evaluating product platform commonality sourcing decisions with two examples. *International Journal of Production Research*, *45*(22), 5285–5308. Retrieved from http://doi.org/10.1080/00207540600710970

Martin, B. R., Nightingale, P., & Yegros-Yegros, A. (2012). Science and technology studies: Exploring the knowledge base. *Research Policy*, *41*(7), 1182–1204. Retrieved from http://doi.org/10.1016/j.respol.2012.03.010

Martínez Sánchez, A., & Pérez, M. P. (2003). Cooperation and the ability to minimize the time and cost of new product development within the Spanish automotive supplier industry. *Journal of Product Innovation Management*, *20*(1), 57–69. Retrieved from http://doi.org/10.1111/1540-5885.201005

Mathews, S. (2010). Innovation portfolio architecture. *Research-Technology Management*, *53*(6), 30–40.

Mathews, S. (2011). Innovation portfolio architecture. Part 2: Attribute selection and valuation. *Research-Technology Management*, *54*(5), 37–46. Retrieved from http://doi.org/10.5437/08956308X5405005

Matzler, K., & Hinterhuber, H. H. (1998). How to make product development projects more successful by integrating Kano's model of customer satisfaction into quality function deployment. *Technovation*, *18*(1), 25–38. Retrieved from http://doi.org/10.1016/S0166-4972(97)00072-2

McGrath, R. N., & Young, S. B. (2002). NASA's small aircraft costs versus automobile costs and the economic value of traveler time. *Technovation*, *22*(5), 325–336. Retrieved from http://doi.org/10.1016/S0166-4972(01)00078-5

Meyer, M. H., & Dalal, D. (2002). Managing platform architectures and manufacturing processes for nonassembled products. *Journal of Product Innovation Management*, *19*(4), 277–293. Retrieved from http://doi.org/10.1016/S0737-6782(02)00145-5

Meyer, M. H., & Mugge, P. C. (2001). Make platform innovation drive enterprise growth. *Research-Technology Management*, *44*(1), 25–39.

Mildenberger, U., & Khare, A. (2000). Planning for an environment-friendly car. *Technovation*, *20*(4), 205–214. Retrieved from http://doi.org/10.1016/S0166-4972(99)00111-X

Moore, W. L., Louviere, J. J., & Verma, R. (1999). Using conjoint analysis to help design product platforms. *Journal of Product Innovation Management*, *16*(1), 27–39. Retrieved from http://doi.org/10.1111/1540-5885.1610027

Muffatto, M. (1999). Introducing a platform strategy in product development. *International Journal of Production Economics*, *60*, 145–153. Retrieved from http://doi.org/10.1016/S0925-5273(98)00173-X

Muffatto, M., & Roveda, M. (2000). Developing product platforms: Analysis of the development process. *Technovation*, *20*(11), 617–630. Retrieved from http://doi.org/10.1016/S0166-4972(99)00178-9

Mukhopadhyay, S. K., & Setoputro, R. (2005). Optimal return policy and modular design for build-to-order products. *Journal of Operations Management, 23*(5), 496–506. Retrieved from http://doi.org/10.1016/j.jom.2004.10.012

Müller-Seitz, G. (2012). Absorptive and desorptive capacity-related practices at the network level – The case of SEMATECH. *R&D Management, 42*(1), 90–99. Retrieved from http://doi.org/10.1111/j.1467-9310.2011.00668.x

Murthy, D. N. P., & Blischke, W. R. (2000). Strategic warranty management: A life-cycle approach. *IEEE Transactions on Engineering Management, 47*(1), 40–54. Retrieved from http://doi.org/10.1109/17.820724

Nepal, B., Monplaisir, L., & Singh, N. (2005). Integrated fuzzy logic-based model for product modularization during concept development phase. *International Journal of Production Economics, 96*(2), 157–174. Retrieved from http://doi.org/10.1016/j.ijpe.2004.03.010

Neto, Q. F., Walther, J., Bloemhof, G., van Nunen, J. a. E., & Spengler, T. (2010). From closed-loop to sustainable supply chains: The WEEE case. *International Journal of Production Research, 48*(15), 4463–4481. Retrieved from http://doi.org/10.1080/00207540902906151

Nobelius, D., & Sundgren, N. (2002). Managerial issues in parts sharing among product development projects: A case study. *Journal of Engineering and Technology Management, 19*(1), 59–73. Retrieved from http://doi.org/10.1016/S0923-4748(01)00046-7

O'Connor, P. (1994). Implementing a stage-gate process: A multi-company perspective. *Journal of Product Innovation Management, 11*(3), 183–200. Retrieved from http://doi.org/10.1111/1540-5885.1130183

Olhager, J., & West, B. M. (2002). The house of flexibility: Using the QFD approach to deploy manufacturing flexibility. *International Journal of Operations & Production Management, 22*(1), 50–79. Retrieved from http://doi.org/10.1108/01443570210412079

Onofrei, M., Hunt, J., Siemienczuk, J., Touchette, D. R., & Middleton, B. (2004). A first step towards translating evidence into practice: Heart failure in a community practice-based research network. *Informatics in Primary Care, 12*(3), 139–145. Retrieved from http://doi.org/Article

Ozer, M., & Cebeci, U. (2010). The role of globalization in new product development. *IEEE Transactions on Engineering Management, 57*(2), 168–180. Retrieved from http://doi.org/10.1109/TEM.2009.2025492

Page, A. L., & Schirr, G. R. (2008). Growth and development of a body of knowledge: 16 years of new product development research, 1989–2004. *Journal of Product Innovation Management, 25*(3), 233–248. Retrieved from http://doi.org/10.1111/j.1540-5885.2008.00297.x

Park, J., & Simpson, T. W. (2005). Development of a production cost estimation framework to support product family design. *International Journal of Production Research, 43*. Retrieved from http://doi.org/10.1080/00207540512331311903

Park, J., & Simpson, T. W. (2008). Toward an activity-based costing system for product families and product platforms in the early stages of development. *International Journal of Production Research, 46*. Retrieved from http://doi.org/10.1080/00207540600825240

Patel, P. C., & Jayaram, J. (2014). The antecedents and consequences of product variety in new ventures: An empirical study. *Journal of Operations Management, 32*(1–2), 34–50. Retrieved from http://doi.org/10.1016/j.jom.2013.07.002

Perdue, R. K., McAllister, W. J., King, P. V., & Berkey, B. G. (1999). Valuation of R and D projects using options pricing and decision analysis models. *Interfaces, 29*(6), 57–74. Retrieved from http://doi.org/10.1287/inte.29.6.57

Perera, H. S. C., Nagarur, N., & Tabucanon, M. T. (1999). Component part standardization: A way to reduce the life-cycle costs of products. *International Journal of Production Economics, 60*, 109–116. Retrieved from http://doi.org/10.1016/S0925-5273(98)00179-0

Perlman, Y. (2012). The effect of risk aversion on product family design under uncertain consumer segments. *International Journal of Production Research, 51*(2), 1–11. Retrieved from http://doi.org/10.1080/00207543.2011.653013

Petersen, K. J., Handfield, R. B., & Ragatz, G. L. (2003). A model of supplier integration into new product development. *Journal of Product Innovation Management, 20*(4), 284–299. Retrieved from http://doi.org/10.1111/1540-5885.00028

Plank, R. E., & Ferrin, B. G. (2002). How manufacturers value purchase offerings. An exploratory study. *Industrial Marketing Management, 31*(5), 457–465. Retrieved from http://doi.org/10.1016/S0019-8501(01)00161-4

Pullan, T. T., Bhasi, M., & Madhu, G. (2012). Object-oriented modelling of manufacturing information system for collaborative design. *International Journal of Production Research, 50*(12), 3328–3344. Retrieved from http://doi.org/10.1080/00207543.2011.575096

Quan, X., & Chesbrough, H. W. (2010). Hierarchical segmentation of R&D process and intellectual property protection: Evidence from multinational R&D laboratories in China. *IEEE Transactions on Engineering Management, 57*(1), 9–21. Retrieved from http://doi.org/10.1109/TEM.2009.2033043

Rabino, S. (2001). The accountant's contribution to product development teams – A case study. *Journal of Engineering and Technology Management, 18*(1), 73–90. Retrieved from http://doi.org/10.1016/S0923-4748(00)00034-5

Rai, R., & Allada, V. (2003). Modular product family design: Agent-based Pareto optimization and quality loss function-based post-optimal analysis. *International Journal of Production Research, 41*(17), 4075–4098. Retrieved from http://doi.org/10.1080/0020754031000149248

Ramachandran, K., & Krishnan, V. (2008). Design architecture and introduction timing for rapidly improving industrial products. *Manufacturing & Service Operations Management, 10*(1), 149–171. Retrieved from http://doi.org/10.1287/msom.1060.0143

Ramdas, K., Fisher, M., & Ulrich, K. (2003). Managing variety for assembled products: Modeling component systems sharing. *Manufacturing & Service Operations Management, 5*(2), 142–156. Retrieved from http://doi.org/10.1287/msom.5.2.142.16073

Ray, P. K., & Ray, S. (2010). Resource-constrained innovation for emerging economies: The case of the indian telecommunications industry. *IEEE Transactions on Engineering Management, 57*(1), 144–156. Retrieved from http://doi.org/10.1109/TEM.2009.2033044

Ray, S., & Ray, P. K. (2011). Product innovation for the people's car in an emerging economy. *Technovation, 31*(5–6), 216–227. Retrieved from http://doi.org/10.1016/j.technovation.2011.01.004

Reitzig, M. (2011). Is your company choosing the best Innovation ideas? *MIT Sloan Management Review, 52*, 47–52.

Riggs, J. L., & Jones, D. (1990). Flowgraph representation of life cycle cost methodology – A new perspective for project managers. *IEEE Transactions on Engineering Management, 37*(2), 147–152. Retrieved from http://doi.org/10.1109/17.53719

Ro, Y. K., Liker, J. K., & Fixson, S. K. (2007). Modularity as a strategy for supply chain coordination: The case of U.S. auto. *IEEE Transactions on Engineering Management, 54*(1), 172–189. Retrieved from http://doi.org/10.1109/TEM.2006.889075

Robertson, D., & Ulrich, K. (1998). Planning for product platforms. *Sloan Managament Review, 39*(4), 19–31.

Romano, P., Formentini, M., Bandera, C., & Tomasella, M. (2010). Value analysis as a decision support tool in cruise ship design. *International Journal of Production Research, 48*(23), 6939–6958. Retrieved from http://doi.org/10.1080/00207540903352686

Romli, A., Prickett, P., Setchi, R., & Soe, S. (2014). Integrated eco-design decision-making for sustainable product development. *International Journal of Production Research, 53*(2), 549–571. Retrieved from http://doi.org/10.1080/00207543.2014.958593

Roy, R., Souchoroukov, P., & Griggs, T. (2008). Function-based cost estimating. *International Journal of Production Research, 46*(10), 2621–2650. Retrieved from http://doi.org/10.1080/00207540601094440

Rücker, A., Jaenicke, P., & Hofer, M. B. (2014). Aktives Vielfaltsmanagement – Ertragssteigerung im automobilen Ersatzteilgeschäft. In B. Ebel & M. B. Hofer (Eds.), *Automotive management* (pp. 207–214). Berlin: Springer Berlin Heidelberg. Retrieved from http://doi.org/10.1007/978-3-642-34068-0_14

Rusinko, C. A. (1999). Exploring the use of Design-Manufacturing Integration (DMI) to facilitate product development: A test of some practices. *IEEE Transactions on Engineering Management, 46*(1), 56–71. Retrieved from http://doi.org/10.1109/17.740038

Salvador, F., Rungtusanatham, M., Forza, C., & Trentin, A. (2007). Mix flexibility and volume flexibility in a build-to-order environment: Synergies and trade-offs. *International Journal of Operations & Production Management, 27*(11), 1173–1191. Retrieved from http://doi.org/10.1108/01443570710830584

Sanchez, R. (1999). Modular architectures in the marketing process. *Journal of Marketing, 63*, 92–111.

Sanderson, S. W. (1991). Cost models for evaluating virtual design strategies in multicycle product families. *Journal of Engineering and Technology Management, 8*(3–4), 339–358. Retrieved from http://doi.org/10.1016/0923-4748(91)90017-L

Sanderson, S. W., & Uzumeri, M. (1995). Managing product families: The case of the Sony Walkman. *Research Policy, 24*(5), 761–782. Retrieved from http://doi.org/10.1016/0048-7333(94)00797-B

Sarangee, K. R., Woolley, J. L., Schmidt, J. B., & Long, E. (2014). De-escalation mechanisms in high-technology product innovation. *Journal of Product Innovation Management, 31*(5), 1023–1038. Retrieved from http://doi.org/10.1111/jpim.12142

Schultz, C., Salomo, S., De Brentani, U., & Kleinschmidt, E. J. (2013). How formal control influences decision-making clarity and innovation performance. *Journal of Product Innovation Management, 30*(3), 430–447. Retrieved from http://doi.org/10.1111/jpim.12009

Sethi, R., & Iqbal, Z. (2008). Stage-gate controls, learning failure, and adverse effect on novel new products. *Journal of Marketing, 72*(1), 118–134. Retrieved from http://doi.org/10.1509/jmkg.72.1.118

Settanni, E., Newnes, L. B., Thenent, N. E., Parry, G., & Goh, Y. M. (2014). A through-life costing methodology for use in product-service-systems. *International Journal of Production Economics, 153*, 161–177. Retrieved from http://doi.org/10.1016/j.ijpe.2014.02.016

Sik Oh, J., O'Grady, P., & Young, R. E. (1995). A constraint network approach to design for assembly. *IIE Transactions, 27*(1), 72–80. Retrieved from http://doi.org/10.1080/07408179508936718

Simonse, L. W. L., Hultink, E. J., & Buijs, J. A. (2014). Innovation roadmapping: Building concepts from practitioners' insights. *Journal of Product Innovation Management*. Retrieved from http://doi.org/10.1111/jpim.12208

Simpson, T. W., Maier, J. R., & Mistree, F. (2001). Product platform design: Method and application. *Research in Engineering Design*, *13*(1), 2−22. Retrieved from http://doi.org/10.1007/s001630100002

Sohn, S. Y., & Kim, Y. (2011). Economic evaluation model for international standardization of correlated technologies. *IEEE Transactions on Engineering Management*, *58*(2), 189−198. Retrieved from http://doi.org/10.1109/TEM.2010.2058853

Song, J.-S., & Zhao, Y. (2009). The value of component commonality in a dynamic inventory system with lead times. *Manufacturing & Service Operations Management*, *11*(3), 493−508. Retrieved from http://doi.org/10.1287/msom.1080.0235

Stevens, G., Burley, J., & Divine, R. (1999). Creativity + business discipline = higher profits faster from new product development. *Journal of Product Innovation Management*, *16*(5), 455−468. Retrieved from http://doi.org/10.1016/S0737-6782(98)00070-8

Stonebraker, J. S., Gil, E., Kirkwood, C. W., & Handfield, R. B. (2012). Impact factor as a metric to assess journals where OM research is published. *Journal of Operations Management*, *30*(1−2), 24−43. Retrieved from http://doi.org/10.1016/j.jom.2011.05.002

Sundgren, N. (1999). Introducing interface management in new product family development. *Journal of Product Innovation Management*, *16*(1), 40−51. Retrieved from http://doi.org/10.1111/1540-5885.1610040

Swaminathan, J. M. (2001). Enabling customization using standard operations. *California Management Review*, *43*(3), 125−135. Retrieved from http://doi.org/CMR203

Swink, M., & Nair, A. (2007). Capturing the competitive advantages of AMT: Design-manufacturing integration as a complementary asset. *Journal of Operations Management*, *25*(3), 736−754. Retrieved from http://doi.org/10.1016/j.jom.2006.07.001

Szengel, R., Middendorf, H., Möller, N., & Bennecke, H. (2012). Der Modulare Ottomotorbaukasten von Volkswagen. *MTZ − Motortechnische Zeitschrift*, *73*(6), 476−482. Retrieved from http://doi.org/10.1007/s35146-012-0363-9

Taipaleenmäki, J. (2014). Absence and variant modes of presence of management accounting in new product development − Theoretical refinement and some empirical evidence. *European Accounting Review*, *23*(2), 291−334. Retrieved from http://doi.org/10.1080/09638180.2013.811065

Tatikonda, M. V. (1999). An empirical study of platform and derivative product development projects. *Journal of Product Innovation Management*, *16*(1), 3−26. Retrieved from http://doi.org/10.1111/1540-5885.1610003

Taylor, G. D. (1997). Design for global manufacturing and assembly. *IIE Transactions*, *29*(7), 585−597. Retrieved from http://doi.org/10.1080/07408179708966368

Thyssen, J., Israelsen, P., & Jørgensen, B. (2006). Activity-based costing as a method for assessing the economics of modularization: A case study and beyond. *International Journal of Production Economics*, *103*(1), 252−270. Retrieved from http://doi.org/10.1016/j.ijpe.2005.07.004

Trygg, L. D. (1993). Concurrent engineering practices in selected swedish companies: A movement or an activity of the few? *Journal of Product Innovation Management*, *10*(5), 403−416. Retrieved from http://doi.org/10.1111/1540-5885.1050403

Tubig, S. B., & Abetti, P. A. (1990). Variables influencing the performance of defense R&D contractors. *IEEE Transactions on Engineering Management*, *37*(1), 22−30. Retrieved from http://doi.org/10.1109/17.45261

Tzokas, N., Hultink, E. J., & Hart, S. (2004). Navigating the new product development process. *Industrial Marketing Management*, *33*(7), 619−626. Retrieved from http://doi.org/10.1016/j.indmarman.2003.09.004

Ulrich, K. (1995). The role of product architecture in the manufacturing firm. *Research Policy*, *24*(3), 419–440. Retrieved from http://doi.org/10.1016/0048-7333(94)00775-3

Usher, J. S., & Whitfield, G. M. (1993). Evaluation of used-system life cycle costs using Fuzzy set theory. *IIE Transactions*, *25*(6), 84–88. Retrieved from http://doi.org/10.1080/07408179308964330

Uskonen, J., & Tenhiälä, A. (2012). The price of responsiveness: Cost analysis of change orders in make-to-order manufacturing. *International Journal of Production Economics*, *135*(1), 420–429. Retrieved from http://doi.org/10.1016/j.ijpe.2011.08.016

Vakharia, A. J., Parmenter, D. a., & Sanchez, S. M. (1996). The operating impact of parts commonality. *Journal of Operations Management*, *14*(1), 3–18. Retrieved from http://doi.org/10.1016/0272-6963(95)00033-X

Van Oorschot, K. E., Akkermans, H., Sengupta, K., & Van Wassenhove, L. N. (2013). Anatomy of a decision trap in complex new product development projects. *Academy of Management Journal*, *56*(1), 285–307. Retrieved from http://doi.org/10.5465/amj.2010.0742

Van Oorschot, K. E., Sengupta, K., Akkermans, H., & Van Wassenhove, L. N. (2010). Get fat fast: Surviving stage-gates in NPD. *Journal of Product Innovation Management*, *27*(6), 828–839. Retrieved from http://doi.org/10.1111/j.1540-5885.2010.00754.x

Vanegas, L. V., & Labib, a. W. (2001). A Fuzzy Quality Function Deployment (FQFD) model for deriving optimum targets. *International Journal of Production Research*, *39*(1), 99–120. Retrieved from http://doi.org/10.1080/00207540010005079

Walwyn, D. R., Taylor, D., & Brickhill, G. (2002). How to manage risk better. *Research-Technology Management*, *45*(5), 37–42.

Wang, H. S., & Che, Z. H. (2008). A multi-phase model for product part change problems. *International Journal of Production Research*, *46*. Retrieved from http://doi.org/10.1080/00207540600999144

Wang, J.-H., & Trolio, M. (2001). Using clustered assembly elements in the estimation of potential design for assembly benefits. *International Journal of Production Research*, *39*(9), 1885–1895. Retrieved from http://doi.org/10.1080/00207540010024087

Wasserman, G. S. (1993). On how to prioritize design requirements during the QFD planning process. *IIE Transactions*, *25*(3), 59–65. Retrieved from http://doi.org/10.1080/07408179308964291

Wouters, M. J. F., Anderson, J. C., Narus, J. a., & Wynstra, F. (2009). Improving sourcing decisions in NPD projects: Monetary quantification of points of difference. *Journal of Operations Management*, *27*(1), 64–77. Retrieved from http://doi.org/10.1016/j.jom.2008.07.001

Wouters, M. J. F., Anderson, J. C., & Wynstra, F. (2005). The adoption of total cost of ownership for sourcing decisions – A structural equations analysis. *Accounting, Organizations and Society*, *30*(2), 167–191. Retrieved from http://doi.org/10.1016/j.aos.2004.03.002

Wouters, M. J. F., & Morales, S. (2014). The contemporary art of cost management methods during product development. In M. J. Epstein & J. Y. Lee (Eds.), *Advances in management accounting* (Vol. 24, pp. 259–346). Advances in Management Accounting. Bingley, UK: Emerald Group Publishing Limited. Retrieved from http://doi.org/10.1108/S1474-787120140000024008

Wouters, M. J. F., Workum, M., & Hissel, P. H. (2011). Assessing the product architecture decision about product features – A real options approach. *R&D Management*, *41*(4), 393–409. Retrieved from http://doi.org/10.1111/j.1467-9310.2011.00652.x

Wu, L., De Matta, R., & Lowe, T. J. (2009). Updating a modular product: How to set time to market and component quality. *IEEE Transactions on Engineering Management*, *56*(2), 298–311. Retrieved from http://doi.org/10.1109/TEM.2008.2005065

Xu, Q. L., Ong, S. K., & Nee, a. Y. C. (2007). Evaluation of product performance in product family design re-use. *International Journal of Production Research*, *45*(18–19), 4119–4141. Retrieved from http://doi.org/10.1080/00207540701440147

Xu, S. X., Lu, Q., & Li, Z. (2012). Optimal modular production strategies under market uncertainty: A real options perspective. *International Journal of Production Economics*, *139*(1), 266–274. Retrieved from http://doi.org/10.1016/j.ijpe.2012.05.009

Yazdifar, H., & Askarany, D. (2012). A comparative study of the adoption and implementation of target costing in the UK, Australia and New Zealand. *International Journal of Production Economics*, *135*(1), 382–392. Retrieved from http://doi.org/10.1016/j.ijpe.2011.08.012

Yeung, J. H. Y., Wong, W. C. K., Ma, L., & Law, J. S. (1999). MPS with multiple freeze fences in multi-product multi-level MRP systems. *International Journal of Production Research*, *37*(13), 2977–2996. Retrieved from http://doi.org/10.1080/002075499190383

Yoshikawa, T., Innes, J., & Mitchell, F. (1994). Applying functional cost analysis in a manufacturing environment. *International Journal of Production Economics*, *36*, 53–64. Retrieved from http://doi.org/10.1016/0925-5273(94)90148-1

Yura, K., Ishikura, H., & Hitomi, K. (2000). Parts-mix analysis in recycling-oriented manufacturing systems for multiple-item production. *International Journal of Production Research*, *38*(2), 447–456. Retrieved from http://doi.org/10.1080/002075400189518

Zengin, Y., & Ada, E. (2010). Cost management through product design: Target costing approach. *International Journal of Production Research*, *48*(19), 5593–5611. Retrieved from http://doi.org/10.1080/00207540903130876

Zeschky, M., Daiber, M., Widenmayer, B., & Gassmann, O. (2014). Coordination in global R&D organizations: An examination of the role of subsidiary mandate and modular product architectures in dispersed R&D organizations. *Technovation*, *34*(10), 594–604. Retrieved from http://doi.org/10.1016/j.technovation.2014.06.001

Zhang, X., & Huang, G. Q. (2010). Game-theoretic approach to simultaneous configuration of platform products and supply chains with one manufacturing firm and multiple cooperative suppliers. *International Journal of Production Economics*, *124*(1), 121–136. Retrieved from http://doi.org/10.1016/j.ijpe.2009.10.016

Zhang, X., Huang, G. Q., & Rungtusanatham, M. J. (2008). Simultaneous configuration of platform products and manufacturing supply chains. *International Journal of Production Research*, *46*(21), 6137–6162. Retrieved from http://doi.org/10.1080/00207540701324150

Zhang, Y. (1999, March). Green QFD-II: A life cycle approach for environmentally conscious manufacturing by integrating LCA and LCC into QFD matrices. *International Journal of Production Research*. Retrieved from http://doi.org/10.1080/002075499191418

Zhou, L., & Grubbström, R. W. (2004). Analysis of the effect of commonality in multi-level inventory systems applying MRP theory. *International Journal of Production Economics*, *90*(2), 251–263. Retrieved from http://doi.org/10.1016/S0925-5273(03)00208-1

Zwerink, R., Wouters, M. J. F., Hissel, P. H., & Kerssens-van Drongelen, I. (2007). Cost management and cross-functional communication through product architectures. *R&D Management*, *37*(1), 49–64. Retrieved from http://doi.org/10.1111/j.1467-9310.2007.00458.x

# ADDITIONAL EVIDENCE ON THE STICKY BEHAVIOR OF COSTS

Chandra Subramaniam and
Marcia Weidenmier Watson

## ABSTRACT

Purpose – *This paper attempts to resolve the conflicting results on sticky cost behavior in prior literature. Large sample studies find that selling, general, and administrative costs (SG&A) and cost of goods sold (CGS) are sticky, that is, costs are less likely to decrease when activity decreases than to increase when activity increases. In contrast, studies limited to one industry find little or no sticky cost behavior.*

Methodology/approach – *We investigate whether SG&A and CGS sticky cost behavior differ across/ four major industry groups (manufacturing, merchandising, financial, and services) characterized by different production, operational, and economic environments. In addition, we study whether sticky cost behavior arises for all changes in activity level (as measured by revenue changes) or for only large changes in activity level. Finally, we investigate whether determinants of sticky cost behavior vary across industries.*

Findings – *Our results suggest that costs in the manufacturing industry are the "stickiest," while costs in the merchandising industry are the*

Advances in Management Accounting, Volume 26, 275–305
ISSN: 1474-7871/doi:10.1108/S1474-787120150000026006

*"least sticky," with financial and service industries exhibiting some level of sticky cost behavior. Further, we find that sticky cost behavior is industry-specific, both in the magnitude of activity changes that give rise to sticky cost behavior and in the determinants that drive the behavior.*

Research limitations/implications *– Our investigation of 20 distinct sub-industries within the "stickiest" manufacturing industry finds that while some sub-industry groupings show significant sticky behavior, most do not. This result may explain why, contrary to large sample studies, single industry studies find little or no sticky behavior in costs.*

Originality/value *– Our research is the first to try and reconcile the conflicting results on sticky cost behavior. Understanding the pervasiveness of stickiness is necessary to move research forward in this domain.*

**Keywords:** Cost behavior; sticky costs; determinants; industry differences

## INTRODUCTION

Anderson, Banker, and Janakiraman (2003) find evidence of sticky cost behavior for selling, general, and administrative costs (SG&A) and cost of goods sold (CGS) in large samples of firms from multiple industries. They define cost behavior as "sticky" if costs increase more for activity increases than they decrease for an equivalent activity decrease.[1] Sticky behavior is the result of decisions made by managers when activity decreases. When activity drops, the manager must decide whether to (a) maintain committed resources and bear the cost of unutilized capacity at least in the short-term or (b) immediately reduce committed resources and incur potentially large retrenching costs in the current period and, if activity increases in the future, incur further costs to replace resources (Anderson et al., 2003) (hereafter ABJ).

In contrast, studies limited to one industry find little or no sticky cost behavior (Balakrishnan, Peterson, & Soderstrom, 2004; Noreen & Soderstrom, 1997) (hereafter BPS and NS, respectively). There are two potential explanations for these contradictory results. Either most firms exhibit some sticky behavior, but small sample studies, like NS and BPS, are not powerful enough to capture this behavior. Or, alternatively, sticky behavior is pronounced in some industries, but not in others due to differences in production, operational, and economic environments. We test this alternative explanation in this paper by investigating whether sticky cost behavior differs across industries. In addition, we study whether sticky cost behavior arises for all changes in activity level (as measured by revenue changes) or for only large changes in activity level. Finally, we investigate whether determinants of sticky cost behavior vary across industries. We conduct our investigation using the two largest and aggregated costs in any firm, SG&A and CGS costs.[2]

Our results suggest that costs in the manufacturing industry are the "stickiest," while costs in the merchandising industry are the "least sticky," with financial and service industries exhibiting some level of sticky cost behavior. Further, we show that the magnitude of activity change before we observe sticky cost behavior varies across industries. Specifically, SG&A is not sticky until activity (revenue) changes by more than 10 percent in manufacturing. Similarly, SG&A is marginally sticky following a 10 percent change in activity for merchandising firms. However, we do not find sticky cost behavior in SG&A in the service, and financial industries when activity change is partitioned based on its magnitude. CGS is not sticky until activity changes by more than 15 percent in manufacturing and 10 percent in the financial industry. CGS is not sticky for the service and merchandising industries following partitioning by activity magnitude. Further analysis reveals that sticky cost behavior in the manufacturing industry is due to high levels of fixed assets and inventory. In contrast, inventory intensity drives sticky cost behavior in merchandising firms, inventory and employee intensity drive sticky cost behavior in the service industry, and greater industry concentration drives sticky behavior in the financial industry.

Finally, having observed that the manufacturing industry exhibits the greatest sticky cost behavior, we investigate if sub-industries within manufacturing also show sticky cost behavior. First, we group firms into 20 distinct industries based on the four-digit SIC code and then repeat our analysis for groups with at least 500 observations. We find that while some sub-industry groupings show significant sticky behavior, most do not. This result may explain why single industry studies, consistent with NS (1997) and BPS (2004), find little or no sticky behavior in costs.

The remainder of the paper is organized as follows. The section "Background and Overview" discusses relevant prior literature and develops the hypotheses. The section "Sample Selection and Empirical Design" describes the sample and the models used to perform hypothesis testing. The section "Empirical Results" presents the results. The section "Conclusion" concludes by discussing the implications of the findings for researchers and managers.

# BACKGROUND AND OVERVIEW

The traditional model of cost behavior assumes strict proportionality between costs and activity as long as costs are within the relevant range, implying that a one percent increase in activity is accompanied by a one percent increase in cost (Noreen, 1991). This assumption is challenged by several empirical studies that show costs do not change proportionately with activity but may exhibit increasing returns to scale (Banker & Johnston, 1993; Noreen & Soderstrom, 1994).

NS (1997) originally test the "folklore" that costs increase more in response to activity increases than they decrease in response to activity decreases, but find insignificant results for a sample of Washington state hospitals. In contrast, ABJ (2003) find support for this "folklore," which they call stickiness, using a large sample of firms from multiple industries. ABJ (2003) argue that the sticky cost behavior is a result of asymmetrical response of managers. If the demand is higher than expected, resources are immediately strained (especially if the firm is currently operating close to capacity) and managers are likely to increase committed resources (and related costs) to fill customer orders. If demand is lower than expected, slack resources exist requiring managers to decide whether to maintain committed resources and incur the cost of operating the firm with unutilized resources or reduce committed resources and incur retrenching costs. However, if demand returns, retrenching firms will incur the costs of replacing these resources. Due to this tension, managers *may be* slow or reluctant to eliminate committed resources from the system if they believe that reduced demand may be temporary (ABJ, 2003). This differential response to activity increases and activity decreases results in costs being sticky.

BPS (2004) test for the existence of sticky cost behavior in their sample of therapy clinics and find that costs exhibit stickiness only when resources are strained. In fact, when there is excess capacity, BPS find the opposite response predicted by stickiness. In conclusion, the authors suggest caution when applying ABJ's findings that costs are sticky for all firms (p. 3).

In this paper, we argue that one potential explanation for the contrary results in prior studies is due to differences in sticky behavior in different industries. Prior research shows that different production environments cause accounting variables to be industry-specific (Ely, 1991). Accordingly, cost behavior is likely to differ among industries because each industry has its own production, operational, and economic environment with its associated technology, product markets, and regulatory environments. Consequently, we study whether sticky cost behavior varies among four broad industry groups – manufacturing, merchandising, service, and financial. In addition, due to the lack of authoritative guidance, the components of SG&A and CGS vary dramatically from one company to another, that is, one company's SG&A may be another company's CGS (Lazere, 1995, 1996; Mintz, 1994). Hence, we examine the stickiness of SG&A and CGS *individually* as well as *jointly* by industry in the following hypothesis:

**Hypothesis 1.** Sticky cost behavior varies across industries.

We investigate whether sticky cost behavior exists for all changes in activity level or only for large changes in activity level. While large increases in activity level usually result in immediate cost increases, large decreases in activity level may not result in immediate cost reductions (even if significant slack exists), because firms may not want to, or can't, reduce assets, employees, and/or other costs in the short term due to the presence of retrenching costs and future replacement cost of these committed resources, if activity rebounds.

BPS (2004) investigate, but do not find evidence, that the magnitude of changes in activity level is related to sticky behavior. We believe their results may be a function of not only the industry they study but also the size of activity changes used in their sample. They define a large activity change as greater than three percent, and 75 percent of all observations in their sample have activity change of less than seven percent. We are better able to assess whether and how the size of activity changes affects sticky cost behavior because activity level changes as much as 30 percent in our sample. In fact, 52 percent of our sample has activity changes greater than 10 percent. Therefore, we investigate whether the magnitude varies across industries by examining whether costs become sticky at different levels of activity change in different industries.

Consistent with our first hypothesis, we argue that different production and regulatory environments across our four industry groupings will lead to different determinants driving sticky cost behavior in SG&A and CGS. The determinants of sticky cost behavior we investigate include fixed asset intensity, employee intensity, inventory intensity, revenue decreases for two consecutive years, and industry competition. High levels of fixed assets, employees, and inventory in an industry should increase stickiness, because they are difficult to reduce quickly when demand decreases. Moreover, managers may not want to immediately reduce these resources as they are expensive and time-consuming to replace if demand increases following a slack period. Industry competition should reduce stickiness because firms in highly competitive industries must have the ability to adapt to changing situations rapidly or lose out to more nimble competitors. Finally, revenue decreases for two consecutive years should reduce stickiness in all industries because managers realize that the decrease in demand is not temporary and they must eliminate excess resources/capacity. Thus, our second hypothesis is:

**Hypothesis 2.** Determinants of sticky cost behavior of SG&A and CGS vary across industries.

# SAMPLE SELECTION AND EMPIRICAL DESIGN

## *Sample Selection*

The sample includes 22 years of annual data from COMPUSTAT during the period 1979–2000. To remain in the sample, observations must have SG&A, CGS, and sales revenue in the current and preceding year. We exclude observations in which the SG&A or CGS exceeds sales revenue or annual sales revenue changes by more than 30 percent to remove effects of acquisitions, mergers, divestitures, and bankruptcy. To eliminate firms that are relatively new or are not consistently reported by COMPUSTAT, sample firms must have at least three usable observations. Using these criteria, the sample consists of 82,118 observations for 9,592 firms with an average of 8.6 observations per firm. We implement industry classification using the following one-digit SIC code industry groups: manufacturing (SIC codes 2 and 3), merchandising (SIC code 5), service firms (SIC codes 4, 7, and 8), and financial services (SIC code 6).[3]

Table 1, Panel A presents descriptive statistics for sales revenue, SG&A, CGS, and Total Costs by industry. Consistent with the population of firms on COMPUSTAT, manufacturing firms represent more than half of our sample, with the remainder evenly distributed among the other three industries. On average, manufacturing and merchandising firms are larger than service and financial firms. The proportion of SG&A-to-revenues is highest, as expected, for service firms at 28.65 percent and lowest for merchandising firms at 22.57 percent. The proportion of CGS-to-revenues is highest for merchandising firms at 71.44 percent and lowest for financial firms at 52.28 percent. The CGS for financial firms represents the interest expense and provision for loan losses as reported by banks and savings and loan firms.

Panel B describes fluctuations in sales revenue, SG&A, CGS, and Total Costs. Manufacturing firms experienced negative changes in revenues more

**Table 1.** Descriptive Statistics.

Panel A: Industry means (medians in parenthesis) of annual revenue, SG&A, CGS, and Total Costs during the period 1979–2000 by industry

|  | Manufacturing | Merchandising | Service | Financial Services |
|---|---|---|---|---|
| Number of firm-years | 43,259 | 12,113 | 11,923 | 8,506 |
| Sales revenue | 1,544.95 | 1,516.17 | 635.32 | 994.44 |
|  | (126.57) | (233.60) | (65.47) | (106.88) |
| SG&A | 279.34 | 251.91 | 147.44 | 202.65 |
|  | (24.28) | (41.00) | (14.23) | (22.17) |
| SG&A % of revenue | 24.71 | 22.57 | 28.65 | 23.47 |
|  | (21.81) | (21.16) | (23.78) | (22.42) |
| CGS | 1,059.66 | 1,172.31 | 356.26 | 569.29 |
|  | (81.89) | (162.54) | (35.77) | (53.70) |
| CGS % of revenue | 65.69 | 71.44 | 58.87 | 52.28 |
|  | (67.84) | (72.96) | (61.51) | (51.82) |
| Total Costs | 1,339.00 | 1,424.22 | 503.70 | 771.94 |
|  | (113.55) | (216.83) | (56.08) | (79.12) |
| Total Costs % of revenue | 90.39 | 94.02 | 87.52 | 75.76 |
|  | (89.91) | (94.44) | (89.54) | (74.63) |

Panel B: Mean (median in parenthesis) fluctuations in revenue, SG&A, CGS, and Total Costs during the period 1979–2000

|  | Manufacturing | Merchandising | Service | Financial Services |
|---|---|---|---|---|
| Percentage of firm-years with negative percentage change in sales revenue from previous period | 31.81 | 26.00 | 29.54 | 22.85 |
| Percentage decrease in sales revenue across periods | 9.92 | 9.08 | 10.40 | 8.97 |
|  | (7.99) | (7.10) | (8.47) | (6.61) |
| Percentage of firm-years with negative percentage change in SG&A from previous period | 27.63 | 23.69 | 29.33 | 18.06 |
| Percentage decrease in SG&A across periods | 10.74 | 11.11 | 13.32 | 11.42 |
|  | (7.42) | (7.16) | (9.46) | (6.51) |
| Percentage of firm-years with negative percentage change in CGS from previous period | 32.41 | 25.91 | 30.98 | 30.83 |
| Percentage decrease in CGS across periods | 10.45 | 10.00 | 12.54 | 13.92 |
|  | (8.06) | (7.27) | (9.31) | (10.25) |
| Percentage of firm-years with negative percentage change in total cost from previous period | 29.95 | 24.91 | 28.30 | 26.29 |
| Percentage decrease in total costs across periods | 9.60 | 9.19 | 10.76 | 11.08 |
|  | (7.37) | (6.80) | (8.02) | (8.06) |

***Table 1.***   (*Continued*)

Panel C: Medians (means) of the determinants (in percent) of sticky cost behavior by industry for the period 1979–2000

|  | Manufacturing ($N = 42{,}511$) | Merchandising ($N = 11{,}900$) | Service ($N = 11{,}659$) | Financial Services ($N = 8{,}222$) |
|---|---|---|---|---|
| Revenue change | 5.91 | 7.12 | 7.10 | 8.78 |
|  | (4.95) | (6.43) | (6.06) | (7.99) |
| SGA change | 7.21 | 8.27 | 8.18 | 8.81 |
|  | (7.52) | (9.29) | (10.41) | (9.99) |
| CGS change | 5.65 | 7.31 | 6.97 | 8.46 |
|  | (5.29) | (6.64) | (7.02) | (8.60) |
| Total cost change | 6.14 | 7.39 | 7.37 | 8.89 |
|  | (5.60) | (6.82) | (7.12) | (8.26) |
| Fixed asset | 20.19 | 12.43 | 21.46 | 17.33 |
| intensity | (26.86) | (19.88) | (50.76) | (31.54) |
| Employee | 0.92 | 0.90 | 1.05 | 0.58 |
| intensity | (1.05) | (1.25) | (1.75) | (0.70) |
| Inventory | 16.39 | 13.39 | 1.67 | 2.19 |
| intensity | (18.32) | (14.77) | (5.11) | (11.36) |
| Concentration | 5.78 | 6.08 | 13.54 | 3.23 |
| ratio (HH1) | (6.32) | (7.02) | (15.05) | (4.94) |
| Interest ratio | 1.66 | 1.19 | 2.02 | 47.78 |
|  | (2.44) | (1.99) | (4.36) | (47.32) |
| Advertising | 0.00 | 0.00 | 0.00 | 0.00 |
| intensity | (1.24) | (1.70) | (1.23) | (0.27) |
| R&D intensity | 0.89 | 0.00 | 0.00 | 0.00 |
|  | (2.95) | (0.14) | (2.52) | (0.14) |

*Notes*: SG&A represents selling, general, and administrative expense. CGS represents cost of goods sold. Total Costs represents the sum of SG&A and CGS. Fixed Asset Intensity is the ratio of the net book value of fixed assets (Compustat #8) to sales revenue. Employee Intensity is the log of the ratio of the number of employees in thousands (Compustat #29) to sales revenue. Inventory Intensity is the ratio of the inventory (Compustat #42) to sales revenue. Concentration Ratio is the Herfindahl–Hirshman Index of industry concentration (HHI) calculated for each two-digit SIC industry group as defined by Defond and Park (1999). Interest ratio is the ratio of interest expense (Compustat #15) to sales revenue for manufacturing, merchandising, and service firms. For financial firms, interest ratio is the ratio of interest expense (Compustat #339) to sales revenue. Advertising Intensity is the ratio of advertising expense (Compustat #45) to sales revenue. R&D Intensity is the ratio of R&D expense (Compustat #46) to sales revenue.

frequently than the other three industries during this period (31.81 percent), while financial services firms reported the lowest number of negative changes in revenues (22.85 percent). Panel C provides some descriptive medians of firm characteristics that potentially drive sticky cost behavior. Using the median measures, we find fixed asset intensity is highest in manufacturing and service industries. Employee intensity is significantly lower in the financial services industry compared to the remaining three industries, implying much greater sales revenue per employee in this industry. Inventory intensity averages 15 percent in the manufacturing and merchandising firms. The Herfindahl–Hirshman Index (HHI) is used as a measure of industry concentration. The HHI is defined as the sum of an industry's squared market share (in percentage) for each two-digit SIC industry group (Defond & Park, 1999). The HHI value assigned to each firm is the five-year industry average prior to the event year in order to minimize year-to-year variations in HHI. Low values of HHI imply low levels of industry concentration or high levels of industry competition. Among the three non-regulated industries, manufacturing is most competitive and service industry is the least competitive.

## Model Specification

Hypothesis 1 states that sticky cost behavior varies across industries. To test this hypothesis, we first determine how cost responds to absolute changes in revenue, and then test for a different response to revenue decreases in each industry. We also test stickiness individually for SG&A and CGS as well as jointly using TOTAL costs, which equals the sum of SG&A and CGS. Accordingly, we estimate Eq. (1), for SG&A, CGS, and TOTAL costs for each industry grouping as follows:

$$
\log\left[\frac{DV_{i,j,t}}{DV_{i,j,t-1}}\right] = \alpha_{0j} + \alpha_{1j} * \log\left[\frac{Revenue_{i,j,t}}{Revenue_{i,j,t-1}}\right] \\
+ \alpha_{2j} * Decrease\_Dummy * \log\left[\frac{Revenue_{i,j,t}}{Revenue_{i,j,t-1}}\right] + \varepsilon_{i,j,t} \quad (1)
$$

where

$DV_{i,j,t}$ = SG&A, CGS, or TOTAL costs for firm $i$, in industry $j$, at time $t$,

$\text{Revenue}_{i,j,t}$ = net sales revenue (Compustat annual item #12) for firm $i$, in industry $j$, at time $t$,

Decrease_Dummy = 1 if revenue decreases from prior year, otherwise 0.

Next, we investigate whether the magnitude of activity change affects sticky cost behavior differently across industries. To do this, we stratify the activity changes in order to identify the level of change in activity that generates sticky behavior. Specifically, we stratify changes in revenue into six bands of increasing amounts of absolute change in revenue.[4] We estimate an expanded version of Eq. (1) that includes these six change bands by industry:

$$\log\left[\frac{DV_{i,j,t}}{DV_{i,j,t-1}}\right] = \beta_{0j} + \sum_{S=1}^{6}\beta_{Sj}*R_{Si,j,t}*\log\left[\frac{\text{Revenue}_{i,j,t}}{\text{Revenue}_{i,j,t-1}}\right]$$
$$+ \sum_{S=1}^{6}\beta_{(S+6)j}*D_{Si,j,t}*R_{Si,j,t}*\log\left[\frac{\text{Revenue}_{i,j,t}}{\text{Revenue}_{i,j,t-1}}\right] + \varepsilon_{i,j,t} \quad (2)$$

where

$DV_{i,j,t}$ = SG&A, CGS, or TOTAL costs for firm $i$, in industry $j$, at time $t$,

$S$ = indicator variable from 1 to 6,

$R_{1i,j,t}$ = 1 if percent change in sales revenue is $[-0.05, 0.05]$,

$R_{2i,j,t}$ = 1 if percent change in sales revenue is $[-0.10, -0.05)$ or $(0.05, 0.10]$,

$R_{3i,j,t}$ = 1 if percent change in sales revenue is $[-0.15, -0.10)$ or $(0.10, 0.15]$,

$R_{4i,j,t}$ = 1 if percent change in sales revenue is $[-0.20, -0.15)$ or $(0.15, 0.20]$,

$R_{5i,j,t}$ = 1 if percent change in sales revenue is $[-0.25, -0.20)$ or $(0.20, 0.25]$,

$R_{6i,j,t}$ = 1 if percent change in sales revenue is $[-0.30, -0.25)$ or $(0.25, 0.30]$,

$D_{1i,j,t}$ = 1 if percent change in sales revenue is $[-0.05, 0)$,

$D_{2i,j,t}$ = 1 if percent change in sales revenue is $[-0.10, -0.05)$,

$D_{3i,j,t}$ = 1 if percent change in sales revenue is $[-0.15, -0.10)$,

$D_{4i,j,t}$ = 1 if percent change in sales revenue is $[-0.20, -0.15)$,

$D_{5i,j,t}$ = 1 if percent change in sales revenue is $[-0.25, -0.20)$,

$D_{6i,j,t}$ = 1 if percent change in sales revenue is $[-0.30, -0.25)$.

The coefficient $\beta_1$ measures the percentage increase in the dependent variable with a one-percent increase in sales revenue when the one-year absolute change in revenue is between zero and five percent. A negative coefficient on the *corresponding* term $\beta_7$ indicates that the dependent variable exhibits stickiness when activity declines within the same range (between zero and five percent). The remaining coefficients $\beta_2$ through $\beta_6$ and their corresponding "sticky" coefficients $\beta_8$ through $\beta_{12}$ follow the same pattern for the indicated revenue changes. The "sticky" coefficients $\beta_7$ through $\beta_{12}$ indicate the magnitude of the activity change that causes managers to differentially change the cost structure of the firm depending on activity increase or decrease.

Hypothesis 2 states that if operational, economic, and production environments are truly different in different industries it is unlikely the same determinants will drive sticky cost behavior in every industry. To test this hypothesis, we estimate the following model:

$$\log\left[\frac{DV_{i,j,t}}{DV_{i,j,t-1}}\right] = \gamma_{0j} + \gamma_{1j}*\log\left[\frac{Revenue_{i,j,t}}{Revenue_{i,j,t-1}}\right]$$

$$+ \gamma_{2j}*Decrease\_Dummy*\log\left[\frac{Revenue_{i,j,t}}{Revenue_{i,j,t-1}}\right]$$

$$+ \gamma_{3j}*Decrease\_Dummy*\log\left[\frac{Revenue_{i,j,t}}{Revenue_{i,j,t-1}}\right]*Fixed\,Asset\,Intensity$$

$$+ \gamma_{4j}*Decrease\_Dummy*\log\left[\frac{Revenue_{i,j,t}}{Revenue_{i,j,t-1}}\right]*Employee\,Intensity$$

$$+ \gamma_{5j}*Decrease\_Dummy*\log\left[\frac{Revenue_{i,j,t}}{Revenue_{i,j,t-1}}\right]*Second\,Decrease$$

$$+ \gamma_{6j}*Decrease\_Dummy*\log\left[\frac{Revenue_{i,j,t}}{Revenue_{i,j,t-1}}\right]*Inventory\,Intensity$$

$$+ \gamma_{7j}*Decrease\_Dummy*\log\left[\frac{Revenue_{i,j,t}}{Revenue_{i,j,t-1}}\right]*Concentration\,Intensity$$

$$+ \varepsilon_{i,j,t}$$

$$(3)$$

As in Eq. (1), DV equals SG&A, CGS, or Total Costs for firm $i$, in industry $j$, at time $t$, and Decrease_Dummy equals one if revenue in period $t$ is less than revenue in period $t-1$. Fixed Asset Intensity is the log of the ratio of the net book value of fixed assets (Compustat #8) to sales revenue and Employee Intensity is the log of the ratio of the number of employees (#29) to sales revenue.[5] The Second Decrease indicator variable equals one if revenue declined for two consecutive periods, else 0. Inventory Intensity is the log of the ratio of the inventory (#42) to sales revenue. The concentration intensity is estimated using the Herfindahl–Hirshman Index described earlier.

## EMPIRICAL RESULTS

### Inter-Industry Differences

To test our first hypothesis, we estimate Eq. (1), by regressing changes in SG&A, CGS, and Total Costs on annual changes in sales revenue for the four selected industries – manufacturing, merchandising, service, and financial services.[6] Table 2 presents the results. For all four industries, the estimated coefficient $\alpha_1$ is significantly positive for SG&A and significantly different from one, implying that SG&A is not proportional to changes in revenues (but exhibits increasing returns to scale). For SG&A, the estimated coefficient for $\alpha_1$ ranges from 0.51 for financial firms to 0.81 in merchandising firms for every one-percent increase in revenues.[7]

For CGS, the estimated coefficient for $\alpha_1$ ranges from 0.97 for manufacturing firms to 1.37 in financial firms for every one-percent increase in revenues. The coefficient $\alpha_1$ is not different from one for manufacturing, merchandising, and service firms, suggesting that CGS increases proportionally to revenues for non-financial firms. On the other hand, $\alpha_1$ for financial firms is significantly greater than one, suggesting that borrowing costs appear to grow faster when the market is improving and revenues are increasing.[8] Ma (1988) provides a potential explanation for this result. He shows that bank managements tend to raise (lower) loan loss provisions in periods of high (low) operating income to smooth earnings. In fact, the SEC has investigated a number of banks for manipulating earnings by increasing loan loss provisions during good financial times and reducing them during bad financial times (Moyer, 1999; Weidner, Ring, & Barancik, 1998).

Manufacturing, merchandising, and service firms show evidence of sticky cost behavior in SG&A, whereas financial firms do not. Specifically, manufacturing firms show the highest level of stickiness in SG&A with the estimated coefficient $\alpha_2$ being $-0.1544$ ($t$-value $= 8.60$), followed by service firms ($\alpha_2 = -0.1051$, $t$-value $= 2.20$) and merchandising firms ($\alpha_2 = -0.0952$,

***Table 2.*** Results of Regressing Annual Changes in SG&A, CGS, and Total Costs on Annual Changes in Sales Revenue for the 22 Year Period 1979–2000 by Industry.[a]

| | Manufacturing Firms | | | Merchandising Firms | | |
|---|---|---|---|---|---|---|
| | SG&A | CGS | Total Costs | SG&A | CGS | Total Costs |
| $\alpha_0$ | 0.0256 | 0.0012 | 0.0072 | 0.0217 | 0.0002 | 0.0049 |
| | (20.99) | (1.69) | (12.11) | (8.60) | (0.14) | (6.15) |
| $\alpha_1$ | **0.7092** | **0.9657** | **0.9013** | **0.8126** | **1.0081** | **0.9621** |
| | **(70.80)** | **(168.05)** | **(183.85)** | **(39.27)** | **(104.76)** | **(146.44)** |
| $\alpha_2$ | **−0.1544** | **−0.0383** | **−0.0771** | **−0.0952** | −0.0008 | −0.0118 |
| | **(−8.60)** | **(−3.72)** | **(−8.77)** | **(−2.42)** | (−0.04) | (−0.95) |
| Adjusted $R^2$ | 0.2523 | 0.6935 | 0.7216 | 0.2576 | 0.7332 | 0.8410 |
| Number of observations | 42,642 | 42,642 | 42,642 | 12,027 | 12,027 | 12,027 |

| | Service Firms | | | Financial Firms | | |
|---|---|---|---|---|---|---|
| | SG&A | CGS | Total Costs | SG&A | CGS | Total Costs |
| $\alpha_0$ | 0.0294 | 0.0039 | 0.0095 | 0.0453 | −0.0363 | −0.0112 |
| | (8.70) | (1.34) | (5.30) | (13.86) | (11.67) | (5.67) |
| $\alpha_1$ | **0.7385** | **0.9749** | **0.9044** | **0.5108** | **1.3666** | **1.0928** |
| | **(28.27)** | **(43.29)** | **(66.44)** | **(20.35)** | **(57.20)** | **(71.89)** |
| $\alpha_2$ | **−0.1051** | −0.0797 | **−0.1064** | 0.0635 | **−0.2863** | **−0.1496** |
| | **(−2.20)** | (−1.93) | **(−4.27)** | (−1.25) | **(−5.90)** | **(−4.84)** |
| Adjusted $R^2$ | 0.1706 | 0.3383 | 0.5379 | 0.1289 | 0.4738 | 0.6012 |
| Number of observations | 11,737 | 11,737 | 11,737 | 8,335 | 8,335 | 8,335 |

*Notes*: The table presents the pooled estimation coefficient estimates with *t*-statistics in parentheses. DV equals selling, general, and administrative expense (SG&A), cost of goods sold (CGS), or Total Costs (sum of SG&A and CGS). Decrease_Dummy equals one if revenue in period $t$ is less than revenue in period $t-1$, zero otherwise. Estimates of coefficients at significance levels greater than 0.05 are given in bold.

[a]Regression specification:

$$\log\left[\frac{DV_{i,j,t}}{DV_{i,j,t-1}}\right] = \alpha_0 + \alpha_1 * \log\left[\frac{Revenue_{i,j,t}}{Revenue_{i,j,t-1}}\right] + \alpha_2 * \text{Decrease\_Dummy} * \log\left[\frac{Revenue_{i,j,t}}{Revenue_{i,j,t-1}}\right] + \varepsilon_{i,j,t}$$

$t$-value $= 2.42$). Conversely, the estimated coefficient $\alpha_2$ for financial firms is positive and not significant.

For CGS, our results reveal sticky cost behavior for manufacturing and financial firms and only marginally for service firms. We do not observe sticky cost behavior in merchandising firms. Specifically, the coefficient $\alpha_2$ is $-0.2863$ ($t$-value $= 5.90$) for financial firms, $-0.0383$ ($t$-value $= 3.72$) for manufacturing firms, and $-0.0797$ ($t$-value $= 1.93$) for service firms. The coefficient, $\alpha_2$ representing sticky behavior in Total Costs is very similar to our CGS results.

These results suggest that production and economic environments play a major role in whether sticky cost behavior is observed for firms in different industries. By examining each industry separately, we show that SG&A is sticky for service firms, but not for financial firms, whereas CGS is sticky for financial firms, but only marginally for service firms. Therefore, the SG&A, CGS, and Total Costs results show that sticky cost behavior varies across industries, supporting Hypothesis 1.[9]

## Sticky Cost Behavior and Magnitude of Activity Change

To investigate whether the sticky cost behavior is dependent on the magnitude of activity change and if the magnitude varies across industries, we estimate Eq. (2), which stratifies revenue changes into absolute five percent intervals, for each industry. Table 3 presents the results. For manufacturing firms, when annual changes in sales revenue are below 10 percent, the linearity of SG&A to revenue changes cannot be rejected. On the other hand, when the absolute change in sales revenue is greater than 10 percent, SG&A exhibits sticky cost behavior ($\beta_9 = -0.1117$, $t = 2.34$). For merchandising firms, sticky cost behavior for SG&A is observed only marginally at the 10 percent level using a one-tail test when the absolute change in sales revenue is greater than 10 percent ($\beta_9 = -0.1324$, $t = 1.32$). Service and financial firms do not show sticky cost behavior for SG&A at any level of change.

Examining the CGS results, we find manufacturing and financial firms exhibit sticky cost behavior. Specifically, CGS is sticky beyond a 15-percent absolute change in sales revenue for manufacturing firms ($\beta_{10} = -0.0584$, $t = 2.80$). For financial firms, CGS is sticky when interest revenue changes by more than 10 percent ($\beta_9 = -0.3250$, $t = 2.51$). The Total Costs results are similar to the CGS results. Specifically, manufacturing and financial firms show that costs are sticky beyond 10 and 15 percent changes of

**Table 3.** Results of Estimating the Model Relating Annual Changes in SG&A, CGS, and Total Costs to Sales Revenue by Industry for the 22-Year Period 1979–2000 after Partitioning the Sales Changes into Five Percent Increments.[a]

| | Manufacturing Firms ($N$ = 42,642) | | | Merchandising ($N$ = 12,027) | | |
|---|---|---|---|---|---|---|
| | SG&A | CGS | Total Costs | SG&A | CGS | Total Costs |
| $\beta_0$ | 0.0320 | 0.0013 | 0.0095 | 0.0207 | 0.0020 | 0.0051 |
| | (12.99) | (0.93) | (7.90) | (4.09) | (0.83) | (3.14) |
| $\beta_1$ | **0.4617** | **0.9298** | **0.8056** | **0.7916** | **0.9603** | **0.9541** |
| | **(4.75)** | **(16.69)** | **(16.95)** | **(4.01)** | **(10.46)** | **(15.22)** |
| $\beta_2$ | **0.5839** | **0.9459** | **0.8483** | **0.8098** | **0.9593** | **0.9529** |
| | **(14.39)** | **(40.63)** | **(42.71)** | **(9.94)** | **(25.31)** | **(36.82)** |
| $\beta_3$ | **0.6555** | **0.9556** | **0.8772** | **0.7941** | **0.9882** | **0.9489** |
| | **(25.22)** | **(64.09)** | **(68.96)** | **(15.15)** | **(40.52)** | **(56.98)** |
| $\beta_4$ | **0.6463** | **0.9636** | **0.8795** | **0.8601** | **1.0027** | **0.9745** |
| | **(32.31)** | **(83.97)** | **(89.83)** | **(21.15)** | **(52.98)** | **(75.42)** |
| $\beta_5$ | **0.6927** | **0.9662** | **0.8943** | **0.7490** | **1.0151** | **0.9539** |
| | **(40.20)** | **(97.73)** | **(106.04)** | **(21.47)** | **(62.53)** | **(86.06)** |
| $\beta_6$ | **0.7002** | **0.9766** | **0.9038** | **0.8761** | **0.9891** | **0.9680** |
| | **(44.27)** | **(107.63)** | **(116.76)** | **(26.71)** | **(64.80)** | **(92.88)** |
| $\beta_{7\ 0-5\%}$ | 0.3252 | −0.0860 | 0.0669 | −0.3364 | 0.1201 | −0.0626 |
| | (1.83) | (−0.84) | (0.77) | (−0.90) | (0.69) | (−0.53) |
| $\beta_{8\ 5-10\%}$ | 0.0682 | −0.0275 | 0.0064 | −0.0957 | 0.0662 | 0.0005 |
| | (0.90) | (−0.64) | (0.17) | (−0.61) | (0.91) | (0.01) |
| $\beta_{9\ 10-15\%}$ | **−0.1117** | −0.0356 | **−0.0598** | −0.1324 | 0.0336 | 0.0110 |
| | **(−2.34)** | (−1.30) | **(−2.56)** | (−1.32) | (0.72) | (0.35) |
| $\beta_{10\ 15-20\%}$ | −0.0456 | **−0.0584** | **−0.0518** | −0.1007 | −0.0244 | −0.0304 |
| | (−1.25) | **(−2.80)** | **(−2.91)** | (−1.28) | (−0.67) | (−1.21) |
| $\beta_{11\ 20-25\%}$ | **−0.1269** | −0.0117 | **−0.0482** | −0.0971 | 0.0189 | −0.0139 |
| | **(−4.19)** | (−0.67) | **(−3.25)** | (−1.45) | (0.61) | (−0.66) |
| $\beta_{12\ 25-30\%}$ | **−0.0985** | **−0.454** | **−0.0651** | −0.1089 | 0.0333 | −0.0059 |
| | **(−3.71)** | **(−2.98)** | **(−5.01)** | (−1.86) | (1.22) | (−0.32) |
| Adjusted $R^2$ | 0.2526 | 0.6936 | 0.7216 | 0.2585 | 0.7322 | 0.8410 |

| | Service Firms ($N$ = 11,737) | | | Financial Firms ($N$ = 8,335) | | |
|---|---|---|---|---|---|---|
| | SG&A | CGS | Total Costs | SG&A | CGS | Total Costs |
| $\beta_0$ | 0.0387 | 0.0102 | 0.0126 | 0.0435 | −0.0431 | −0.0130 |
| | (5.57) | (1.70) | (3.47) | (6.49) | (6.76) | (3.19) |
| $\beta_1$ | 0.1415 | **0.7749** | **0.7352** | **0.5759** | **1.7318** | **1.2741** |
| | (0.51) | **(3.26)** | **(5.12)** | **(2.27)** | **(7.18)** | **(8.30)** |
| $\beta_2$ | **0.5617** | **0.7876** | **0.7876** | **0.4865** | **1.5592** | **1.1557** |
| | **(4.97)** | **(8.08)** | **(13.38)** | **(4.56)** | **(15.36)** | **(17.88)** |
| $\beta_3$ | **0.6209** | **0.9213** | **0.8695** | **0.4465** | **1.4606** | **1.0995** |
| | **(8.57)** | **(14.74)** | **(23.02)** | **(6.60)** | **(22.69)** | **(26.82)** |

***Table 3.***   (*Continued*)

| | Service Firms ($N = 11,737$) | | | Financial Firms ($N = 8,335$) | | |
|---|---|---|---|---|---|---|
| | SG&A | CGS | Total Costs | SG&A | CGS | Total Costs |
| $\beta_4$ | **0.7246** | **0.9251** | **0.9002** | **0.5150** | **1.4002** | **1.1001** |
| | **(13.17)** | **(19.49)** | **(31.39)** | **(9.96)** | **(28.45)** | **(35.11)** |
| $\beta_5$ | **0.6926** | **0.9437** | **0.8860** | **0.5226** | **1.4191** | **1.1122** |
| | **(15.21)** | **(24.02)** | **(37.33)** | **(12.18)** | **(34.77)** | **(42.80)** |
| $\beta_6$ | **0.7054** | **0.9781** | **0.9067** | **0.5751** | **1.3337** | **1.0829** |
| | **(17.41)** | **(27.99)** | **(42.95)** | **(14.70)** | **(35.84)** | **(45.71)** |
| $\beta_7$ 0–5% | 0.8991 | 0.2169 | 0.1104 | −0.4330 | −0.6848 | −0.3009 |
| | (1.79) | (0.50) | (0.42) | (−0.91) | (−1.51) | (−1.04) |
| $\beta_8$ 5–10% | 0.0202 | 0.2063 | −0.0143 | −0.2667 | −0.2246 | −0.1344 |
| | (0.10) | (1.13) | (−0.13) | (−1.28) | (−1.13) | (−1.06) |
| $\beta_9$ 10–15% | −0.0304 | −0.0632 | **−0.1340** | 0.3122 | **−0.3250** | −0.0361 |
| | (−0.23) | (−0.54) | **(−1.90)** | (2.29) | **(−2.51)** | (−0.44) |
| $\beta_{10}$ 15–20% | 0.0423 | −0.0384 | −0.0534 | 0.0371 | **−0.5573** | **−0.2955** |
| | (0.42) | (−0.44) | (−1.02) | (0.36) | **(−5.67)** | **(−4.72)** |
| $\beta_{11}$ 20–25% | −0.1019 | 0.0310 | **−0.1061** | 0.03827 | **−0.3678** | **−0.1693** |
| | (−1.23) | (0.43) | **(−2.45)** | (0.44) | **(−4.47)** | **(−3.23)** |
| $\beta_{12}$ 25–30% | 0.0385 | −0.0474 | **−0.492** | 0.0351 | **−0.2900** | **−0.1585** |
| | (0.55) | (−0.78) | **(−1.34)** | (0.45) | **(−3.87)** | **(−3.32)** |
| Adjusted $R^2$ | 0.1716 | 0.3384 | 0.5385 | 0.1312 | 0.4757 | 0.6021 |

*Note*: Estimates of coefficients at significance levels greater than 0.10 using the one-tail test are given in bold.

[a]Regression specification:

$$\log\left[\frac{DV_{i,j,t}}{DV_{i,j,t-1}}\right] = \beta_0 + \sum_{S=1}^{6}\beta_S * R_{Si,j,t} * \log\left[\frac{Revenue_{i,j,t}}{Revenue_{i,j,t-1}}\right]$$
$$+ \sum_{S=1}^{6}\beta_{(S+6)} * D_{Si,j,t} * R_{Si,j,t} * \log\left[\frac{Revenue_{i,j,t}}{Revenue_{i,j,t-1}}\right] + \varepsilon_{i,j,t}$$

where
$DV_{i,j,t}$ = SG&A, CGS, or TOTAL Costs for firm $i$, in industry $j$, at time $t$,
$R_{1it}$ = 1 if percent change in sales revenue is $[-0.05, 0.05]$,
$R_{2it}$ = 1 if percent change in sales revenue is $[-0.10, -0.05)$ or $(0.05, 0.10]$,
$R_{3it}$ = 1 if percent change in sales revenue is $[-0.15, -0.10)$ or $(0.10, 0.15]$,
$R_{4it}$ = 1 if percent change in sales revenue is $[-0.20, -0.15)$ or $(0.15, 0.20]$,
$R_{5it}$ = 1 if percent change in sales revenue is $[-0.25, -0.20)$ or $(0.20, 0.25]$,
$R_{6it}$ = 1 if percent change in sales revenue is $[-0.30, -0.25)$ or $(0.25, 0.30]$,
$D_{1it}$ = 1 if percent change in sales revenue is $[-0.05, 0)$,
$D_{2it}$ = 1 if percent change in sales revenue is $[-0.10, -0.05)$,
$D_{3it}$ = 1 if percent change in sales revenue is $[-0.15, -0.10)$,
$D_{4it}$ = 1 if percent change in sales revenue is $[-0.20, -0.15)$,
$D_{5it}$ = 1 if percent change in sales revenue is $[-0.25, -0.20)$,
$D_{6it}$ = 1 if percent change in sales revenue is $[-0.30, -0.25)$.

revenue ($\beta_9 = -0.0598$, $t = 2.56$ for manufacturing firms and $\beta_{10} = -0.2955$, $t = 4.72$ for financial firms), respectively. Only Total Costs is (consistently) sticky for Service firms beyond 20 percent changes of revenue, while merchandising firms do not show sticky cost behavior when activity change is partitioned by its magnitude.

In general, the results show that even in industries where we observe sticky cost behavior, costs are sticky only for large activity changes, implying that for small changes in revenues, costs are linearly related to revenue changes. These results suggest that proportionality of costs to revenue changes is valid as long as activity is within the current operating (or relevant) range as discussed in many accounting textbooks (Hansen & Mowen, 2003; Horngren & Foster, 1991). The relevant range appears to be different by industry.

### Inter-Industry Determinants of Sticky Cost Behavior

To test our second hypothesis, we estimate Eq. (3), by regressing changes in SG&A, CGS, and Total Costs on the five selected determinants for each industry. The five determinants include fixed asset intensity, employee intensity, inventory intensity, industry concentration intensity, and an indicator variable to represent two consecutive years of activity decline to proxy for long-term decline. Table 4 presents the results. For manufacturing firms, fixed asset intensity ($\gamma_3$) is significant and appears to drive the stickiness of each type of costs (SG&A, CGS, and Total Costs). However, that is not the case for the other three industries except for SG&A costs for merchandising and service firms, even though service firms are as asset-intensive as manufacturing firms as shown in Table 1, Panel C. Employee intensity ($\gamma_4$) appears to drive sticky behavior of CGS in merchandising and service firms, whose sales are generated by employees, but not in manufacturing and financial firms.[10] In contrast, employee intensity ($\gamma_4$) does not drive sticky behavior of SG&A in any industry.

Inventory intensity ($\gamma_6$) increases the stickiness of SG&A and CGS in manufacturing, merchandising, and service firms. This result implies that while inventory increases when revenue increases, firms are unable or are reluctant to reduce inventory by the same proportion when revenue is declining. Industry concentration ($\gamma_7$), a proxy for industry competitiveness, appears to reduce sticky behavior in CGS and Total Costs only in the financial services industry.[11] Finally, the positive coefficient on the second decrease variable ($\gamma_5$), representing two consecutive years of revenue reduction, shows that over the long-term managers do reduce costs when revenue declines for each type of cost (SG&A, CGS, and Total Costs) in every industry, implying stickiness is a short-run phenomena. The results here

***Table 4.***   Results of Estimating the Model Relating Annual Changes in SG&A, CGS, and Total Costs on Annual Changes in Sales Revenue to Identify the Drivers of the Stickiness Coefficient for the 22-Year Period 1979–2000 for Each Industry.[a]

| | Manufacturing Firms | | | Merchandising Firms | | |
|---|---|---|---|---|---|---|
| | SG&A | CGS | Total Costs | SG&A | CGS | Total Costs |
| $\gamma_0$ | 0.0248 | 0.0009 | 0.0069 | 0.0232 | 0.0008 | 0.0051 |
| | (20.17) | (1.35) | (11.61) | (9.09) | (0.81) | (7.08) |
| $\gamma_1$ | **0.7124** | **0.9646** | **0.9025** | **0.8142** | **1.0018** | **0.9650** |
| | **(69.58)** | **(167.28)** | **(182.08)** | **(38.63)** | **(129.22)** | **(162.91)** |
| $\gamma_2$ | **−0.5178** | **−0.3450** | **−0.3038** | **0.4394** | −0.0911 | **−0.0932** |
| | **(−6.51)** | **(−7.70)** | **(−7.89)** | **(2.66)** | (−1.50) | **(−2.01)** |
| $\gamma_3$ | **−0.0578** | **−0.0504** | **−0.0335** | **−0.1041** | **0.0424** | **−0.0152** |
| | **(−6.15)** | **(−9.53)** | **(−7.38)** | **(−4.63)** | **(5.13)** | **(−2.40)** |
| $\gamma_4$ | 0.0218 | 0.0013 | 0.0077 | **0.1558** | **−0.0365** | −0.0035 |
| | (1.63) | (0.17) | (1.19) | **(5.90)** | **(−3.76)** | (−0.47) |
| $\gamma_5$ | **0.3517** | **0.1033** | **0.1814** | **0.2584** | **0.1041** | **0.1206** |
| | **(20.12)** | **(10.49)** | **(21.43)** | **(5.88)** | **(6.44)** | **(9.76)** |
| $\gamma_6$ | **−0.1176** | **−0.0751** | **−0.1007** | **−0.0473** | **−0.0210** | **−.0337** |
| | **(−9.13)** | **(−10.35)** | **(−16.16)** | **(−2.36)** | **(−2.85)** | **(−5.98)** |
| $\gamma_7$ | 0.0014 | −0.0158 | **0.0198** | **0.0823** | 0.0276 | **0.0391** |
| | (0.07) | (−1.45) | **(2.12)** | **(1.98)** | (1.80) | **(3.34)** |
| Adjusted $R^2$ | 0.2697 | 0.7191 | 0.7375 | 0.2773 | 0.8220 | 0.8774 |
| Number of observations | 38,878 | 38,878 | 38,878 | 10,811 | 10,811 | 10,811 |

| | Service Firms | | | Financial Firms | | |
|---|---|---|---|---|---|---|
| | SG&A | CGS | Total Costs | SG&A | CGS | Total Costs |
| $\gamma_0$ | 0.0263 | −0.0012 | 0.0081 | 0.0451 | −0.0439 | −0.0169 |
| | (6.57) | (0.47) | (4.19) | (11.44) | (12.35) | (7.37) |
| $\gamma_1$ | **0.7486** | **0.9706** | **0.9062** | **0.5293** | **1.3683** | **1.1174** |
| | **(23.48)** | **(47.99)** | **(58.60)** | **(17.65)** | **(50.62)** | **(63.97)** |
| $\gamma_2$ | **−0.4779** | **−0.5438** | **−0.6515** | 0.1363 | **−1.5764** | **−1.1537** |
| | **(−2.45)** | **(−4.40)** | **(−6.89)** | (0.60) | **(−7.63)** | **(−8.65)** |
| $\gamma_3$ | **−0.0644** | 0.0109 | −0.0022 | −0.0374 | 0.0044 | −0.0057 |
| | **(−2.70)** | (0.72) | (−0.19) | (−1.71) | (0.22) | (−0.45) |
| $\gamma_4$ | 0.0584 | **−0.0946** | **−0.0647** | −0.0432 | −0.0519 | **−0.0897** |
| | (1.68) | **(−4.28)** | **(−3.84)** | (−1.18) | (−1.57) | **(−4.20)** |
| $\gamma_5$ | **0.3993** | 0.0627 | **0.2005** | **0.3829** | **0.1654** | **0.2326** |
| | **(7.00)** | (1.73) | **(7.25)** | **(5.90)** | **(2.83)** | **(6.16)** |
| $\gamma_6$ | **−0.0790** | −0.0262 | **−0.0429** | | | |
| | **(−3.72)** | (−1.94) | **(−4.14)** | | | |

**Table 4.** (*Continued*)

|  | Service Firms | | | Financial Firms | | |
| --- | --- | --- | --- | --- | --- | --- |
|  | SG&A | CGS | Total Costs | SG&A | CGS | Total Costs |
| $\gamma_7$ | −0.0016 | 0.0121 | −0.0033 | **0.2268** | **−0.3171** | **−0.1130** |
|  | (−0.04) | (0.41) | (−0.15) | **(4.89)** | **(−7.58)** | **(−4.18)** |
| Adjusted $R^2$ | 0.1761 | 0.5194 | 0.5984 | 0.1469 | 0.5426 | 0.6579 |
| Number of observations | 7,039 | 7,039 | 7,039 | 5,328 | 5,328 | 5,328 |

*Notes*: The table presents the pooled estimation coefficient estimates with *t*-statistics in parentheses. DV equals selling, general, and administrative expense (SG&A), cost of goods sold (CGS), or Total Costs (sum of SG&A and CGS). Decrease_Dummy equals one if revenue in period *t* is less than revenue in period *t* − 1, zero otherwise. Fixed Asset Intensity is the log of the ratio of the net book value of fixed assets (Compustat #8) to sales revenue. Employee Intensity is the log of the ratio of the number of employees (Compustat #29) to sales revenue. Second Decrease takes the value of one if revenue also declined in the previous period. Inventory Intensity is log of the ratio of the inventory (Compustat #42) to sales revenue. Concentration Ratio is the Herfindahl−Hirshman index of industry concentration calculated for each two-digit SIC industry groups (Defond & Park, 1999). Estimates of coefficients at significance levels greater than 0.05 are given in bold.
[a]Regression specification:

$$\log\left[\frac{DV_{i,j,t}}{DV_{i,j,t-1}}\right] = \gamma_{0j} + \gamma_{1j} * \log\left[\frac{Revenue_{i,j,t}}{Revenue_{i,j,t-1}}\right] + \gamma_{2j} * Decrease\_Dummy * \log\left[\frac{Revenue_{i,j,t}}{Revenue_{i,j,t-1}}\right]$$

$$+ \gamma_{3j} * Decrease\_Dummy * \log\left[\frac{Revenue_{i,j,t}}{Revenue_{i,j,t-1}}\right] * Fixed\ Asset\ Intensity$$

$$+ \gamma_{4j} * Decrease\_Dummy * \log\left[\frac{Revenue_{i,j,t}}{Revenue_{i,j,t-1}}\right] * Employee\ Intensity$$

$$+ \gamma_{5j} * Decrease\_Dummy * \log\left[\frac{Revenue_{i,j,t}}{Revenue_{i,j,t-1}}\right] * Second\ Decrease$$

$$+ \gamma_{6j} * Decrease\_Dummy * \log\left[\frac{Revenue_{i,j,t}}{Revenue_{i,j,t-1}}\right] * Inventory\ Intensity$$

$$+ \gamma_{7j} * Decrease\_Dummy * \log\left[\frac{Revenue_{i,j,t}}{Revenue_{i,j,t-1}}\right] * Concentration\ Intensity + \varepsilon_{i,j,t}$$

suggest that the drivers of sticky cost behavior do vary by industry consistent with Hypothesis 2.

## Sensitivity Analysis

Consistent with previous studies, we use aggregated costs (SG&A and CGS) to test for sticky cost behavior in the prior section. In this section, we examine whether sticky cost behavior is also prevalent in two other more detailed costs incurred by firms, for example, research and development (R&D) and advertising costs. While sales revenue is not the primary driver for most detailed costs available in COMPUSTAT (e.g., interest, depreciation), we argue that sales revenue is the cost driver for R&D and advertising costs. R&D cost is available separately for about half of the manufacturing sample, while advertising is available for a third of the manufacturing firms and a half of the merchandising sample. In addition, we study sticky cost behavior in interest expense and provision for loan losses (CGS components) for financial firms.

Our results are presented in Table 5. We find both R&D and advertising costs are sticky. Specifically, $\gamma_1$ is positive and significant and $\gamma_2$ is negative and significant for both costs. These results suggest that managers are reluctant to reduce these costs, even though R&D and advertising costs are normally classified as discretionary, which could potentially be reduced in the short term when activity declines. Further, we find fixed asset intensity increases sticky cost behavior in R&D costs, whereas employee intensity increases sticky cost behavior in advertising costs. The proxy representing two consecutive years of revenue declines behaves as expected in both cases.

For financial firms, $\gamma_1$ is positive and significant for both interest expense and provision for loan losses, but $\gamma_2$ is negative and significant only for interest expense suggesting that interest expense exhibits sticky behavior but provision for loan losses does not. None of the determinants we examine appear to increase sticky behavior, but the proxy for two consecutive years of revenue declines and industry competitiveness significantly decreases sticky cost behavior. In an unreported regression, we also include a variable for debt intensity (total liabilities divided by sales). Debt intensity, as expected, increases the sticky cost behavior of interest expense.

Our analysis so far uses major industry groupings based on a one-digit SIC code. Because intra-industry differences among firms within a one-digit SIC code are substantial, we regroup the firms into 20 separate and distinct industries using their four-digit SIC codes.[12] This methodology allows for greater refinement and minimization of intra-industry differences, to better understand the sticky behavior of costs. Table 6 presents a summary of the results. To understand the sticky behavior of these new industry groupings, we obtained information on the production and economic environment of specific industries from several sources including: the *2000 Datamonitor Industry Market Research*, *2001 Encyclopedia of American Industries*, and the *2003 Encyclopedia of Global Industries*. Our primary focus is to

**Table 5.** Results of Estimating the Model Relating Annual Changes in Selected Costs that Comprise CGS and SG&A on Annual Changes in Sales Revenue to Identify the Drivers of the Sticky Cost Behavior in These Costs for the 22-Year Period 1979–2000 for Non-Financial and Financial Firms.[a]

| | Non-Financial Firms | | Financial Firms | |
| --- | --- | --- | --- | --- |
| | R&D | Advertising | Interest | Provision for loan losses |
| $\gamma_0$ | 0.0241 | 0.0080 | −0.0670 | 0.0454 |
| | (5.95) | (1.61) | (22.77) | (2.08) |
| $\gamma_1$ | **0.5725** | **0.7820** | **1.5694** | **0.7416** |
| | **(14.33)** | **(17.92)** | **(71.49)** | **(4.55)** |
| $\gamma_2$ | **−1.0813** | **−0.7634** | **−3.2311** | 11.4261 |
| | **(−3.93)** | **(−2.72)** | **(−3.08)** | (1.35) |
| $\gamma_3$ | **−0.1224** | 0.0159 | −0.0738 | 0.2967 |
| | **(−3.12)** | (0.33) | (−1.19) | (0.54) |
| $\gamma_4$ | −0.1031 | **−0.1534** | **0.2701** | 0.9485 |
| | (−1.78) | **(−2.57)** | **(3.14)** | (1.32) |
| $\gamma_5$ | **0.5302** | **0.5853** | **0.3035** | 0.6797 |
| | **(8.02)** | **(7.50)** | **(4.44)** | (1.29) |
| $\gamma_6$ | −0.0775 | 0.0201 | | |
| | (−1.78) | (0.52) | | |
| $\gamma_7$ | −0.4175 | 0.1102 | **−1.1405** | 1.552 |
| | (−0.75) | (0.21) | **(−4.17)** | (0.72) |
| Adjusted $R^2$ | 0.0371 | 0.0775 | 0.7419 | 0.0240 |
| Number of observations | 20,881 | 16,489 | 3,661 | 3,399 |

*Notes*: The table presents the pooled estimation coefficient estimates with $t$-statistics in parentheses. DV equals research and development, advertising for manufacturing and merchandising firms, and interest expense and provision of loan losses in financial firms. Decrease_Dummy equals one if revenue in period $t$ is less than revenue in period $t-1$, zero otherwise. Fixed Asset Intensity is the log of the ratio of the net book value of fixed assets (Compustat #8) to sales revenue. Employee Intensity is the log of the ratio of the number of employees (Compustat #29) to sales revenue. Second Decrease takes the value of one if revenue also declined in the previous period. Inventory Intensity is log of the ratio of the inventory (Compustat #42) to sales revenue. Concentration Ratio is the Herfindahl–Hirshman index of industry concentration calculated for each two-digit SIC industry groups (Defond & Park, 1999). Estimates of coefficients at significance levels greater than 0.05 are given in bold.
[a]Regression specification:

$$\log\left[\frac{DV_{i,t}}{DV_{i,t-1}}\right] = \gamma_0 + \gamma_1 * \log\left[\frac{Revenue_{i,t}}{Revenue_{i,t-1}}\right] + \gamma_2 * Decrease\_Dummy * \log\left[\frac{Revenue_{i,t}}{Revenue_{i,t-1}}\right]$$

$$+ \gamma_3 * Decrease\_Dummy * \log\left[\frac{Revenue_{i,t}}{Revenue_{i,t-1}}\right] * Fixed\,Asset\,Intensity$$

$$+ \gamma_4 * Decrease\_Dummy * \log\left[\frac{Revenue_{i,t}}{Revenue_{i,t-1}}\right] * Employee\,Intensity$$

$$+ \gamma_5 * Decrease\_Dummy * \log\left[\frac{Revenue_{i,t}}{Revenue_{i,t-1}}\right] * Second\,Decrease$$

$$+ \gamma_6 * Decrease\_Dummy * \log\left[\frac{Revenue_{i,t}}{Revenue_{i,t-1}}\right] * Inventory\,Intensity$$

$$+ \gamma_7 * Decrease\_Dummy * \log\left[\frac{Revenue_{i,t}}{Revenue_{i,t-1}}\right] * Concentration\,Intensity + \varepsilon_{i,j,t}$$

*Table 6.* Results of Estimating the Model Relating Annual Changes in SG&A, CGS, and Total Costs on Annual Changes in Sales Revenue after Partitioning the Sample into 20 Sub-Industries.[a]

| Industry Number | Industry Name | Sample Size | SG&A | CGS | Total Costs |
|---|---|---|---|---|---|
| 1 | Agriculture & Food<br>100–799, 2000–2099 | 2,867 | No | No | No |
| 2 | Mining<br>1000–1299, 1400–1499 | 642 | No | No | No |
| 3 | Construction<br>1500–1799 | 1,009 | No | No | No |
| 4 | Oil & Petroleum<br>1300–1389, 2900–2999 | 3,120 | No | No | No |
| 5 | Small Scale Manufacturing<br>2100–2690 | 5,367 | No | No | No |
| 6 | Printing & Publishing<br>2700–2799 | 1,779 | No | No | **Yes** |
| 7 | Chemicals/Related Manufact.<br>2800–2899, 3000–3299 | 7,224 | **Yes** | No | **Yes** |
| 8 | Industrial Manufact.<br>3300–3569 | 7,416 | No | No | No |
| 9 | Computers & Electronic Parts<br>3570–3699 | 9,078 | **Yes** | No | **Yes** |
| 10 | Transportation Equipment<br>3700–3799 | 2,201 | No | No | No |
| 11 | Measuring & Specialty Instrument<br>3800–3899 | 5,070 | **Yes** | **Yes** | **Yes** |
| 12 | Misc. manufacturing industries<br>3900–3999 | 1,123 | **Yes** | No | **Yes** |
| 13 | Transportation<br>4000–4790 | 1,470 | No | No | No |
| 14 | Telecommunication<br>4800–4899 | 1,195 | **Yes** | No | No |
| 15 | Utilities<br>4900–4999 | 721 | **Yes** | No | No |
| 16 | Wholesale<br>5000–5190 | 4,456 | **Yes** | No | No |
| 17 | Retail<br>5200–5799, 5900–5990 | 5,809 | No | No | No |
| 18 | Services<br>5800–5820, 7000–7363,<br>7380–8748 | 7,709 | No | **Yes** | **Yes** |

***Table 6.*** *(Continued)*

| Industry Number | Industry Name | Sample Size | SG&A | CGS | Total Costs |
|---|---|---|---|---|---|
| 19 | Financials 6000–6999 | 8,278 | No | **Yes** | **Yes** |
| 20 | Software & Technology Svcs 7370–7379 | 2,920 | No | No | **Yes** |

*Notes*: DV equals selling, general, and administrative expense (SG&A), cost of goods sold (CGS), or Total Costs (sum of SG&A and CGS). Decrease_Dummy equals one if revenue in period $t$ is less than revenue in period $t-1$, zero otherwise. If the significance level of the estimate of $\alpha_2$ is greater than 0.05, than we report as "Yes," otherwise "No." Estimates of coefficients at significance levels greater than 0.05 are given in bold.
[a]Regression specification:

$$\log\left[\frac{DV_{i,j,t}}{DV_{i,j,t-1}}\right] = \alpha_0 + \alpha_1 * \log\left[\frac{Revenue_{i,j,t}}{Revenue_{i,j,t-1}}\right] + \alpha_2 * Decrease\_Dummy * \log\left[\frac{Revenue_{i,j,t}}{Revenue_{i,j,t-1}}\right] + \varepsilon_{i,j,t}$$

understand why large sample studies (ABJ, 2003) show sticky cost behavior but specific industry studies (BPS, 2004; NS, 1997) as well as why most of the detailed groupings in our Table 6 do not.

The measuring and specialty instruments industry (#11) is the only industry grouping exhibiting sticky behavior in SG&A, CGS, and Total Costs. This industry consists primarily of firms in the search, detection, navigation, and guidance systems (SIC 3812) and surgical and medical instruments (SIC 3823–3845). The primary customer for the SIC 3812 industry is the U.S. government, in particular the Department of Defense, Federal Aviation Administration, and National Aeronautics and Space Administration. Contracts are usually awarded in a "winner-take-all" competition and using cost plus fixed fee contracts. The timing of these contracts is erratic and contractors incur high costs to maintain skilled and highly paid employees, with a need for continual retraining of employees and retooling of facilities due to untried technologies and advanced designs. Both the search and navigation industry and the medical instruments industry are one of the most technologically sophisticated industries with large R&D expenditures, independent of the revenue stream. The consequence of this operational environment is firms are unable to shift costs as revenues change resulting in costs being sticky.

The chemicals, pharmaceuticals, and related manufacturing industry (#7), computer and electronic parts industry (#9), and miscellaneous manufacturing industry (#12) exhibit sticky behavior in SG&A and Total Costs. Firms in chemicals, pharmaceuticals, and related manufacturing industry must make large expenditures to remain viable and reduce the threat of new entrants. For example, pharmaceutical firms (SIC 2834) have high research and development costs (20 percent of sales, which are higher than any other industry), high marketing costs (24 percent of sales), and strong barriers-to-entry due to patent protection. Perfume and cosmetic firms (SIC 2844) rely on extremely expensive marketing and promotion campaigns to keep out new competitors. Rubber and plastic products firms (SIC 3000) are highly consolidated with deeply entrenched market leaders. As a result, there are major barriers-to-entry for new competitors due to massive start-up costs and technological expertise.

The computer and electronic parts industry (#9) faces intense domestic and international competition. To sustain competitiveness, firms must spend large amounts on research and technology to develop high-tech, value-added machinery. During the 1980s and 1990s, these firms invested heavily in productivity, quality, customer service programs, and new plants and equipment. The industry also incurred unusually high costs to obtain skilled employees, retrain employees, and retool facilities. The high levels of expenditures that firms must make to reduce the threat of new competition allow firms in these industries opportunities to maintain some amount of slack in their cost structure.

We find SG&A costs are sticky in the telecommunication (#14), utilities (#15), and wholesale industries (#16). At first glance, these industries do not seem related, but an in-depth analysis reveals that monopolistic power connects the three. For example, while some sectors of the telecommunications industry may be open to competition, other sectors like telephone service are handled by a single monopoly. Similarly, utilities were primarily run as regional monopolies and regulated during most of the 1980s and 1990s, the time period of our study. In wholesaling, size dominates. Efficiency is determined by economies of scale; links with producers; automated ordering, shipping, and inventory systems; and the ability to provide customers with the best prices, service, convenience, and quality. Size gives wholesalers buying clout with suppliers and allows them to spread fixed costs over a wider sales base. Moreover, size and computer technology allow wholesalers to restrict entry and reduce competition, resulting in their ability to maintain short-term slack when it arises.[13]

Now, we turn to some industry groupings that do not show sticky cost behavior. The small-scale manufacturing industry grouping (#5), which includes the tobacco (SIC 2100), textile (SIC 2200), apparel (SIC 2300), lumber (SIC 2400), furniture and fixture (SIC 2500), and paper products (SIC 2600), experienced declining growth during the 1990s. Health and environmental risks, lawsuits, and protests depressed both the tobacco and lumber industries. With many firms leaving the textile industry, remaining firms tried to reduce costs as quickly as possible through mill closures and layoffs as revenues were declining. In 2001 alone, at least 100 U.S. textile mills closed, firing 60,000–75,000 U.S. textile workers. As expected, we do not find any sticky behavior in these sub-industries.

In another non-sticky industry grouping, industrial manufacturing (#8), firms experienced severe downturns in demand during the 1980s. In fact, industrial, commercial, and electrical equipment manufacturers were extremely vulnerable to foreign competition, particularly on price and quality. In response, many firms moved most of their manufacturing overseas where labor is significantly cheaper. In this highly competitive industry, where members move quickly to meet changing environmental and economic demands, sticky cost behavior should not be expected. In addition, we find firms in the agriculture, food, mining, construction, oil and petroleum industry groupings (#1, 2, 3, and 4) do not show any sticky cost behavior for SG&A, CGS, and Total Costs as they dealt with decreasing (or cyclical) demand and extra capacity.

In general, our results suggest that sticky cost behavior is observed only when the industry is growing and firms within the industry are able to create barriers-to-entry through significant research and development, marketing costs, patents, high capital investments, size, institutional knowledge or other such criteria giving the firm the flexibility of maintaining short-term slack. Therefore, we find that the industry and operating environment of the firm is critical in determining whether cost behavior exhibits stickiness.

We conclude our sensitivity tests with two robustness tests. To ensure that the size of the activity change bands (five percent) did not affect the results, we tested several other ranges with similar qualitative results. Next, we tested significance of the coefficients using the White's (1980) heteroskedasticity-corrected statistics and found them qualitatively unchanged. Since our tests are performed on a panel data, we tested for autocorrelation. Virtually all firms indicated that no correction was needed for autocorrelation based on the Durbin–Watson test statistic (Durbin & Watson, 1951). In addition, we estimated the model separately for each year and tested $z$-statistics as described in Healy, Kang, and Palepu (1987) and also estimated a fixed panel model with separate dummies for each year. The results are qualitatively unchanged using both tests.[14]

# CONCLUSION

This study attempts to reconcile the conflicting results of extant research by examining sticky behavior in four new ways. First, the study tests whether cost stickiness varies across four industries – manufacturing, merchandising, service, and financial services. Second, the study examines the sticky behavior of SG&A and CGS, individually and jointly. Third, the study examines if the sticky behavior of costs is dependent on the absolute magnitude of revenue changes, indicating the size of the relevant range. Finally, the study tests how selected determinants affect the sticky behavior of costs differently across industries.

Exploring each industry separately gives us greater insights into cost behavior, relevant range, and determinants. Costs in the manufacturing industry are the "stickiest" due to high levels of fixed assets and inventory as shown in Table 4. In addition, in many cases, firms are able to restrict entry by other firms through size, technological expertise, patents, maintenance of high costs in research and development and marketing through promotions and advertising. SG&A and CGS are individually and jointly sticky for activity changes greater than 10–15 percent. Our results suggest that for revenue increases greater than 10–15 percent, managers must expand the capacity of the firm by changing the firm's committed resources. However, if revenues decrease by more than 10 percent, managers may not want or be able to reduce the capacity of the firm, causing the sticky behavior of costs.

Costs in the merchandising industry are the least "sticky." Relatively low levels of fixed assets and temporary help allow firms to respond quickly to changes in revenues. A high inventory level is the only determinant consistently increasing the sticky behavior of costs in this industry. The merchandising industry is also a competitive industry observed by its low Herfindahl–Hirshman Index, so firms must be able to react quickly to the economic environment to remain viable.

For service firms, a simple analysis without stratifying revenue changes shows that SG&A and CGS are individually and jointly sticky. However, only Total Costs is sticky beyond 20 percent when the revenue stratification analysis is performed. Appropriately, employee and inventory intensity are the main drivers of sticky behavior in this industry, where success is determined by employees' ability to satisfy customers with the right product/service.

The financial industry manifests some interesting behavior. The CGS, representing interest expense and provision of loan losses, is sticky beyond a 10-percent change in interest revenue whereas Total Costs shows sticky behavior beyond a 15-percent change in revenues. While employee intensity increases the stickiness of costs, the main driver of sticky behavior is the total liabilities maintained by the firms. These results are not surprising given that financial firms must pay interest (borrowing costs) even during periods of revenue declines. Industry competition and two consecutive declines in revenues decrease sticky behavior of costs.

This paper explains some of the conflicting results of prior literature. Using a sample of firms known to exhibit sticky cost behavior in the aggregate, we show that sticky cost behavior is not present in all industries. Our evidence also suggests that the magnitude of activity changes when sticky costs behavior arises can vary across industries. Finally, we show that the determinants of sticky cost behavior also vary by industry. In addition, while we find the manufacturing industry to be stickiest industry among the four major groupings, we are unable to show sticky cost behavior for most sub-industries within the manufacturing industry. These results may explain why single industry studies do not report sticky behavior (BPS, 2004; NS, 1997). Our results support BPS's (2004) statement that caution must be applied when applying ABJ's (2003) conclusion that costs are sticky (BPS, 2004, p. 3). Future research can explore additional industry characteristics that affect cost behavior to better understand sticky cost behavior.

# NOTES

1. This differential change in cost structure for activity increases and decreases was reported earlier by Cooper and Kaplan (1998) and Noreen and Soderstrom (1997).

2. Other studies examine the determinants of sticky cost behavior (Banker & Byzalov, 2014; Banker, Byzalov, & Chen, 2013; Banker, Byzalov, Ciftci, & Mashuwala, 2014; Calleja, Steliaros, & Thomas, 2006; Cannon, 2014; Chen, Lu, & Sougiannis, 2012; Dierynck, Landsman, & Renders, 2012; Kama & Weiss, 2013), consequences of sticky cost behavior (Anderson, Banker, Huang, & Janakiraman, 2007; Banker, Basu, Byzalov, & Chen, 2015; Banker & Chen, 2006; Ciftci, Mashruwala, & Weiss, 2015; Weiss, 2010), and informativeness of sticky cost behavior to forecasting earnings and understanding earnings management in financial accounting research (Banker & Chen, 2006; Weiss, 2010). Other studies show that sticky cost behavior is a pervasive global phenomena (Banker & Byzalov, 2014; Banker, Byzalov, & Threinen, 2013; Calleja et al., 2006).

3. Within the one-digit SIC code, production environments, including the technology, product markets, and regulatory environment, are assumed to be highly

correlated. While two-, three-, and four-digit SIC codes may provide finer partitions in classification, they (1) significantly increase the number of the industries to be studied without substantial addition to our understanding and (2) decrease the sample size for each industry. In addition, we exclude utilities (SIC 4900–4999) from the sample of service firms because they were regulated during the 1980s and most of the 1990s. However, for completeness, we test sticky cost behavior for these finer partitions in the sensitivity analysis (Section "Empirical Results").

4. 24.86 percent of the observations have absolute change in revenues of less than 5 percent, 23.12 percent have absolute change in revenues of between 5 percent and 10 percent, 19.21 percent between 10 percent and 15 percent, 14.46 percent between 15 percent and 20 percent, 10.61 percent between 20 percent and 25 percent, and 7.78 percent between 25 percent and 30 percent. Within each range, on average, 30.3 percent of the observations are negative.

5. Fixed Asset Intensity is usually defined as the log of the ratio of the net book value of fixed assets (Compustat #8) to total assets (#6). Therefore, we repeated our tests with this definition with no qualitative change in the results.

6. To minimize the effect of extreme observations, observations in the top or bottom 0.5 percent distribution of any variable are excluded (Chen & Dixon, 1972). This trimming procedure results in a sample of 80,778 firm-year observations.

7. Aggregate results without industry groupings are similar to ABJ (2003).

8. As discussed earlier, Compustat identifies CGS for financial firms as interest expense and provision for loan losses. Stickiness is found for financial firms because they have to continue to pay their borrowing costs even as revenues decline.

9. In addition, we run a single regression model with all four industries included and perform the joint test that $\alpha_2$ for all industries are the same. It is rejected at greater than 0.0001 level for SG&A, CGS, and Total Costs.

10. To obtain a more precise measure of employee intensity, we attempted to use the actual labor (and related) expense (Compustat #42). Unfortunately, this measure is not given for most observations and reduces our sample by more than 90 percent, making estimation unreliable.

11. We regressed CGS for all firms against the five determinants and found the coefficient on industry concentration is negative and significant. Given this result we assumed the lack of variability in HHI index within industry classifications using the two-digit SIC might be the reason for not finding any relationship. Hence, we re-estimated HHI index based on a four-digit SIC code and repeated the test with no change in results.

12. In addition, we perform a similar test for sticky cost behavior within each two-digit, three-digit, and four-digit SIC codes when there are at least 200 observations available. For example, we find SG&A is sticky in 8 of 19 sub-industries and CGS is sticky in 4 of 19 sub-industries in the two-digit classification of manufacturing firms. When we refine industry grouping further to three-digit SIC code, we find SG&A is sticky in 14 of 62 sub-industries and CGS is sticky in 6 of 62 sub-industries. Further refinement to a four-digit SIC code results in SG&A being sticky in 22 of 76 sub-industries and CGS is sticky in 8 of 76 industries. A low probability of sticky cost behavior is also observed for the other three one-digit industry groupings. These results suggest that when we test individual industries with small

samples for sticky behavior, it is more than likely we will not detect sticky behavior, a result consistent with NS (1997) and BPS (2004).

13. In fact, a study co-sponsored by Canada's Ministry of Industry, Science and Technology found that the communications and wholesale industries were more likely than any other service industries to introduce computer-based technologies.

14. Multicollinearity tests using the Belsley, Kuh, and Welsch (1980) diagnostic also indicated this is not a concern. The condition index in each of the tests was no more than five.

# ACKNOWLEDGMENTS

The authors would like to thank Mary Stanford, Robert Vigeland, Larry Walther, and workshop participants at the University of Kentucky, Mississippi State University, Virginia Commonwealth University and the 2003 AAA Management Accounting Conference. Professor Weidenmier Watson gratefully acknowledges financial support from the Charles Tandy American Enterprise Center at Texas Christian University. All errors are our own.

# REFERENCES

Anderson, M. C., Banker, R. D., Huang, R., & Janakiraman, S. (2007). Cost behavior and fundamental analysis of SG&A costs. *Journal of Accounting Auditing and Finance, 22*(1), 1–28.

Anderson, M. C., Banker, R. D., & Janakiraman, S. (2003). Are selling, general, and administrative costs "sticky"? *Journal of Accounting Research, 41*(1), 47–63.

Balakrishnan, R., Peterson, M., & Soderstrom, N. (2004). Does capacity utilization affect the "stickiness" of cost? *Journal of Accounting, Auditing and Finance, 19*(3), 283–300.

Banker, R. D., Basu, S., Byzalov, D., & Chen, J. (2015). The confounding effect of cost stickiness on conservatism estimates. *Journal of Accounting and Economics*, forthcoming.

Banker, R. D., & Byzalov, D. (2014). Asymmetric cost behavior. *Journal of Management Accounting Research, 26*(2), 43–79.

Banker, R. D., Byzalov, D., & Chen, L. (2013). Employment protection legislation, adjustment costs and cross-country differences in cost behavior. *Journal of Accounting and Economics, 55*(1), 111–127.

Banker, R. D., Byzalov, D., Ciftci, M., & Mashuwala, R. (2014). The moderating effect of prior sales changes on asymmetric cost behavior. *Journal of Management Accounting Research, 26*(2), 221–242.

Banker, R. D., Byzalov, D., & Threinen, L. (2013). *Determinants of international differences in asymmetric cost behavior*. Working Paper. Temple University.

Banker, R. D., & Chen, L. (2006). Predicting earnings using a model based on cost variability and cost stickiness. *The Accounting Review, 81*(2), 285–307.

Banker, R. D., & Johnston, H. H. (1993). An empirical study of cost drivers in the U.S. airline industry. *The Accounting Review*, *68*(3), 576–601.

Belsley, D., Kuh, E., & Welsch, R. (1980). *Regression diagnostics: Identifying influential data and collinearity*. New York, NY: Wiley.

Calleja, K., Steliaros, M., & Thomas, D. (2006). A note on cost stickiness: Some international comparisons. *Management Accounting Research*, *17*(1), 127–140.

Cannon, J. N. (2014). Determinants of sticky costs: An analysis of cost behavior using United States air transportation industry data. *The Accounting Review*, *89*(5), 1645–1672.

Chen, C. X., Lu, H., & Sougiannis, T. (2012). The agency problem, corporate governance, and asymmetrical behavior of selling, general, and administrative costs. *Contemporary Accounting Research*, *29*(1), 252–282.

Chen, E. H., & Dixon, W. J. (1972). Estimates of parameters of a censored regression sample. *Journal of the American Statistical Association*, *67*(139), 664–671.

Ciftci, M., Mashruwala, R., & Weiss, D. (2015). Implication of cost behavior for analysts' earnings forecasts. *Journal of Management Accounting Research*, forthcoming.

Cooper, R., & Kaplan, R. S. (1998). *The design of cost management systems: Text, cases and readings* (2nd ed.). Upper Saddle River, NJ: Prentice Hall.

Defond, M. L., & Park, C. W. (1999). The effect of competition on CEO turnover. *Journal of Accounting and Economics*, *27*(1), 35–56.

Dierynck, B., Landsman, W. R., & Renders, A. (2012). Do managerial incentives drive cost behavior? Evidence about the role of the zero earnings benchmark for labor cost behavior in private Belgian firms. *The Accounting Review*, *87*(4), 1219–1246.

Durbin, J., & Watson, G. S. (1951). Testing for serial correlation in least-squares regression. *Biometrika*, *38*(3–4), 159–177.

Ely, K. M. (1991). Interindustry differences in relation between compensation and firm performance variables. *Journal of Accounting Research*, *29*(1), 37–58.

Hansen, D. R., & Mowen, M. M. (2003). *Management accounting* (6th ed.). Cincinnati, OH: SouthWestern.

Healy, P., Kang, S., & Palepu, K. (1987). The effect of accounting procedure changes on CEOs' cash salary and bonus compensation. *Journal of Accounting and Economics*, *9*(1), 7–34.

Horngren, C. T., & Foster, G. (1991). *Annotated instructor's edition cost accounting: A managerial emphasis* (7th ed.). Englewood Cliffs, NJ: Prentice Hall.

Kama, I., & Weiss, D. (2013). Do earnings targets and managerial incentives affect sticky costs? *Journal of Accounting Research*, *51*(1), 201–224.

Lazere, C. (1995). Spotlight on SG&A. *CFO*, *11*(December), 39–45.

Lazere, C. (1996). Spotlight on SG&A. *CFO*, *12*(December), 28–34.

Ma, C. K. (1988). Loan loss reserves and income smoothing: The experience in the U.S. banking industry. *Journal of Business Finance and Accounting*, *15*(4), 487–497.

Mintz, S. L. (1994). Spotlight on SG&A. *CFO*, *10*(December), 63–65.

Moyer, L. (1999). SEC reviews bankers trust's loan loss reserve practices. *American Banker*, *164*(95), 30.

Noreen, E. W. (1991). Conditions under which activity-based costs provide relevant costs. *Journal of Management Accounting Research*, *3*(Fall), 159–168.

Noreen, E. W., & Soderstrom, N. S. (1994). Are overhead costs strictly proportional to activity? *Journal of Accounting and Economics*, *17*(1–2), 255–278.

Noreen, E. W., & Soderstrom, N. S. (1997). The accuracy of proportional cost models: Evidence from hospital service departments. *Review of Accounting Studies, 2*(1), 89–114.

Weidner, D., Ring, N., & Barancik, S. (1998). 'Earnings management' found in all businesses, SEC chief says. *American Banker, 163*(215), 1–2.

Weiss, D. (2010). Cost behavior and analysts' earnings forecasts. *The Accounting Review, 85*(4), 1441–1471.

White, H. (1980). A heteroskedasticity-consistent covariance matrix estimator and a direct test for heteroskedasticity. *Econometrica, 48*(4), 817–838.